Women and War in the 21st Century

Women and War in the 21st Century

A Country-by-Country Guide

Margaret D. Sankey

ABC-CLIO™

An Imprint of ABC-CLIO, LLC
Santa Barbara, California • Denver, Colorado

Copyright © 2018 by ABC-CLIO, LLC

All rights reserved. No part of this publication may be reproduced, stored in a retrieval system, or transmitted, in any form or by any means, electronic, mechanical, photocopying, recording, or otherwise, except for the inclusion of brief quotations in a review, without prior permission in writing from the publisher.

Library of Congress Cataloging-in-Publication Data

Names: Sankey, Margaret D. (Margaret Diane), 1974- author.
Title: Women and War in the 21st Century : A Country-by-Country Guide / Margaret D. Sankey.
Description: Santa Barbara, California : ABC-CLIO, An Imprint of ABC-CLIO, LLC, [2018] | Includes bibliographical references and index.
Identifiers: LCCN 2018014307 (print) | LCCN 2018027725 (ebook) | ISBN 9781440857669 (ebook) | ISBN 9781440857652 (hard copy : alk. paper)
Subjects: LCSH: Women and war. | Women and the military.
Classification: LCC UB416 (ebook) | LCC UB416 .S36 2018 (print) | DDC 355.0082—dc23
LC record available at https://lccn.loc.gov/2018014307

ISBN: 978-1-4408-5765-2 (print)
      978-1-4408-5766-9 (ebook)

22 21 20 19 18   1 2 3 4 5

This book is also available as an eBook.

ABC-CLIO
An Imprint of ABC-CLIO, LLC

ABC-CLIO, LLC
130 Cremona Drive, P.O. Box 1911
Santa Barbara, California 93116-1911
www.abc-clio.com

This book is printed on acid-free paper ∞

Manufactured in the United States of America

Contents

Regional Guide to Entries	ix
Introduction	xi
Chronology	xvii
Afghanistan	1
Algeria	9
Argentina	15
Australia	19
Brazil	25
Canada	27
Chile	35
China	39
Cuba	47
Denmark	51
Egypt	55
Eritrea	59
Ethiopia	63
Finland	67
France	71
Germany	79

Great Britain	87
Greece	97
Hungary	101
India	105
Iran	113
Iraq	119
Ireland	127
Israel	135
Italy	145
Japan	151
Korea	161
Kurds	169
Liberia	175
Libya	181
Nepal	185
New Zealand	193
Nigeria	197
Norway	203
Pakistan	209
Palestine	215
Philippines	221
Poland	229
Russia	235
Sierra Leone	243
South Africa	249
Sri Lanka	253
Sweden	261
Turkey	265

Contents

United Arab Emirates	271
United States	273
Vietnam	289
Index	297
About the Author	321

Regional Guide to Entries*

Africa (Sub-Sahara)

Eritrea
Ethiopia
Liberia
Nigeria
Sierra Leone
South Africa

East Asia and the Pacific

Australia
China
Japan
Korea
New Zealand
Philippines
Vietnam

Europe and Eurasia

Denmark
Finland
France
Germany
Great Britain
Greece
Hungary
Ireland

---

*Regions defined by the U.S. Department of State.

Italy
Norway
Poland
Russia
Sweden
Turkey

Near East

Algeria
Egypt
Iran
Iraq
Israel
Kurds
Libya
Palestine
United Arab Emirates

South and Central Asia

Afghanistan
India
Nepal
Pakistan
Sri Lanka

Western Hemisphere

Argentina
Brazil
Canada
Chile
Cuba
United States

Introduction

Political scientist and feminist theorist Cynthia Enloe famously demanded of the field of international relations: where are the women? In speaking of women and war, they increasingly appear as heads of state and general officers formulating policy and as the uniformed ship captains, infantry platoon leaders, and fighter pilots carrying out their nation's commands. At the same time, in a continuity from the earliest human beings, women are also the family members of combatants, the ones who care for the wounded and the dead, the residents displaced by conflict, and the labor that provides fighters with their food, clothing, and sexual release. Since the 1990s, what brought about this tremendous shift, in which large numbers of women have assumed recognized roles within the power structure, rather than as outliers and unsung supporters or acted-upon populations?

The end of the Cold War presented militaries, particularly those in the wealthy Global North, an opportunity to recalibrate their forces for the 21st century. With war planning no longer calibrating resources for a massive land war against the Soviet Union, their tax-paying and voting populations did not want to pay for conscription of a large standing army, and threats like the breakup of the former Yugoslavia did not respond to traditional military application of force. Military sociologists predicted the development of a "postmodern" military, in which planners would confront risks that recognized no national borders and in which nations would need to act, not necessarily out of their own Realist interests but in solidarity to preserve international peace and conduct humanitarian operations. In these situations, the warrior orientation of traditional militaries would be superseded by peacemaking and peacekeeping. From existing, limited inclusion of women into armed forces, experience suggested that the logistics, medical, diplomatic, and administrative skills of women might not just be acceptable in the new configuration but also particularly adapted to winning hearts and minds and conducting stability operations.

Meanwhile, international institutions increasingly recognized the role war was playing in the lives of women. Introduced in 1998 and law in 2002, the Rome Statute of the International Criminal Court specifically identified crimes against women (coerced prostitution, sterilization, trafficking, and forced pregnancy) during war as crimes against humanity and in some cases as genocide. This was in response to the mass rapes and sexual torture carried out in Rwanda and in the former Yugoslavia and represented a departure from the view that these offenses were against an individual and the honor of the family but were instead weapons.

The United Nations followed this with Security Council Resolutions 1325 and 1820. Resolution 1325, based on work done in the 1995 Beijing Platform for Action, recognized that conflict had a disproportionate effect on women and girls and called for all responses to take into account their presence. From preventing violation to supporting participation in ending the fighting, women and girls should be shielded from gender-based offenses; refugee camps should be planned with their needs in mind; disarmament, demobilization, and reintegration programs should be initiated with women assumed to be among the combatants; and women should be encouraged to take part in legitimate political processes following the peace. Countries supplying peacekeeping troops were to examine their recruiting and training and make it a point to increase the number of women deployed on these missions, and observers were tasked to specifically search out information on the experiences of women and girls during conflicts and make that information available. United Nations Security Council Resolution (UNSCR) 1820, issued in 2008, reiterates many themes of 1325 as well as the Rome Statute, in denouncing rape as a tactic of warfare and calling on governments and their militaries to take responsibility for protecting the civilian population and educating their forces about refraining from sexual coercion and violence. Despite lofty intentions, only 40 of the 192 signatories to 1325 have presented National Action Plans as of 2013, and the proclamations have had little effect on guerrilla forces or on harassment and assault within military organizations.

Nonetheless, many nations were proceeding with integrating their armed forces and opening all roles, including combat, to women. Part of this was outright necessity. Smaller families and shrinking populations meant that, in absence of universal male conscription, the only way to provide a quality pool of voluntary personnel was to invite women into the service's most highly regarded and competitive jobs. A military competing with civilian employers could not restrict women to clerical duties when corporate airlines had women pilots or private security companies sent women as armed bodyguards. Women already regularly worked in nonmilitary jobs, requiring physical risk, long hours, and travel far from home, which were common arguments against military inclusion. Additionally, in the late 20th-century conflicts, having women among the soldiers, sailors, and airmen offered a sense of legitimacy

Introduction

and national commitment of the whole population lacking when the boots on the ground belonged entirely to men.

Development of military technology also offered opportunities unavailable to women in the past. Certainly, there would be infantry patrols in which participants would be carrying heavy rucksacks of supplies and bulky weapons and ammunition for long distances, but many other military trades had no real physical demands that women could not perform. Flying a drone, monitoring electronic networks, processing intelligence reports, or operating construction equipment could be done just as well by women as men, with women seen as having an advantage at tasks requiring information sharing, collaboration, or soft skills like empathy and networking. As guerrillas have always known, there is no secured home front where women are safe, and since World War I, technology has allowed enemies to reach out and attack civilian populations with increasing ease, making bright lines between combat and noncombat trades extremely difficult to police. In the Global North's corporate world, quotas on the representation of women in business boards and union leadership were recognized as bringing useful diversity of opinions and perceived as having greater ethical weight. Since the early 20th century, these countries had held up women's rights and education as a benchmark of modernity, especially in comparison to their imperial possessions, and continuing to do so through charities and aid priorities needed to be reflected in not just civilian but also military practice.

Since ancient Athenian citizens met to practice the phalanx, military service, especially the broad conscription of men, has formed a vital marker of both maturity and inclusion into the body politic. The time the state has in which young men are a captive audience is used not just for physical drills but also for inculcating a powerful vision of the nation's history, goals, and values, carefully structured to meet current defense needs. This formative bonding translates to friendships, business partnerships, and political alliances after service, conveying intangible advantages to the men who participate. In some democracies, military service is still one of the first things mentioned by a candidate for office, shorthand for patriotism, maturity, and experience. This public perception has not easily transferred over to women who served voluntarily, and there is little in women's public life that forms a ready alternative when measured against men and medals. This argument surfaced many times in the transition to women's greater inclusion in the military, that to be full citizens, they must be subject to the same obligations as men and have access to the same civic indoctrination and communal experience. It has even been claimed that it is ethically wrong to place the full burden of defense of the state on men when there are women mentally and physically capable of shouldering it alongside them.

Changes in the military met ferocious resistance from people inside and outside the institutions. One of the most powerful and enduring stereotypes is that women are innately peaceful, and as the givers of life, they cannot be takers of it. The dual system of men as protectors, women and children as protected, lies at the core of gender roles so persistent that many people insist that they are innate qualities of male and female human beings, with divergence from them constituting monstrous aberrations of nature. This venerated status, though, has been a way to exclude women from sharing political power, as they are ostensibly shielded from the ugliness of public life, and women have pointed out that motherhood is anything but peaceful, bloodless, and pristine. In fact, being the vessel of cultural transmission and symbol of identity of a people makes enemies of that people target women, for death or for wombs that can be filled with another's people's offspring via rape. Some 20th-century feminists have objected to women participating in the military at all, seeing it as an institution coopting women and masculinizing them to its benefit, rather than women having the opportunity to change (or end) the institution to the benefit of society. This argument overlooks the speed with which women often come to support wars and rally to national messages of aggression and use of force.

Another powerful objection has been that women disrupt military effectiveness and make male personnel less able to concentrate on their jobs, because they are sexually distracted or because they hesitate and prioritize saving a woman rather than charging ahead. Asking men to do violence for a cause, this argument goes, must be paid for by allowing them the intense and compensating emotional bond of male comradeship, in which women can never have a place. Publicly cherished visions of heroes are male, "bands of brothers" who cannot admit women, whose average physical strength and raw ability to project force are admittedly less than average men. Militaries that have studied effectiveness as part of their transformations have found a radically different reality. Outside of some intensely physical trades, many tasks can be mitigated by working together to lift heavy things, corrected with ergonomically designed equipment, and the emotional bond replaced by the "swift trust" of shared doctrine, demonstrated competence, and "buddyship." Deep biases, however, are hard to shift, as problems of harassment and assault meant to demonstrate to women that they do not belong manifest even as the stock insults of "ladies" and "girls" shouted by drill instructors to shame male recruits.

Unless a nation is entirely independent of public opinion (and some of them are), any changes to an institution as central to national identity as the military run hard up against the feelings of millions of people with no firsthand experience. The introduction of all volunteer forces has widened the gap between civilian and military backgrounds and exacerbated the anxiety civilians feel at involving women in organizations, which, in popular culture and in their minds, must be male to survive. It is still common to see people insist that the public will not tolerate women coming home in body bags, maimed by combat, or as prisoners of war, when these events have happened with increasing frequency. Military women are often the targets of slander campaigns, accusing them of being sexually promiscuous, lesbians, man-haters, or meant to weaken the institution from the inside as a scheme by cultural leftists. Twenty-first-century people are still products of thousands of years of enculturation that women are "beautiful souls" and men are violent brutes, and the thought of women pulling a trigger or dropping a bomb is profoundly uncomfortable, if not unthinkable. Women who voluntarily sign up must be damaged in some way, forced to join because of the bad economy, or lacked female role models and thus wish to ape men. The public is a long way from widespread acceptance that women who join feel the same call as their male colleagues—a desire to serve patriotically, have access to training and jobs, and do meaningful work in an interesting environment.

Declarations like UNSCR 1325 remind us that in the 21st century, where conflicts lack neat and discrete endings, women must be considered after the shooting stops. In general, wars bring women under more state control, not less, despite expansions of economic and social roles, as their labor is demanded and their freedom constrained. Nationalism is almost always framed as men's vision of the country, along with their ambitions for its future and their memories of its perceived humiliations. Ending a war, for a victor, is the accomplishment of that vision, which often overlooks the women who helped to make it possible. For the losing country, this may trigger widespread frustration on the part of the men, which finds its way into both the domestic space and the next set of moves toward neighboring countries. The relief at the end of wars has almost always meant a "return to normalcy," which, even in massive mobilizations like World War II, signals that women leave the factories, sniper's nests, and tank hatches to go back to the kitchen and nursery. As those roles change, the comforting standard of "before the war" is far slower to keep up. As many women guerrillas have learned, when the fighting is for power, not a change in power relations, the end of the war sees women, who may have been 30 percent of the fighters, relegated to secondary positions in the postwar administration.

We are still early in the 21st century, but these tensions and transformations are unlikely to stop, each playing out in a way informed by the historical, social, religious, and economic context of the country involved. These entries offer case studies of individual nations and their experience with women and war leading up to the present, in an effort to understand commonalities and disparities in the acceptance, integration, and potential of women at war.

Further Reading

Addis, Elisabetta, ed. *Women Soldiers: Images and Realities*. New York: Macmillan, 1994.

Caforio, Giuseppe. *Handbook of the Sociology of the Military*. New York: Springer Science Business Media, LLC, 2006.

Chapkis, W. *Loaded Questions: Women in the Military*. Amsterdam: Transnational Institute, 1981.
Cohn, Carol. *Women and Wars*. Cambridge: Polity, 2013.
Duncanson, Claire, and Rachel Woodward. *The Palgrave International Handbook of Gender and the Military*. Basingstoke: Palgrave Macmillan, 2017.
Enloe, Cynthia. *Bananas, Beaches and Bases: Making Feminist Sense of International Politics*. Berkeley: University of California Press, 2014.
Enloe, Cynthia H. *Maneuvers: The International Politics of Militarizing Women's Lives*. Berkeley: University of California Press, 2000.
Feinman, Ilene Rose. *Citizenship Rites*. New York: New York University Press, 2000.
Francke, Linda Bird. *Ground Zero: The Gender Wars in the Military*. New York: Simon & Schuster, 1997.
Gilligan, Carol. *In a Different Voice: Psychological Theory and Women's Development*. Cambridge, MA: Harvard University Press, 2016.
Isaksson, Eva, ed. *Women and the Military System: Proceedings of a Symposium Arranged by the International Peace Bureau and Peace Union of Finland*. Brighton: Wheatsheaf, 1988.
Lorentzen, Lois Ann, and Jennifer E. Turpin, eds. *The Women and War Reader*. New York: New York University Press, 1998.
Peach, Lucinda. *Women at War: The Ethics of Women in Combat*. Bloomington: Indiana University, 1993.
Sjoberg, Laura. *Gendering Global Conflict: Toward a Feminist Theory of War*. New York: Columbia, 2013.
Smith, Hazel, ed. *Diasporas in Conflict: Peace-Makers or Peace-Wreckers?* Tokyo: United Nations University Press, 2007.
Snyder, R. Claire. *Citizen-Soldiers and Manly Warriors: Military Service and Gender in the Civic Republic Tradition*. Lanham, MD: Rowman & Littlefield, 1999.
Williams, Cindy. "From Conscripts to Volunteers: NATO's Transitions to All-Volunteer Forces." *Naval War College Review* 58, no. 1 (Winter 2005): 35–62.

Chronology

1791
Olympe de Gouges writes "Declaration of the Rights of Women and the Female Citizen" as rebuttal to French Revolutionary "Declaration of the Rights of Man and Citizen"

1793
Attempting to speed the French armies into battle, the government passes "Law to Rid the Army of Useless Women" but fails to replace the nursing, supply, and support services they provided

1804
Marie-Angelique-Josephine Duchemin pensioned as a lieutenant in French Army for her defense of Corsica during Napoleonic Wars, later buried in Les Invalides, Paris

1807
Nadezhda Durova discovered serving in men's clothing as a soldier in the Russian Army, rewarded by Czar Alexander I and allowed to continue

1812
During War of 1812, American Lucy Brewer discovered serving in men's clothing in the crew of USS *Constitution*

1823
Maria Quiteria de Jesus is the first woman to serve in the Brazilian military during their War of Independence, later made patron/mascot of modern logistics corps

1830
Women like Emilia Plater from the Polish landowning class lead local militias in rebellion against the Russians

1847
Hong Xiuquan begins Taiping Rebellion in China, with platform of rejecting oppression of women and liberation of peasantry, recruits and arms women's units

1854
Florence Nightingale organizes nursing corps to attend British troops in the Crimean War, creating modern nursing profession

1858
Lakshmi Bai, a widowed Indian ruler, takes up arms against the British and dies in battle during the Mutiny of 1857–1858

1861
Clara Barton, Dorothea Dix, and others organize a nursing response to Union Army needs in the American Civil War. Approximately 400 women served in the Civil War on the Union and Confederate sides, posing as men.

1863
Polish Maria Piotrowiczowa raises troops from her family's lands to fight against the Russians

Harriet Tubman given command of U.S. Army raid on the Combahee River, attacking Confederate plantations and freeing 750 enslaved people

1880
Afghan women tribal leaders Malalai and Ghazi Adi lead their people against the British Army

1888
Indian Military Nursing Service created to enroll women for service in military hospitals and attending to Indian soldiers

1890
Henrik Ibsen publishes *A Doll's House*, critiquing the role of women in modern society

1893
New Zealand becomes the first nation in the world with suffrage for adult women

Gregoria de Jesus founds the women's division of the Katipunan or anti-Spanish independence movement in the Philippines

1898
Wealthy Korean women found the Korean Women's Rights Organization to agitate for suffrage and education

1899
In response to the Boer War, Canada, Australia, and New Zealand create women's nursing services and send personnel to South Africa to care for injured soldiers

1900
Righteous Fists of Heaven (the "Boxers") attack westerners in China, women serve as Red Green and Blue Lantern Corps. Future First Lady Lou Hoover present at siege of Beijing's diplomatic Quarter.

1901
United States forms Army Nurse Corps in response to Spanish-American War

Women gain suffrage in Australia

1907
Bar Giora formed in Israel to defend Jewish settlers, women prominent as fighters

1908
Young Turks take power in Ottoman Empire, initiating western-style reforms, including expansion of women's rights

United States founds the Naval Nurse Corps

1909
Bar Giora evolves into Hashomer, or "Watchman," who patrol Jewish settlements on horseback, prominent members Manya Shochat and Rachel Yanait

Constance Markievicz cofounds the paramilitary Fianna Eireann in Ireland

1910
French general staff recognize women's support services as crucial to future war planning

1911
Women's Suffrage Alliance formed in China

1913
Women in Norway gain suffrage

1914
World War I begins:

Women called up as nurses, thousands more work in factories in all of the participating nations

In Russia, Maria "Yashka" Bochkareva joins Russian Second Army, distinguishes herself as noncommissioned officer (NCO) under fire

1915
New Zealand nursing corps re-formed, sends nurses to Egypt, Salonika, and hospitals in United Kingdom

Women gain suffrage in Denmark

Women in Britain join "forage corps" to address food shortages

British "right to serve" rallies by women demanding to enlist in military capacities

First women's university in the Ottoman Empire opens

1916
Irish volunteers, including 77 women like Markiewicz and Helena Molony, seize the Dublin Post Office to begin the Easter Rising against British Authority

U.S. secretary of the navy creatively uses definition of "yeoman" to preemptively recruit women for clerical and administrative work prior to U.S. entry into World War I

1917

Russian Provisional Government authorizes 1st Women's Battalion of Death, which outperforms male soldiers

Women gain suffrage in Canada

Finland declares independence, women's "Lotte Svard" auxiliary crucial in supporting efforts

French women in wartime factories successfully strike for equal pay

United Kingdom creates women's military uniformed auxiliaries

Ottoman women enlisted in worker battalions for factory and agricultural work

1918

Women gain suffrage in United Kingdom, Poland

Spanish flu epidemic, women's nursing corps vital in handling public health crisis

Huge numbers of women in combatant countries left widowed or without possibilities of marriage because of male casualties, driving significant social change in views toward women in the workforce and in politics

1919

Canadian women gain suffrage everywhere but Quebec

U.S. women gain suffrage rights

Italian parliament passes law banning women from military service

1920

Joan of Arc becomes a saint, bolstered by support from French military

1924

Swedish branch of "Lotta Svard" women's auxiliary raises money to pay for male national defense training

1926

Forced to seek shelter with Chinese peasants, Mao and his Communist guerrillas deprioritize women's rights to blend in

1930

Indochinese Communist Party founds Women's Union with support from Ho Chi Minh

1934

Women gain suffrage in Cuba

Women gain suffrage in Turkey

Women join Danish Ground Observer Corps for civil defense and to locate civilian air crashes

Chronology

1935
In response to Italian invasion of Ethiopia, women form Armed Forces Wives' Association and other humanitarian and support groups

Sabiha Gokcen, Ataturk's adopted daughter, becomes the first woman in the Turkish Air Academy

1936
All civilian occupations opened to women in Denmark

Hundreds of French, British, and American women volunteer as members of the International Brigades fighting fascism in the Spanish Civil War

Ioannis Metaxas of Greece adopts fascist social policies placing women in traditional, passive roles in Greek society

1937
Women gain suffrage in the Philippines

1938
Norway opens civil defense jobs and some military medical and administrative trades to women

UK commissions engineer Caroline Haslett to study effectiveness of women in antiaircraft gun crews

Polish government authorizes Maria Wittek to form an armed Women's Auxiliary

1939
World War II begins in Europe

French government enlists women in military auxiliary

Polish Home Army, with a large proportion of women, fights German invasion

Red Cross and Women's Volunteer Service begun in Canada

1940
Women's suffrage in Quebec

Auxiliary Territorial Service in United Kingdom begins

Red Army in Russia mobilizes 800,000 women

Nguyen Thi Minh Khai executed by the French as a Vietnamese Communist guerrilla

1941
United States joins World War II officially after Pearl Harbor Attack

New Zealand forms Women's Auxiliary Air Force, Naval Auxiliary, and Army Auxiliary

Australia forms Women's Auxiliary divisions of air force, army, and navy

U.S. Representative Edith Nourse Rogers introduces bill to create women's divisions within the U.S. military, fails

1942
British garrisons in the Far East fall to the Japanese, women military nurses and civilians taken prisoners of war

Australian women join in civil defense, factory, and agricultural labor organizations

In North Africa, Susan Travers, driving for the French Army and Foreign Legion, shows such bravery in leading a retreat across the desert that she is accepted as the only woman in the Legion

Rogers reintroduces bill for women's auxiliaries in the United States, supported by Eisenhower and Marshall, succeeds in authorizing women's branches of army, navy, and marines

Women in the Philippines join the armed Huk resistance to the Japanese

1943
Women in vital roles as codebreakers and radar operators in British service

Indian Nationalist Subhas Chandra Bose created a women's regiment

Brazil sends 72 nurses to work in American field hospitals in the European theater of World War II

Germans recruit 450,000 women to work in noncombat support roles

The British Home Guard, meant for World War I male veterans, includes women

A planeload of 13 American women nurses crashes in Albania, survivors trek 600 miles to Italy

Greek partisan women comprise at least 25 percent of the partisan resistance

1944
Women in the resistance crucial to coordinating sabotage activity in advance of Normandy landings, including train derailments

Women in Poland participate in Warsaw uprising as armed combatants

Women's fascist military auxiliary formed in Italy

Charles de Gaulle declares, as leader of the Free French, that women have suffrage rights in recognition of their war service

U.S. Army nurse Frances Slanger first woman on the Normandy beaches, dies later that year when her hospital shelled

1945
Most women demobilized at war's end

Iraqi Women's Union formed

1946
Danish Home guard creates women's auxiliaries for army and air force

Women gain suffrage in Japan under new constitution

1947
Women enroll at the University of Kabul, Afghanistan

Australian women's auxiliary military services disbanded after World War II

Creation of Israel as a nation, war of independence fought with women combatants

Partition of India–Pakistan, organization of women's groups to handle refugee crises

1948
Women removed from combat duties in Israel

Postwar Italian constitution recognizes legal and social equality of women, several former women anti-fascist partisans elected to the parliament

1949
Women gain suffrage in Chile

Begum Ra'ana, First Lady of Pakistan, creates the Army Women's National Guard, followed by the Naval Reserve for Women

1950
North Korea invades South Korea, beginning Korean War

Australian Women's Divisions of the army, navy, and air force permanently restored after manpower shortage in the Korean War

Chinese women of the People's Liberation Army (PLA) serve in Korean War as medical, communications, and propaganda jobs

Armies of the UN forces in the Korean War utilize women nurses, often in field hospitals and as flight nurses on routes to Japan

1951
French government organizes women's service in the military, creating separate auxiliary branches

Chinese PLA Air Force begins training women pilots

1952
Army Nursing Corps founded in Japan

1953
Danish Home Guard add a Women's Auxiliary to the navy

East German women receive civil defense training and expected to be part of factory-based "battle groups" for conflict with the west

Mao's Great Leap Forward expects women to take part in rapid industrialization projects in China

1954
Women in the Communist Vietnamese forces vital to the fall of French position at Dien Bien Phu

1955
China promotes Li Zhen, a guerrilla on the Long March, to major general in honor of her service

China demobilizes 750,000 soldiers, many of them women, from uniformed to civil service jobs

South Korea founds Army Women's Training Center

Turkish women use loophole in laws to gain admission to military academy as "Turkish students" until loophole closed to specify "male Turkish students"

Women join resistance movement in Algeria against the French

1956
Celia Sanchez operates a network of rural guerrillas to aid Fidel Castro and his cadre in the Cuban mountains

1959
Italian National Police form a Women's Auxiliary Service

Marta Hillers publishes *A Woman in Berlin* anonymously, recounting the mass rapes and abuses by Russian troops in Germany at the end of World War II

Fidel Castro overthrows the Cuban Batista government with the armed support of revolutionary women

1960
Federation of Cuban Women founded, active in national defense

Eritrean Liberation Front founded, recruits women

Sirimavo Bandaranaike becomes first woman prime minister in the world, Sri Lanka

1961
Finland recruits women's auxiliary for radar operators, coastal artillery, and administration jobs

Pakistan's Family Law Ordinance offers a modern, secular role for women in public life

1962
Women allowed to join Chilean military

Women allowed in Danish military in noncombat roles

1963
Italy opens all civil service jobs to women

Women's Auxiliary of the Philippine Army created

1964
Women's suffrage in Afghanistan

Palestine Liberation Organization founded, women active in operations

1965
Canadian government caps number of women in its military at 1,500

1966
Indira Gandhi becomes prime minister of India

1967
President Lyndon B. Johnson announces intention to use Civil Rights Act applications to civil service to lift promotion and number caps on women in the U.S. military

1968
Japan forms Women's Army Corps

Tet attack in Vietnam places U.S. military women under direct fire

1969
Golda Meir becomes prime minister of Israel

1970
Canada lifts cap on number of women in its military forces

United States promotes first women general officers, Brigadier Generals Anna Mae Hays of the Army Nurse Corps and Elizabeth Hoisington of the Women's Army Corps

Afghan women stage protests against attempts to limit their dress and educational opportunities

1971
U.S. Air Force and Navy promote first women general officers, Brigadier General Jeanne Holm and Rear Admiral Alene Duerk

South Africa begins to recruit white women for its military

1972
Sri Lanka forms women's auxiliary services to all of its military branches

France amalgamates its women's services with their parent military branches

1973
Elizabeth Reid appointed to study the role of women in Australian society, including the military

West German government commissions study of women and society

1974
Beginning of the "Dirty War" in Argentina, women activists specifically targeted

Major General Wendy Clay, Canadian Air Force, first woman to earn pilot wings

Eritrean People's Liberation Front explicitly recruits women and arms them for combat

U.S. Navy begins to allow women pilots

1975
Cuban women present on military missions to Angola

The UN's International Year of the Woman sparks discussions of the role of military women worldwide

Australian military women allowed to wear their uniforms while pregnant

Military medical service opened to West German women

All-woman special operations unit formed in South Korea for intelligence gathering and handling women prisoners

Tigrayan People's Liberation Front formed, operates with significant number of women combatants

1976

Women receive complete equality in Cuban constitution

Brigadier Valerie Andre becomes France's first woman general officer

U.S. Federal Courts end military bans on women serving after having children

Congress opens U.S. military academies to women

1977

Cuban women soldiers present in missions to Ethiopia

Australian Air Force amalgamates women's auxiliary

Women enrolled in French War Colleges

U.S. Coast Guard opened to women

Italian parliament lifts gender-based restrictions on all civilian employment

1978

Canadian Human Rights Act

First women drill instructors in French Air Force

Foundation of Kurdish Worker's Party, significant women's rights platform and participation in guerrilla activities

United States allows women on noncombat ships

United States amalgamates women's services into their parent military service, combines ranks and promotion lists

1979

Soviet invasion of Afghanistan

Australian Army amalgamates women's auxiliary into main service

Canadian Air Force selects three women, Captains Deanna Brasseur, Leah Mosher, and Norah Bottomly, for pilot training

Margaret Thatcher becomes prime minister of Great Britain

Iranian Revolution overthrows the Shah

Creation of Sri Lankan Army Women's Corps

U.S. military women allowed to join missile crews

1980
Canadian Royal Military College admits women

Iran–Iraq War begins

1981
U.S. Commission on the Future of Women in the Armed Forces convenes

Iranian protesters, many of them women from the Mujahideen, march against the Revolutionary Islamic Government, are forcibly suppressed

Demilitarization of the Italian police amalgamates women's auxiliary into main force

1983
End of "Dirty War" in Argentina, women protesters demand accounting of missing and tortured

Operation Urgent Fury, 100 U.S. military women serve during invasion of Grenada

1984
Military service exempt from Australian Sex Discrimination Act

Elsa Yacob paints "Woman Hero" memorializing role of women in the Eritrean Civil War

Indira Gandhi assassinated

1985
Australian Navy amalgamates separate women's auxiliary

Women gain complete occupational equality in Norwegian military branches

1986
U.S. women fly refueling tankers in Libyan operations, technically eligible for air combat medals

Iran and Iraq recruit women's units to fight in the Iran–Iraq War and serve in support services

1987
Taliban assassinates Meena Kamal, of the Revolutionary Women of Afghanistan

Canadian government orders CREW trials to gauge capabilities of women in combat roles

First Palestinian Intifada starts, women in largely support roles

1988
Denmark opens all military roles to women

European Union ends gender restrictions on civilian jobs

South Korea ceases to dismiss women from its military when they marry or become pregnant

1989
End of the Cold War, fall of the Berlin Wall

Canadians Georgia Ann Brown, Isabelle Gauthier, Marie-Claude Gauthier, and Joseph Houlden bring discrimination case to Human Rights Tribunal over combat exclusion of women

Canadian Private Heather Erxleben becomes the first woman to pass combat infantry course

British Royal Air Force begins training women to fly combat aircraft

U.S. women serve in Operation Just Cause in Panama, Captain Linda Bray, MP, leads unit in combat during seizure of Panamanian military kennel

1990
Australia opens combat-related trades to women

Aparthied dismantled in South Africa, amalgamation of military begins, includes women from African National Congress (ANC) guerrilla wing

British Navy conducts trial deployments of women on HMS *Brilliant*

UAE opens Khawlah bint al-Azwar military academy for women, Abu Dhabi

Iraq invades Kuwait, beginning First Gulf War

1991
Canadian officers Anne Reiffenstein, Holly Brown, and Linda Shrum take command of combat arms units

Noncombat roles available to Finnish women on peacekeeping missions

UK Royal Air Force has women pilots and navigators

All trades in medical and musical services open to women in German military

Tailhook Scandal, Las Vegas

U.S.-led Coalition invades Iraq, U.S. forces involve 41,000 military women, two women prisoners of war (POWs)

Civil War begins in Sierra Leone

Tamil Tiger woman suicide bomber assassinated Rajiv Gandhi, India

Poland promotes World War II resistance leader Maria Wittek to general

1992
Women begin to serve on ships in French Navy

British Ministry of Defense begins amalgamation from women's auxiliaries to full integration

Turkish military academies admit women

Japan graduates its first women from military academies

Russia encourages women to enlist in its military as contract soldiers

1993
Republic Act 7192 opens all military trades to Philippine women

1994
Nie Li becomes first woman major general in China, heading scientific research division

Hungary admits women to its military colleges

Major General Aderonke Kale, a psychiatrist, becomes the first Nigerian woman to hold that rank in her nation's army

1995
Leyla Zana, Kurdish Worker's Party (PKK) guerrilla leader imprisoned in Turkey, awarded Andrei Sakharov Prize for free thought

All military trades open to women in Finland

First woman fighter pilot in French military

1996
Taliban forces take Kabul, women forced out of government and military of Afghanistan

Fidel Castro promotes revolutionary veteran Tete Puebla of the Mariana Grajales to brigadier general, the first woman in Cuba at general officer rank

Hungary opens all military trades, including combat, to women

Maoist insurgency begins in Nepal, large presence of women among rebels

Courage Under Fire, starring Meg Ryan, explores the possibility of women receiving the Congressional Medal of Honor and dying in combat

Scandal at U.S. Army training grounds, Aberdeen, Maryland, as drill sergeants coerce sexual relationships from women recruits

1997
Women integrated into Australian submarines

Lt. Jennifer Daetz becomes first Australian woman in command of a naval vessel, HMAS *Shepparton*

South Africa opens all military ranks and trades to women

South Korea promotes first woman colonel, then first woman commands an infantry company

G.I. Jane, starring Demi Moore, sparks debate over women in American combat roles

1998
All military trades open to women in Israel, graduation of first women combat navigators

Gender quotas abolished in French military

In Hungary, graduation of first 29 women officers from Janos Bolyai Military Technical College

Indian military forms Rapid Action Force, including women

South Korea has first woman commander of training center

Benazir Bhutto elected prime minister of Pakistan

1999

Brazil allows women into military academies

UK Royal Marines reject Angela Maria Sirdar, appealed to the EU Court of Justice, which upheld military right to exclude women on the grounds of military effectiveness

Philippine military academy admits women

2000

United Nations Security Council Resolution (UNSCR) 1325 on Women, Peace, and Security, calls on nations to consider the disproportionate effect of conflict on women and girls in all phases of warfare

Australian Air Commodore Julie Hammer is the first woman to reach one-star rank in her nation

Italian military academies open to women

EU Human Rights Act enters British legal use, applies to women in the armed forces

2001

9/11 attacks on the United States, military women killed at the Pentagon

United States invades Afghanistan, women medical support soldiers accompany first deployed troops

Canadian submarines fully integrated with women

CHEN dissolved in Israel, women integrated into Israeli Defense Force (IDF)

First women combat pilots in Israel

2002

Argentine Navy opens enlistment to women

Major General Shahida Malik of Pakistan becomes the first woman of that rank in her country

Civil War ends in Sierra Leone, women enter first disarmament, demobilization, and reintegration (DDR) programs under UNSCR 1325

Rome Statute becomes law

Arafat gives "Army of Roses" speech, calling on Palestinian women to be suicide bombers, they immediately respond

2003

All career fields open for Chilean military women

South Korean women allowed on battleships

Pakistan Air Force places women in pilot training

In Liberia, women organize Mass Action for Peace

Chronology

U.S. invasion of Iraq (Second Gulf War), Private Jessica Lynch's injury, capture, and rescue publicized

Private Lori Piestewa, a member of the Hopi Tribe, is the first Native American woman killed in combat, Iraq

2004
Eliana Maria Krawczyk becomes the first woman serving on an Argentinian Navy submarine

Formation of the Israeli Defense Force Caracal Battalion, mixed-gender combat unit

Women in the Pakistani military receive limited combat training

Role of U.S. military women in abuses at Abu Ghraib Prison in Iraq becomes public

2005
Argentina's Debora Pontecorvo becomes that nation's first woman military pilot

Leigh Ann Hester, a military police officer from the U.S. National Guard, earns a silver star for bravery in close combat in Iraq

2006
U.S. rules limiting military women to support functions implemented in Afghanistan

In Brazil, first women qualify as military pilots

Canadian Captain Nichola Goddard commands firing position at Battle of Panjwaii, killed in action in Afghanistan

2007
Iraqi MP Malalai Joya removed from Parliament for criticizing her male colleagues

Argentina drops requirements that officers get permission to marry from commanding officers and recognizes same-sex and civil marriages

India sends an all-woman police battalion to Liberia as peacekeepers

2008
U.S. Army General Ann Dunwoody becomes the first female four-star general officer of her service

UNSCR 1820 condemns rape as a weapon of war

2009
Danish Colonel Susanne Bach Bager becomes the first to reach that rank in her country

U.S. Marine Corps (USMC) creates Female Engagement Teams in Afghanistan and Lioness Program in Iraq to include women on combat patrols

2010
South Korea opens college Reserve Officer Training Corps (ROTC) detachments to women

Pakistan makes sexual harassment and acid attacks against women a crime

2011
Australia opens all roles except special operations to women

Germany becomes an all-volunteer force, ending conscription

The Indian military offers permanent contracts to women in professional fields

In Nigeria, Blessing Liman becomes the first woman air force pilot

Major General Margaret Woodward of U.S. AFRICOM (U.S. Africa Command) directs 11-day air campaign against Libya as commander of Operation Odyssey Dawn

2012
First woman suicide bomber in Afghanistan

Rear Admiral Dalva Maria Carvalho is Brazil's first female general officer

Norway's Colonel Ingrid Gjerde, first to lead a Norwegian combat command

Establishment of the Nordic Center for Gender in Military Operations

Rear Admiral Itunu Hotonu becomes the first female general officer in Nigeria

In the United States, Janet Wolfenbarger becomes the first four-star woman general

Four U.S. women, joined by the American Civil Liberties Union (ACLU), sue the Department of Defense over bans from combat service, after which the Obama administration announces that it plans to open all fields to women by 2016

2013
All career fields in the Argentinian military open to women

Pakistan trains 24 women from the medical and IT corps to be paratroopers

Philippines sends its first woman-commanded peacekeeping mission to Haiti, under Navy Captain Luzviminda Camacho

U.S. Representative Tulsi Gabbard, a major in the Army National Guard, elected to Congress from Hawaii

2014
U.S. Navy Admiral Michelle Howard is the first woman promoted to that rank, also the first African American woman to hold it

In UAE, Major Mariam al-Mansouri becomes the first woman qualified to pilot military aircraft

Israeli Defense Force begins second mixed-gender combat battalion, the Lions of Jordan, with woman in command

Palestinian Presidential Guard trains 22 women in commando course

2015
U.S. secretary of defense Ash Carter announces that all roles will be open to women by 2016

First women serve on U.S. submarines

Chronology

2016
Women allowed into Australian Army special operations
Brigadier General Lone Traeholt named chief of Danish Air Force Tactical Staff
Women become available for conscription in Norway
In the United Kingdom, ban lifted on women in close combat roles
In Iraq, Shia militias enlist women
Tammy Duckworth, a disabled U.S. veteran, elected to the Senate from Illinois
U.S. Army Infantry course graduates first women

2017
First U.S. woman graduates from USMC Infantry Officer Course
First women fighter pilots in Australian Air Force
Indian Air Force places a small number of women in its pilot training program

2018
North Korea's Kim Jong-un names his sister, Kim Yo-jong to head the intelligence service, and she represents him diplomatically at the Winter Olympics

Afghanistan

Background

Since the invasion of Alexander the Great, the people of Afghanistan have used the challenging landscape and their tribal networks of alliances to expel intruders. The harsh life of rural agriculture and herding required women to be shrewd managers of resources and hard workers, although the Pashtunwali, or tribal code, limits their legal rights and contradicts many aspects of Islamic Sharia Law, especially in areas like dowries and inheritance. Nazo Tokhi, a poet and noblewoman, led troops into battle to avenge the death of her father, then became the mother of Mirwais Hotak, who drove the Safavids out of Afghanistan and founded a dynasty in the early 18th century. Another royal lady, Zarghuna Alamo, engineered the rise to power of her son Ahmad Shah Durrani (1747–1772), chosen King of Afghanistan. Women like Malalay and Ghazi Adi also fought with their tribespeople against the British in 1880. Rudyard Kipling, reflecting on the brutal fighting in Afghanistan, suggested not only that women are the deadlier sex but also that a young British soldier wounded in the mountains should "blow out" his brains rather than face the Afghan women who would come out after battles to finish off the enemy.

Both Abdur Rahman Khan (1880–1901) and his successor Amanullah Khan (1919–1929) attempted significant reforms to education and the status of women; Amanullah assisted by the example of his wife, western-educated Queen Soraya, and his sister, Suraj el-Banat. His changes, however, including unveiling women, provoked conservative tribal leaders into a coup, which forced him out of power and into exile. After his removal, women's rights eroded, although women were allowed to enroll at the University of Kabul in 1947, largely to provide the skilled medical care required in a society where women could not consult men from outside their families.

The prime ministership (1953–1963) and, after he overthrew his brother-in-law, the King, presidency (1973–1978) of Mohammad Daoud Khan, a member

> **War Reporting**
>
> Beginning in the mid-19th century, with the work of Jane Cazneau reporting from the Mexican-American War in 1846 and Margaret Fuller's accounts of the Revolutions of 1848 in Rome, women have covered every modern conflict and humanitarian crisis for mass media as reporters and photographers. In many cases, this role involved risk, physical hardship, and working through the mistrust of public and militaries, which both resented women's interference in a masculine world and craved the good public relations (PR) and human-interest details they provided. In October 1965, this danger was highlighted by the death of Georgette "Dickey" Chapelle, an experienced photojournalist since World War II, after stepping on a landmine in Vietnam.
>
> Lynsey Addario (b. 1973) began her photojournalism career in 1996 for the *Buenos Aires Herald* as an expert on Cuba, before working for *National Geographic, Associated Press,* and *The New York Times* covering post-9/11 engagements in Iraq, Afghanistan, Sudan, and West Africa, with a special focus on the role of women and traditional societies in conflict. She has been kidnapped twice, in 2004 in Iraq and 2011 in Libya, and recounts the harassment and groping faced by women at the hands of security forces and rebels. She received a MacArthur Genius grant in 2009, as well as being part of the *New York Times* (NYT) Pulitzer-winning team covering the Waziri Valley in Afghanistan. Addario's memoir, which will be filmed by Steven Spielberg, wrestles with her balancing of danger with her marriage and pregnancy, as well as the special access accorded to women in the conservative locations where she works.

of the Afghan royal family, saw a significant liberalization in social mores and economic growth as Afghanistan formed diplomatic ties to the Soviet Union and received aid in their development and as opposition to U.S. ally Pakistan. This included suffrage for women in 1964, along with educational exchange programs and the adoption of western dress. Women organized major marches in 1968, when conservatives threatened to end study abroad, and they pressured the government in 1970, when tribal leaders condoned acid attacks on women who wore miniskirts or unveiled their faces.

1978–1996

In April 1978, the People's Democratic Party of Afghanistan (PDPA), concerned that Daoud was reversing his secular, progressive policy and planned to eliminate them from the government, and wanting to establish a fully

Communist state, staged a coup with the help of the Afghan army against Daoud, killing him and his family and installing Nur Mohammad Taraki as president. Over the next year, the PDPA engaged in a bloody purge of both Daoud's supporters and factions within its own party, executing as many as 25,000 people. Meanwhile, they began a series of Soviet-style rapid modernization programs, including literacy and land reform, which enraged traditionalists. With civil war spreading and endangering the PDPA regime, the Soviet Union intervened in 1979, sending 100,000 troops in to quell the threat. This invasion destabilized the rapprochement reached between the United States and Soviet Union in the 1970s, as the United States and Pakistan backed mujahideen rebels for the next decade.

While the Afghan army and the Soviets fought in the countryside, Kabul and other cities modernized with injections of Soviet money and advisors. The Afghan Women's Council acted on the communist government's declaration that women were fully equal and should participate in society and the economy to run outreach programs against illiteracy and domestic violence and for vocational training. Women were recruited into and served in the military, police force, and civil service, as well as in civilian jobs in the national airline and television stations. The press usually commented at the vast gulf between urban Afghanistan and the tribal lands, where the status quo was still in the 19th century. There was also a drastic contrast between the government working in partnership with the Soviets and the brutality exercised by Soviet troops toward the population, including carpet bombing and torture of prisoners.

The resistance was a loose coalition of actors, from warlords of the Northern Alliance to the nascent Taliban, joined together as mujahideen or "holy warriors" to defeat the secular and communist government. The sense that this was an existential, national struggle allowed the rebels to draw on Afghan historical conflicts for reference, and their desperation allowed them to include women in functions like nursing, supply, and luring Soviet soldiers into ambushes, although they avoided arming or using them in combat roles. The proper place of women, an ideology in which the United States never interfered, was one of segregation and second-class status, reinforced in the experiences of mujahideen, who left their families in refugee camps and existed without women for extended periods of time. This alarmed many of the members of the resistance who had been purged PDPA members, significantly to the left of mujahideen fighting as religious opponents of the state, but it was the mujahideen who received aid from Islamic Pakistan and from Ronald Reagan's America. Mujahideen reach extended to the diaspora community in India and Iran, silencing women writers and politicians like Meena Kamal, of the Revolutionary Women of Afghanistan, who was assassinated in 1987.

The Soviet Union had begun to withdraw from Afghanistan before its collapse in 1989, due to the unpopularity of the drawn-out war and the unsustainability of the massive troop commitment. The loss of support emboldened the mujahideen, and the PDPA government fought to survive from 1992, when the final Russian aid ended, and 1996, when the Taliban-dominated forces took Kabul. At the end, the PDPA armed and trained all of its women members to defend the city, but they did not succeed. The Taliban immediately reversed the gains achieved under the secular government—40 percent of teachers were women, as were 40 percent of doctors, and 50 percent of civil servants, with 34 percent of women in the paid workforce, usually as tailors or skilled carpet weavers. This ended with prohibitions against women being in public without male escort and dismissal from all government employment. Public health crises, including resurgent tuberculosis, malaria, and skyrocketing maternal mortality, were an immediate result of the social regression. Some women and their families fled, in a new wave of diaspora, while others went underground to conduct schools and provide secret networks of medical care, but most donned burqas and painted their windows black in accordance with the new regime's rules.

21st Century

In November 2001, in response to the Taliban and Al-Qaeda's involvement in the 9/11 attacks, the United States invaded Afghanistan and launched a series of air strikes, which toppled the Taliban government in Kabul. To replace it, the Bonn Agreement installed Hamid Karzai and a cabinet of ministers drawn from the Afghan diaspora. Among them, three women held ministerial portfolios, including Dr. Sima Samar, as head of women's affairs. In the ensuing elections for a bicameral legislature, women were guaranteed quotas of 20 percent in the upper and 27 percent in the lower house, and the turnout of women voters was enthusiastic and large. In Kabul, and among the government planners, a kid of "strategic essentialism" made women's participation palatable—it pleased the Americans and nongovernmental organizations (NGOs), and portraying women as peacemakers and community-builders offered roles that did not threaten male dominance of society or politics. This did not play nearly so well in the rural regions, where women candidates suffered intimidation, harassment, and threats. Eventually, Dr. Samar would be forced out of the cabinet, after which the United Nations sent her as a special envoy to the Sudan, and MP Malalai Joya was removed from her seat after giving an interview in 2007, calling her male colleagues "donkeys," under a rule that MPs may not criticize one another.

U.S. and the North Atlantic Treaty Organization (NATO) advisers began programs to upgrade the bureaucracy, sending groups of women to training in America and Europe as judges, health workers, and civil servants. In some areas, like Herat, where the ethnic group is Shia and closely tied to Iran, there was acceptance of a revival of women in public life. In others, elders only

Afghanistan

Dr. Sima Samar, who fled the communist regime in Afghanistan in 1984, ran medical programs for women in exile in Pakistan until her return home in 2001. After serving as minister of women's affairs from 2001–2003, she has continued to denounce and work against Taliban restrictions on women, especially the lack of access to medical care and education. (MARCOS TOWNSEND/AFP/Getty Images)

allowed women's *shuras*, or councils, to get NGO money and refused the services offered when the women returned from training. A few NGOs made active use of women's networks, training midwives, who had intimate access to family homes, to talk to women about strategies useful in discouraging their male relatives from joining extremist groups. In response to the weakness of the government, and the inability of Karazi to provide security or development, the Taliban resurfaced with a vengeance, especially targeting women, schools, and modernization projects. In 2005 alone, 756 people died because of improvised explosive devices (IEDs) planted to terrorize the population, while 3,000 more were killed to cow resistance to the Taliban.

The National Army, which had fallen apart in the last years of fighting the Taliban in the mid-1990s, received massive investment in training and equipment. The military still seeks to recruit women but has found only several hundred of the thousands anticipated. The most promising pool of recruits are those who served in the PDPA and were trained originally by the Soviets, like Brigadier General Khatool Mohammadzai, who was a paratrooper and instructor until 1992, when forced out by the death of her husband, a fellow officer, and the Taliban's refusal to allow women public jobs. She survived running a secret school for girls and has been reinstated as the Department of Defense's head of Women's Affairs, although she has not been allowed to do combat jumps since 2006 because of rules limiting women to support functions. Niloofar Rahmani, a younger woman, answered the call for pilot recruits and learned to fly the C-208, then the C-130 transport plane in 2012. On one mission, she broke taboos and picked up wounded men, what any male pilot would have done, for which she was sharply criticized. The star of a publicity trip to the United States, Rahmani, revealed that her family was being harassed, her brother beaten up and her sister divorced for her actions, and she requested asylum in America. The Afghan Air Force moved quickly to revoke her pilot's rank and classified her as a deserter. The case is unresolved as of 2017.

The National Police have an even more urgent need for women, as traditional families will not allow their women to interact with unrelated men, making house searches and interviews impossible without women officers. Despite investing $93.5 million in encouraging women to don the uniforms of the military and police, the Americans have found it difficult to fill quotas, with only 105 women signing up for training in 2008. Initially, German military police conducted the program, superseded by U.S. contractor DynCorp. The most successful recruitment, like the military's, has been in locating women who served under the PDPA and updating their skills. General Aziza Nazari, head of the Human Rights Department in the interior ministry, served as a police officer for 31 years before 1996. Zarif Shaan Naibi, warden of a women's prison, was trained in that job by Soviet advisers in the 1990s. The police force struggles with corruption, including prostitution rings involving women officers, and the women find it difficult to get to work due to the lack of transportation and the dangers of wearing their uniforms when not armed and on duty.

Rural Afghans remain frustrated with the elite in Kabul and see their reconstruction benefiting a few wealthy and politically connected families. Resistance to change, either by the Taliban and its splinter groups or conservative village elders, remains a stumbling block. In 2012, connected to a global jihadi change in tactics, Afghanistan saw its first female suicide bomber, acting in the name of the group Hezb-e-Islami, but it is unlikely Afghan groups will embrace the use of women to the degree others have. In an extreme example of taking matters into their own hands, Reza Gul, her daughter Fatima, and daughter-in-law Seema were present when extremists killed her son, a policeman working a checkpoint. The three women armed themselves in the chaos and carried on a seven-hour gun battle, in which they killed 25 attackers and wounded 5 more. The more frequent reality is women placed back in the isolation of their homes and under the stifling authority of Pashtunwali's version of honor culture.

Further Reading

Addario, Lynsey. *It's What I Do: A Photographer's Life of Love and War*. New York: Penguin Books, 2016.

Bernard, Cheryl, Seth G. Jones, Olga Oliker, Cathryn Quantic Thurston, Brooke K. Sterns, and Kristen Cordell. *Women and Nation-Building*. Santa Monica, CA: Rand, 2008.

Bezhan, Faridullah. *Women, War and Islamic Radicalization in Maryan Mahboob's Afghanistan*. Clayton, VI: Monash, 2008.

Blau, Max. "First Female Afghan Air Force Pilot Asks US for Asylum." *CNN*. December 27, 2016. https://www.cnn.com/2016/12/27/politics/female-afghan-military-pilot-asylum/index.html.

Edy, Carolyn M. *The Woman War Correspondent, the U.S. Military, and the Press, 1846–1947*. Lanham, MD: Lexington Books, 2017.

Hedström, Jenny, and Thiyumi Senarathna. *Women in Conflict and Peace*. Stockholm: International IDEA, 2015.

"In Afghanistan, an Elite Female Police Officer Battles Cultural Taboos as well as the Taliban." *Los Angeles Times*. May 3, 2017. http://www.latimes.com/world/la-fg-afghanistan-female-police-2017-story.html.

Magnus, Ralph H. "The Military and Politics in Afghanistan: Before and after the Revolution." In *The Armed Forces in Contemporary Asian Societies*, edited by Edward Olsen and Stephen Jurika, 325–46. Boulder, CO: Westview, 1986.

Moghadam, Valentine. "Reform, Revolution and Reaction: The Trajectory of the 'Woman Question' in Afghanistan." In *Gender and National Identity: Women and Politics in Muslim Societies*, edited by Valentine Moghadam, 81–109. London: Zed Books, 1994.

Moghadam, Valentine M. "Revolution, Islamist Reaction and Women in Afghanistan." In *Women and Revolution in Africa, Asia and the New World*, edited by Mary Ann Tetrault, 211–35. Columbia: University of South Carolina Press, 1994.

Moorcraft, Paul L. *Dying for the Truth: The Concise History of Frontline War Reporting*. Barnsley, South Yorkshire: Pen & Sword Military, 2016.

Rubin, Barnett. *Fragmentation of Afghanistan: State Formation and Collapse in the International System*. New Haven, CT: Yale University Press, 2002.

Shahrani, M. Nazif Mohib, and Robert Leroy. *Revolutions & Rebellions in Afghanistan: Anthropological Perspectives*. Berkeley: Institute of International Studies, University of California, 1984.

Skaine, Rosemarie. *Women of Afghanistan in the Post-Taliban Era: How Lives Have Changed and Where They Stand Today*. Jefferson, NC: McFarland & Company, 2008.

Algeria

Background

Before Algerian independence, it was a French colony dominated by a settler class of about a million people of European and Catholic descent. Under their rule, the 9 million members of the indigenous Algerian population, speaking Arabic, and majority Sunni Muslims were subject to strict limitations on their access to education and political power. Part of France's "civilizing mission" included attempt to unveil Algerian women, producing a backlash that further entrenched traditional patriarchal families, and restrictions on women in the public sphere. At the outbreak of the war in 1954, female literacy was extremely low, especially in rural areas.

The Algerian War

Women played a significant role in the Algerian War (1954–1962), with an estimated 11,000 taking part, and 3.1 percent of those seeing active combat. This percentage is parallel to the experience of European women in World War II. Most of the women who joined the National Liberation Front (FLN) were under the age of 25 years, drawn from about 22 percent urban and 78 percent rural backgrounds. Their participation tended to be in one of three categories: *fidaiyet* (women who participated in armed action, like bombings or raids), *mussabilet* (those who were hosting and nursing combatants), and *maquisards* (those who lived with men in the field as cooks and camp logistical support). Because of their veiling, and their long service in European households as maids and servants, Algerian women could pass far more easily among the urban population. Women were also effective ambassadors of the independence movement from the FLN to the rural population and conducted educational sessions about politics, revolutionary struggle, and current events. For those whose male family members became militants, the war pushed them to

> **Counterinsurgency (COIN)**
>
> The U.S. Army Counterinsurgency manual, FM 3-24, revised in light of experiences in Iraq and Afghanistan, and meant for use in that continuing conflict, draws significant lessons learned from the experience of the French military in the Algerian War. One of the most significant lessons learned was the role of women as both agents of insurgency and as potential allies to a counterinsurgent force. Frantz Fanon (1925–1961), an Afro-Caribbean psychiatrist and National Liberation Front (FLN) diplomat, and David Galula (1919–1967), a French army officer, both wrote about the war in the Kabyle region and observed the role of women in that traditional, rural area.
>
> Fanon's view was through the lens of his experience in Vichy Martinique, as a nonwhite Free French soldier and Marxist. He observed the ways in which racial and sexual stereotypes were being taken advantage of by Algerian women to move among European quarters of urban areas, to hide weapons and supplies under their voluminous robes, and that their veils were an effective disguise against a society, which found them repulsive and homogeneous. Galula, whose troops pacified Kabyle, saw the other side of the COIN: women were the network of support holding rural society together. When assured physical security, medical care, and education for their children, and treated respectfully by the French soldiers, the village women were found to be excellent sources of intelligence and conduits for the distribution of information. Additionally, offering equality and liberation was an attractive counterweight to the political goals presented by the insurgents. Both Fanon's and Galula's views found their way into 21st-century American COIN doctrine and informed the creation of units like Team Lioness concept and Female Engagement Teams for culturally sensitive outreach to women in Iraq and Afghanistan.

assume family and community duties left undone by the fighters, including monitoring the locations in which their male relatives were imprisoned and notifying others of the often short-notice execution schedules offered by the French.

Women paid a high price for their participation. One in five who associated themselves with the FLN died, and after the Battle of Algiers in 1957, the French routinely arrested and tortured suspected FLN women, and there are official reports from at least 2,200 women of this treatment. At the end of the conflict, many women found it difficult to reintegrate into society, as their families considered them unmarriageable for their unchaperoned association with men, their status as rape survivors, or their expectations of political service.

The independent government's 1962 foundation promised equality, coeducation, and health care, but the FLN excluded women from its planning councils and ignored specific demands for programs like childcare and compensation for injuries during the war.

The Civil War

Between 1962 and 1991, the Algerian government's pursuit of modernity led to gains for women as programs for increasing literacy and reducing traditional barriers for women achieved their steadily greater access to education at the primary, secondary, and university levels, especially in fields like education, law, and medicine. In 1995, 46 percent of primary students were girls, rising to 50 percent of secondary students because of higher male dropout rates. Modernity, however, competed with Arabization and a version of Islamization that called for traditional gender roles, leading President Chadli Bendjedid to make increasing accommodations to his political rivals, including the 1984 Family Code, which reduced women to the legal status of minors and guaranteed polygamy. Women organized against many provisions of the law and successfully pushed back on elements like men casting proxy votes for their wives.

These tensions exploded into civil war in 1991; when the government canceled elections, Islamist parties were likely to win. Over the next decade, militants killed 80,000–100,000 people, particularly targeting the secular educated class and women who did not conform to their traditional roles. In 1994, the Islamic Salvation Front, one of several salafi-jihadist organizations participating in the war, issued a fatwa allowing for the murder of unveiled women. Other groups routinely kidnapped women for use as cooks, laundry workers, and sex slaves via "temporary marriages." Even after the rebels lost public support because of their brutality, and the hostilities cooled in the early 2000s, the government refuses to recognize children born of these "temporary marriage" rapes as legitimate for legal purposes, nor do they acknowledge the women as victims of terrorism, which would entitle them to financial compensation.

21st-Century Military

Houari Boumédiène, president of the Revolutionary Council and then president of Algeria from 1965 to his death in 1978, sponsored the recruitment of women into the nation's armies beginning in 1978, as a mark of national modernization. This reform ended in 1986, and women were excluded from the Algerian military until 2001. In February 2006, laws passed establishing the legal equality of military men and women. Although Algeria conscripts men, women's service must be entirely voluntary, and bans remain on service in the infantry, artillery, armor, or any unit facing combat. The military service remains deeply paternalistic toward women soldiers, allowing them to consider participation in field exercises alongside men optional, on the basis that they will never see combat and are thus protected from needless risks. Women officers at or above the grade O-5 (lieutenant colonel) are allowed to retire three years before their male counterparts and may request extended leave to follow a spouse's employment or care for a family member. Except for those in the medical fields, women are not assigned night duty, and they may break their enlistment contracts if the reason is family disapproval of their service.

Most of the women in the Algerian military concentrate in the communications, social service, and medical fields. In 2009, Fatima Zohra Ardjoune, director general of the Ain Naadja hospital, was the first woman promoted to the rank of general, followed by Fatima Boudouani in 2012. As of 2017, there are five women with the rank of general officer in the Algerian military, and a pipeline of approximately 18 percent of the cadets in the country's military academies. Although restricted to noncombat roles, demographic factors like continued increase in women's higher education, later marriage, smaller families, and male preference for entrepreneurial and international remittance work suggests that access to military service plays an important role in Algeria's view of itself as modern and cognizant of its revolutionary history.

Further Reading

Amrane, Djamila. *Femmes au combat: la guerre d'Algérie (1954–1962)*. Algiers: Éditions Rahma, 1993.
Amrane, Djamila, and Farida Abu-Haidar. "Women and Politics in Algeria from the War of Independence to Our Day." *Research in African Literatures* 30, no. 3 (Fall 1999): 62–77. doi:10.1353/ral.1999.0003.
Bouatta, Cherifa. "Feminine Militancy: *Moudjahidates* during and after the Algerian War." In *Gender and National Identity*, edited by Valentine Moghadam, 18–39. London: Zed Books, 1994.
Cherifati-Merabtine, Doria. "Algeria at a Crossroads: National Liberation, Islamization and Women." In *Gender and National Identity*, edited by Valentine Moghadam, 40–62. London: Zed Books, 1994.
Decker, Jeffrey Louis. "Terrorism (Un)Veiled: Frantz Fanon and the Women of Algiers." *Cultural Critique* 17 (Winter 1990–1991): 177–95. doi:10.2307/1354144.
Fanon, Frantz. *Studies in a Dying Colonialism*. Translated by Haakon Chevalier. New York: Monthly Review Press, 1965.
Galula, David. *Pacification in Algeria, 1956–1958*. Santa Monica, CA: RAND Corporation, 2006.
Ghanem-Yazbeck, Dalia. "Women in the Men's House: The Road to Equality in the Algerian Military." *Carnegie Middle East Center*, November 4, 2015, 1–14.

Ladewig, Nicole. "Between Worlds: Algerian Women in Conflict." In *A Soldier and a Woman: Sexual Integration in the Military*, edited by Gerard de Groot and Corinna Peniston-Bird, 240–55. London: Pearson, 2000.

Petraeus, David Howell, and James F. Amos. *Counterinsurgency: FM 3-24 (2006)*. Boulder, CO: Paladin, 2009.

Slackman, Michael. "A Quiet Revolution in Algeria: Gains by Women." *New York Times*, May 26, 2007.

Turshen, Meredeth. "Algerian Women in the Liberation Struggle and the Civil War: From Active Participants to Passive Victims?" *Social Research* 69, no. 3 (Fall 2002): 889–911.

Argentina

Background

In the 19th-century Wars of Independence, women accompanied Argentine troops, acting as nurses, laundresses, and sutlers, although the uniformed military remained an all-male prerogative until the late 20th century. The military's association with and support of *junta* governments and participation in the "dirty war" of 1974–1983 seriously tarnished the prestige of the armed forces and their relationship with the civilian population. In response to leftist political movements and protests, the military government kidnapped, tortured, and disappeared as many as 20,000 citizens, using techniques learned from French actions in Algeria and the United States in Vietnam, taught at the U.S. School of the Americas. This period of state-sponsored violence against its own people came to an end in 1983, when the government miscalculated British response to an invasion of the Falkland Islands meant to burnish Argentine patriotism and military morale. In the wake of losing the Falklands War, the Argentine population restored democracy in 1983 with the election of Raul Alfonsin.

The first major military change came in 1993, as Argentina joined UN Peacekeeping forces in Cyprus, beginning a reorientation of the military to coalition and humanitarian operations. In 1994, in response to the hazing murder of Omar Carrasco, a young army conscript, the military suspended mandatory service in favor of a transition to an all-volunteer force. As part of this shift, Argentine planners studied the unification of the German army, increased the presence of liberal arts in the military academies, and in 1995, accepted the first women volunteers. Women have been rapidly included in the services, with the air force open to women in 2001, then the navy in 2002. By 2013, all career fields in the Argentine military were available to women. Since 1995, 341 women have served in Argentina's peacekeeping detachments.

> **Protest in Conflict**
>
> During Argentina's "Dirty War" (1976–1983), one of the tactics of the regime was the kidnapping, torture, and disappearance of dissidents, students, and labor leaders. As the numbers mounted with no answers, and repression of those who asked, an extraordinary protest movement emerged. Beginning in April 1977, every Thursday, dozens, then hundreds of women wearing white head scarves (many of them children's diapers, embroidered with the names of the missing) gathered in the Plaza de Mayo in Buenos Aires, across the square from the presidential palace, demanding to know the whereabouts of their missing children. Their protest drew international attention, especially during the 1978 Soccer World Cup, and the women traveled to Rome to confront Pope John Paul II over the inaction of the Catholic Church to support them in Argentina. The regime's response was brutal, with at least four of the women (whose bodies were identified by DNA analysis in 2005) kidnapped and murdered themselves.
>
> Despite this, and the 1986 Ley de Punto Final, which ended investigations into the Dirty War, the women continued to protest, publish lists of the missing, and expand their organization to women in Chile and other Latin American countries with repressive regimes. In 2005, the Argentine Supreme Court ruled the pardons and Ley de Punto Final unconstitutional and reopened searches for the bodies of the missing, eventually admitting to 9,000 (the Madres estimate 30,000 missing), and the kidnapping and illegal adoptions of more than 500 children of prisoners. One hundred and thirteen children have been found, with 31 returned to their biological families. The organization held its last march in 2006 but continues to advocate for human rights, social services for the poor, and increased participation by women in Latin American civic life.

The 21st Century

Now under more civilian control, and with strategic doctrine focused on protecting natural resources, peacekeeping in the Spanish-language world, working against transnational crime and investing in national energy independence, the military in Argentina is a generation removed from their antagonistic relationship with the civilian public. In 2007, the army formally dropped the obsolete requirement that officers get permission from their commanders to marry and agreed to recognize the "irregular relationships" of unmarried and same-sex couples. In 2005, Debora Pontecorvo, sister of a male fighter pilot, made her first solo flight in an Air Force B-45 Mentor, hoping to fly an A-29 Super Tucano, having become the first woman to pass the harsh pilot survival

Wearing their missing children's diapers as headscarves, the Mothers of the Plaza de Mayo march in Buenos Aires to demand the Argentine government reveal the whereabouts of thousands of dissidents kidnapped, tortured, and murdered by the military during the "Dirty War" of 1976–83. (Miguel Mendez/AFP/Getty Images)

course in the desert. Eliana Maria Krawczyk, who joined the Argentine Navy in 2004, became the first woman to serve on a submarine, the ARA *Salta*, and was tragically onboard the ARA *San Juan*, which was lost in an accident in November 2017.

Argentine commanders, who used to be able to count on military families moving smoothly 10–12 times over a career, assuming stay-at-home spouses and the cooperation of the national school system, are now dealing with a generation of new subordinates who have working spouses, who do not want to live in remote garrison towns, and who chafe at old paternal traditions. As more women enlist and accept commissions, this framework is likely to evolve into more family- and women-friendly policies.

Further Reading

Bosco, Ferdinand. "The Madres De Plaza De Mayo and Three Decades of Human Rights' Activism." *Annals of the Association of American Geographers* 96, no. 2 (2006): 342–65.

Bouvard, Marguerite Guzman. *Revolutionizing Motherhood: The Mothers of the Plaza de Mayo*. Lanham, MD: SR Books, 2004.

"Buen debut de la primera mujer piloto de la Fuerza Aérea." *La Nacion*, May 27, 2005. http://www.lanacion.com.ar/707876-buen-debut-de-la-primera-mujer-piloto-de-la-fuerza-aerea.

"Cualquier Mujer Que Quiera, Puede." Ministerio de Defensa – Argentina. https://www.facebook.com/MindefArg/videos/832524733554286/.

Feinsilber, Marina Malamud. "Latin American Peacekeeping Operations: A Sociopolitical Overview." In *Advances in Military Sociology: Essays in Honor of Charles C. Moskos*, edited by Giuseppe Caforio, 139–55. Bingley, UK: Emerald, 2009.

Frederic, Sabena, and Laura Masson. "Profession and the Military Family: Generational Differences and Socio-Cultural Changes." In *Military Families and War in the 21st Century*, edited by Rene Moelker, Manon Andres, Gary Bowen, and Philippe Manigart, 73–83. London: Routledge, 2015.

"Grandmothers' President Recovers Grandson Taken Away under Dictatorship." *Buenos Aires Herald*, August 5, 2014. http://buenosairesherald.com/article/166359/grandmothers-president-recovers-grandson-taken-away-under-dictatorship.

Gutierrez, Oman. "Changes in the Military Profession in Latin American Countries." In *Advances in Military Sociology: Essays in Honor of Charles C. Moskos*, edited by Guisseppe Caforio, 65–96. Bingley, UK: Emerald, 2009.

Masson, Laura E. "Women in the Military in Argentina: Nationalism, Gender, and Ethnicity." In *Gender Panic, Gender Policy (Advances in Gender Research, Volume 24)*, edited by Vasilikie Demos and Marcia Texler Segal, 23–43. Bingley, UK: Emerald Publishing Limited, 2017.

McLaughlin, Eliott C. "Search for Argentine Submarine Enters 'Critical Phase'." *CNN*, November 23, 2017. http://www.cnn.com/2017/11/22/americas/argentina-missing-submarine/index.html.

Robben, Antonius C. G. M. "Mourning and Mistrust in Civil-Military Relations in Post-Dirty War Argentina." In *The Soldier and the State in South America: Essays in Civil-Military Relations*, edited by Patricio Silva, 109–126. London: Palgrave, 2001.

Salguero, Miguel. "Civil Military Relations in the Modern Democratic Argentina Era: Army Soldiers as Military Professionals versus Civilians in Uniform." Master's thesis, U.S. Army War College, 2011.

Australia

Background

Triggered by the loss of the American Colonies in 1783, the British government sent out the "First Fleet" to Australia in order to claim the land they had previously surveyed. Part of the pressure was to have a place to send convicted criminals from overcrowded urban jails, as well as to allow dislocated farmers pushed off the land from the Highland Clearances and enclosure to resettle elsewhere. Clashes with the aboriginal inhabitants, as well as the dangerous plants and animals, made it necessary for women, as well as men, to defend and care for themselves on remote stations. This frontier mentality has often positioned Australia to be used as a comparison to the United States on issues like gun ownership and perception of personal freedoms.

As part of the British Commonwealth, Australia sent troops to the Boer War in South Africa in 1899. The Australian Army Nursing Service was created to serve the New South Wales military force, later augmented by the Army Nursing Reserve. At the end of that war, as part of the foundation of the Commonwealth of Australia in 1901, women received the right to federal suffrage, building on earlier voting in individual states. During World War I, Australian nurses were called up, with 2,000 sent overseas to provide medical care for soldiers in the Middle Eastern theater and on the Western Front. Fifteen of the 129 Australian women with medical degrees also joined the military, which, in need of skilled medical personnel, was friendlier to the new phenomena of women practitioners than the general public. At a field station in Abbeville, France, Dr. Phoebe Chapple survived a German aerial bombardment that killed 10 of her nurses and worked through the night by the light of a burning ambulance, earning recognition in the form of the Military Medal. Olive King, who had been famous as a mountain climber and rally driver before World War I, funded her own ambulance, which she drove in the Balkans as an auxiliary to the Serbian army. After the Armistice, the

> **Contractors**
>
> Since 2002, many countries have dealt with strained personnel numbers and multiple deployments by outsourcing logistical and support services like laundry and mess halls to private military-contracting companies, leading to one estimate that in 2012, the proportion of soldiers to contractors is 10:1. Companies often hire poorly paid third-party nationals from countries like Namibia and Uganda to do the cooking and cleaning, while recruiting former military personnel for armed security, prison staff, body-guarding, and asset protection of oil wells. Companies pay contractors more than they would receive as uniformed personnel, but the contracts and arrangements often include nondisclosure agreements, binding arbitration, and no responsibility for injuries suffered on the job.
>
> Neryl Joyce, a former Australian army officer, joined Blackwater and served rotations in Iraq from 2004 to 2006, working to protect members of the Iraqi Elections Commission. She had previously been trained by the military to do protection of dignitaries, and as a single mother, the significant increase in pay was attractive. She, like many other women contractors, found that lax supervision and a macho culture of risk-taking, drinking, and sexual abuse were endemic, with few recourses to report these transgressions to a responsible jurisdiction, and that the dangers were as acute as those for active duty military. Some critics of private contracting argue that in order to downplay the less traditionally male activities they undertake (protection, guards, and supply), they amp up an image of action, mega-masculinity, and heroics, leading to harassment of women coworkers and abuse of local people.

women were demobilized, although some, like Chaple and King, parlayed their experiences into work in public health, the Red Cross, and the Girl Guides.

World War II and Cold War

Australia once again joined Great Britain in preparing for war in 1939, but the swift collapse of British garrisons in the Far East in 1942 raised real possibilities of Japanese invasion. Women moved into factory and farmwork to free men for service and volunteered as air-raid wardens and trained to give first aid by organizations like the Women's National Emergency Legion. Beginning in 1941, the air force, army, and navy created women's auxiliary services, recruiting an eventual 50,000, all of whom were paid 68 percent of the rate of their male peers.

The army service was under the command of Lt. Colonel Sybil Irving, a social worker from a military family, who carefully began with a core cadre of 29 women and insisted both that her women soldiers be able to be deployed overseas, but should never be armed, and that they do noncombat jobs as clerical, administrative, and communications staff. The military bent this rule in the case of antiaircraft work, assigning 3,618 women as crews to defend the coastline.

Because of the nearness of hospitals to the battlefield, nurses were most endangered, with 41 dying on active duty, from disease and enemy fire, and 8 as prisoner of war camps. One extraordinary nursing sister, Vivian Bullwinkel, was evacuated from Singapore in advance of the Japanese invasion, but was on the SS *Vyner Brooke*, which sank after being torpedoed. She and other survivors made it to land but were captured by the Japanese, who machine gunned the prisoners. Bullwinkel, wounded, escaped into the jungle, evading Japanese search parties for 12 days before being recaptured and sent to a prison camp. She later testified at the Tokyo War Crimes Trials about the execution of her shipmates. Australian Nancy Wake joined the clandestine British Special Operations Executive (SOE) and operated an escape network, courier service, and maquis squad in southern France. Major Mabel Josephine Mackerras, an entomologist, working for the Land Headquarters Medical Research Unit, did research to test the efficacy of malaria prevention drugs, as disease-bearing mosquitos were a major problem for troops in Southeast Asia.

By 1947, the Australian military had demobilized its World War II personnel and disbanded the women's auxiliaries. Three years later, as the nation contributed forces to the Korean War, the manpower shortage prompted a reestablishment of permanent women's divisions of the army, navy, and air force, largely drawn from World War II veterans, with numbers capped at 4 percent of the total number of men, later lifted to 10 percent by the air force and navy during the 1960s. The women attended separate officers' schools, first at Mildura in 1952, replaced by Georges Heights, Sydney, in 1957. Women from these divisions served in Vietnam, usually as nurses and medical aides, and civilian Australian women were present as religious missionaries, Red Cross volunteers, and entertainers recruited by the United Service Organizations (USO), including an aboriginal rock and soul group, the Sapphires. The Vietnam War was not widely supported by the Australian public, with many protests organized by feminist groups and antinuclear activists.

Social change and the women's movement began to catch up with the military in the early 1970s. In 1973, the prime minister appointed a special adviser, Elizabeth Reid, an expert on international development, to examine the role of women in Australian society. As part of the 1975 International Year of the Woman, the military implemented reforms, which allowed women to remain in uniform after becoming pregnant, although they continued strict no-combat limitations. The air force merged its women's division into the mainstream service in 1977, followed by the army in 1979 and the navy in 1985. At their request, the services were granted exemption from the Sex Discrimination Act in 1984, allowing women to be paid 80–85 percent of men's salaries and for 60 percent of trades to remain off limits on the grounds that they were combat or combat-related.

The 21st Century and Integration of Women

At the end of the Cold War, Australia examined its forces in light of new defense strategies and another wave of personnel shortages to the all-volunteer force. A government review in 1990 recommended all positions be available to women, but instead, the military opened combat-related jobs, including service on warships and as pilots. One of the first to earn wings was Linda Corbould, who had represented Australia at international competitions as a skydiver. Infantry, engineer, diver, armor, and artillery roles remained off-limits. During the 1990s, Australia sent troops to Iraq, including women on the HMAS *Westralia*, which was in a combat zone, and to Peacekeeping Missions in Western Sahara (1993), Rwanda (1994–1995), and East Timor (1999), where 440 of the 5,500 deployed were women. Captain Carol Vaughan-Evans, a doctor, earned the Medal of Gallantry for her coolness under fire during an attack on her hospital in Rwanda. The acquisition of Collins-class submarines allowed for the integration of women to crews in 1997. Realizing that the military support systems needed to evolve along with the personnel demographics, separate service centers were merged into the Defense Community Organization in 1996 and reoriented to the needs of more diverse military families. In the late 1990s, women moved into high ranks, with Lt. Jennifer Daetz commanding the HMAS *Shepparton* in 1997, then Lt. Colonel Tracy Dobis as commanding officer of the army training command in 1998. The first woman general officer was Air Commodore Julie Hammer, who pinned on her first of two stars in 2000, after a career in electronic warfare.

Entering the 21st century, Australia's armed forces were 13.8 percent women. This change, however, had not eradicated traditional attitudes or lifted restrictions on combat jobs. At public ceremonies, women in uniform and veterans wearing their medals were frequently challenged by civilians unfamiliar with the presence of women in the military at all about their service. A commissioned study found harassment and incidents of discrimination out of proportion to the civilian population, and scandals on the HMS *Swan* and at the Australian Defense Force Academy eroded women's interest in joining at a time when women were finding greater success in the civilian workforce. The Academy case, in which a cadet secretly transmitted video feed of himself on Skype having sex with a fellow cadet, prompted an investigation by the chair of the Sex Discrimination Committee of the Australian Human Rights Commission, Elizabeth Broderick, whose team recommended major changes. Additionally,

Lt. General David Morrison recorded a scathing critique of harassment culture that went viral on YouTube around the world, insisting "the standard you walk past is the standard you accept" as a challenge to commanders and bystanders tolerating abuse in their units.

Morrison oversaw the implementation of Plan Beersheba, which included opening all roles except special operations in 2011, then lifting that last barrier in 2016. Although women had been flying, including Flight Lt. Joanne Mein, who served on the prestigious acrobatic flying team, the Roulettes, the first women fighter pilots graduated from training in December 2017. Morrison retired in 2015, but the structure he put in place is a strong response to a persistence culture of resistance to women's inclusion, and the forces have set ambitious recruitment targets to further involve women. Already, by 2016, the percentage of women had increased to 15.8, largely credited to these changes.

Further Reading

Beaumont, Joan. *Australia's War, 1938–1945*. St. Leonard's, NSW: Allen & Unwin, 1995.

Carroll, Luke. "Raising a Female-Centric Battalion: Do We Have the Nerve?" *Australian Army Journal* 11, no. 1 (Winter 2014): 34–56.

"Chief of Army Fires Broadside at Troops." *ABC News*, June 14, 2013. http://www.abc.net.au/news/2013-06-14/chief-of-army-fires-broadside-at-army-over-email-allegations/4753208.

Downs, Cathy. "Australia and New Zealand: Contingent and Concordant Militaries." In *The Postmodern Military: Armed Forces after the Cold War*, edited by Charles Moskos, 182–204. Oxford: Oxford University Press, 2000.

Doyle, Jeff, Jeffery Grey, and Peter Pierce. *Australia's Vietnam War*. College Station: Texas A&M Press, 2002.

Eichler, Maya. *Gender and Private Security in Global Politics*. New York: Oxford University Press, 2015.

Horner, David. *Making the Australian Defense Force*. Oxford: Oxford University Press, 2001.

Joachim, Jutta, and Andrea Schneiker. "Of 'True Professionals' and 'Ethical Hero Warriors': A Gender-Discourse Analysis of Private Military and Security Companies." *Security Dialogue* 43, no. 6 (2012): 495–512. doi:10.1177/0967010612463488.

Joyce, Neryl. *Mercenary Mum: My Journey from Young Mother to Baghdad Bodyguard*. Strawberry Hills, NSW: ReadHowYouWant, 2016.

McHugh, Siobhan. *Minefields and Miniskirts: Australian Women and the Vietnam War*. South Melbourne, Victoria: Lothian Books, 2005.

Raphael, Beverly, Susan Neuhaus, and Samantha Crompvoets. "Women and War: Australia." In *Women at War*, edited by Elspeth Cameron Ritchie and Anne L. Naclerio, 34–48. Oxford: Oxford University Press, 2016.

Schreuder, Deryck, and Stuart Ward, eds. *Australia's Empire*. Oxford: Oxford University Press, 2008.
Seigel, Matt. "Australia Says It Will Open Combat Roles to Women." *The New York Times*, September 28, 2011. http://www.nytimes.com/2011/09/28/world/asia/australia-will-allow-women-to-serve-in-frontline-combat.html.
Siebler, Philip. "Down Under Support for Military Families from an Australian Perspective." In *Military Families and War in the 21st Century: Comparative Perspectives*, edited by Rene Moelker and Manon Andres, 287–301. London: Routledge, 2015.
Wadley, J. "Gendering the State: Performativity and Protection in International Security." In *Gender and International Security*, edited by Laura Sjoberg, 38–58. London: Routledge, 2010.

Brazil

Background

The first woman to serve in the Brazilian army was Maria Quiteria de Jesus, who joined the War of Independence in 1823, disguised in male dress. Her father outed her to the authorities, but she persisted, winning medals for bravery and honors from the Brazilian Emperor. In 1996, the army named her patron of staff officers, but in the 19th century, strictly forbade any further participation by women in military affairs. In 1943, because the military junta of Getulio Vargas was as an ally of the United States, Brazil sent 73 nurses to serve in 4 American field hospitals in the European theater of World War II. In Brazil, the military and its academies had long been a vehicle for technological innovation and one of the few engineering schools, as well as one of the few paths to social mobility for talented recruits from the lower classes. In the 1960s, after the restoration of civilian political control, the Escola Superior de Guerra, teaching a curriculum of "new professionalism" and supported by the U.S. Cold War policy, encouraged military officers to once again intervene in the democratic process. From 1964 to 1985, a series of military regimes ruled Brazil, engaging in the kinds of anti-leftist tactics practiced in Argentina and Chile, which included kidnappings, torture, and deportations.

The 21st Century and the Integration of Women

One of the features of restored democracy in the 1980s was the inclusion of women into the military, as a separate reserve corps. Men are still required to do mandatory service as conscripts, but in the 21st century, Brazil is moving to a more professionalized volunteer force, under increased civilian control. In the 1990s, the military amalgamated its separate women's reserve into the active duty military, opening spaces at the Army Administration School to women in 1992. Further personnel needs have led to, in 1996, opening service to women already qualified as medical officers, then accepting women students to the military medical schools in 1997. The success of specialized technological service internships for women systems analysts, architects, accountants, and lawyers led to the opening of the Air Force Academy to women in 1999, with the first women qualifying as pilots in 2006.

Brazil's first woman general officer was Rear Admiral Dalva Maria Carvalho, who achieved that rank in 2012. The Brazilian military currently enjoys substantial public approval for their actions undertaken to control urban organized crime and combat public disorder. The strategic planning of the Brazilian armed forces focuses on joint peacekeeping, especially in the Lusophone world, control of the Amazon basin and its resources, and prevention of neighboring threats, like the Revolutionary Armed Forces of Colombia (FARC) guerrillas, from having safe havens in Brazil's borderlands. As peacekeepers, Brazilian military participants believe that, being from a developing nation, they better understand the origins of conflict in inequality and social disorder and can be more effective in situations like the 2006 Haitian elections. The continued requirements of the country for a large, professional, and increasingly STEM-oriented (science, technology, engineering, and math) military argue for increased participation by women and their promotion.

Further Reading

Castro, Celos. "The Army as a Modernizing Actor in Brazil, 1870–1930." In *The Soldier and the State in South America: Essays in Civil-Military Relations*, edited by Patricio Silva, 53–70. London: Palgrave, 2001.

Estrada Portales, Isabel. "Brazil Boosts Female Officers to Leadership Positions within the Military." *Dialogo Americas*. https://dialogo-americas.com/en/articles/brazil-boosts-female-officers-leadership-positions-within-military.

Feinsilber, Marina Malamud. "Latin American Peacekeeping Operations: A Sociopolitical Overview." In *Advances in Military Sociology: Essays in Honor of Charles C. Moskos*, edited by Giuseppe Caforio, 139–55. Bingley, UK: Emerald, 2009.

Gutierrez, Oman. "Changes in the Military Profession in Latin American Countries." In *Advances in Military Sociology: Essays in Honor of Charles C. Moskos*, edited by Guiseppe Caforio, 65–96. Bingley, UK: Emerald, 2009.

Ministry of Defense. "Quitéria lutou pelo Exército, mas só 120 anos depois mulheres foram admitidas." *O Jornol de Todos os Brasil*, January 28, 2015. https://jornalggn.com.br/noticia/quiteria-lutou-pelo-exercito-mas-so-120-anos-depois-mulheres-foram-admitidas.

Stepan, Alfred. *Rethinking Military Politics: Brazil and the Southern Cone*. Princeton, NJ: Princeton University Press, 1988.

Canada

Background

Since settlement in the 17th century, Canada's vast size has fostered an ethos of responsibility of citizens to be responsible for their own security and to take part in providing defense for their neighbors as part of local militias. Women on rural homesteads were expected to be able to defend the family while male relatives were with the militia, which they did in the face of the French in the Seven Years' War, Americans during the Revolutionary War, and Americans again in the War of 1812, as well as in conflicts with the First Nations people. During the Metis Rebellion (1871–1885), a movement of mixed-race French-First Nations people against the authority of the Hudson's Bay Company and the Confederation, both the Metis and the government of Canada relied on women for support functions, especially nursing the wounded and providing succor to displaced people.

When Canada sent troops to fight in the Anglo-Boer war in 1899, the government created the Canadian Army Medical Department and dispatched four nurses, who were assigned the status of lieutenants. By the end of the war in 1902, this number had doubled to 8 nursing sisters, who worked alongside British medical staff to care for 7,000 Canadian soldiers sent to South Africa. The service retained 5 women as permanent personnel and maintained a roster of 57 reserve nurses who could be called up in emergencies.

The World Wars

Canada quickly joined Great Britain in declaring war on the Central Powers in 1914. Like the recruitment of young men, enlistment materials for women stressed the duty to serve as well as the adventure and independence offered by overseas deployment. Women who chose to stay at home played a vital role in the rationing and war production work necessary to supply the forces, while more than 3,000 women answered the call to be nurses. Recognized as skilled

> **War Memorials**
>
> As part of the 1992 Canada 125 celebrations, the Department of National Defense and National Capital Commission jointly sought a memorial design commemorating the service of 120,000 Canadians in UN Peacekeeping missions. The winning design, from Jack Harmon, Richard Henriquez, and Cornelia Hahn Oberlander, is unusual among the other memorials in Ottawa's Confederation Square for featuring a uniformed military woman. Other markers, like the National War Memorial (1939), the National Aboriginal War Memorial (2001), and Valiants Memorial (2006), feature women but in roles as nurses and civilian patriots on the home front.
>
> The memorial features three peacekeepers standing watch on an austere wall, tiled to evoke the local style of Nicosia, Cyprus. The three military figures look toward a serene grove of trees, representing a secure life for survivors of conflict. The two male figures stand guard and gaze into the distance with field glasses while the female figure kneels to use the radio and communicate what they see. The statue, which cost $2.8 million, is titled "Reconciliation: In the Service of Peace" and is inscribed with a quote from Lester Pearson's 1956 proposal for a UN Peacekeeping force and a list of 48 locations where Canadians have served as peacekeepers.

professionals, their pay of $4 a day was significantly higher than a male infantryman and underscored their value and scarcity. Because nurses worked on ships and at frontline casualty clearing stations, they were often under enemy fire. By 1918, 47 Canadian nurses had died from disease or enemy fire, including 4 who drowned in the torpedoing of the HMHS *Llandovery Castle*. In 1916, in an attempt to recruit more Asian and First Nations soldiers, the government lifted the ban on suffrage for these groups, prompting women's organizations to demand the same in recognition of patriotic service. Women with relatives in the military gained suffrage in 1917, followed by universal adult female voting in 1919 in all of Canada except Quebec, which waited until 1940.

The outbreak of World War II in 1939 prompted the revival of many women's organizations, like the Red Cross and the Women's Volunteer Service, to support the nation's military efforts. During the Great Depression of the previous decades, women had already been practicing the frugality, recycling, and informal economy of part-time work, which the government now needed officially. War work was especially appealing to women who had been pushed out of teaching or manufacturing in the effort to limit families to one paid job, and women eagerly lined up to work as "bomb girls" and step into the jobs left

Volunteers in the Women's Royal Canadian Naval Service ("Wrens") traveling aboard the HMCS *Sudbury* in 1943. Wrens served in shore assignments as administrators, maintained map plots in headquarters, and performed signals intelligence jobs until their WWII service was demobilized in 1946. (Corel)

open as men were called up. In June 1941, the British Mechanized Transport Corps began recruiting women in Canada to drive trucks and act as drivers for senior leaders, and Canada followed by creating the Canadian Women's Army Corps (21,000 personnel), the Women's Royal Canadian Naval Service (7,000), and the Canadian Women's Auxiliary Air Force (17,000), along with deploying 5,000 nurses from the medical corps. Recruiting women was meant to make more men available for combat service and resulted in women who had been trained to be photograph analysts, telegraph and telephone operators, mechanics, military police, laboratory assistants, and medical aides. Most women were demobilized in 1945, with small numbers, usually medical personnel, clerks, and food service workers remaining in uniform.

Approximately 5,000 women in the auxiliary forces served in support jobs during the Korean War, to which Canada sent 25,000 men, but remained a small minority in separate women's divisions of the services. In 1965, the government mandated that no more than 1,500 women in total might serve and amalgamated those who stayed into the regular army, navy, or air force. In 1970, however, the general feeling of anti-militarism engendered by the Vietnam War among young people, and the growing presence of the women's rights movement strained the ability of recruiters to find potential soldiers in the Canadian population. The Royal Commission on the Status of Women issued recommendations, accepted by the military, that the cap of 1,500 women be lifted, 33 of 95 trades be available, women be allowed to remain in service after they married, and they would not be dismissed when they became pregnant. In 1974, Major Wendy Clay, a military doctor, was the first woman in the Canadian Air Force to earn pilot wings, furthering her expertise in aeronautical medicine and medical evacuation. In 1994, as a major general, Clay became Canada's 14th surgeon general.

The passage of the Human Rights Act in 1978 raised questions about the limits placed on women's service, and the government ordered Service Women in Non-Traditional Environments and Roles (SWINTER) trials to determine where gender exclusion was necessary for a military occupation to be effective. After these experiments, the navy chose to allow women on noncombat vessels, and the air force found that they could field women air crew effectively. Ahead of the other services, the air force selected three women captains, Deanna Brasseur, Leah Mosher, and Nora Bottomley, for pilot training in 1979. In 1980, the Royal Military College accepted its first women students and faculty, although hazing was rampant and rarely reported by women who feared that complaints would end their inclusion all together. In Gallup polling done in this period, about half of the Canadian public supported women serving in expanded military roles. Civilians in Canada expected increased equality, as reflected in the 1982 Equal Employment Law and Charter of Rights and Freedoms. Activists made the case that excluding women from full military service damaged their prospects for jobs in the civilian workforce that favored veterans, like airline pilots and police officers. In 1987, the government ordered Combat Related Employment of Women (CREW) trials on a destroyer and in armor, engineering, and signals units to determine if there were jobs for which the military could seek exemption from the equal employment law on the grounds of operational effectiveness.

In 1989, Georgia Ann Brown, joined by Isabelle Gauthier, Marie-Claude Gauthier, and Joseph G. Houlden, petitioned the Canadian Human Rights Tribunal, claiming that the ban on women from some military trades was in violation of the Charter. The women had all been blocked from transfer or promotion because of quotas, while Houlden, a pilot, alleged it was unfair to place the burden on combat entirely on men. The Tribunal ruled that restrictions on women in the military were unsupportable and that the limits were in place because of traditional beliefs, not deficits in the women's ability. Affirming that the Canadian Forces should reflect the population, they ordered immediate integration, and the use of the CREW trials as a vehicle to accomplish it, with oversight remaining in place for a decade. Private Heather Erxleben became the first woman to pass the infantry training course in 1989, with Lieutenants Anne Reiffenstein and Holly Brown and Captain Linda Shrum completing artillery training and taking command of combat arms units in

1991. Reiffenstein later deployed with peacekeeping units to Cyprus, Uganda, and Rwanda in the 1990s.

Despite these advances, the military had not fully reckoned with resistance and hazing. As Canadian women soldiers served in the First Gulf War, they had to deal with harassment and sexual assault, as well as negligent oversight by military authorities. When Colonel Romeo LaLonde was court-martialed in 1994 for actions during his command in the Gulf, the court found him guilty and demoted him in rank, only to have an appeal overturn the judgement. Sandra Perron, who was the first woman infantry officer and deployed as a peacekeeper in Yugoslavia, detailed extensive harassment and abuse in her 2017 memoir, *Out Standing in the Field*. The title refers both to her striving for excellence and to the night her training colleagues, simulating a prisoner of war (POW) scenario, left her tied to a tree in freezing weather. Canadians were further scandalized in 1993, when members of the Canadian Airborne Regiment, acting as peacekeepers in Somalia, killed Ahmed Arush, a Somali teenager caught in the process of stealing from their base. Days later, two other members of the unit confronted Shidane Abukar Arone on suspicion of attempting to sneak into the Canadian base, and then beat him to death after sodomizing him with a broomstick. Investigations revealed a culture of toxic masculinity, white supremacy, and aggression, which undermined Canadians' sense of themselves as supporters of a humanitarian mission and social justice. Similar shockwaves emerged when *Maclean's* magazine published accounts from women in the forces whose rapes, eventually totaling 24, and harassment by fellow military personnel had gone unpunished and tolerated.

In response, the Canadian Forces developed anti-harassment and assault prevention training, but women continue to report struggling with double standards like being punished for crying, while men hit walls in frustration and escape reprimand. Supports have evolved to include single parents, same-sex couples, and extended families, but resentment of women who take pregnancy leave and systems designed for male heads of households continue to cause friction. Women have demanded the design of ergonomic equipment like the new rucksack and the discontinuation of demeaning training videos, like a hypothermia film that demonstrated symptoms on a woman in a bikini. The last barrier to full integration, the absence of women on submarines because of the lack of facilities for them, ended in 2001 with the acquisition of Victoria Class vessels.

After 9/11, Canada joined the United States in invading Iraq and Afghanistan as part of the Coalition. The presence of women in combat roles created friction with allies who were not prepared for this reality, even though only 8 percent of the women deployed were in those jobs. Additionally, Afghanistan represented the first time that Canadian troops had been in firefights since the Korean War. On May 17, 2006, Captain Nichola Goddard, commanding a Light

Armored Vehicle (LAV) in her place as a Forward Operating Observer at the Battle of Panjwaii, called in artillery fire on enemy positions before being killed when a rocket-propelled grenade (RPG) struck the LAV. Prime Minister Stephen Harper announced her death, the first of a Canadian woman in combat, during Parliament's vote to extend the mission to Afghanistan, which subsequently passed 149–145.

Goddard's parents and husband allowed her letters to be published, familiarizing Canadians with a young woman who joined the forces for college money and to serve in humanitarian missions, but whose hand pinpointed the use of the nation's deadly force. Goddard's service record was also an example of a woman serving under austere conditions at close quarters with men and earning the admiration and loyalty of her enlisted male subordinates. Because Goddard herself had downplayed her status as a trailblazer, supporters of women in the military praised her for normalizing combat experience, while critics saw her death as an exploitation of women by an imperialist government. Afghan president Hamid Karzai issued a statement mourning the death of a "lady from Canada" who had been killed protecting Afghans when she should have been protected as a guest. Unprepared for the death of a woman, the government had to adjust the regulations to award her widower, Jason Beam, the silver cross medal usually awarded to a mother or wife of a fallen soldier.

Since 2006, there have been further women casualties. Master Corporal Kristal Giesbrecht and Trooper Karine Blais, a medic, were killed by improvised explosive devices (IEDs) in 2009–2010, and Major Michelle Mendes's suicide in Kandahar was connected to the stress of her second tour of Afghanistan. Major Eleanor Taylor, in 2010, took command of an infantry company, making her the first woman to lead a frontline combat unit and was consulted by the U.S. Marine Corps on the process of integrating women. Taylor has explained in interviews that Afghan men not only had mentally compartmentalized her as "foreign" rather than female, allowing her to work with them in ways unavailable to local woman, but also saw her as being more compassionate and approachable than armed men. Infantry Captain Ashley Collette earned the Medal of Military Valour, Canada's third highest military honor, for "fortitude under fire" during intense combat in Panwajii. The nearly 30 years since integration began mean that women are climbing to senior leadership positions, like Colonel Jennie Carignan, who was Task Force Kandahar's senior combat engineer in 2009. Defense planners believe not just that the armed forces of Canada should reflect the diverse population but also that maintaining the high quality of the nation's volunteer soldiers mandates the recruitment and retention of women across all military occupations. As a reflection of this, 21st-century commemorations of historical events, including the new Juno Beach Museum in Normandy, opened in 2003, are conscientious about celebrating the military contributions of all Canadians in a multicultural society.

Further Reading

Charbonneau, Bruno, and Wayne S. Cox. *Locating Global Order: American Power and Canadian Security after 9/11.* Vancouver: UBC Press, 2014.

Davis, Karen D. *Women and Leadership in the Canadian Forces: Perspectives and Experience.* Kingston, Ontario: Canadian Defence Academy Press, 2007.

Davis, Karen D., and Stéphanie A. H. Bélanger. *Transforming Traditions: Women, Leadership and the Canadian Navy, 1942–2010.* Kingston, Ontario: Canadian Defence Academy Press, 2010.

Dundas, Barbara. *A History of Women in the Canadian Military.* Montreal: Art Global and Department of National Defense in Cooperation with Department of Public Works and Government Services Canada, 2000.

Fortney, Valerie. *Sunray: The Death and Life of Captain Nichola Goddard.* Toronto: McArthur, 2011.

Fremeth, Howard. "Searching for the Militarization of Canadian Culture: The Rise of a Military-Culture Memory Network." *TOPIA: Canadian Journal of Cultural Studies* 23–24 (2010): 52–76.

Gill, Ritu, and Angela R. Febbraro. "Experiences and Perceptions of Sexual Harassment in the Canadian Forces Combat Arms." *Violence against Women* 19, no. 2 (2013): 269–87. doi:10.1177/1077801213478140.

Gossage, Carolyn. *Greatcoats and Glamour Boots: Canadian Women at War (1939–1945).* Toronto: Dundurn, 2016.

Gough, Paul. " 'Invicta Pax': Monuments, Memorials and Peace: An Analysis of the Canadian Peacekeeping Monument, Ottawa." *International Journal of Heritage Studies* 8, no. 3 (2002): 201–23. doi:10.1080/1352725022000018903.

Harrison, Deborah, and Patrizia Albanese. *Growing up in Armyville: Canada's Military Families during the Afghanistan Mission.* Waterloo, Ontario: Wilfrid Laurier University Press, 2016.

"Juno Beach Centre." 2018. http://www.junobeach.org/.

Kitchen, Brenda Lee. "Ma'am, Yes Ma'am: Gender Relations and Institutional Change in the Royal Newfoundland Regiment." Master's thesis, Memorial University of Newfoundland, 2003.

McLaurin, Kathleen. "Organizational Values and Cultural Diversity in the Canadian Forces: The Case of Aboriginal Peoples." In *Challenge and Change in the Military: Gender and Diversity Issues*, edited by Franklin Pinch, 146–70. Winnipeg: Canadian Forces Leadership Institute, 2004.

O'Hara, Jane, Brenda Branswell, John Geddes, Shanda Deziel, Sharon Doyle Driedger, and Stephanie Nolen. "Rape in the Military." *Macleans.ca.* April 23, 2014. http://www.macleans.ca/news/canada/rape-in-the-military/.

Perron, Sandra. *Outstanding in the Field: A Memoir of Military Service.* Toronto: Cormorant Books, 2017.

Pinch, Franklin. "Canada: Managing Change with Shrinking Resources." In *The Postmodern Military: Armed Forces after the Cold War*, edited by Charles Moskos, 156–81. Oxford: Oxford University Press, 2000.

Poulin, Grace. *Invisible Women: WWII Aboriginal Servicewomen in Canada*. Ottawa: Library and Archives Canada, 2007.

Symonds, Ellen. "Under Fire: Canadian Women in Combat." *Canadian Journal of Women and the Law* 4, no. 2 (1991): 477–511.

Taber, Nancy. "Learning How to be a Woman in the Canadian Forces/Unlearning It through Feminism: An Autoethnography of My Learning Journey." *Studies in Continuing Education* 27, no. 3 (2005): 289–301. doi:10.1080/01580370500376630.

Weinstein, Laurie Lee, and Christie C. White. *Wives and Warriors: Women and the Military in the United States and Canada*. Westport, CT: Bergin & Garvey, 1997.

Winslow, Donna, and Jason Dunn. "Women in Canadian Forces." In *Proceedings of the Challenge of Continuity, Change and the Military, ISA RC 01*, edited by Gerhard Kummel, 15–56. 2015.

Chile

Background

As one of the most conservative of the Catholic Latin American states, the participation of women in military service is of extremely recent vintage. Throughout the Spanish colonial period and Wars of Independence, women existed on the periphery of conflicts and were sidelined entirely with the professionalization of the military in the 19th century, as Chile sought out European advisers to train, supply, and organize their forces in the wake of Chile's 1879–1884 War of the Pacific against its Peruvian and Bolivian neighbors. It was, however, acceptable for women to attend institutions of higher education, particularly those preparing them for the highly gendered occupations of teaching and nursing, so that beginning with the founding of women's academies in the 1870s, women comprised a large proportion of college enrollment by the 1960s. Women earned the right of suffrage in Chile in 1949 and reliably voted Conservative via highly organized women's workshops patronized by wealthy oligarchs.

Crisis came to Chile in the form of the 1970 election of socialist Salvador Allende. Although many women, especially students, supported Allende, others did not—the Socialist and Communist parties had women's auxiliaries rather than full inclusion of women's concerns, and their reforms on divorce, legitimizing children and property, threatened the familiar social order and economic crises caused runs on staple food products. When trucking companies went on strike against the government (which the U.S. Central Intelligence Agency had a hand in funding, under the 1972 "September Plan"), drivers' wives organized demonstrations, manufactured spikes to sabotage replacement trucks, and goaded the military by throwing chicken feed at them as an accusation of cowardice. In September 1973, the Chilean military turned decisively against Allende, murdering him in an invasion of the presidential palace and installing General Augusto Pinochet as the head of a right-wing *junta*. For the next 17 years, the armed forces in Chile were key to Pinochet's campaign of repression and terror, in which the regime tortured, kidnapped, and killed thousands of dissidents.

In 1988, Pinochet, whose government had been gradually relaxing their restrictive controls on the press, speech, and assembly, allowed a plebiscite to approve an eight-year continuation of his rule but was voted down and replaced by a democratically elected president. The subsequent constitutional reforms have placed the military under civilian control and engaged the institution in a truth and reconciliation process. The appointment of socialist politician Michelle Bachelet, the daughter of an air force general assassinated by Pinochet's regime in 1973, as the first woman minister of defense, and then president, has led to significant changes in the Chilean military and women's role in Chilean society.

The 21st Century and Integration of Women

Women had joined the military police in 1962, after an earthquake overstretched the capabilities of existing personnel, advancing to jobs in criminology, the horse-mounted police, and gained entry to the police academy in 1990. Chile's first woman general officer was Brigadier General Mireya Perez of the Carabineros Department for Protection of the Family, dealing with domestic violence and sexual assault. Since 1974, Pinochet's regime allowed women to serve in educational and administrative support jobs but with caps on advancement.

In the 1990s, as part of the Alcazar Plan process of scaling back reliance on conscripts and transitioning to high-tech weaponry, women were allowed to serve in support functions, then admitted to academies and, in 2000, aviation schools. The government was surprised when, having opened 1,000 places in the military for women, they received 3,000 applications. In 2003, Chile opened all career fields to women. Like its neighbors, Chile has shifted from strategic planning for border warfare to positioning itself as a provider of peacekeepers and readied to fight transnational crime and deal with humanitarian disasters. Chile's armed forces face an ongoing process of retaining the trust of the civilian population, while adjusting a deeply conservative and paternal organization to the reality of dual-career soldiers, working mothers, and a globalized officer class used to working with international allies.

Further Reading

Feinsilber, Marina Malamud. "Latin American Peacekeeping Operations: A Sociopolitical Overview." In *Advances in Military Sociology: Essays in Honor of Charles C. Moskos*, edited by Giuseppe Caforio, 139–55. Bingley, UK: Emerald, 2009.

Gonzales, Gustavo. "First Female General, a Landmark in Gender Equality." Inter-Press Service. November 17, 1998. http://www.ipsnews.net/1998/11/women-chile-first-female-general-a-landmark-in-gender-equality/.

Gutierrez, Oman. "Changes in the Military Profession in Latin American Countries." In *Advances in Military Sociology: Essays in Honor of Charles C. Moskos*, edited by Guiseppe Caforio, 65–96. Bingley, UK: Emerald, 2009.

Larrain, Sergio. "The Chilean Army, Its History, Organization, Regional Environment and Challenges over the Next 25 Years." Master's thesis, U.S. Army War College, 2002.

Mani, Kristina. *Democratization and Military Transformation in Argentina and Chile*. Boulder: Lynne Rienner, 2011.

Ross, Jen. "In Traditional Chile, Meet the Soldiers with Pearl Earrings." *The Christian Science Monitor*. November 7, 2005. https://www.csmonitor.com/2005/1107/p01s04-woam.html.

Suppler, Joan. "Women and the Counter-Revolution in Chile." In *Women and Revolution in Africa, Asia and the New World*, edited by Mary Ann Tetreault, 394–412. Columbia: University of South Carolina Press, 1995.

Weeks, Gregory. *The Military and Politics in Post-Authoritarian Chile*. Tuscaloosa: University of Alabama Press, 2003.

China

Background

Chinese history memorializes brave and dutiful women who, in times of great national emergency and family crisis, have stepped up to lead armies. Among the ancient tombs of the Shang Dynasty, one is of Fu Hao, whose name appears on oracle bones as a royal woman who commanded 13,000 soldiers. During the Warring States Period, Sun Tzu offered the example of King Wu's palace concubines, not advocating for the inclusion of women but making the point that it was discipline and proper training that made good soldiers, rather than individual bravery or skill. Women of the Confucian administrative class sometimes acquired martial arts training along with the mastery of household management and were expected to assist their husbands, like Liang Hongyu, who "beat the battle drum" for Marshal Shi Zhong Hang in an 1130 engagement at Gold Mountain. Peasant women, accustomed to a much harsher life of village agricultural work, could also emerge as military leaders, often because they had little to lose. The mythologized Hua Mulan, who donned men's clothes to take her father's place in military conscription, remains a national heroine (and a global one, thanks to Disney), but Mu Lu's rebellion in 18 AD, seeking revenge for her wrongly executed son, and Shuo Zhen Chen, who seized territory and declared herself a "peasant emperor" in 653 AD, exist in official documents as dangerous problems for the state. In peacetime, Confucian values confined women to the private sphere of the home, as obedient daughters, wives, and mothers, with prosperous families taking pride in a daughter's bound feet, demonstrating her submissiveness and unsuitability for outside work.

The strain of imperialism exploded in two major 19th-century movements with large female participation. In 1847, Hong Xiuquan, an ethnic Hakka, raised a rebellion of peasants under the banner of the Heavenly Kingdom of Great Peace, or Tai-ping. Hong's ideology, a blend of exposure to Christian missionary work and Chinese classics, made Hong the second son of the King

> **Military Performance Art**
>
> During the Cultural Revolution, Jiang Qing, Mao Zedong's wife, dictated that only eight model operas could be performed. One of them, *The Red Detachment of Women* (1964), was based on a novelization of the exploits of the Special Company of the 2nd Independent Division of the Chinese Red Army, formed in 1931 and comprised entirely of women. Premiering a week before China's atomic bomb test, and in a period when Sino-Soviet relations were at a nadir, the overt show of guns, aggression, and patriotic fervor were meant to remind audiences of the Party's class enemies and victory through gender solidarity. The heroine, Wu Qinghua, is enslaved by an evil landlord, Nanbatian, for the debts of her peasant father. Escaping after a brutal whipping, she encounters the detachment, who take her in and train her as a soldier. Wu endangers a later surprise attack on Nanbatian by selfishly firing on him in revenge rather than acting as a member of the unit. In a final battle with the landlord and his henchmen, hero commissar Hong Changqing is captured and burned to death as a martyr, leaving Wu to take up his job, chastened and reformed as a member of the army.
>
> At the time, the scenes of whipping and enslaved dancing girls, as well as the Bermuda shorts costumes of the soldiers, were scandalous. In more recent productions, including the one attended by Nixon in 1972 and parodied in John Adams's 1987 opera,*Nixon in China*, the effect is campy. Chinese national companies continue to produce the work, including international tours, and a television series aired in 2006. Its continued resonance may also include the setting in Hainan, a major launching point for Chinese forces in the South China Sea region.

of Heaven (Jesus Christ being the first) and promised liberation from both the corrupt Qing government and the corruption of imperialism's exploitation of China. Hong banned plural marriages, opium, foot binding, and prostitution and undertook wealth and land redistribution, issues popular enough to draw hundreds of thousands to his cause. In gender-segregated units, women fought on the front lines against Qing troops and held bureaucratic office during the decade the Tai-ping controlled much of southern China. After Hong's death in 1864, the Qing brutally suppressed the rebellion and restored the social status quo. In 1900, with the encouragement of the Dowager Empress, the secret peasant society of the Righteous Fists of Heaven (interpreted by westerners as the "Boxers") attacked American and European missionaries and diplomats, laying siege to the embassy quarter of Beijing. Age-divided women, the Black (elderly), Blue (middle-aged), and Red (young) women accompanied them.

The Red Lanterns, believing sincerely in folk magic, were on the battlefield to deflect bullets with their fans and access powers unavailable to the men. This failed in the face of modern weaponry, and the Boxer Rebellion collapsed.

However, western missionaries and their insistence on educating women had created a growing middle class of Chinese feminists who were active in early 20th-century movements to bring modernity and democracy to China. As a member of Sun Yat-sen's Revolutionary Alliance, Jin Qiu ran a camp in Shaoxing for secretly training revolutionaries under the cover of a girls' school and wore men's clothes to lead armed raids on Qing garrisons before being captured and executed in 1907. Other women joined the Women's Suffrage Alliance, founded in 1911, or marched with the May Fourth Movement, which rejected China's acceptance of the disadvantageous terms of the Treaty of Versailles in 1919. During the 1920s, more than 1.5 million women joined groups along the political spectrum from communism to nationalism, seeing their own liberation as a key element of the modernization of China.

Famous in the west for the Disney film, the legendary Chinese military heroine Hua Mulan donned male clothing to replace her ailing father and serve in the conscript forces of the emperor. Set in varying time periods including the Northern Wei (386–536 CE) and the Tang (618–907 CE), the tale is most likely fictional, but has been used to inspire women to fierce filial devotion to family and the Chinese state. (Verdelho/Dreamstime.com)

Women, Nationalists, and Communism

The Chinese Communist Party rejected feminism detached from class warfare, with Xiang Jian Gou and Cai Chang denouncing it as a western and bourgeois concept that would undermine the revolution if allowed to subsume solidarity with the peasantry. In 1927, forcefully driven out by the Nationalists,

Mao and the Communist Party took shelter in the countryside, where this concept was immediately implemented. Rather than offend the conservative sensibilities of the peasants, women were to work for the liberation of all society rather than specifically feminist issues, accepting support roles and not challenging the patriarchal village system. The Nationalists, under Chiang Kai-shek, also took a hard turn to the right after 1927. Before this, Sun Yat-sen's widow, Soong Qing Ling, and other prominent women, had roles in the Wuhan government, including running the Central Military and Political Institute, which trained 200 women cadets, and the Huangpo military Academy, which graduated 130, expecting them to serve in the Nationalist forces. A purge of leftist elements in the Nationalist Kuomintang eliminated these powerful women and ended the educational programs, although, during the anti-Japanese War beginning in 1937, the Nationalists used women like Zheng Pingru (whose life inspired Ang Lee's 2007 movie, *Lust, Caution*) as spies and others as nurses and support auxiliaries. When they encountered Communist women in arms, the Nationalists treated them harshly, including using them in forced prostitution and marriages to their soldiers.

Meanwhile, the Communists began the Long March, withdrawing 4,000 miles into the north to avoid the Nationalist army. Women were crucial to this operation, with at least 3,000 known participants. The Women's Independent Brigade worked logistics, often with wheelbarrows, while the Women's Engineer Battalion was entrusted by Mao Tse-tung with the transport of the party's hard currency. The march was extremely difficult, and some of the women suffered from tuberculosis. Women who became pregnant, or who had small children, sometimes left them with villagers along the way, unable to bring them on the arduous trek. Members of the party who were on the Long March had special status as companions of Mao and especially trusted comrades, including the women who survived. Li Zhen, a fierce guerrilla scout, was promoted to major general in 1955 in recognition of her service on the Long March, the only woman to reach general officer rank until the 1990s.

Women in the Red Army fought the Japanese throughout World War II, serving as frontline infantry as well as conducting grueling foraging and supply operations, once forming a human chain across an icy river in Shandong to deliver food and ammunition. Donations from women were the major source of transfused blood for medical use during the war, and women both taught and were trained at the Eighth Route Army Anti-Japanese University. The Red Army made special use of illiterate women who were trained to decode and memorize Morse telegraph messages, which, because they could not be written down, were more secure. Japanese treatment of prisoners, whether the seizure of Chinese civilians as "comfort women" or the mass rape at Nanjing, fueled many women's participation in the armed resistance to the invasion. At the end of World War II, the Nationalists and Communists turned their armies on one another to fight for control of China, with women on both sides continuing their established roles. In 1949, the Nationalists withdrew to Taiwan, and Mao proclaimed the establishment of the People's Republic of China.

Women and the PLA

Postwar China, like many societies, saw a return to normalcy as one in which women would leave the military. Women of the People's Liberation Army (PLA) served as medics, communications personnel, and propagandists with the soldiers sent to fight with North Korea in 1951 in the Korean War but were treated badly when they returned, especially those who had been captured and held as prisoners of war by the Americans. "Speak bitterness" sessions held in 1948 had been the first time many women had the opportunity to discuss the inequalities and oppressions of their lives, and they expected further advancement in the new communist society. Instead, modeling the PLA after the Soviet Red Army, China began a massive transformation in 1955, shifting 750,000 soldiers, many of them women, to civilian jobs. Women who remained in uniform as volunteers were restricted to noncombat roles, while the core of the army became the huge number of young male conscripts drafted every year. A change in the marriage laws in 1950, allowing divorce and ending any remaining plural marriages, sparked a wave of suicides from women who were now abandoned by their spouses. The Great Leap Forward, Mao's 1953 industrialization program, instructed women to serve the nation by smelting steel in backyard furnaces and engaging in pest eradication programs rather than carrying a gun or campaigning for women's issues.

The Red Army fought repeatedly during the Cold War, against India (1962), the Soviet Union (1969), and twice in Vietnam (1974 and 1979). Women medical personnel and political commissars were present in these conflicts, usually organized under the name "May 8th" units in recognition of International Women's Day. The PLA Air Force trained 208 women as pilots between 1951 and 1987, although they served as test pilots and instructors rather than in combat. During the Cultural Revolution (1966–1976), while Mao encouraged the youth of China to attack tradition, women found the PLA attractive as an alternative to being sent to rural areas as agricultural workers and a vehicle to acquire urban registration and move away from the countryside. During the 1960s and 1970s, the PLA began specifically recruiting women who could excel on their cultural or sports teams, fielding basketball, volleyball, badminton, and drill teams to compete in China and around the world as a mark of the military's prestige.

Beginning in the 1990s, the demographic results of the one-child policy instituted in 1978 became significant to the PLA and, as in other countries facing a decline in quality recruits, turned to a new emphasis on women, who made up approximately 4.5 percent of the PLA in 1993. Nie Li, the daughter of a marshal, and educated in the Soviet Union as a scientist, became a major general in 1994, heading the PLA's research and development division. Eight other women were promoted to general officer and head the PLA Art Institute, the August First Film Studio, and major medical institutions. Other women senior officers are faculty at the more than 100 PLA schools. Women make up about 3 percent of Chinese peacekeeping units, as the PLA believes that they enhance the harmony of the group and can interact effectively with the local population and are often in military police and border guard detachments, where their presence allows their units to search local women without offending traditional sensibilities.

The 21st Century

At the 2009 National Day Parade, observers were surprised by a PLA woman's drill team clad in pink and go-go boots, with many accusing the military of using actresses rather than real women soldiers. However, in the yearly recruitment meetings, where the PLA selects women for military academies and enlisted service, the process includes a 2.5-minute question and answer portion and a 2-minute talent demonstration, favoring singing, dancing, and athletic prowess. Women in the PLA receive equal pay to their male peers, along with a 6 yuan/month addition to pay for "hygiene products," an addition brought to national attention by the release of the 2011 military action film "Sky Fighters," in which a heroic male commander demonstrates his modernity, comradeship, and leadership by making sure the women in his unit have tampons. As China reckons with its demographic future and desire to maintain a large PLA force, they are likely to expand the presence of women further, although whether into combat roles is unknown.

Further Reading

Bailey, Paul. *Women and Gender in Twentieth-Century China*. London: Palgrave Macmillan, 2012.

Canaves, Sky. "China's Military Women Hold up Half the Sky (and Dance, and Sing, and. . .)." *The Wall Street Journal*, December 1, 2009. https://blogs.wsj.com/chinarealtime/2009/11/30/chinas-military-women-hold-up-half-the-sky-and-dance-and-sing-and%e2%80%a6/.

Daven, Delia. "Gender and Population in the People's Republic of China." In *Women, State and Ideology: Studies from Africa and Asia*, edited by Haleh Afshar, 111–29. Albany: State University of New York Press, 1987.

Dreyer, June Teufel. "The Role of the Armed Forces in Contemporary China." In *The Armed Forces in Contemporary Asian Societies*, edited by Edward Olsen and Stephen Jurika, 25–54. Boulder, CO: Westview, 1986.

Edwards, Louise P. *Women Warriors and Wartime Spies of China*. Cambridge, UK: Cambridge University Press, 2016.
Guttry, Andrea De, Emanuele Sommario, and Lijiang Zhu. *China's and Italy's Participation in Peacekeeping Operations: Existing Models, Emerging Challenges*. Lanham, MD: Lexington Books, 2014.
Li, Xiaolin. "Chinese Women in the Peoples Liberation Army: Professionals or Quasi-Professionals?" *Armed Forces & Society* 20, no. 1 (1993): 69–83. doi:10.1177/0095327x9302000105.
Li, Xiaolin. "Chinese Women Soldiers: A History of 5,000 Years." *Social Education* 58, no. 2 (February 1994): 67–71.
Park, Kyung Ae. "Women and Revolution in China: The Sources of Constraints on Women's Emancipation." In *Women and Revolution in Africa, Asia and the New World*, edited by Mary Ann Tetrault, 137–60. Columbia: University of South Carolina Press, 1994.
Rigdon, Susan. "Women in China's Changing Military Ethic." In *A Soldier and a Woman: Sexual Integration in the Military*, edited by Gerard De Groot and Corinna Peniston-Bird, 275–93. London: Longman, 2000.
Segal, Mady Wechsler, Xiaolin Li, and David R. Segal. "The Role of Women in the Chinese People's Liberation Army." *Minerva* 10, no. 1 (Spring 1992): 48–55.
Young, Helen Praeger. "Women at Work: Chinese Soldiers on the Long March." In *A Soldier and a Woman: Sexual Integration in the Military*, edited by Gerard De Groot and Corinne Peniston-Bird, 83–99. London: Longman, 2000.
Yunzhu, Yao. "Chinese Women's Role in the People's Liberation Army." *Army Quarterly and Defense Journal* 126, no. 1 (1996): 414–19.

Cuba

Background

By the 1940s, the position of women in Cuba was equal to or, in some cases, ahead of their Latin American neighbors. Ramon Grau's government had granted women suffrage in 1934, and the trend toward urbanization saw large numbers of women who were literate, working outside the home and using birth control and civil divorce. The 1940 constitution, one of the most progressive in the Western Hemisphere at the time for women, promised land reform, access to education, and health care, although many of these promises were not realized. Women were unusually well represented in the legal profession as judges, possibly because the civil service pay was low and men preferred to be in practice. Existing simultaneously with this modern evolution, Cuba remained a traditional Catholic, Spanish, patriarchal society, especially in rural areas.

1953–Present

Women were a significant presence in the Cuban Revolution from its beginnings. Haydee Santamaria and Melba Hernandez, among others, acted as nurses as Castro mounted an unsuccessful attack on the Moncada Barracks in 1953, and it was a woman reporter, Marta Rojas, who smuggled out images of the attack for publication and attended Castro's subsequent trial as a journalist. When Castro and his cadre returned in 1956, Celia Sanchez, a doctor's daughter from Manzanillo, used her network of rural contacts to hide them and supply their guerrilla hideouts in the mountains. Women fought under arms in both mixed units and as all-woman platoons, like the *Mariana Grajales*, named for a 19th-century Afro-Cuban revolutionary, and proved to be fierce and capable soldiers, mentioned frequently by Castro for their bravery and tenacity. At the Battle of Holguin, armed with new M-1 rifles, women ambushed a truck, continuing to fight after their male comrades fled in retreat.

Fidel Castro frequently praised the armed women who joined the Cuban Revolution, seeing them as vital partners not just in winning the conflict, but in building a new society. These fighters are riding an armored vehicle into Havana on January 1, 1959, as Castro seized power from Batista. (Lester Cole/Corbis via Getty Images)

Women like Lidia Doce and Clodomira Acosta Ferrals, who were killed by Batista's forces, became revolutionary martyrs.

Once in control of Cuba, Fidel Castro turned to making revolutionary policy about women. Seeing them as "nature's workshop" for their capacity as mothers, he also saw them as partners in the Cuban revolution, and a necessary workforce and military pool. Some women remained under arms as the rebels coalesced into the new Cuban military, while others, under the newly founded (1960) Federation of Cuban Women, organized into militias to prevent sabotage and counterrevolutionary burning of the cane fields, set up block watches for arson and spies, and formed teaching brigades to teach literacy to rural women and children and offer retraining to former prostitutes and maids whose employers had fled the island. These civil defense preparations were vital in the Cuban response to the Bay of Pigs, as well as to Hurricane Flora in 1963. Women soldiers were part of Cuban missions to Angola (1975) and Ethiopia (1977), where they instructed other women in guerrilla warfare, and teaching and medical battalions of women served in Nicaragua and as doctors in Chavez's Venezuela as part of exchange programs to gain Cuba access to oil resources.

In 1976, the new revolutionary constitution recognized women as full legal equals. However, Cuba has never entirely shed its traditional machismo. Aside from extraordinary women like Vilma Espin, Raul Castro's wife, few have reached senior positions in the government, and not even Fidel Castro's repeated speeches motivated Cuban men to take up equal home responsibilities for children and traditional women's housework. Women continue to serve in all branches of the Cuban military, although numbers are not available. There are a few prestigious all-women units, like the antiaircraft regiment defending Havana, and the Border Guards who face the American installation at Guantanamo. In 1996, Castro promoted Tete Puebla of the Mariana Grajales to brigadier general, the highest rank any woman has earned up to the present.

The end of the Cold War catastrophically disrupted the Cuban economy, which had relied on 85 percent of its trade with the Soviet Union and Eastern European satellites for consumer goods and a stable market for Cuban sugar. Subsequent rationing of food and gasoline affected women disproportionately, as they had to invest time securing food, walking to their jobs, and shopping instead of having transportation available and having childcare and new housing frozen in a spate of 1990s' budget cuts. The military, guided by Raul Castro, began a process in the 1980s of taking over state enterprises like hotels, beaches, and former casinos, sending officers to international hospitality and accounting training programs, and investing funds to modernize and open tourist sites to European and Latin American guests. These Grupo Empresarial S.A. (GAESA), or military business enterprises, employ many Cuban military women in management and service jobs. It is not clear how much of the profits go back into the Cuban economy to support the social welfare programs and how much finds its ways to senior officials' lifestyles. For women in general, working in tourism for hard currency is increasingly an attractive alternative to poorly paid manual labor or little reward for advanced educational or medical training, even if the job involves prostitution. Cuba is unlikely to be invaded or to again play a significant role in training or supplying global revolutionaries, so the future of its military, and the women in it, balances between attempting to preserve the revolution and engaging in a measured way with capitalistic tourism.

Further Reading

Abrahams, Harlan, and Arturo Lopez-Levy. *Raúl Castro and the New Cuba: A Close-up View of Change*. Jefferson, NC: McFarland & Co., 2011.

Azicri, Max. *Cuba Today and Tomorrow: Reinventing Socialism*. Gainesville: University Press of Florida, 2000.

Bunck, Julie Marie. "Women and Post-Cold War Socialism: The Cases of Cuba and Vietnam." In *Cuba in Transition*, 21–31. Proceedings of Association for the Study of the Cuban Economy, Miami, Florida. 1997. https://ascecuba.org//c/wp-content/uploads/2014/09/v07-bunck.pdf.

Castro, Fidel, and Vilma Espín Guillois. *Women and the Cuban Revolution: Speeches and Documents*, edited by Elizabeth Stone. New York: Pathfinder Press, 2004.

Farmer, Ann. "Rojas Swims against Machismo Tide in Cuba." *Women's eNews*, September 18, 2009. http://womensenews.org/2004/12/rojas-swims-against-machismo-tide-cuba/.

Lutjens, Sheryl L. "Remaking the Public Sphere: Women and Revolution in Cuba." In *Women and Revolution in Africa, Asia, and the New World*, edited by Mary Ann Tétreault, 366–93. Columbia: University of South Carolina Press, 1994.

Puebla, Teté, and Mary-Alice Waters. *Marianas in Combat: Teté Puebla and the Mariana Grajales Womens Platoon in Cuba's Revolutionary War, 1956–58*. New York: Pathfinder, 2016.

Roca, Alicia. "The Old Cuban Cadre: Four Women Survive Manzanillo." In *Capitalism, God and a Good Cigar: Cuba Enters the 21st Century*, edited by Lydia Chavez and Mimi Chakarova, 31–44. Durham, NC: Duke University Press, 2006.

Denmark

Background

Since the early modern era, women in Denmark benefitted from the country's Lutheranism and trade orientation under laws that permitted them to run businesses and join guilds in the place of deceased spouses and have had a high degree of literacy stemming from the need for education to read the Protestant Bible in Danish. Denmark's 19th-century wars were not prolonged and did not involve the home front to any significant degree, so Danish women were not associated with ongoing auxiliary work. Women were included in higher education in 1875, gained suffrage in 1915, and, with the exception of the military, had all occupations opened to them by 1936. In 1934, women joined the voluntary Danish Ground Observer Corps for civil defense and to locate civilian air crashes.

During World War II, women made up at least 7 percent of the Resistance forces, first operating as a passive resistance against the Nazi occupation, helping 7,000–8,000 Danish Jews to escape to neutral Sweden, hiding downed allied pilots until they could be rescued, and then taking part in an escalation of violence and sabotage after 1943. Because the Germans wished to use Denmark as a model Aryan protectorate, Danish women skillfully took advantage of orders to treat the civilian population carefully and smuggled people, supplies, and documents under the cover of their daily routines. In 1944, a coordinated resistance action sabotaged the Danish railroads to prevent German reinforcements from reaching the Normandy landing sites.

Postwar

In response to the Cold War, Denmark in 1946 formed a Home Guard, with separate branches for women as auxiliaries to the army and navy, adding an air force contingent in 1953. Men over the age of 18 were required to perform

4–12 months of conscripted national service, served if physically able in the armed forces. From 1946 to 1962, women made up 14–17 percent of the Home Guard personnel, forming a cost-effective way to maintain a part-time reserve force, especially for civil defense and emergency management. In 1962, the Danish parliament legalized the admission of women to the Danish military, although women could not serve in combat-oriented units. This began a steady expansion of access, with women enlisting as noncommissioned officers (NCOs) in 1971, then accepted to military academies in 1974. After a series of studies on the feasibility of women in combat roles, the Danish Armed Forces opened all jobs to women in 1988.

Despite these opportunities, Danish women make up only 6.4 percent of the forces as of 2016, and few have reached senior levels of command. The first colonel, Susanne Bach Bager, made rank in 2009, and the first general office was Brigadier General Lone Træholt, named chief of the Air Force Tactical Staff in 2016. The Danish military sets its physical requirements to individual jobs and is deeply invested in recruiting women, holding "defense days" to explore careers and "inspirational days for women" to allow prospective candidates to talk to women in the current forces, seeing women who want to join without the pressure of conscription as "particularly motivated." The forces augment the generous national parental leave and childcare with arrangements to avoid deploying parents at the same time if both are military and providing extra days off for parents to attend school events and aid in deployment adjustment.

However, the high level of social equality in Denmark and women's participation in the civilian workforce, especially in jobs with rapid promotions and high financial compensation, like IT, provide few incentives for women to join. Danish military planners see the integration of women, like their integration of homosexuals, as a demonstration of the democracy of Danish society and a move that will further the innovation and flexibility of the armed forces by providing a diverse pool of thinkers and practitioners. How they will attract women to military service remains a crucial question for the 21st century.

Further Reading

Finnedal, Martin. "Lone Træholt er Danmarks Første Kvindelige General." *Forsvarets*, September 29, 2016. https://www2.forsvaret.dk/nyheder/overige_nyheder/Pages/LoneTr%C3%A6holterDanmarksf%C3%B8rstekvindeligegeneral.aspx.

Kanstrup, Henrik. "An Examination of Gender Diversity in the 21st Century Royal Danish Armed Forces: Can the US Experience Contribute to the Future Danish Armed Forces?" Master's thesis, United States Air Force, Air Command and Staff College, 2001.

Sorenson, Henning. "Denmark: From Obligation to Option." In *The Postmodern Military*, edited by Charles Moskos, John Allen Williams, and David R. Segal, 121–36. Oxford: Oxford University Press, 2000.

Sorensen, Henning. "Denmark: The Small NATO Nation." In *Female Soldiers— Combatants or Noncombatants: Historical and Contemporary Perspectives*, edited by Nancy Loring Goldman, 189–202. New York: Praeger, 1982.

Thomas, John Oram. *The Giant Killers: The Story of the Danish Resistance 1940–1945*. New York: Taplinger, 1975.

Egypt

Background

Until 1953, women in Anglo-Colonial Egypt led lives similar to those of others in traditional Arab societies. Both as resistance to colonial rule and as an element of Islamic practice, women outside of the imperial upper class veiled, had little access to education, and lived within tightly controlled patriarchal households. Egypt's independence in 1953, and the regime of Gamal Abdel Nasser, saw significant legal and social gains for women, including explicit equality in the 1956 Constitution. Nasser pursued a policy of "state feminism" with extensive social welfare benefits to women and children, including birth control campaigns and promotion of women's suffrage. Although these gains faced erosion in the 1970s under Sadat and Mubarak, whose economic liberalization policies severely reduced the social welfare state, women's expectations of participation in Egyptian civic life had increased substantially.

Following the disastrous Six-Day War against Israel in 1967, Saad el-Shazly, the new chief of staff, needed to substantially rebuild and enlarge the military. The crucial shortage was a 30–40 percent shortfall in the officer corps, prompting him to both engage in the promotion of enlisted volunteers and the first commissioning and enlistment of women in 1971. His championing of women's service extended to allowing his daughter, Shahdan el-Shazly, to undertake parachute training. Since then, women have been allowed to serve in noncombat, rear echelon capacity in the fields of administration, medicine, nutrition, and social work. Their numbers remain small in a military establishment of 450,000, and women are not admitted to the service academies.

Arguments against great admission of women come from both traditionalists who believe the women's place in the nation is in the home and the position that Egypt's military functions as an education and socialization mechanism for the more than 80,000 male conscripts inducted every year as mandatory national service. The military owns and operates extensive farms and

This woman, protesting at Cairo's Tahrir Square in December 2011, is in the vanguard of Egyptian women demanding greater representation and participation in the government, including the possibility of service and even conscription in the Egyptian military. (FILIPPO MONTEFORTE/AFP/Getty Images)

companies that employ conscripts not chosen for field duties, providing them with literacy and other vocational training. Downsizing the army, or admitting more women, jeopardizes the stabilizing function the military plays in the society with very high male unemployment and rural isolation.

21st Century

However, women's highly visible participation in 2011 Tahrir Square protests (and their abuse by military forces, including beatings and virginity tests) has sparked interest in greater female presence in Egypt's military institutions. A group, *Moganada Masreya* (Female Egyptian Conscripts), has been campaigning since 2014 to allow volunteer service in a wider spectrum of military service, perhaps even mandatory conscription. This has gained further traction through the prominence of UAE women fighter pilots in social media in the Arab world and a 2017 revival of a 1973 law requiring university graduates to perform public service. *Moganada Masreya* argues that this requirement should include military enlistment. However, Egypt is a country with continued high rates of public and domestic violence against women, honor killings, and female genital mutilation, suggesting that integration will require careful planning and mitigation for dislocated men and significant cultural shifts.

Further Reading

Aboul-Enein, Youssef H. *Reconstructing a Shattered Egyptian Army: War Minister General Mohamed Fawzi's Memoirs, 1967–1971*. Annapolis, MD: Naval Institute Press, 2014.

Higgins, Michael. "Police Beating of 'Girl in the Blue Bra' Becomes New Rallying Call for Egyptians." *National Post*, December 20, 2011. http://nationalpost.com/news/beating-of-blue-bra-woman-reignites-egyptian-protests.

Marshall, Shana. "The Egyptian Armed Forces and the Remaking of an Economic Empire." *Carnegie Middle East Center*, April 2015, 1–38.

Meky, Shounaz. "Egyptian Group Challenges Norm, Calls for Female Military Service." *Al Arabiya News*, December 13, 2014. http://english.alarabiya.net/en/perspective/features/2014/12/13/Egyptian-group-challenges-norm-calls-for-female-military-service.html.

Eritrea

Background

Italy, coming late to the colonization scramble, claimed the coastal area of East Africa as its first possession in 1882, quickly setting up an administration that suppressed indigenous people and was engineered to extract natural resources, including palm oil, leather, tobacco, and dom nuts, which can be carved into durable buttons. Under this regime, Eritrean people had no representation, were excluded from education, and were prevented from forming labor unions or political parties to protest their exploitation. During World War II, the British army liberated the country and took over colonial administration, leaving many Italian business owners in place but opening floodgates by setting up a school system that admitted both boys and girls, legalizing unions and encouraging preparation for political participation.

Under pressure to withdraw from expensive and manpower-intensive oversight of a far-flung global empire, the British arranged for Eritrea to be federated with Ethiopia in 1952. Although the two regions had many similarities, and several ethnic groups overlapped the border, generations of colonization in Eritrea had introduced sufficient differences with the Kingdom of Ethiopia and its Emperor, Haile Selassie, that Eritreans resisted. Over the next decade, Ethiopia interfered in the internal politics of Eritrea, relocated factories, and outlawed anti-Ethiopian trade organizations and political groups, until finally annexing Eritrea outright in 1962.

Civil War

As early as 1958, defiant Eritreans began planning to oppose Ethiopian domination, founding the Eritrean Liberation Movement (ELM) and planning to undertake infiltration of the government, a plan made moot by the annexation. The Eritrean Liberation Front (ELF), created in 1960, took an openly militant stance, seeking arms and aid from Arab Islamic states, eventually gaining support from the Chinese and the Palestine Liberation Organization (PLO), who sent arms and instructors. Both the ELM and ELF, typical of the conflict, transcended Eritrea's ethnic and religious divides to unite Muslims, Orthodox Christians, Tigrinya, Tigre, and Saho people to fight for their freedom. The ELF also had the advantage of a large body of men who had been conscripted into the World War II Italian army and already had training in arms and tactics.

However, it was not until 1974, seeing the overthrow of Haile Selassie by a Marxist coup, and subsequent infusion of Soviet arms and advisers, that the various splinter groups of the ELM and ELF coalesced into the Eritrean People's Liberation Front (EPLF) and took the advice of their own Maoist advisers to explicitly call for the participation of women, launching the campaign with the slogan "no liberation without women's participation." The first to answer the call were urban, educated women, but they were quickly joined by rural rebels, eventually making up half of the ELF's membership. This was an extraordinary response in a society that was still deeply traditional and enmeshed in separate, gendered kin networks and backbreaking farm labor.

Much of this appealing doctrine came from a Maoist rejection of "bourgeois" family culture and roles. After a six-month, gender-segregated training period, meant to inoculate the volunteers against their retrograde upbringing and backward customs, complete with self-criticism sessions and separation from home, ELF "tegadelti" or fighters were expected to function as soldiers, not men or women. Those comrades who met and wished to marry had to gain the permission of their leaders, who often separated them soon afterward, and any children resulting from these guerrilla marriages were raised communally in revolutionary nurseries. Breaking with custom, the ELF forbade female genital mutilation and ridiculed the taboo that required women to be virgins when they married. In camp, both men and women did assigned chores, which, back home, were the work of one or the other—cooking, wood gathering, laundry, or nursing sick comrades. In one popular marching song, EPLF women chanted, "Farewell kitchen, I've broken your shackles!"

These EPLF guerrilla women presented an electrifying sight to international media and their enemies. Originally sent into combat because they lacked the specialized skills more educated men brought to the organization, they proved adept at mastering the captured guns, tanks, boats, and electronic equipment captured from Ethiopian troops. Photos capture women with an unmistakable swagger, marching in tire-tread-soled sandals, with practical natural hair and AK-47s slung casually over their shoulders. Elsa Yacob, a veteran of the EPLF, painted "Woman Hero" (1984) to commemorate this iconic figure. Another of Yacob's works, the 1988 "The Tanks Crushed My Mom," pays tribute to the women who sacrificed their lives in the liberation struggle and their orphaned children, who are given into the hands of other revolutionary comrades.

The war dragged on for 30 years, consuming an entire generation of people. By the time the Eritreans won the Battle of Afabet in 1988, the Soviets were withdrawing aid to Ethiopia as their own nation imploded. In 1991, the EPLF was in possession all of the major cities and began setting up a provisional government, drafting a constitution and planning for a postwar world.

21st Century

The world the EPLF won was devastated, with 60,000 dead, 700,000 Eritreans living in exile around the world, and the land wracked with the environmental devastation of floods, droughts, agricultural sabotage, and famine. The surviving population lives with food insecurity and poor infrastructure. The provisional constitution, which had women on the drafting committee, promised equality, education, and relief from subsistence farming via labor-saving technology. Tragically, a resurgent border war between Eritrea and Ethiopia in 1998–2000 caused tens of thousands of casualties and put an end to the ratification of the constitution. Reformers were detained and have disappeared.

Women, who had been the backbone of the EPLF, did not see substantial change after the war. Reforms dissipated with the failed constitution, and many male fighters returned to their families, seeking young, conservatively raised women, who would be obedient wives and take care of a home and family in the segregated way of the past. EPLF women, often trained as doctors, dentists, electricians, and engineers, refuse to return to their ancestral villages and do not want to settle down into a prescribed role, while their society is willing to see them in traditional women's jobs but not in the skills for which they trained. The egalitarianism and potential state feminism of the EPLF had been dictated from the top by male leaders who gave little thought to how it might be carried through in the postwar society.

Technically, Eritrea requires national service of all citizens aged 18–45, with exceptions for the sick, pregnant, and disabled, but it is unknown if they are enforcing this conscription. One estimate, made by the Red Cross in 2000, was that Eritrea's national army was one-fifth women. Eritrea currently refuses foreign aid, so the inner workings of their military are opaque to outsiders, and there are no good numbers on the proportion of women who have remained under arms or what they are doing with their military training and experience.

Further Reading

Barth, Elise F. *Peace as Disappointment: The Reintegration of Female Soldiers in Post-Conflict Societies, a Comparative Study from Africa.* Oslo: International Peace Research Institute (PRIO), 2002.

Bernal, Victoria. "Equality to Die For: Women Guerilla Fighters and Eritrea's Cultural Revolution." *PoLAR: Political and Legal Anthropology Review* 23, no. 2 (November 2000): 61–76.

Eritrean Women's Association. *Women and Revolution in Eritrea*. Rome: National Union of Eritrean Women, 1980.

Hale, Sondra. "The Soldier and the State: Post-Liberation Women, the Case of Eritrea." In *Frontline Feminisms: Women, War and Resistance*, edited by Marguerite R. Waller and Jennifer Rycenga, 349–70. New York: Garland, 2000.

Mehreteab, Amanuel. *Veteran Combatants Do Not Fade Away: A Comparative Study on Two Demobilization and Reintegration Exercises in Eritrea*. Bonn: BICC, 2002.

Muller, Tanja R. *The Making of Elite Women: Revolution and Nation Building in Eritrea*. Leiden: Brill, 2005.

Pateman, Ray. *Eritrea: Even the Stones Are Burning*. Lawrenceville, NJ: Red Sea Press, 1990.

Tesfagiorgis G., Mussie. *Eritrea*. Santa Barbara, CA: ABC-CLIO, LLC, 2011.

Wilson, Amrit. *The Challenge Road: Women and the Eritrean Revolution*. London: Earthscan, 1991.

Zerai, Worku. "Participation of Women in the Eritrean National Liberation Struggle." Master's thesis, Institute of Social Studies, The Hague, 1994.

Ethiopia

Background

Ethiopian tradition placed the now-deposed royal family in a direct line of descent from the Queen of Sheba and King Solomon, allowing a series of Empresses and Dowager Empresses to play significant roles in the government of the nation, including Queen Menen Asfaw, wife of Haile Selassie. Beginning in 1935, powerful elite women founded and ran organizations like the Ethiopian Women's Welfare Association, the Armed Forces Wives' Association, and committees of the Young Women's Christian Association (YWCA), all ended by the Derg after 1974. However, despite land tenure in the traditional *risi* system of inheritance tracing maternal and paternal family lines, the power of elite court women never trickled down to women in the vast majority of Ethiopia's population.

The invasion of Ethiopia by fascist Italy in 1935 led to five years of rapid modernization as the invaders built roads and other modern infrastructure. The British, backing deposed Emperor Haile Selassie, not only returned him to the throne after defeating the Italians in 1941 but also backed the Tigrayan people, who had aided them as guerrillas. During the Cold War, the United States stepped in to support the monarchy, especially against Marxist-Leninist movements like the one which formed in Eritrea to oppose Ethiopian federation and annexation. The strain of the war in Eritrea exacerbated the Emperor's inability to adapt and his tight grip on power, leading the Ethiopian Communist party to approach the Soviet Union for assistance, which arrived in the wake of the 1972 famine. The coalition of intellectuals, students, and reformers opposed to the monarchy was quickly hijacked by the Ethiopian military, headed by Colonel Mengistu Haile Mariam, who overthrew the Emperor and established a government called the "Derg." The totalitarian Derg seized church land and conducted a massive purge of opponents in 1977, the "red terror," as well as expelled the American military mission and replaced it with Soviet and Cuban advisers.

Civil War

In 1975, the Tigrayan People's Liberation Front (TPLF) formed to fight back against the Derg, taking advantage of remote region and its challenging landscape, as well as the ongoing wars with Eritrea and Somalia. The TPLF would eventually head a coalition of resistance groups, the Ethiopian People's Revolutionary Democratic Front (EPRDF), often working with allies in the Eritrean insurgency. From 1977 to 1991, the Derg committed more than half of the nation's budget to military spending, becoming dependent on Soviet aid to wage war. Although figures are speculative, the Derg enlisted women, who made up perhaps 3–4 percent of their forces, based on the demobilization of 13,000–17,000 women in 1991.

The TPLF was founded with an explicit agenda of liberation for both the Ethiopian people in general and women in particular. Women joined in the fighting at the nadir of the cause, earning respect for their ferocity and tenacity while the campaign struggled the most to survive. Women made up at least 30 percent of the TPLF, mastering the captured Ethiopian equipment they used, including guns, tanks, and trucks and creating networks of tunnels and logistical conveys of camels for supply. The commitment to equality extended to military discipline, with units sharing cooking tasks and decision-making and celebrating their role with marching song lyrics like "we were only speaking tools/now we as well as men have guns."

In their contact with the population, the TPLF worked to educate rural women in literacy, contraception, and political information campaigns. Potential recruits attended boarding schools that taught the "double oppression" of being a Tigrayan and a woman. Fighting women sat on local elected *baitos* councils operating as a parallel government, making decisions about land use, rural administration, and application of laws, including marriages, divorce, and property inheritance. However, an attempt by the TPLF to train women to plough, in an attempt to relieve widows and orphans from dependence on others to keep their lands in production, foundered on overwhelming opposition from traditionalists who saw that specific job as being exclusively male and who blamed famines and difficulties on women upending the proper order.

Postwar

In 1991, beset with defeats from Eritrea and the collapse of their Soviet backers, the Derg regime fell as the EPRDF advanced on the capital, Addis Ababa. The transitional government, which knew it had to deal with 455,000 Derg soldiers, had a demobilization plan in place very quickly, including its own people in a stabilization project. Fearing banditry and alienation of segments of the population, the new government downsized the EPRDF by 20,000 soldiers to make room for a new Ethiopian military drawn from the whole spectrum of people, including former Derg. Many of those downsized were TPLF women. For those whose husbands remained in the military, this meant separation or transplantation to a new base, while others received a cash payment and encouragement to start businesses. Women veterans can receive support for education up to grade 12, and there are quotas to guarantee them places in teacher training colleges. The government went so far as to start a textile factory to employ former fighters, but the women found it difficult to take orders from a manager and the business found it easier to hire tractable young women without combat experience.

Although Ethiopia has attempted more programs to assist the reintegration of its women fighters than Eritrea, poverty and lack of resources keep the outlook for women bleak. Only 32 percent are literate, with major outbreaks of HIV/AIDS and tuberculosis. Many former soldiers believed rumors that there were international laws against women bearing arms and went along with disarmament as a token of the TPLF's transition into a legitimate national army. Women who had spent a decade or more in the field found themselves at odds with demanding in-laws who criticized their cooking, lack of filial obedience, and outspoken ways, and they were at a disadvantage starting businesses or getting jobs in tight local networks. Practicing contraception during their time in the TPLF, women made a deliberate decision to have small families, which are out of the norm in rural Ethiopia, and which both motivates the women to push for a better future for their children and disappoints their in-laws.

Post-Derg Ethiopia has an increased number of women serving in Parliament (7 percent) and as international representatives, although that number is low by developed world comparison. Demands by women, which were first carried out in local councils, have been encoded as law, setting a later age for marriage, providing women over 17 with land, and offering access to education. The Ethiopian Women Lawyers Association and Women's Affairs Office press for further reforms and enforcement of existing laws on domestic violence and abuse. Perhaps the most visible former TPLF women guerrilla is Azeb Mesfin, the widow of Prime Minister Meles Zenawi (d. 2012), founder of the National Initiative for Mental Health, a campaigner against HIV/AIDS, and who is currently serving as the chief executive officer (CEO) of the Endowment Fund for the Rehabilitation of Tigray.

Further Reading

Burgess, Gemma. "A Hidden History: Women's Activism in Ethiopia." *Journal of International Women's Studies* 14, no. 3 (July 2013): 96–107.

Colletta, Nat J., Markus Kostner, and Ingo Wiederhofer. *Case Studies in War-to-Peace Transition: The Demobilization and Reintegration of Ex-combatants in Ethiopia, Namibia, and Uganda.* Washington, DC: World Bank, 1996.

Coulter, Chris, Mariam Persson, and Mats Utas. *Young Female Fighters in African Wars: Conflict and Its Consequences*. Uppsala: Nordiska Afrikainstitutet, 2008.

Dercon, Stefan, and Daniel Ayalew. "Where Have All the Soldiers Gone: Demobilization and Reintegration in Ethiopia." *World Development* 26, no. 9 (1998): 661–75. doi:10.1016/s0305-750x(98)00077-1.

Hammond, Jenny, and Nell Druce, eds. *Sweeter than Honey: Ethiopian Women and Revolution: Testimonies of Tigrayan Women*. Trenton, NJ: Red Sea, 1990.

Negewo-Oda, Beza, and Aaronette M. White. "Identity Transformation and Reintegration Among Ethiopian Women War Veterans: A Feminist Analysis." *Journal of Feminist Family Therapy* 23, no. 3–4 (2011): 163–87. doi:10.1080/08952833.2011.604536.

Tareke, Gebru. *The Ethiopian Revolution: War in the Horn of Africa*. New Haven: Yale University Press, 2009.

Tronvoll, Kjetil. *War & the Politics of Identity in Ethiopia: Making Enemies & Allies in the Horn of Africa*. Woodbridge, Suffolk: James Currey, 2009.

Veale, Angela. *From Child Soldier to Ex-fighter: Female Fighters, Demobilisation and Reintegration in Ethiopia*. Pretoria: Institute for Security Studies, 2003.

Young, John. *Peasant Revolution in Ethiopia: The Tigray People's Liberation Front, 1975–1991*. Cambridge, UK: Cambridge University Press, 2006.

Finland

Background

Until 1809, Finland was part of Sweden and enjoyed the legal reform of the 18th-century kingdom, including suffrage for women who were tax-paying members of professional guilds. The thinly populated and rural nature of the region led to highly independent women who expected significant consideration in local and family affairs and, as Finland lacked a large upper or middle class with Victorian sensibilities of a "women's sphere," worked on farms and in businesses as a necessity. From 1809 to 1917, Finland was a Grand Duchy of Russia, ruled under laissez-faire governors until the implementation of Russification policies of the late 19th century began to alienate Finnish people and spark a nationalist consciousness differentiating them from Russians. Russia expected Finland to field a militia to protect itself, a system that was accepted by the population as they were not required to leave to participate in Russia's conflicts elsewhere, and the officer class was drawn from fellow Finns.

In 1917, Finland seized the opportunity presented by the Bolshevik Revolution and declared independence on December 6, fighting a Civil War until May 1918. General Carl Mannerheim, commanding the "white," or anti-Bolshevik forces, called upon his sister, Baroness Sophie Mannerheim to create a women's nursing and support auxiliary, drawing on an image from Johan Ludvig Runeberg's poem "Lotta Svard," about a soldier's wife who follows him into an 1809 battle and stays after his death to succor the troops as a sutler. Sophie Mannerheim, who had been trained in London in the Florence Nightingale tradition of public health and nursing, quickly organized women to assist in hospitals, run canteens, sort supplies, and provide morale-boosting entertainment for the troops, under strict supervision and morals regulations. These strictures were in contrast to the women serving with the "reds," fighting with the Bolsheviks as full participants under

Founded in 1918 and copied across Scandinavia, the Lotta Svard volunteers mobilized during the Finnish War of Independence to perform auxiliary nursing and supply work while freeing up men to join the military. During WWII, the role of "Lottas" expanded to staffing anti-aircraft guns, air raid warning stations, and search lights. (Hulton-Deutsch Collection/Corbis via Getty Images)

arms and in male uniforms and drawing horrified disapproval from the Finnish mainstream.

Between the wars, the Lotta Svard continued as a voluntary organization, taking care of the graves of veterans, doing public service, and working as aides in hospitals, old-age homes, and for people with disabilities. In 1939, the Soviet Union invaded Finland, touching off the "Winter War," in which Finland mobilized most of its male reserves and engaged the Red Army along the vast Finnish–Russian borderlands. Calling up more than 242,000 "Lottas" allowed 100,000 men to leave factory and food-production jobs to defend the homeland while women stepped into their places. One Lotta unit, operating an antiaircraft gun in the 1944 Battle of Helsinki, was armed with rifles for self-defense, making them the first women to serve under arms in the Finnish military. By 1944, 291 Lottas had died from disease, air raids, and accidents and 66 killed in direct contact with the enemy. As part of the peace treaty with the Soviets, the organization was disbanded that year as "paramilitary," although it resumed charitable activities after the war and currently has branches in Sweden, Denmark, and Norway.

Postwar

Finland did not join NATO in 1949 but had obvious concerns about the Soviet Union as a neighbor. Finland requires young men to be subject to conscription and do a term of national service, seeing the military as a way to instill a national consciousness and bridge class and educational differences, taking as a model Infantry Regiment 11, officered by wealthy urban men commanding rural and blue-collar soldiers. This deliberate mixing of people also helped Finland to manage the presence of a Communist party in the 1950s through parliamentary democracy rather than exclusion or radical political action. In 1956, Finland volunteered for UN Peacekeeping missions, sending to the Suez the first of what are now more than 40,000 Finnish soldiers to have served in that capacity. In 1961, they opened the enlisted jobs of radar operator, coastal artillery, and administrative jobs to women in a special auxiliary, amalgamating them with the regular force in 1994. Noncombat support roles on peacekeeping missions became available to women in 1991.

In 1995, Finland opened all military jobs to women volunteers, although women are not subject to conscription. Finnish peacekeepers have a reputation for having rules of engagement with a very high threshold for lethal force and strict anti-fraternization encampments that divide men and women and impose curfews, amusing and frustrating colleagues from more socially liberal countries like Norway and Germany. Finland regards the presence of women in combat positions to be a positive moderating force and an asset in interacting with local people. In 2016, women made up only 2.9 percent of the Finnish armed forces, with about 500 women volunteering each year. In an attempt to recruit more, Finland has invested in campaigns with a message of "do work that has a purpose" and one in which a woman soldier is fashionably attired in camouflage pants, scarf, and belt with tags on them identifying their origins as London, Paris, and the Helsinki Military Supply Depot in an attempt to show the military as cool and attractive as a career. For women in military service, Finland provides the same generous maternity and family leave as available for civilians, as well as policies designed to avoid separating families or deploying a parent internationally unless he or she volunteers.

Further Reading

Ellefson, Merja. "The Hero's Mother: Lotta Svard and Mediated Memories." In *Dynamics of Cultural Borders*, edited by Anu Kannike and Monika Tasa, 147–68. Tartu, Finland: University of Tartu Press, 2016.

Harinen, Olli, and Jakka Leskinen. "General Conscription in Finland after 2008: Some Reasons behind Finland's Population's and Conscript's Attitudes towards General Conscription." In *Advances in Military Sociology: Essays in Honour of Charles C. Moskos*, edited by Guiseppe Caforio, 51–65. Bingley, UK: Emerald Group Publishing, 2009.

Henriksson, Lea. "Sisterhood's Ordeals: Shared Interests and Divided Loyalties in Finnish Wartime Nursing." *DYNAMIS* 19 (1999): 305–27.

Jukararainen, Pirjo. "Men Making Peace in the Name of Just War: The Case of Finland." In *Making Gender, Making War: Violence, Military and Peacekeeping Practices*, edited by Annica Kronsell and Erika Svedberg, 103–20. London: Routledge, 2011.

Valenius, Johanna. "A Few Kind Women: Gender Essentialism and Nordic Peacekeeping Operations." *International Peacekeeping* 14, no. 4 (2007): 510–23. doi:10.1080/13533310701427785.

France

Background

Since the 15th century, France has lauded Joan of Arc, the young woman whose divine inspiration and military acumen helped push the English out of medieval France. Joan became a Saint in 1920, after World War I military devotion to her a patron, but she was an outlier in a system that barred women's participation until modern times. Women followed soldier husbands into the field as laundresses, vivandieres, and amateur nurses, allowed by the army rather than have men foraging or buying alcohol from civilians in occupied territory. In 1793, the French Revolutionary government attempted to remove them, passing the Law to Rid the Armies of Useless Women, but it was practically impossible for the military to function without the services they provided, and many women resurfaced as "cantinieres" running taverns and supply wagons near any encampment or garrison. Cantinieres, wearing a skirted version of the uniform of the regiment they provisioned, followed French troops to Algeria, the Crimean War, Mexico, and Indochina. A few women, dressed in men's clothing, served in the ranks undetected until wounded, like Marie-Angelique-Josephine Duchemin, who fought in the defense of Corsica (1792–1799) and was pensioned in 1804 as a lieutenant. Emperor Napoleon III promoted her as the first woman admitted to the French Legion of Honor in 1851, and she received a military funeral at Les Invalides in 1859.

During the French Revolution, women emerged as a potent radical force, marching on Versailles to demand bread and reform and organizing into mobs harnessed by Jacobin politician Georges Danton. The revolution officially discouraged women's participation in government, refusing Olympe de Gouges's Declaration of the Rights of Women and the Female Citizen (1791) on the grounds that it was the duty of men to bear arms, vote, and be elected, while women fulfilled their duty to France as mothers. Women activists during the 1830s' "war of the streets" against the restored French monarchy threw bombs,

> **Military Medicine**
>
> As French experts gathered in 1981 to debate the future of women in their military, their chair was a woman whose service could not be questioned—General Valérie André (b. 1922). André worked with the French Resistance before resuming medical school at the end of World War II and spending time with a local flight and parachute club. These hobbies, and her surgical expertise, earned her recruitment as a contract physician with the French Army in Indochina, where she would parachute in to treat wounded soldiers in remote locations. In 1950, seeing a demonstration of two Hiller 360 helicopters in Saigon, she became determined to train as a pilot and use the craft as air ambulances. Taking her first solo flight in August 1950, she returned to Indochina and began a flight log totaling more than 4,000 hours and 500 missions, often under fire. Her reputation for fearlessness and commitment to serving the wounded led to her nickname among the Vietnamese, Mrs. "Quekat" (Helicopter).
>
> Rising through the French military medical ranks, she served again in Algeria, piloting both medical and armed commando flights in H-19 and H-34 aircraft. She achieved the rank of medical Colonel in 1970, then physician general of the French Armed Forces in 1976. Although she had been awarded the Grand Cross, Legion of Honor, most profiles of her called her a "girl" and praised her cooking and her long marriage to Alex Santini, her former flight instructor. In 1981, when she was asked to chair the commission, she was also inspector general of medicine. André still lives outside Paris, near the municipal heliport.

distributed pamphlets, and planned attacks but had little representation in the leadership of the 1830 or 1848 Revolutions. During the Franco-Prussian War of 1870–1871, women organized emergency responses to the shelling of Paris, but during the subsequent Commune, working-class women remaining in the city freed prisoners, helped seize the artillery guns of Montmarte, and took up weapons to defend the city and its new communard government from the French army. Louise Michel, an anarchist and teacher, operated an ambulance and joined the Commune's National Guard, joining them in their last stand in the Montmarte Cemetery. She and thousands of other communard women were exiled to Algeria and New Caledonia as political prisoners.

The World Wars

War plans drawn up by the French General Staff in 1910 recognized that women had to be included in the support system of the military, and they assumed the participation of Red Cross nurses, who had served effectively in the French response to the Boxer Rebellion in 1900 and the 1907 Moroccan crisis. At the outbreak of World War I, the military was able to call up 100,000 women as nurses, who worked in 1,480 hospitals, casualty clearing stations, and sanitariums, often under fire from long-range artillery and air attacks. Factories took on women workers to free men for service, granting them equal pay in 1917 after a series of strikes. Under intense criticism that they were indulgently profiting from the war, sexually available, or stealing jobs from men, the women labored under dangerous conditions, handling chemicals in munitions factories and working without safety regulations, which had been abandoned for war efficiency. Others, missing their own sons, became "war godmothers" for troops near their homes, providing letters, care packages, and home visits.

The armed forces, needing a vast expansion of their bureaucracy, also turned to women, employing 120,000 by 1918, with priority given to the widows and orphans of soldiers. In order to keep the women, who received expensive and time-consuming training, the military provided crèches for children and flexible working hours. At the end of the war, as industry sent women home, French manpower losses meant that the bureaucracy needed to keep many of its wartime women clerks, secretaries, telephone operators, and managers. Additionally, when judged against mutinous men, many of whom would have to be retrained in new procedures and technologies, docile office women were very appealing, especially if supporting them paid a debt owed for their widowhood. French soldiers chafed at restrictions on their political participation, set in place in the 19th century as a guard against the possibility of a general's coup d'etat, but women in France, unlike Britain and the America, did not win suffrage in 1918 and could remain apolitical. France conservative social mores and panic about postwar population loss led to policies designed to prioritize motherhood and the replacement of a generation of men lost in the war, even approving a provision for pregnant women to marry, with the special permission of the president of the republic, a soldier fiancée posthumously in order to claim his name and benefits for the child. This law remains on the books and was last used in 2017 for the male partner of a policeman killed in a terrorist attack on Paris.

Hundreds of French women joined the International Brigades to fight fascism in Spain in 1936, after the Blum government announced that it would not intervene. Growing pressure from Nazi Germany, and worry about the demographic damage World War I had wrought on the pool of men who could be called up, moved the government to allow French women to enlist in the armed forces in 1939. The swiftness of the Fall of France in May 1940 meant that few took part except for as managers of the mass evacuation of Paris or those who retreated with de Gaulle and what would become the Free French

Army. The Vichy regime, despite the traditionalist views of Marshal Petain, had no alternative but to continue to employ women in its bureaucracy in the absence of the men captured at the surrender of the French forces and sent to Germany as internees or prisoner-labor.

De Gaulle encouraged women to join the Free French Forces as well as the Resistance within France and the British-run Special Operations Executive. Along with nursing, clerical work, and drivers, General Lucien Merlin organized a Women's Signal Corps, nicknamed the "Merlinettes," to operate radios, work cryptography, and manage intelligence documents. These women were often recruited for parachute and explosive training and sent into occupied Europe as liaisons with the maquis and saboteurs, a dangerous job in which those captured were tortured and usually executed by the Gestapo. Across the political spectrum of the resistance, women comprised probably 20 percent of the total agents and were particularly effective because the Nazis devalued women's agency and overlooked many of their activities hidden in everyday banal tasks. In North Africa, Susan Travers, an ambulance driver and medic, was serving as General Pierre Koenig's driver at Bir Hakeim, where his command included the 13th Demi-Brigade of the French Foreign Legion. On June 10, 1942, forced to retreat, Koenig ordered Travers to drive at the head of the column, guiding the rest through a minefield and machine gun fire. For this extraordinary performance, the Legion enrolled her as an adjudant-chef, the only woman ever allowed to join. In recognition of their valiant service, de Gaulle ordered that as of April 1944, women had the right to vote.

The Wars of Decolonization and Cold War

Following World War II, French women returned to traditional roles in the home, although some veterans, including Travers and Valerie Andre, went on to serve in France's wars of decolonization in Vietnam and Algeria, most often as contract medical personnel. Legislation in 1951 regularized their presence in the military, although in separate, women's services, and on renewable contracts with slow promotion. In the 1950s and 1960s, the growing French feminist movement was largely anti-military and saw little reason to campaign for women to be included or to enter combat trades. Those women who joined skewed conservative and, although if unhappy with their unequal status, made few waves about it. In 1972, the separate women's branches were merged with the regular French Army, Navy, and Air Force, with caps placed at 20 percent of the total allowed to be women, broken down into 7 percent of the transportation, signal, or ordinance corps; 3 percent of the marines; and 30 percent of the technology and administration specialties.

The effect of these decisions began to appear in the 1970s, as Valerie Andre, an aeromedical helicopter pilot and neurosurgeon, became the first woman general officer in 1976. Women were admitted to the French War Colleges in

1977, followed by the end of separate training schools in 1983. The French Air Force introduced women drill instructors in 1978, noting that women could exert a feminized coercive power over men through charisma and competence in the model of "manager" rather than the expected heroic example of previous generations. The Commission on the Future of Women in the Armed Forces, convened in 1981 and headed by Andre, produced recommendations that opened transport aircraft and helicopter jobs to women, as well as navy non-commissioned officer (NCO) ratings. In civilian France, a 1988 European Court of Justice ruling applicable across the European Union (EU) ended gendered restrictions on careers like primary school teachers and athletic trainers, raising questions about the legality of combat bans in the military.

Reviewing French performance in the First Gulf War, the forces determined that they should improve command and control, strategic intelligence, and informational warfare for future conflicts and that the wars for which they wanted to prepare would be ones in which women could play a greater part. In 1992, women began serving on naval vessels and were admitted to the French Naval Academy, and in 1995, the air force pinned wings on its first woman fighter pilot. During this period, politicians decided to begin scaling down the conscription system in France, transitioning to an All-Volunteer Force that would depend on women for a competitive pool of recruits.

The 21st Century and the Full Integration of Women

Claire Aldige, a 1996 candidate for the supply corps, was rejected because the cap on women had already been met, and her place went to a man whose test scores and application were of lesser quality. Aldige appealed to the Council of State for Public Affairs, which found in her favor in May 1998. Subsequently, Secretary of State for Defense Charles Million, presided over the end of quotas and the opening of all trades except those involving "extensive contact with the enemy," with determination made on the qualifications of each specialty. Training as commandos became available in 1998, then naval fighter pilot and riot police in 1999. A study done of these changes found that, to the advantage of women, they handled altitude and adapted to field conditions well, but that as a disadvantage, they had less overall strength and stamina than male peers. The consideration, as France approached a full volunteer force in 2002, was to what degree this mattered in warfare requiring resilience and high-tech expertise. The decision was to open all trades except submarines and riot police NCOs, although both of these have been lifted with the construction of new barracks and, in 2017, the assignment of women to the nuclear-weapons carrying subs with sufficient room to quarter women separately.

France arrived at its integration of women through bureaucratic decisions and the needs of the military in the 21st century rather than popular politics and support. France strongly believes that its armed forces are a key feature of national prestige, as is their ability to act as stabilizing peacekeepers and manage conflicts over the long term. Women responded to recruiting for similar reasons men did: steady jobs, interesting work, adventure, and their family and child-rearing needs can be dealt with through solutions already used in the civilian sector. In 2016, women comprised 15 percent of the French forces, and the military has programs in place to recruit and retain women in scarce specialty fields like cyber and nuclear engineering.

Further Reading

André, Valérie. *Ici, Ventilateur!: (Excerpts from a Flight Log)*. Paris: Calmann-Lévy, 1954.

Boene, Bernard, and Didier Danet. "France: Farewell to the Draft and All That." *Military and Society in the 21st Century: A Comparative Analysis*, edited by Jurgen Kuhlmann, 227–57. Berlin: Lit Verlag, 2000.

Boene, Bernard, et al. "France: In the Throes of Epoch-Making Change." *The Postmodern Military: Armed Forces after the Cold War*, 53–79. Oxford: Oxford University Press, 2000.

Boulègue, Jean. " 'Feminization' and the French Military: An Anthropological Approach." *Armed Forces & Society* 17, no. 3 (1991): 343–62. doi:10.1177/0095327x9101700302.

Dubois, Thierry. "Fighting Girl: Valérie André." *Vertical*, June 15, 2017. https://www.verticalmag.com/news/fighting-girl-valerie-andre/.

Faupin, Alain. "Defense Sector Reform: The French Case Study." In *Post-Cold War Defense Reform: Lessons Learned in Europe and the United States*, edited by Istvan Gyarmati and Theodor Winkler, 44–60. Washington, DC: Brassey's, 2002.

Holden, Henry M. *Hovering: The History of the Whirly-Girls, International Women Helicopter Pilots*. Mt. Freedom, NJ: Black Hawk Pub. Co., 1994.

Martin, Michel L. "From Periphery to Center: Women in the French Military." *Armed Forces & Society* 8, no. 2 (1982): 303–33. doi:10.1177/0095327x8200800208.

Martin, Michel L. *Warriors to Managers: The French Military Establishment since 1945*. University of North Carolina Press, 1981.

McKechnie, Rosemary. "Living with Images of a Fighting Elite: Women and the Foreign Legion." In *Images of Women in Peace and War*, edited by Sharon Macdonald et al., 122–41. Madison: University of Wisconsin Press, 1987.

Orr, Andrew. *Women and the French Army during the World Wars, 1914–1940*. Indiana University Press, 2017.

Sorin, Katia. "Women in the French Forces: Integration vs. Conflict." In *Challenge and Change in the Military: Gender and Diversity Issues*, edited by Franklin Pinch, 76–96. Winnipeg: Canadian Forces Leadership Institute, 2002.

Weitz, Margaret Collins. "Soldiers in the Shadows: Women of the French Resistance." In *A Soldier and a Woman: Sexual Integration in the Military*, edited by Gerard De Groot and Corinne Peniston-Bird, 135–51. New York: Longman, 2000.

Yalom, Marilyn. *Blood Sisters: The French Revolution in Women's Memory*. New York: Basic Books, 1995.

Germany

Background

German women, except those who followed soldiers as wives, sutlers, and camp followers in the Thirty Years' War and the 18th-century conflicts in which German states produced mercenary troops, had little contact with the military. In the Revolutions of 1848–1849, women reformers had interests in the nationalistic, liberal, and educational freedoms espoused by the rebels but did not reach the leadership of the movement in any German state. The quick succession of wars engineered by Otto von Bismarck to unite the Second Reich—against, Denmark, Austria, and France, concluded in short order and did not demand women's additional labor or substantial homefront support. German war planning, mindful of the limits to population and resources, sought to avoid two-front and prolonged wars and not call on women.

World War I

These plans shattered against the reality of World War I, as the mass mobilization of men year after year required women to take their places in factories and in farm labor. The lack of access to imported goods because of the sea blockade meant that ersatz versions of coffee, wool, soap, and leather became the norm, along with harsh rationing of food by 1916, which was termed the "turnip winter" because people turned to eating livestock feed. Women's work was necessary for the war effort, but conservative women's groups opposed it, as did the powerful German trade unions, which considered the women interlopers and job thieves and insisted that their pay reflect their status as temporary replacements. Eventually 700,000 women voluntarily came to work centers for placement industry, while 100,000 nurses provided treatment for soldiers at the battlefront and in hospitals and sanitariums, while women

> **Political Leadership**
>
> In 2013, Chancellor Angela Merkel appointed Dr. Ursula Albrecht von der Leyen (b. 1958) as the first woman defense minister in Germany. Dr. von der Leyen, who grew up in a German political and diplomatic family, trained as a doctor at the University of Hanover, specializing in women's health. After marrying a fellow doctor, she followed him to Stanford, where she was a stay-at-home parent to their seven children. Returning to Germany, she won a seat in the Parliament of Lower Saxony for the Christian Democratic Union, quickly coming to the attention of Angela Merkel, who made her a member of the shadow cabinet in 2005. When Merkel became chancellor, von der Leyen served as minister of family affairs and youth (2005–2009) and labor and social affairs (2009–2013), achieving reforms in parental leave, childcare, and emigration of needed health-care workers.
>
> Her appointment in 2013 to the Defense Ministry signaled a desire to clean up a department troubled by scandal and plagued by recruiting and acquisitions problems. Von der Leyen applied many of her civilian policies to the military, offering recruits family-friendly policies for deployment and hazard pay, forcing Airbus to pay substantial compensation for contract delays, and in 2017, fired Major General Walter Spindler for failing to curb military hazing. She has been an advocate of a strong German military presence, visiting troops in Afghanistan and committing resources to German troops at Incirlik Air Base in Turkey, UN Peacekeeping and North American Treaty Organization (NATO) defense of the Baltic. In 2014, she broke a long-standing taboo by sending arms to Iraqi and Kurdish security forces and has overseen Germany's continued transition to an all-volunteer force. Von der Leyen, whom the media nicknamed "Flinten-Uschi" (Ursula the Rifle), is an advocate for a united EU military.

teachers, who had pioneered interventions for blind and deaf children applied them to wounded servicemen. The last year of the war, the army trained 500 women to do signals work, but was careful to specify that they worked *for* the military but were not *in* the military.

The war left 2 million "extra women" who were widowed or single because of the loss of men, and their pensions and support strained the new Weimar government. The new constitution gave women the right to vote and was substantially more liberal than the Kaiser's government, but the cultural shift of women working and loosening of social control caused profound unease. Women on the radical left participated in the violent aftermath of the war as

Spartacists, like Rosa Luxemburg, fighting in the streets against the Freikorps soldiers co-opted by the government to restore order. Men felt alienated and displaced in a severely depressed economy and believed that their military service was going unheralded. This clash of values underlay the conservative view of women offered by the Nazi Party, which promised a return to Germany's glory days and a restoration of women focused on Kinder, Kirche, and Kuche (children, church, and kitchen).

World War II

Because of this core feature of the National Socialist ethos, and the labor force available from the hundreds of thousands of prisoners of war captured in Russia and France, the Nazis attempted to avoid calling up women during World War II. Only a few celebrities, like Olympic athletes, filmmaker Leni Riefenstahl, and the pilot Hanna Reitsch, were able to defy the expectation of domesticity. Orders in 1935 and 1939 set in place measures for conscription and labor exchanges, but instead, the government used the model of the Finnish Lotta organization to attract women volunteers beginning in 1941. The pressure of the war led to Albert Speer instigating full mobilization in 1943, after which 450,000 women went to work as clerical, administrative, and financial support personnel in all branches of the regime. Women with experience in aircraft could join an auxiliary to provide skilled mechanics to the Luftwaffe, and volunteer "blitz-madchen" crewed the many antiaircraft guns and searchlights protecting cities from bombing raids, although the authorities feared that women, having pulled the trigger on an artillery piece, would be psychologically damaged or incapable of submitting to her proper place in the Nazi gender hierarchy. The Nazis, having encountered Soviet women in combat, wanted their women to be as different as possible.

Women in Nazi Germany were never official combat troops but played a key role in carrying out the regime's plans. Medical personnel in the 1930s acquiesced to and implemented euthanasia programs, and civilians informed on their neighbors to the police or stood by as the Nuremburg laws forced them out of jobs and schools. In one of the most heinous of roles for women, volunteers enlisted to be prison guards and concentration camp administrators. A small minority actively defied the government, like teenaged Sophie Scholl, who incited others to resist and was guillotined as an enemy of the state. In the last year of the war, a woman in Pomerania used Home Guard equipment to destroy three Soviet tanks with a bazooka, for which she earned an Iron Cross, but this and the other 39 Iron Crosses awarded to women were rare. A last ditch effort was made to deploy a women's battalion but largely as a measure to shame men into fighting to the death. As the Russians occupied Berlin, soldiers raped and looted on an epic scale, described in the anonymous diary, *A Woman in Berlin* (1959), whose author, Marta Hillers, demanded that her name

One of the few women to escape gendered restrictions on professional work, film director Leni Riefenstahl became a vital part of the Nazi propaganda machine, producing powerful visions of the Nuremburg Rallies and the 1936 Olympic Games. A close associate of Hitler's, Reifenstahl accompanied film crews to occupied Poland and France, and used Romani concentration camp prisoners as forced extras in her film, *Tiefland*. (Library of Congress/Corbis/VCG via Getty Images)

be withheld until her death in 2001 because of the social shame of violation by the Russians.

East and West Germany

The postwar repatriation of tens of thousands of German prisoners meant that women took the lead in clearing and beginning to reconstruct German cities, which had been reduced to rubble. During the Berlin Airlift of 1948–1949, the Americans at Tempelhof Airport relied on women to construct and maintain runways to make the constant cycle of takeoffs and landings possible. Despite these demonstrations of women's ability to undertake labor under harsh conditions, Cold War East and West Germany shied away from using it further and instead prized a narrative of women's innate pacifism and role as mother and family peacemaker.

Germany

East Germany followed the model of the Soviet Union, preferring that women enter the professions and science, technology, engineering, and math (STEM) fields in the civilian sector, although many defaulted to the traditional female occupations as nurses and teachers. After 1953, women received civil defense training as member of factory "battle groups" preparing for conflict with the West and could volunteer to serve in the military, unlike men, who were conscripted. Even in the Ministry for State Security (STASI) secret police, the government recruited very few women because it drew from a pool of conscripted soldiers. Even in its espionage operation, the STASI overwhelmingly sent male agents to seduce and compromise western European women rather than the traditional female "honeypot" of spycraft. Almost all of the women still serving in the East German military and border guards in 1990 were retired or squeezed out in an amalgamation that accepted only one-fifth of East Germany's military.

The Bundeswehr, West Germany's armed forces, followed the Constitution's section 12a, which forbade women to bear arms, blocking their participation. Instead, women entered the civilian workforce during the restructuring and modernized industrialization that yielded the West German "economic miracle" of the 1960s, gaining ground in unions and workplace protections and rising into management positions. In 1966, the government granted military personnel the right to be represented by a trade union, which is active in negotiating their benefits today. In light of modern social changes, including women's liberation and the student movement, the government commissioned a study by the Women and Society Commission in 1973. This study, and the German public, had to take into account the actions of women members of terrorist organizations like the Baader-Meinhof Gang and Red Army Faction. Ulrike Meinhof, Friederike and Hanna-Elise Krabbe, Barbara Meyer, and Andrea Klump took equal part in the kidnappings, bank robberies, and extortions and proved so fearsome in their determination that the West German counterterrorism unit had a standing order to "shoot the women first."

A severe shortage in medical personnel moved the Bundeswehr to open the medical service to women in 1975, along with training in small arms for the purpose of protecting patients if necessary in the field. This was followed soon after by admission to the military's musical bands, which have traditionally been seconded to medical units as extra hands in emergencies. Throughout the 1970s and 1980s, more than 50,000 women (28% of Ministry of Defense civilian workers) worked for the Bundeswehr as clerks, accountants, and instructors, which slowly made it more palatable that they might someday join as uniformed personnel. The reunification of Germany in 1990 required an amalgamation of East and West forces, which ended up accepting only a small percentage of East German soldiers, very few of them women. In 1991, all musical and medical trades opened to women, with Brigadier General Verena von Weymarn reaching general officer rank in 1994 as surgeon general.

1989–21st Century

With the Cold War over, Germany reoriented its defense establishment away from the prospect of a World War III with the Soviet Union and into a global projection of power in the interest of peace and security. Still under restrictions about offensive capabilities, Germany deployed medical, peacekeeping, and stability operations troops to the 1991 Gulf War and missions to Yugoslavia and Somalia in 1992 and joined the NATO reaction force in 1994. However, the turning point in the German public's attitude toward the Bundeswehr came in 1998, when the majority approved of the use of force for intervention in Kosovo, and the military significantly improved its standing as a trustworthy institution in the eyes of civilians.

Back in 1986, Tanja Kreil, a 19-year-old electrician, applied to join the Bundeswehr as a maintainer, which fell under the classification of combat support. Rejected because these jobs were closed to women, she appealed the decision to the German federal court in Hanover. Kreil moved on with her life as the case moved slowly through the German court system and into the European Court of Justice, which had also taken up cases about gendered employment in France. Their 1998 finding overruled German laws and placed the exclusion of women not as a military matter but as workplace labor practices. After conducting polling and a study, the Bundeswehr Institute for Social Research recommended opening all trades to women, and the Bundestag responded by amending section 12a of the Constitution to allow women to serve under arms.

In general, the soldiers viewed the integration of women as a positive development, citing women's ability as negotiators and diplomats, and judged that women added legitimacy and prestige to overseas operations. Traditionalists feared that sexual tensions would interfere with military effectiveness and believed that they would be at a disadvantage for promotion and jobs. Most German men had already worked closely with women before joining the military, and a majority had no problem seeing women as their bosses and were familiar with gendered quotas in civilian jobs. The 2008 global financial crisis and its effect on the German budget moved the Bundestag to end the practice of male conscription or mandatory national service and transition to an all-volunteer force by 2011, making the recruiting and retention of women especially valuable. Women currently serve in all trades of the German military, including paratroopers, fighter pilots, and, as of 2014, when suitable vessels were available, submarines. In recent peacekeeping deployments, they have made up 6 percent of the personnel.

The German public supports the foreign policy that averts problems globally before they can affect domestic safety, and despite several terrorist incidents, like the truck attack on a Berlin Christmas Market in 2016, they feel secure. The German social welfare system offers parental leave and childcare to all citizens, but the military's deployment schedules complicate family life and childbearing. Few German military personnel live on bases, creating a "commuter force" in which spouses and children prefer to remain in one location while the military member deploys or moves from base to base. For those serving in Iraq or Afghanistan, the German postal service has been vital in providing a conduit for communication and goods, while the military sponsors Internet forums for family concerns. When assigned to an exchange position, like a post in the United States, the Bundeswehr takes special care that dual-career military families are not disadvantaged by a gap in the trailing spouse's record, finding complimentary jobs for them or other mitigations. As of 2016, 11.3 percent of the German military comprises women.

Further Reading

Barnes, Tiffany D., and Diana Z. O'Brien. *Defending the Realm: The Appointment of Female Defense Ministers Worldwide*. University of California Berkeley Working Papers. cpd.berkeley.edu/wp-content/uploads/2016/10/AJPSBarnes OBrien2016RR.pdf.

Campbell, D'Ann. "Women in Combat: The World War II Experience in the United States, Great Britain, Germany, and the Soviet Union." *The Journal of Military History* 57, no. 2 (1993): 301–23. doi:10.2307/2944060.

Collmer, Sabine. "Between Alliance and Homefront Considerations: The German Armed Forces and Security-Related Opinions Polls." In *Advances in Military Sociology: Essays in Honor of Charles C. Moskos*, edited by Guiseppe Caforio, 145–69. Bingley, UK: Emerald, 2008.

Dittmer, Cordula, and Maja Apelt. "About Intervening in Vulnerable Societies: Gender in Military Peacekeeping of the Bundeswehr." In *Women in the Military and in Armed Conflict*, edited by Helena Carreiras and Gerhard Kummel, 63–80. Wiesbaden: Sozialwissenschaften, 2008.

Henley, Jon. "Europe's Defence Minister Roles Become Female Stronghold." *The Guardian*, May 19, 2017. https://www.theguardian.com/world/2017/may/19/europes-defence-minister-roles-become-female-stronghold-sylvie-goulard.

Klein, Paul. "Coping with the Peace Dividend: Germany and Its Armed Forces in Transition." In *Military and Society in 21st Century Europe: A Comparative Analysis*, edited by Jurgen Kuhlmann, 183–225. Berlin: Lit Verlag, 2000.

Kümmel, Gerhard. "Complete Access: Women in the Bundeswehr and Male Ambivalence." *Armed Forces & Society* 28, no. 4 (2002): 555–73. doi:10.1177/0095327x0202800403.

Liebert, Ulrike. "Europeanizing the Military: The European Court of Justice and the Transformation of the Bundeswehr." In *Equity in the Workplace: Gendering Workplace Policy Analysis*, edited by Heidi Gottfried, 325–48. Lanham, MD: Lexington Books, 2004.

MacDonald, Eileen. *Shoot the Women First*. London: Arrow Books, 1992.

Michel, Hildegard Maria. "Women in the German Democratic Republic and in the New Federal States." In *Gender Politics and Post-Communism: Reflections from Eastern Europe and the Former Soviet Union*, edited by Nanette Funk and Magda Mueller, 138–50. London: Routledge, 1993.

Policy Planning and Advisory Staff of the German Ministry of Defense. "The Bundeswehr on Its Way into the Twenty-First Century." In *Post-Cold War Defense Reform: Lessons Learned in Europe and the United States*, edited by Istvan Gyarmati and Theodor Winkler, 224–46. Washington, DC: Brassey's, 2002.

Reuschmeyer, Marilyn, ed. *Women in the Politics of Postcommunist Eastern Europe*. Armonk, NY: M.E. Sharpe, 1998.

Siebrecht, Claudia. "Martial Spirit and Mobilization Myths: Bourgeois Women and the 'Ideas of 1914'." In *The Women's Movement in Wartime: International Perspectives, 1914–1919*, edited by Allison Fell and Ingrid Sharp, 38–52. New York: Palgrave, 2007.

Totaro, Paola. "Defense Minister and Mother to Seven, Ursula von der Leyen, Shares Some Hard-Won Wisdom." *The New York Times*, October 8, 2015. http://nytlive.nytimes.com/womenintheworld/2015/10/08/ursula-von-der-leyen-mother-of-all-multi-taskers/.

Great Britain

Background

Britain's geographic advantages as an island have reduced the opportunities and the necessity of women following armies into continental Europe on the same scale as their neighbors' premodern modes of supply. Medieval queens like Margaret of Anjou during the Wars of the Roses headed armies, although field command was in the hands of male generals, and Catherine of Aragon, the daughter of Crusader Isabella of Castile, acting as regent, dispatched troops to defeat the Scots while Henry VIII was in France for diplomatic meetings. Henry VIII's daughter, Elizabeth I, put on an armored breastplate at Tilbury and inspired the troops there waiting to repel the Spanish Armada in 1588, but women did not see direct conflict until the English Civil War, when women from both Parliamentary and Royalist family defended castles against enemy attack. Naval captains during the 18th century were allowed to bring their wives onboard with them, and there were scattered reports of women serving in the army of that period in male dress, but these were very unusual.

During the long 19th century, women immigrated to British colonies as the wives of soldiers and bureaucrats, especially after the government forced the British East India Company to allow missionaries from the Anglican Church into India, where they disrupted the practice of single male officials forming relationships with Indian women. Instead, the wave of "memsahibs" replicated respectable British life in the imperial tropics from India to Africa. This inevitably placed them in harm's way, in the 1857 Sepoy Mutiny and in the Boer War. During this period, the head of state was Queen Victoria, who revived the public image of the Celtic chieftain Boudica (whose name translated to "victory"), who attacked Roman London in revenge for the usurpation of her husband's kingdom and the rape of her daughters. This feminine ferociousness suited Victoria's paternalist interest in the empire and the troops who garrisoned it.

> **LGBTQ Women in the Military**
>
> In 1998, after serving in the Royal Air Force (RAF) for 18 years, Caroline Paige made a momentous decision and asked for medical consultation to begin transition and serve as a woman. Born in 1959 and raised in a British army family, Paige joined the RAF in 1980 and served as an F-4 navigator on Cold War intercepts of Soviet planes over Europe before retraining to fly Merlin helicopters. As a flight officer, she served in Saudi Arabia in the First Gulf War and in Anglo-French and North Atlantic Treaty Organization (NATO) deployments to Bosnia in 1995. As other personnel challenged British bans on gay military service at the EU Human Rights Court, Paige asked for and received permission to become the first transgender officer in the British armed forces.
>
> After medical procedures and recovery lasting 45 days, Paige subsequently served another 16 years in the RAF, including 4 tours each in Iraq and Afghanistan as a highly regarded helicopter pilot and trainer. Her memoirs recount incidents of abuse, like the *Sun* newspaper's front-page outing in 2000, wrenching family tensions and slurs from the public, but the military valued keeping the expertise and loyal service of a long-serving asset in whom they had invested. From very early in her transition, Paige volunteered and received training as a mentor to other lesbian, gay, bisexual, transgender, and queer (LGBTQ) personnel, was a key member of the RAF LGBT Freedom Network, acted as a consultant to the military and the government on the inclusion, recruitment, and retention of diverse populations, and in 2012, received recognition on the New Year's Honours List from the commander in chief of Air Command. Paige retired in 2014 after 35 years of service, 34 of them on active flight duty, and now works as a speaker, consultant, and author.

During the Crimean War, Florence Nightingale was so incensed by the poor medical care available to British soldiers, who were dying of neglect and disease in unsanitary field hospitals, that she formed a nursing corps and went to the Ottoman Empire. Nightingale, although sentimentally praised as the "Lady of the Lamp," was also a hard-nosed, scientifically grounded professional, who confronted male doctors with statistics showing the mortality rates connected to cleanliness practices and insisted on strict standards for the women who worked for her. Before this point, nursing had been the job of camp followers, sometimes prostitutes, or the military unit of an injured man, and Nightingale's reforms created nursing as a modern profession open to middle-class women and deserving of royal patronage. Ironically, one of the highest ranking doctors in the British military in the mid-19th century was Dr. James Barry, who was actually an Irish woman who had donned men's clothing and adopted a man's name to attend medical school and then join the army as a surgeon, remaining in disguise the rest of her life.

In the years leading up to World War I, women took part in increasingly violent demonstrations demanding suffrage. To defend themselves, some studied the recently arrived and exotic Japanese martial art ju-jitsu, tailored for women as "suffrajitsu." In response to their tactics of chaining themselves to railings and cars, breaking windows, and disrupting horse races by charging onto the field, the police escalated arrests, beating, and force feedings while the women were in custody. Trades union women took part in strikes and protests, also meeting rough response at the hands of the police. When World War I began, the government feared that women's suffrage leaders' political orientation would be toward international pacifism and that could disrupt mobilization to the detriment of national defense. Instead, the government made an agreement with the most prominent of the leaders, Emmeline Pankhurst, who declared a stop to suffrage demands for the duration of the conflict in return for a promise of postwar suffrage. Additionally, women aided recruiting with acts of humiliating public theater, approaching men not in uniform and handing them white feathers, which was an accusation of cowardice. Men, especially after the war, resented this pressure and many blamed women for having helped the government send men to their deaths.

The World Wars

World War I drew on manpower and industrial capacity that could not be sustained without massive injections of labor. Factories took on 1.25 million women as replacement workers, usually at a fraction of male salaries, while women signed up in 1915 as part of the forage corps led by Queen Mary, gathering edible plants and cultivating gardens. To supplement the wartime bureaucracy, 80,000 worked as typists, clerks, telephone operators, and assistants, usually assigned by social class. In 1915, "Right to Serve" rallies by women demanded the opportunity to enlist in a uniformed capacity, and the government responded in 1917 by creating auxiliary versions of the army, navy, and air force. Volunteer nurses, from the Red Cross and the Voluntary Aid Detachment, including Agatha Christie and Vera Brittain among thousands, served in clearing stations in France and in British institutions. English nurse Edith Cavell had been in Belgium when the Germans invaded and, against the orders of the occupying Germans, aided wounded British and Belgian soldiers. Her execution, and the mistreatment of women and children by German soldiers, inflamed British public opinion toward supporting the war.

The postwar world was a place of shattered social conventions. Britain's huge losses of men meant that many women, who had expected to marry and have children, were single and in need of jobs to support themselves. The social mores of the Edwardian Era, in which women needed chaperones and dressed in constricting corsets, collapsed as the 1920s saw women wearing the short skirts of flappers, driving their own cars, and remaining in some of the jobs left open by the lost generation of men. Women indeed earned suffrage, voting for the first time in 1918, and Nancy Astor was the first woman member of parliament (MP) seated in the House of Commons. During the 1926 General Strike, trade union women joined men in walking picket lines for nine days, while middle- and upper-class women volunteered for the jobs left undone, especially in public transport, undermining the effect of the strike. Watching the ominous events in Europe, British women joined International Brigades and fought in Spain, like Felicia Browne, an artist and Communist, who became the first British casualty, and only British woman to die in the fighting. Other women, especially those in the networks of socially connected club women, organized the Kindertransport, placing German Jewish children in British homes.

The "Phoney War" of 1939–1940, in which the British had declared war on Nazi Germany, Italy, and Japan, but fighting had only taken place in Poland, offered the British government space to revive the women's auxiliaries disbanded after World War I and recruit women for St. John's ambulance service, civil defense wardens, and industrial work. The Auxiliary Territorial Service, in which Queen Elizabeth II served as a young woman, placed women as mechanics, drivers, and antiaircraft crews as well as in clerical and administrative positions. Engineer Caroline Haslett had been asked, in 1938, to study whether women could operate antiaircraft guns, and she assured the government that they could. Dispatched in mixed crews, the women proved to their male commanders that they were cool under fire, working even after being hit by debris and mastering complex targeting procedures. To the end, the government refused to let the women pull the trigger on the guns, fearing that being responsible for the kill would coarsen the women and make men uneasy. The women pointed out that they lived under the threat of aerial bombing and could not be sheltered from a front line that had come to them. The Home Guard, designed to employ World War I male veterans, broke regulations locally and enrolled women, forcing the government to allow an auxiliary in 1943. The Women's Institute, which joking referred to themselves as "Jambusters," after the dam-busting bombing runs of the air force, taught the public how to conserve food, garden, and best use ration coupons through mending and recycling.

By the end of the war, 430,000 women had volunteered for war work, and an additional 125,000 single women between the ages of 20 and 30 were conscripted and assigned to labor in factories, on farms, and in the bureaucracy. Others were more directly under fire, as nurses, including on hospital ships during the evacuation of Dunkirk. The Special Operations Executive prized the participation of women agents sent into occupied Europe, like Nancy Wake and Violette Szabo, because they, unlike male agents, could pass unnoticed in a world stripped of men by conscription and prisoners of war taken by the Germans. The First Aid Nursing Yeomanry (FANY) did recruit and train nurses, but it was also co-opted by the British Intelligence Service, which used its personnel as code clerks and agents. Women with talents for mathematics and cryptography were also the backbone of secret projects at Bletchley Park to break German codes using early computers.

The Cold War

Great Britain demobilized the thousands of women who served in World War II but, under the pressure of the Soviet threat to Western Europe, founded the Women's Royal Army Corps to replace the Auxiliary Territorial Service (ATS) on a permanent basis and parallel navy and air force auxiliaries. These women made up about 2.5 percent of the total British forces and performed noncombat jobs with no weapons training. Their uniform, designed by a man more interested in smart and attractive office workers than in practicality, featured a tight-tailored jacket and skirt, which drew the attention of the Queen, who asked, on a visit to one installation, why the Women's Royal Army Corps (WRAC) women were not available to march for her review. The uniform was revised. With the advent of the National Health Service, and the availability of birth control in the 1960s, more women wanted careers and put off or limited their childbearing, which had been one of the major arguments against investment in training or enlisting women. Small numbers of women medical personnel accompanied British troops to the Korean War. Britain ended male national service and conscription in 1960, in favor of an all-volunteer force, which necessarily cut into the pool of potential soldiers.

Women in the 1950s and 1960s participated in the anti-militarism and anti-nuclear movements, marching against British intervention in the Suez Crisis and in the acceptance of American Polaris missiles placed in bases on British soil. Feminist and pacifist women created the Golders Green encampment as an ongoing demonstration, which also evolved into a protest of the Vietnam War. Barbara Castle, a powerful Labour MP, supported reforms for women in the workplace, intervening on behalf of striking women at an American-owned Ford Assembly plant, where they negotiated for 92 percent of male salaries. Because of the philosophy of the British police that the force should reflect the people they serve, women had become uniformed officers in 1918 and had increasingly left clerical duties for expansions into the motorcycle police, overseas service with British police units in Cyprus, and armed duty in Northern Ireland. Under an exemption to the Sex Discrimination Act, however, the military retained the ability to treat women differently and bar them from combat and arms training.

Tory politician Margaret Thatcher became prime minister in 1979, after a campaign that saw her referred to as "Attila the Hen" and many voiced doubts that a woman could fulfill the obligations of a national leader. Although reviled for her attacks on the social welfare system and unions, the military quickly came to respect her. The Argentine junta invaded the Falkland Islands in 1982, challenging the British to respond. Thatcher was cool and decisive, authorizing the sinking of the *General Belgrano*, and responded to the loss of lived on the HMS *Sheffield* with compassion, but resolve. Soviet press mockingly called her the "Iron Lady," but she solidified this image appearing defiant after the Irish Republican Army (IRA) bombing of the Conservative Party's meeting in Brighton and visiting Belfast, where she wore a bulletproof vest during her walking tour and asserted that the government would not negotiate with terrorists.

During her government, women began to receive weapons training, and Sandhurst, the army's academy, opened a fifth college in order to admit women into a parallel program. Advocates for women's further inclusion used these pilot programs to collect data which suggested that women produced less "training wastage" and performed as well as their male peers. Advocates also pointed out the ridiculousness of regulations keeping women a set distance from front lines, especially since it meant that women attached to the British Army of the Rhine in Western Europe had to stay in France's Channel ports. Women in civil aviation had been flying helicopters and airliners for decades, making the restrictions on pilot training less supportable. In 1989, the Royal Air Force began training women in its auxiliary service to fly combat aircraft, while the navy started trials putting women on ships, beginning with the HMS *Brilliant* in 1990. Some of the wives of male sailors protested this, but the trial was largely a success. There was a single court-martial for fraternization, and one woman was investigated for becoming pregnant, although she had done so on shore leave with her fiancé, a shipmate, and subsequently married him. The British military ended its policy of dismissing women when they became pregnant and retroactively paid substantial damages to the 4,500 women affected by this practice between 1978 and 1990.

Women made up 1,100 of the military personnel Britain contributed to the First Gulf War, drawing the derisive comment that "the infidel has brought his wife" from Saddam Hussein. Still under restrictions about how close they could be to an official battlefield, they were 8 km away, at Divisional Rear Headquarters. The reality of Iraqi-launched tactical ballistic SCUD missiles made this, like the World War II Blitz, a pointless separation of behind and on the front line. Women military personnel and their doctors worked out solutions to complaints that they required ongoing care by deploying with six-month supplies of contraceptives and using hygiene supplies sent as donations by a sympathetic public. Women chafed at the requirement that they keep their fatigue jackets on for modesty in the desert heat, a gesture to Saudi customs, when men stripped down to t-shirts. On their return in 1992, the British Ministry of Defense began the process of amalgamating the women's services into the mainstream army, navy, and air force, retaining some of the senior leadership as gender advisers to mitigate and disadvantage to the women affected. The Royal Air Force had its first women pilots and navigators in 1991, followed by the navy in 1995.

The 21st Century

Military planners in the mid-1990s faced a stark problem. Demographic changes during the 1980s resulted in a severe decline in the number of 18-year-old men. The military could no longer count on a recruiting pool of underemployed, white, working-class northern Englanders. Sir Peter Harding, chief of the air staff, pointed out that by accepting women the services could assure a pool of their highest quality personnel, rather than reaching for substandard men. Echoing this, Captain Alan West's report, using studies of Dutch and Canadian deployments of women, debunked myths that premenstrual syndrome (PMS) would debilitate women physically or mentally or that men would hesitate in combat in order to protect women in their units. In his judgment, good leadership and teamwork would mitigate problems, and that because there was no systematic data on women's ability to kill in combat, there was also no way to prove that they could not. As of 1995, women were moving into more trades in the military, but because of exclusion from jobs with high likelihood direct combat with an enemy, units like the Household Cavalry, Armor, and the Royal Marines were closed. In 1999, the Royal Marines rejected Angela Maria Sirdar, and she appealed the decision to the European Court of Justice, which upheld the right of a force to exclude women if it believed they compromised the effectiveness of the organization. However, the European Union's Human Rights Act entered British legal use in 2000, along with an increasing reliance on civilian-style human resources workforce management.

Great Britain's participation in the Global War on Terror has accelerated the inclusion of women in the 21st century. The women deployed to Iraq and Afghanistan represented 70 percent of the trades in the army, 73 percent in the navy, and 96 percent in the air force. There was no way to keep them from inevitably engaging with the enemy directly, challenging the logic of existing restrictions. Three women, all medics, performed acts of heroism in tending to and saving colleagues under fire, Private Michelle Norris (2006), Able Seaman Kate Nesbitt (2009), and Lance Corporal Sarah Bushbye (2010) have all been awarded Military Crosses in recognition of their valor. Flight Lieutenant Helen Seymour flew repeated seven-hour sorties over Libya protecting the no-fly zone, disproving critics that women could not manage extended flight times. Concern was raised in 2007 when Acting Leading Seaman Faye Turney along with 14 of her fellow sailors on the HMS *Cornwall* were seized by Iran and held for 13 days. The British public was incensed that Turney, the only woman in the crew, was forced to wear a headscarf. Although subjected to psychological stress and questioning, the sailors were not physically harmed and were returned to Britain, where they, unusually, received permission from the Ministry of Defense to sell their stories to the press. Turney's was the most sought after, and she may have received 100,000 pounds.

Prime Minister David Cameron lifted the ban on close combat roles in 2016, and the forces began training for implementation of women in all trades over the next year. As of 2016, women made up 10 percent of the British military, which seeks to balance its powerful and cohesion-building traditions with the integration of women and the values of modern volunteers. The British have been leaders in developing policy for lesbian, gay, bisexual, transgender, and queer (LGBTQ) personnel and have set targets to recruit underrepresented populations in an attempt to have the military reflect the composition of the British public.

Further Reading

Campbell, D'Ann. "Women in Combat: The World War II Experience in the United States, Great Britain, Germany, and the Soviet Union." *The Journal of Military History* 57, no. 2 (1993): 301–23. doi:10.2307/2944060.

Dandeker, Christopher, and Mady Wechsler Segal. "Gender Integration in Armed Forces: Recent Policy Developments in the United Kingdom." *Armed Forces & Society* 23, no. 1 (1996): 29–47. doi:10.1177/0095327x9602300102.

Drury, Ian. "Female Army Medic Awarded Military Cross for 'Extreme Courage' as She Treated Injured Colleagues amid 'Bullets and Bombs'." *Daily Mail Online*, November 9, 2010. http://www.dailymail.co.uk/news/article-1328175/Female-Army-medic-Sarah-Bushbye-awarded-Military-Cross-extreme-courage.html.

Eulriet, Irene. *Women and the Military in Europe 2012*. London: Palgrave Macmillan, 2014.

German, Lindsey. *How a Century of War Changed the Lives of Women*. London: Pluto Press, 2013.

Goldman, Nancy Loring, and Richard Stites. "Great Britain and the World Wars." In *Female Soldiers—Combatants or Non-Combatants? Historical and Contemporary Perspectives*, edited by Nancy Loring Goldman, 21–45. London: Praeger, 1982.

Kennedy-Pipe, Caroline, and Stephen Welch. "Women in the Military: Future Prospects and Ways Ahead." In *New People Strategies for the British Armed Forces*, edited by Alex Alexandrou, Richard Bartle, and Richard Holmes, 49–69. London: Frank Cass, 2002.

Macdonald, Sharon. "Bodicea: Warrior, Mother and Myth." In *Images of Women in Peace and War*, edited by Sharon Macdonald, Pat Holden, and Shirley Ardener, 40–61. Madison: University of Wisconsin Press, 1987.

Muir, Kate. *Arms and the Woman*. London: Coronet, 1993.

Paige, Caroline. "The Transgender Top Gun: How an RAF Hero Who Flew Perilous Missions in Two Wars Has Become the First Combatant to Change Sex after Dreaming of Waking up as a Woman for 40 Years." *Daily Mail Online*, February 25, 2017. http://www.dailymail.co.uk/news/article-4260110/How-RAF-hero-combatant-change-sex.html.

Paige, Caroline. "Transitioning Gender in the UK Military." *HuffPost UK*, May 24, 2015. http://www.huffingtonpost.co.uk/caroline-paige/transgender-in-the-military_b_6926072.html.

Paige, Caroline. *True Colours: My Life as the First Openly Transgender Officer in the British Armed Forces*. London: Biteback Publishing, 2017.

Wildman, Helen. "Military Culture under Fire." In *New People Strategies for the British Armed Forces*, edited by Alex Alexandrou, Richard Bartle, and Richard Holmes, 25–36. London: Frank Cass, 2002.

Greece

Background

Although Greece takes pride in a classical mythology with heroines and ancient women military commanders like Queen Gorgo of Sparta, as well as fictional peacekeepers like Lysistrata of Aristophanes's comedy or Antigone of Sophocles' drama, the reality of women's life in Greece was far more restrictive. During the 1820s' War of Independence, wealthy women stepped up to liberate the country from Ottoman rule, Manto Mavrogenous and Laskarina Bouboulina raising crews and sailing in command of family ships, although their service did not translate into political power after the war. Instead, woman, aside from a small elite, remained largely illiterate, barred from professions, and tied to a traditional kin network of arranged marriages, dowries, and patriarchal control. Folk songs valorized the heroines who took up arms to resist invaders and defend their homes and personal honor, but the opportunities to do so officially were limited to volunteer work in the Hellenic Red Cross, founded in 1877.

During World War I, women, particularly from the middle and upper class, did nursing and voluntary work to support the Greek military. In the aftermath of the war, and the Treaty of Sevres, hundreds of thousands of refugees moved from the new nation of Turkey to Greece (and in the opposite direction, depending on ethnicity and religion), creating a staggering humanitarian crisis and change in population demographics. Although the newly founded League for the Rights of Women attempted to capitalize on other nations' recent enfranchisement of women, even the liberal Venizelos government used concerns over "social order" and undready new emigrants to deny suffrage. This became even less likely in 1936, as Ioannis Metaxas adopted fascist policies that placed women in a passive position as the object of "Mother Worship," although this inadvertently laid the later foundation for a generous social welfare state.

Unusual in the ancient Greek world, Spartan women occupied a significant place in their society, expected to raise strong children, manage land, and participate in public life, especially in the absence of men at war. Spartan women took part in fierce athletic training and, although not allowed to compete, sponsored teams in the Olympic games. (Sergey Galushko/Dreamstime.com)

World War II Resistance

In October 1940, Italy invaded and occupied Greece, followed by Nazi Germany in April 1941 when Italians could not keep control of the country. The Greek Communist Party (KKE) and an alliance of other left-wing organizations recruited and began to field partisans and resistance fighters, using support from the British Special Operations Executive and the American Office of Strategic Services and turning Greece's mountainous landscape to their advantage. By 1944, women were at least 25 percent of the *ardartissa*, or mountain commandos, hauling supplies up the steep hillsides, liberating villages, and sabotaging roads, bridges, and communication lines. Their bravery forced men in their units to match them, and partisan leaders maintained strict rules of behavior and respect for women who were capable of knifing an enemy in the darkness. Because women were vital to the production of food, links to peasant women proved vital to keeping the partisans fed and able to operate in the harsh conditions of the mountains. In villages liberated by the partisans, women undertook educational literacy programs, set up women-led councils, and introduced self-government to areas that had been ignored and exploited.

In the aftermath of the German defeat, civil war broke out between the restored conservative monarchy, which had the support of the victorious allies, and the Communist Party, which sought and received support via Yugoslavia from the Soviet Union. Many women partisans continued to fight alongside their comrades in an increasingly savage insurgency that saw both "Red" (communist) and "White" (monarchist) Terror Campaigns of reprisal, forced movement of people, imprisonments, and mass murders. The Conservative government used the KKE and the participation of women in its activities to paint itself as the savior of decency, the church, and a normalized postwar home life. Marshall Plan funds went toward projects that sent men back to work, and persecution of communists reversed all of the gains women had made through their service.

Cold War

Women remained on the periphery of military service in Greece until the 1970s, although a nurse corps, which served in Greece's contingent to the Korean War, was authorized in 1946. During the military junta of 1967–1974, the authorities attacked and imprisoned leftist activists, at least 2,000 of them women, often justifying their suspicions and torture on the women rejecting traditional gender roles. By the mid-1970s, ongoing hostilities with Turkey and a falling birthrate forced planners to consider allowing women into the armed forces, bearing arms if they would not bear children, in the thinking of one male politician. However, few Greek feminists equated military service with opportunity, but with violent oppression, and they did not campaign for inclusion. Within the military, there were debates about the physical ability of women to do military tasks, particularly to move heavy tank shells, but others pointed out that among the rural women likely to enlist, heavy farm work was commonplace and far harder. In 1977, Parliament passed a law allowing for women's conscription and opening voluntary enlistment, while men continued to serve a mandatory conscription.

Since then, women have made progress in the Greek military, demanding less lax training, and integration with men's programs, opening the military academies to a beginning quota of no more than 10 percent of the students and, in 1996, raising to brigadier general the highest rank a woman could hold. For a brief period in 1982–1987, women were not allowed into the service because of conservative political objects, but enlistment and commissions resumed and accelerated with pressure from the EU and NATO.

21st Century

In 2016, Greek women represented 15.4 percent of the country's military forces, serving without restrictions or quotas. In 2002, the government added several nursery schools for the use of military parents, with leave given for parents to attend school functions and maintain good connections with their children. In 2004, the military created the Gender Equality Office, following the recommendations of NATO and United Nations Security Council Resolution (UNSCR) 1325. Since the financial crisis of 2008, many women see the Greek military and police forces as stable and advantageous employment, which has significantly boosted the proportion of women in the last decade. Greece has become the frontline of the Syrian refugee crisis, a situation which demands that Greek military personnel be adept at humanitarian and emergency management, skills drawn from the logistical and medical career fields where women have begun to outpace men. It is likely that Greek women will continue to find military service a rewarding and attractive choice in the 21st century.

Further Reading

Amokovitis, Demitrios. "Greek Contributions to the Korean War." In *Advances in Military Sociology: Essays in Honor of Charles C. Moskos*, edited by Giuseppe Caforio, 225–32. Bingley, UK: Emerald, 2009.

Brown, James, and Constantina Safilios-Rothschild. "Greece: Reluctant Presence." In *Female Soldiers: Combatants or Non-Combatants? Historical and Contemporary Perspectives*, edited by Nancy Loring Goldman, 165–78. London: Praeger, 1982.

Gerolymatos, André. *Red Acropolis, Black Terror: The Greek Civil War and the Origins of Soviet-American Rivalry, 1943–1949*. New York: Basic Books, 2004.

Mathiopoulos, Margarita. "Greece Ventures onto New Ground: The New Greek Security and Defense Policy, 2000-2015." In *Post-Cold War Defense Reform: Lessons Learned in Europe and the United States*, edited by Istvan Gyarmati and Theodor Winkler, 297–304. Washington, DC: Brassey's, 2002.

Nikolau-Smokoviti, L. "Women in the Military Profession: The Greek Case." In *Advances in Military Sociology: Essays in Honor of Charles C. Moskos*, edited by Giuseppi Caforio, 195–211. Bingley, UK: Emerald, 2008.

Poulos, Margaret. *Arms and the Woman: Just Warriors and Greek Feminist Identity*. New York: Columbia University Press, 2009.

Stefatos, Katerina. "The Female and Political Body in Pain: Sexual Torture and Gendered Trauma during the Greek Military Dictatorship." In *Gendered Wars, Gendered Memories Feminist Conversations on War, Genocide and Political Violence*, edited by Ayse Gul Altınay and Andrea Peto, 69–92. London: Routledge, 2016.

Hungary

Background

Hungary recognizes a long history of influential women who took up arms for their families' dynastic advantage. Fifteenth-century King Matthias Hunyadi owed his throne to the devoted machinations of his mother, Erzsebet Szilagyi, while the women of Eger Castle helped hold off an Ottoman army for 39 days of brutal siege in 1552. Even the Habsburgs met with women-led resistance, as Countess Ilona Zrinyi continued her husband Imre Thokoly's rebellion for three years after his 1685 arrest. The Habsburg rulers of Austria and Hungary did not allow women to serve in their armies aside from the unofficial mass of camp followers who trailed premodern armies. In the 19th century, women in the field of education pressed for nationalism through promotion of the Hungarian language, joining the 1848 Revolution of Louis Kossuth with a publicly printed "Demands of Radical Hungarian Women" that included modernized laws on marriage and education. Among the armed Hungarian rebels in 1848–1849, women served as nurses and there are mentions of women serving as uniformed "order guards." These demands, like the nationalist independence movement, were crushed by Russian troops and restoration of Habsburg authority.

Hungarian women, looking to the Magyar-phile Empress Elisabeth of Austria, often framed their requests for modernization in terms of national character and a need to preserve Hungarian language and culture. The 1904 founding of the Feminist Association advocated for women's suffrage, legal equity, career training, and education as a matter of national strength, although, like many women's organization of the time, it held strong beliefs in pacifism and the futility of war. In 1914, when World War I broke out, women took part in support activities through the Austro-Hungarian Red Cross as nurses, worked producing war materials, and joined the government bureaucracy as clerks and administrative functionaries. The short-lived 1919 Communist regime of Bela

Kun formed alliances with women's groups and included suffrage and legal reforms that did not entirely survive Kun's fall and replacement by the conservative government of Admiral Miklos Horthy. The interwar period saw Horthy's policies edge from the tradition of the old monarchy into fascism, with the corresponding expectations that women's place was, like that of his own spouse, as mothers and wives.

The Cold War

World War II ended with the Soviet occupation of Hungary and installation of a Communist satellite government that expected women to take a much larger role working outside the home and espoused a political doctrine of gender equality, although, like many Eastern-bloc countries, the rhetoric was a far cry from the reality of shortages, state control of personal matters, and continued imbalance of household labor. In 1956, protests against Soviet interference and in solidarity with reform demands in Poland swelled into a national uprising. Women bravely took to the streets, some as nonviolent protesters, others using weapons taken from the police or carefully hidden since the end of the war. They joined in blocking tanks, throwing Molotov cocktails, toppling statues, and calling for freedom, only to be crushed by the arrival of the Red Army, which did not hesitate to shoot women, and the restoration of the Communist regime.

Although part of the Warsaw Pact, Hungary was one of the most peripheral of the Soviet Union's satellites. Hungary's Cold War position was as the least combat ready of any Eastern bloc nation, without its own strategic culture, or long tradition of independent military success. During the 1980s, young men increasingly evaded conscription in order to participate in the informal economy, and military careers in remote garrisons were undesirable. These personnel concerns were sufficiently concerning for the government to open specialist jobs in the medical, signal, and administrative corps to civilian woman, usually the wives of officers, in order to secure qualified workers, and the army offered scholarships to women who studied law, engineering, and medicine in exchange for service to the military.

After the collapse of the Soviet Union, Hungary underwent a dramatic realignment, shifting its ambitions to NATO and its military concern from western Europe to Russia in the east. Through the Partnership for Peace program, Hungary explored the requirements for entering NATO, which included a commitment to defense spending, a critical evaluation of national male conscription, civilian control of the military, and further integration of women. The early 1990s saw Hungary voluntarily join the United States and its coalition in the First Gulf War, sending a 40-member medical team, but years of junior ministers holding the portfolio for defense and little attention paid to developing a modern force meant that Hungary struggled to assign 300 soldiers to participate in NATO's 1999 intervention in Kosovo and found that although they had planes, they lacked the identification (ID) systems to fly patrols with allies.

The 21st Century and Integration of Women

Unlike countries where the addition of women sparks heated political debate, Hungary matter-of-factly presented it as an expectation of much-desired NATO membership and proceeded without fanfare. Hungary admitted women to its military colleges in 1994, beginning with Janos Bolyai Military Technical College, which graduated a first class of 29 women in 1998, all qualified as electrical engineers, mechanical engineers, or economists. During their time at the school, the Ministry of Defense made great efforts to include them, in uniform, at state events, with political spokespeople instructed to chide the press for asking stereotypical gendered questions. These women students were also extensively surveyed and studied by military psychologists and educational specialists, who wanted to use their experience to design better and more inclusive programs. Some of the hitches to the plan came from Hungary's limited resources, as when they had trouble supplying uniforms sized for women and had to paint the available brown shoes black in order to have parade gear that matched male colleagues. The commandant of the school, Major General T. Farkas, was so confident in the mainstreaming of the women students that he encouraged his own daughters to join the military, with two of three agreeing.

Hungary opened all military career fields to women in 1996, including combat lines like anti-tank operations, airborne and infantry. This measured and publicly supported investment in personnel development paid off in 1999, when the military's prominent role in flood relief raised public opinion of the forces, with women soldiers featured prominently in humanitarian activities. In 2001, as a consequence of transition to an all-volunteer force (completed in 2002), more than half of the billets were open, making it necessary to accelerate accessioning women into the jobs. As of 2016, 20 percent of Hungary's armed forces are women, an unusually high number among the alliance, and the government hopes that this will translate into greater participation of women in national politics, in which, without quotas, women represent only 7.3 percent of parliamentary seats.

Since 2003, Hungary has sent a contingent of soldiers, including women, to International Security Assistance Force (ISAF) Afghanistan and had taken over as lead country at the Kabul Airport and in the Provincial Reconstruction Team for Baghlan Province. Two women soldiers have died during these deployments. Hungary's replacement birth rate remains low, and men continue to find opportunities with civilian employers, making it important that the military offer women solid reasons to join, through enlistment, military colleges, or as directly commissioned professionals. The Women's Section of the Military Trade Union represents women soldiers and has negotiated retention points like maternity leave and job stability that allow the armed forces to recruit excellent talent. As Hungary positions itself as a reliable ally and source of intelligence, the mainstreaming of women into high-tech and intellectually demanding specializations will only increase.

Further Reading

Acsady, Judit. "In a Different Voice: Responses of Hungarian Feminists to the First World War." In *The Women's Movement in Wartime: International Perspectives, 1914–1919*, edited by Alison Fell and Ingrid Sharp, 105–23. London: Palgrave, 2007.

Arpad, Susan S., and Sarolta Marinovich. "Why Hasn't There Been a Strong Women's Movement in Hungary?" *Popular Culture* 29, no. 2 (Fall 1995): 77–96.

Békés, Csaba, János Rainer, and Malcolm Byrne. *The 1956 Hungarian Revolution: A History in Documents*. Budapest: Central European University Press, 2003.

Bolgar, Judit. "Women in the Hungarian Armed Forces." *Minerva* 17, no. 3/4 (December 1999): 92.

Cox, Terry. *Hungary 1956: Forty Years On*. London: Frank Cass, 1997.

Dunay, Pál. "The Half-Hearted Transformation of the Hungarian Military." *European Security* 14, no. 1 (2005): 17–32. doi:10.1080/09662830500042429.

Eberhart, Eva. "Situation of Women in Hungary." *Commission of the European Communities* 32 (1991): 153–58.

Fabian, Katalin. *Contemporary Women's Movements in Hungary: Globalization, Democracy and Gender Equality*. Baltimore, MD: Johns Hopkins University Press, 2009.

Kiss, Zoltan Laszlo. "Hungarian Experiences from Peacekeeping in Afghanistan." In *Advances in Military Sociology: Essays in Honor of Charles C. Moskos*, edited by Guiseppe Caforio, 189–224. Bingley, UK: Emerald, 2009.

Lajtai-Szabó, Gergely, Alexandra Béni, Lilla Mezei, Blanka Marianna Györgyi, and Kitti Erdő-Bonyár. "The Heroes of 1956: The Girl, Who Was Already Dead When Her Photo Went around the World." *Daily News Hungary*, July 20, 2017. https://dailynewshungary.com/heroes-1956-girl-already-dead-photo-went-around-world/.

Martinusz, Zoltan. "Defense Reform in Hungary: A Decade of Strenuous Efforts and Missed Opportunities." In *Post-Cold War Defense Reform: Lessons Learned in Europe and the United States*, edited by Istvan Gyarmati and Theodor Winkler, 269–96. Washington, DC: Brassey's, 2002.

Obradovic, Lana. *Gender Integration in NATO Military Forces*. Burlington, VT: Ashgate Publishing Group, 2014.

Reuschmeyer, Marilyn. *Women in the Politics of Postcommunist Eastern Europe*. Armonk, NY: M.E. Sharpe, 1998.

Szabo, Andrea. "Establishment of the Hungarian Women Soldiers' Section and Its Justification." *Minerva* 17, no. 3–4 (Fall 1999): 68–73.

India

Background

The Hindu pantheon of gods offers fierce deities like Shakti, the primordial cosmic energy, and her most popular incarnation Durga, portrayed riding into battle with each of her eight arms holding a weapon. In reality, even wives of rulers usually lived lives modeled after the heroine Sita, whose fidelity, chastity, and obedience to her husband Rama extended even to passing through fire to prove her purity after being kidnapped by an evil king. The coming of Islam to India with the invading armies of the Mughal introduced the practice of Purdah, which sheltered women in the home and away from men outside the family. A few royal women, like Nur Jahan, wife of Shah Jehangir, exercised significant administrative power or acted as regents and defended a husband or son's territory, like Chand Bibi at Ahmednagar in the 16th century. Among the tribal people of northern India, the royal families produced women expert in cavalry tactics and conflict, like Tarabai, the Regent of the Maratha Empire in the early 18th century, who fended off the Mughal Empire.

After the establishment of the British Raj, a few women, outraged by the high-handed and oppressive administration forced on them, took advantage of the 1857 Sepoy Mutiny to take up arms and rebel. The Rani of Jhansi, Lakshmi Bai, a young widow, refused the annexation of her kingdom by the British at her husband's death. She took up arms, led troops, and died from wounds suffered in battle in 1858. Other Indian women campaigned more traditionally for reform, advocating for education, women's public life, and Indian nationalism. In 1888, the Indian Military Nursing Service enrolled women to staff military hospitals, especially to provide religiously appropriate care and food for Muslims, Hindus, and Sikhs.

> **Conflict Policing**
>
> In the wake of sexual abuse scandals among UN Peacekeeping troops, the first all-woman Indian Formed Police Unit (FPU) arrived in Liberia in 2007 as one of four policing units meant to stabilize the country and assist in reforming its law enforcement community. The initial contingent of 108 (in subsequent rotations, 125) women were drawn from the paramilitary Central Reserve Police Force and had extensive experience in urban riot control and counterinsurgency in Jammu and Kashmir, as have their rotations of replacements. Initially aloof from Liberians, the FPU troops quickly earned the trust of local people through infrastructure projects like clean water access and installing streetlights to reduce instances of crime against women walking at night. This evolved into additional interactions like computer classes and summer camps for girls in which the police officers taught self-defense, traditional Indian dance, and personal health.
>
> Although the 2014 Ebola outbreaks strained the capabilities of the peacekeeping forces, by the time the FPU left Liberia in 2016, they had proven the ways in which women might more easily intervene in domestic and community problems, avoid sexual improprieties, and offer medical services in a traditional society. Their position as role models has led to Liberian police academy classes by 2009 being 13 percent women and to a swell in reports of domestic violence and sexual assault, crimes previously underreported to male police. India and Bangladesh remain the only UN Peacekeeping countries to have deployed all-women units.

The World Wars

India, long a jewel in the crown of the British Empire for its trade goods and vast taxed population, proved a vital resource in World War I, supplying a million men in the desperate war of attrition. The British were anxious to secure the support of leading members of Indian society, especially women, to give legitimacy to their demands for men and materials, especially in the fraught campaign activists like Gandhi were waging for Indian autonomy. Tara Devi, a Hindu princess, and the Maharani of Bhopal, a Muslim queen, supported the war because the British appealed to them as members of a traditional warrior class. It was especially important to have the approval of Muslim aristocrats in order to challenge the Ottoman Empire's claim on the loyalty of Islamic people. Women organized the Jhansi Girls Brigade, among other charities, to knit, sew, raise money, and dispatch morale-raising gifts to Indian soldiers, as well as arranging ambulance trains and convalescent places for wounded men sent home to India. Sarojini Naidu, the "Nightingale of India" for her poetry, fully embraced the war effort, seeing service to the British Empire as the key to later independence. When this expectation was not met, and protests, strikes, and the "Quit India" movement rocked cities, the British authorities authorized hiring women police in Kanpur to deal with women jute workers.

World War II caused Great Britain to call on India again for massive numbers of men. Accompanying them were Indian nurses, some of whom died on the SS *Kuala*, which was evacuating military hospital patients and dependents from Singapore when it came under aerial attack and sank. Women living in the Eastern border regions of India feared Japanese invasion and prepared for attack, while hundreds of thousands of poor women and their families were devastated by the 1943 famines resulting from British decisions to prioritize sending an already poor harvest for consumption in wartime Britain rather than feeding the nation that produced it. Under these harsh economic conditions, women turned to prostitution around military garrisons and a drastic shortage in textiles, again because the British consumed the whole of production, left women literally without clothing to wear outside their homes.

Among the enemies of the British Raj, a daring experiment was afoot. Subhas Chandra Bose, whose nationalist ambitions led him to accept help from Nazi Germany and Japan, created a women's regiment in 1943 to compliment the male troops he was raising from prisoners of war held by the Japanese and volunteers. This Rani of Jhansi Regiment, commanded by Captain Dr. Lakshmi Swaminathan, attracted 1,500 women of all religions and castes, who underwent full military training in Japanese-occupied Singapore. Their shorn hair and Jodhpur uniforms shocked conservative Indians and their Japanese sponsors. The women fought alongside Bose until 1945, when the Regiment was forced to retreat from Rangoon into Thailand. Swaminathan, who continued to work as a doctor, led a relief team to Bhopal after the Dow Chemical Emergency in 1984.

After the partition of India in 1947, the mass and often forced migration of millions of people to India, Pakistan, and East Pakistan disrupted the lives of women significantly. To keep the peace in cities crowded with refugees, the Calcutta police recruited women officers, followed by most other major urban areas, finding that women could gain entry to homes where women remained in purdah and would be allowed to speak to them in ways a nonrelated man could not. This inclusion did not extend to the military. India followed a very British model for its postwar army and did not enlist women or create separate auxiliary services.

While India pursued a Cold War policy of nonalignment, the most prominent women politician in the country was Indira Gandhi, the daughter of former prime minister Jawaharlal Nehru. Widowed in 1960, she had acted as first lady and her father's hostess, showing initiative and great charisma by flying to the border area in 1962 as the Sino-Indian war broke out, calming the civilians and establishing the confidence and authority of the government. She was a cabinet minister and on vacation in Kashmir in 1966 when Pakistani invaders in the form of tribal raiders crossed the border, and she quickly established contact with the military and the prime minister, rallied resistance, and helped drive off the threat. She became prime minister in 1966, with Congress party leaders assuming that they could control her, but by 1969, she had taken over the organization. She along with Golda Meir were unusual 20th-century women leaders who headed their countries in times of war, projecting both maternal authority and the steel of a decisive commander. Gandhi directed the government to aid refugees from East Pakistan in 1971, as the region broke free from Pakistan, and intervened militarily, even defying an American fleet sent to the Indian Ocean. She fought off attempts to remove her for charges of corruption and nepotism, but in 1984, two of her Sikh bodyguards assassinated her in retaliation for using the military to remove Sikh militants from the Golden Temple in Amritsar.

Contemporary Military Issues

Most city police forces followed the lead of Calcutta and hired women police, and in 1998, the government formed a Rapid Action Force including women officers to respond to terrorist attacks and national emergencies. Since 1988, three women's battalions serve as part of the Central Reserve Force, handling riots and other situations with large numbers of women participants. This willingness to diversify the police, who often patrolled combat zones in Kashmir, Assam, and Bengal, did not translate to the military, although in 2007, India sent an all-woman police battalion to Liberia as part of its humanitarian mission. Planners insisted that having women in uniform threatened to demoralize men if there was a chance the women might be captured and mistreated by an enemy. The United Nations urged India to incorporate women into its peacekeeping troops, and under this pressure, India began recruiting women to nonnursing jobs on 5-year contracts, later expanded to 7, and then 14. Unlike men, who might be kept on after 14 years, women would be dismissed from the service before the 20-year mark required for pensions.

Women objected, pointing to the disruption caused in leaving a career at middle age rather than retirement. When the women brought a case to the Delhi High Court, the justices found the military's policy discriminatory. The air force agreed to comply, the army refused, and the navy found reasons to delay implementation. In 2011, the military began offering permanent contracts to women in the fields of legal, educational, finance, and medical specialties, although the women cannot hold command positions or be in jobs that will deploy them in combat trades. Surprisingly, in 2017, the air force placed a small number of women into the pilot-training pipeline, with Avani Chaturvedi, Bhawana Kanth, and Mohana Singh preparing to graduate and join squadrons flying the MiG-21 Bison Intercept Fighter, a notoriously temperamental airframe. The current percentages of women in the Indian military are very small with 8.5 percent of the air force, 3 percent of the army, and 2.8 percent of the navy.

Naxalites

In the Naxalbari region of West Bengal, a long-running Communist agricultural rebellion has significant numbers of women participants. Founded in 1969 by Comrade Charu Majumdar, a Maoist who died in police custody in 1972, the Naxalites armed themselves to resist exploitation by land owners. At one time, the Naxalite cause spread across India, but Indira Gandhi used the army in Operation Steeplechase to crush most of their campaign in 1971. In West Bengal, however, a core of approximately 10,000 supporters kept the cause alive and, in the 21st century, have established a parallel administration in the "Compact Revolutionary Zone." Until the end of the Sri Lankan civil war, advisers from the Tamil Tigers provided Naxalites with military training.

Observers who have been to their camps report that the Naxalite demands include land redistribution, egalitarianism, and an abolition of the caste system. They usually target police stations and security personnel, and women play a leading role in commanding units, planting mines, scouting potential attacks, and maintaining the day-to-day life of the rebels, who live austere lives in the jungle. Naxalites treat one another as brothers and sisters, addressing women as "didi," or "elder sister," although they are allowed to marry if they satisfy the Naxalite leadership it does not endanger the cohesion or the security of the group. Women are encouraged to use birth control and not to raise children in the harsh circumstances in which the group operates.

Since 2005, the Naxalites have become far more violent than they have been since the 1970s, with 300 women attacking a police reserve training camp in Karnataka. In April 2010, a massive operation involving 1,000 Naxalites ambushed and killed 76 Central Reserve Police officers. They followed this with a bus bombing, the kidnapping of Italian tourists, and an attack on a Congress party rally. It is unknown why their campaign has escalated. The regional and national government rely on a combination of rural development programs to wean people away from supporting them on economic and social grounds and military force to engage and defeat them.

Kashmir

The strategic region of Kashmir, populated by 13 million people, is a major source of conflict between India and Pakistan. In 1846, a Hindu royal family acquired the area, which was majority Muslim, supported by the British. During the 1920s, its Maharajah, Hari Singh, so favored Hindus over Muslims, interfering in every aspect of daily life, that the social tolerance between groups frayed badly, with leading political activists leaving Kashmir for education elsewhere. When they returned, it was to demand reforms and religious accommodation. In 1947, Singh attempted to keep Kashmir independent, rather than part of India or Pakistan. Encouraged by Pakistan, tribal raiders invaded, causing the people of Kashmir to form defense units in response. Among them was a women's militia of women from Muslim, Hindu, and Buddhist families, who armed themselves and trained to provide first aid and refugee services. Because of the fighting, Singh asked to be absorbed into India, which then intervened in the conflict. At the ceasefire in 1949, India retained 63 percent of Kashmir, including the Kashmir Valley, but the hostilities continued to reoccur, including an incident in 1965 involving Indira Gandhi.

The withdrawal of the Soviet Union from Afghanistan in the late 1980s freed a wave of Islamist fighters to flow out into other countries, including the Philippines and Pakistan. Their arrival in Kashmir pushed tensions in the region into resurgent violence. Many married into Kashmiri families, forming a broad network of contacts, and they began to insist on an Islamization of public life. Before this, women in Kashmir did not veil and took part in public life. In the early 1990s, women's groups, like the Daughters of Faith, insisted that women take a conservatively defined proper place in the home and abandon the colorful local dress for burqas. Some women threw acid on those dressed "immodestly," while others raised money or smuggled weapons. The insurgents also proclaimed that the greatest contribution the women could make was as mothers of fighters and that this sacrifice counted far more than money. The Indian government's response was to pass the Armed Forces Special Powers Act and the Disturbed Areas Act, allowing the police and the military to detain suspected terrorists. These arrests, beatings, and disappearances drove more Kashmiris into extremist organizations in revenge for their humiliation and suffering. It became common for women to march in large groups to police garrisons to demand the release of prisoners or to know their whereabouts. Estimates are that 60,000 have been killed, 20,000 gone missing, and 15,000 widowed, while as many as 300,000 Indian military and police garrison the area.

This ongoing conflict has devastated Kashmir. In the 21st century, Kashmiri women have gone without full access to medical and social services for three decades because of the disruption. Splinter groups demand "taxes" to support their activities, making it difficult to operate businesses or support families. None of the groups have reached a consensus on their goals for Kashmir, so the chaos continues. Groups like the Association of Parents of Disappeared Persons span the spectrum of religious and secular bereaved, but most join groups that have distinct ideas about the role of women and the methods to pressure

India and operate an Islamist society. Asiya Andrabi, of the Daughters of the Faith, disapproves of women taking an active, armed part in the conflict but boycotts the secular world and refuses to let her son play cricket for an Indian team. At the other end of the spectrum, Banat-e-Ayesha (Daughters of Ayesha) and Lashkar-e-Taiba use women as couriers and the latter runs a 21-day training camp for women to learn weapons, tradecraft, and religious indoctrination. In 2008, Yasmeena Akhter exploded a bomb, killing herself and bystanders, making it the first woman suicide bomber in Kashmir, although the authorities suspect it might have been an accident during a courier run. The Lashkar-e-Taiba were responsible for the 2008 Mumbai Massacre, almost certainly planned and executed with the assistance of women members of the group.

Muslim women are not alone in engaging in violence. Also in 2008, the police arrested Hindu Pragya Singh Thakur, who bombed a series of Muslim targets. Major protests ensued when, in that same year, the Amarnath Shrine Board voted to set aside land in Kashmir to build shelter for Hindu pilgrims traveling to the shrine. Muslim saw this as the first step in encroachment and settlement, and Farida Behenji, sister of Bilal Ahmed Beg, a commander in the Jammu and Kashmir Islamic Front, herself jailed from 1996 to 2002, organized and directed the marches. As these networks of jihadi fighters become more enmeshed with those engaging in suicide bombing and use of women, it is likely that Kashmir will become even more deadly for the women who live there.

Further Reading

Banerjee, Paula. "Between Two Armed Patriarchies: Women in Assam and Nagaland." In *Women, War and Peace in South Asia: Beyond Victimhood to Agency*, edited by Rita Machanda, 131–76. Thousand Oaks, CA: Sage, 2001.

Chakraborty, Ananya. "Women in Calcutta Police: Femininity in the Male World." Master's thesis, University of Burdwan, 2006.

Cordell, Kristen. "Liberia: Women Peacekeepers and Human Security." *OpenDemocracy*, October 8, 2009. https://www.opendemocracy.net/content/liberia-women-peacekeepers-and-human-security.

Das, Santanu. "'Indian Sisters! Send Your Husbands, Brothers and Sons': India, Women and the First World War." In *The Women's Movement in Wartime*, edited by Alison Fell and Ingrid Sharpe, 18–37. London: Palgrave, 2007.

Goswami, Namrata. *Indian National Security and Counter-Insurgency: The Use of Force vs Non-Violent Response*. London: Routledge, 2015.

Hills, Carol, and Daniel C. Silverman. "Nationalism and Feminism in Late Colonial India: The Rani of Jhansi Regiment, 1943–1945." *Modern Asian Studies* 27, no. 4 (1993): 741–60. doi:10.1017/s0026749x00001281.

Karat, Brinda. "Opinion: Indian Army's Shameful Treatment of Women Recruits." *NDTV.com*, December 1, 2014. https://www.ndtv.com/opinion/indian-armys-shameful-treatment-of-women-recruits-706717.

Kember, Olivia. "The Impact of the Indian Formed Police Unit in the United Nations Mission in Liberia." Master's thesis, Georgetown University, 2010.

Khan, Nyla Ali. *Islam, Women, and Violence in Kashmir: Between India and Pakistan*. London: Palgrave Macmillan, 2016.

Lebra, Joyce. *The Rani of Jhansi: A Study in Female Heroism in India*. Bombay: Jaico, 1988.

Machanda, Rita. "Guns and Burqa: Women in the Kashmir Conflict." In *Women, War and Peace in South Asia: Beyond Victimhood to Agency*, edited by Rita Machanda, 42–101. Thousand Oaks, CA: Sage, 2001.

Pandit, Rajat. "India's First-Ever Women Fighter Pilots Gear Up for Solo MiG-21 Flights—Times of India." *The Times of India*, January 23, 2018. https://timesofindia.indiatimes.com/india/indias-first-ever-women-fighter-pilots-gear-up-for-solo-mig-21-flights/articleshow/62609283.cms.

Pandit, Rajat. "Military Dead against Permanent Commission for Women across the Board." *The Times of India*, November 6, 2011. https://timesofindia.indiatimes.com/india/Military-dead-against-permanent-commission-for-women-across-the-board/articleshow/10635729.cms?referral=PM.

Parashar, Swati. "Aatish-e-Chinar: In Kashmir, Where Women Keep Resistance Alive." In *Women, Gender and Terrorism*, edited by Laura Sjoberg and Caron Gentry, 96–119. Athens: University of Georgia Press, 2011.

Parashar, Swati. "Women in Militant Movements: (Un)Comfortable Silences and Discursive Strategies." In *Gendered Wars, Gendered Memories: Feminist Conversations on War, Genocide and Political Violence*, edited by Aysa Gul Altinay and Andrea Peto, 192–210. London: Routledge, 2016.

Parashar, Swati. *Women and Militant Wars: The Politics of Injury*. Milton Park, Abingdon, Oxon: Routledge, 2014.

Pruitt, Lesley J. "All-Female Police Contingents: Feminism and the Discourse of Armed Protection." *International Peacekeeping* 20, no. 1 (2013): 67–79. doi:10.1080/13533312.2012.761836.

Sreedharan, Chindu. "Notes from the Diary of Chindu Sreedharan, Who Spent 82 Hours with People's War Guerrillas." 1998. http://www.rediff.com/news/1998/aug/25pwg.htm.

Wood, Glynn L. "Civil-Military Relations in Post-Colonial India." In *The Armed Forces in Contemporary Asian Societies*, edited by Edward Olsen and Stephen Jurika, 271–84. Boulder, CO: Westview, 1986.

Iran

Background

Upper-class women in Iran, especially those around the royal court, began to have extraordinary opportunities for education and influence in the 19th century. Fath Ali Shah (1797–1834) appointed his daughters to be treasurer, secretary, and political advisers to his administration. Nasir al-Din Shah's (1848–1896) daughter Taj al-Saltaneh was a leading feminist and nationalist. The daughters of aristocratic families, tutored at home until the establishment of elite schools in the early 20th century, absorbed western political arguments about women's suffrage and modernization. In the 1906–1911 Constitutional Revolution, women played a leading and forceful part. Angry at the high price and low availability of bread, they threw rocks at the Shah's carriage, and when he tried to complain to women in his harem about this disdainful treatment, his concubines agreed with the rioters. Wealthy women staked their jewelry to capitalize the Iran National Bank, so that the nation would be less dependent on foreign funds. In 1908, as the Shah, urged by the Russians, wavered on reform, women armed themselves and took to the barricades, and after street fighting, 20 of the dead were found to be women in men's clothing. As the Russians called in loans in 1911 as a threat if the Constitution was not revoked, women marched to Parliament and held legislators at gunpoint to prevent them from giving in.

Despite achieving some movement away from the feudal past through these actions, traditional Islamic authorities held sway in the countryside, and liberal men did not prioritize the freedom of women over their nationalistic goals. Afraid of the Bolshevik Revolution in Russia, the British and French assisted in the overthrow of the Shah and the installation of Reza Pahlavi to protect their interest in Iran's vast oil resources. Reza Shah, an admirer of Ataturk's modernization program in Turkey, attempted a similar process in Iran. In 1936, he outlawed women's veiling, using police to forcibly uncover them. While some of

> **War on Film**
>
> Framed by the end of the Iran–Iraq War in 1988 and the 2003 U.S. invasion of Iraq, the film *Gilane*, directed by Iranian filmmaker Rakhshan Bani-Etemad (b. 1954), explores the effect of conflict on a woman in an isolated Caspian village. Gilane, a widow, has a daughter, Maygol, whose husband was drafted and who subsequently disappeared after deserting his post in Tehran. Her son, Ismail, the most promising man in the village, volunteered to fight after seeing his friends with a recruiter. In an attempt to find her son-in-law, Gilane journeys to Tehran, seeing for the first time the damage from rocket attacks, and suffers the scorn of Tehrani boys whose wealthy families bought them out of conscription. Flashing forward to 2003, Ismail is back from the war, having become an invalid suffering from posttraumatic stress disorder (PTSD) and epileptic fits from surviving a chemical weapons attack. Gilane is trapped as his caregiver, aided only by a local doctor, himself an amputee veteran, and hoping that Ismail can be admitted to a state-run veteran's hospital.
>
> Bani-Etemad, whose documentaries and feature films have centered on the daily experiences of Iranian women, wanted to contrast the idealized state narrative glorifying the mothers of martyrs with the reality of women who must deal with the consequences of military actions on their families and communities. She set the scene in a rural area both to highlight the contrast between Tehran and the periphery and to offer a universal experience of suffering in the aftermath of violence. At screenings, she found that veterans who wanted to attend were often stymied because the theaters had no wheelchair access.

his modernizations were celebrated by Iranian women, it was an authoritarian regime that, unlike Ataturk, never handed over power to a genuine democracy, and rural women who chose to veil became further isolated from public life.

During World War II, the Americans and the British, concerned about Reza Shah's sympathies for Nazi Germany, deposed him in favor of his son, Mohammad. Hoping that the new ruler would be more amenable to reform, Fatima Sayyah, a leading feminist, campaigned for women's suffrage. These demands took a distant place behind economic change, which came in the form of the appointment of Mohammad Mosaddegh as prime minister in 1951. Mosaddegh nationalized the Anglo-Iranian Oil Company and instituted significant land reform, as well as mandated benefits for employees. With the help of the U.S. Central Intelligence Agency (CIA), the Iranian army and elements of the wealthy landowners staged a coup and removed him in 1953. To control dissent from women, all feminist organizations were combined under the leadership of the Shah's twin sister, Princess Ashraf Pahlavi, who forced them to become middle-class social clubs rather than hotbeds of reform talk.

The Shah launched his White Revolution in the late 1950s, finally giving women suffrage, opening universities, investing in modernization, and turning Tehran into the Paris of the East, where the upper class dressed, socialized, and spent money as if they were Europeans. The Shah's army and the police force promoted women officers, and his wife, Empress Farah Pahlavi, sincerely advocated for the advancement of women. This drastic change was still the work of an authoritarian, and elections, although open to more voters, offered no real choices. Those unhappy with the regime were the targets of the SAVAK, an Israeli and American-trained secret police, whose methods included kidnapping, rape, torture, and assassination.

Three Modes of Opposition

The Marxist Fedaian

Secular nationalists, the Fedaian were an evolution of social democratic groups of the early 20th century. They sought class solidarity with rural peasants and workers to overthrow the Shah and picked up guerrilla training and weapons from the Chinese, Cubans, and Eastern European Soviet satellites. Ashraf Dehghani, whose brother was kidnapped and killed by the SAVAK, shocked westerners by publishing a graphic account of her own torture at the hands of the Shah's secret police. Marzieh Ahmadi Oskouei discovered Marxism during her time at a teacher's college and went to prison for participating in a large student strike in 1972. She died in a shootout with the military in 1974. Fedaian pamphlets attempted to stress that comrades must practice egalitarian divisions of household labor, but this broke down when the group had to live underground in rural areas, where this alienated them further from the traditional population.

The Mujahedin

Ali Shariati, a colleague and friend of Frantz Fanon, and a fellow anti-colonialist, offered a compelling new reading of Islam. By approaching it as sociology rather than metaphysics, Shariati especially appealed to women, to whom this offered a liberation grounded in authentic personal experience as the "new Iranian woman," instead of either a fundamentalist-dominated drudge or a westernized slave of materialism and sexual exploitation. Fatimah, the Prophet's daughter, offered a model of fierce devotion, as did Zaynab, her daughter. In the aftermath of the disastrous battle of Karbala, Zaynab took command of the survivors, including saving Hussein's son and preserving the dynasty, and retreated to safety. Some

Mujahedin received training from the Palestine Liberation Organization (PLO), with women forming "Zaynab's Commandos" to attack SAVAK personnel, bomb police stations, and assassinate prominent supporters of the regime. In 1975–1976, their targets included two American Air Force Colonels in Iran on an advisory mission and an employee of Rockwell, the defense contractor. Estimates are that, between the Marxists and the Mujahedin, 10,000 women died and 25,000 were arrested and tortured.

Khomeini and Islamic Theocracy

Ayatollah Khomeini, from his mosque in Qom, offered a religious critique of the Shah, but one which appealed to the rural poor, and the unmoored people who had come to the boom cities of an oil-rich country and found only more poverty and dislocation. In the 1970s, despite literacy campaigns, only 17 percent of women could read. Khomeini excoriated "westoxification" and promised to cleanse the country of Americans and western corruption that had caused such misery to the people.

The Islamic Revolutionary State

Ultimately, it was Khomeni's faction that overthrew the Shah in 1979, establishing the Islamic Republic of Iran and shattering the idea that the three strains of resistance had remotely similar goals other than the end of the old regime. In one of its signature acts, seizing the American Embassy and keeping its personnel hostage, women, dressed in hijab, took active part and appeared in the media denouncing the United States. It quickly became apparent that the new government was as authoritarian as the old, with the Revolutionary Guard replacing the SAVAK for crushing dissent. In June 1981, 500,000 protesters, many of them women from the Mujahedin, marched demanding the version of Islam they had found through Shariati. The Revolutionary Guards opened fire, massacring them. Many members of the Mujahedin fled, with a significant number seeking shelter in France, Iraq, and among the Kurdish people in northern Iran.

The Iran–Iraq war began in 1980, with Khomeini calling for women to volunteer to take up arms as a home guard. Additionally, the regime recruited 450,000 Basij, or militia volunteers, from religious schools. These young men, who wore yellow keys around their necks to symbolize their entry to paradise, were used as human wave attacks against the Iraqis and to clear minefield. The deaths of these men were often commemorated with Pieta-like images of their mothers cradling their bodies and rejoicing at their martyrdom. As celebrated in the Tehran Martyrs Museum, at least 69 women died in the war as combatants. Any women civilians near a battle were expected to set up and staff field kitchens and to take on small-scale manufacturing of needed war materials like shoes and uniforms.

Led by Maryam Rajavi, the National Liberation Army of Iran trained in Iraq under the protection of Saddam Hussein. This armed wing of the Mujahedin rejected the conservative vision of women espoused by Ayatollah Khomeini in favor of the liberation theology of Ali Shariati. (Jacques Pavlovsky/Sygma/COR-BIS/Sygma via Getty Images)

The Mujahedin, meanwhile, accepted assistance from Saddam Hussein to outfit the National Liberation Army (NLA), which contained large numbers of women under Maryam Rajavi. The women trained to drive tanks, fire mortars, and conduct an invasion, which launched in 1987 with operations Shining Sun, Forty Stars, and Eternal Light. The NLA claims to have killed 55,000 Iranians before being forced to retreat. The Mujahedin are still in existence with Rajiv as spokesperson, living in Paris.

The long war devastated the Iranian population, with losses upward of 300,000 killed and 500,000 wounded. Khomeini insisted that women owed the modesty and wearing of the hijab and chador as respect to the soldiers and that they had an obligation to marry and care for the disabled and maimed, especially since the regime paid no pensions for their support. The surviving Basij were empowered to act as morals police, accosting and harassing women on the street for being insufficiently modest. The huge losses also made polygamy necessary for many women to find spouses. Women have had little representation in the Republic's legislature, although Khomeini's daughter sat in the Parliament in the 1980s, advocating for women. Successors to Khomeini have managed to strike a balance between allowing the middle class to enjoy private luxuries like cable TV, alcohol, and un-Islamic popular culture from the west, in exchange for not openly dissenting. How long this will last and the role women will play is unknown.

Further Reading

Davis, Joyce. *Martyrs: Innocence, Vengeance and Despair in the Middle East.* New York: Palgrave Macmillan, 2004.

Farhi, Farideh. "Sexuality and the Politics of Revolution in Iran." In *Women and Revolution in Africa, Asia and the New World*, edited by Mary Ann Tetrault, 252–71. Columbia: University of South Carolina Press, 1994.

Gilane. Directed by Rakhshan Bani-Etemad. Performed by Fatemah Motamed-Aria, Baran Kosari, and Bahram Radan. Iran: Fadak Film, 2004. DVD.

Haddad, Yvonne Yazbeck, and John L. Esposito. *Islam, Gender, & Social Change.* Milton Keynes, UK: Lightning Source UK Ltd., 2010.

"Interview with Rakhshan Bani-Etemad, Co-director of Gilaneh." World Socialist Website. October 3, 2005. http://www.wsws.org/articles/2005/oct2005/bani-o03.shtml.

Johnson, Robert. *The Iran-Iraq War.* Basingstoke, UK: Palgrave Macmillan, 2011.

Reeves, Minou. *Female Warriors of Allah: Women and the Islamic Revolution of Iran.* New York: Athena, 1993.

Shahidian, Hammed. *Women in Iran: Emerging Voices in the Women's Movement.* Westport, CT: Greenwood Press, 2002.

Tohidi, Nayereh. "Modernity, Islamization and Women in Iran." In *Gender and National Identity: Women and Politics in Muslim Societies*, edited by Valentine Moghadam, 110–47. London: Zed Books, 1994.

Varzi, Roxanne. "Iran's Pieta: Motherhood, Sacrifice and Film in the Aftermath of the Iran-Iraq War." *Feminist Review* 88, no. 1 (April 2008): 86–98.

Varzi, Roxanne. *Warring Souls: Youth, Media, and Martyrdom in Post-Revolution Iran.* Durham, NC: Duke University Press, 2006.

Waller, Marguerite R., and Jennifer Rycenga. *Frontline Feminisms: Women, War, and Resistance.* New York: Routledge, 2012.

Ward, Steven R. *Immortal: A Military History of Iran and Its Armed Forces.* Washington, DC: Georgetown University Press, 2014.

Iraq

Background

The kingdom of Iraq was a creation of the breakup of the Ottoman Empire at the end of World War I. Under a British Mandate, Faisal I was installed as the ruler, and he attempted to create a government reflecting Iraq's diverse religious and ethnic population. Faisal was also unusually open to women's education, more so than some of his British advisers, including Gertrude Bell, who believed most women incapable of academic and political accomplishments on par with her own achievements and limited to motherhood and the home. During the 1920s, Iraq had a women's magazine, *Layla*, edited by Paulina Hassoun, and the poet Jamal al-Zahawi and his sister Asma began the Awakening movement, which attracted the participation of middle- and upper-class Iraqi women interested in education, charity, and humanitarian volunteering through the Red Crescent. A more radical women's movement emerged after independence in 1932, with the Iraq Women's Union being formed in 1945 to advocate for changes to divorce, suffrage, punishments for prostitution, and women's inheritance of property. Massive student protests in 1952 were the formative moment for a generation of young, educated women who opposed the monarchy and were choosing from Communist, Nasserist, and Ba'athist Arab Nationalist plans for the future.

Brigadier General Abd al-Karim Qasim overthrew the monarchy in a coup in 1958 and set up a liberal government (1958–1963) with significant socialist elements, including land redistribution. Dr. Naziha al-Dulaimi, a gynecologist and communist, was a leading member of the Women's Union and served as minister of municipalities. This, in turn, suffered overthrow by a more conservative faction of the military, led by Colonel Abdul Salam Arif, who subsequently purged the government of Ba'athist officers and undertook a Nasserist program of technocratic infrastructure improvement and relationships with Egypt. After his suspicious death in 1966, a helicopter flight possibly

> **Wartime Cultural Preservation**
>
> World War I unleashed unexpected destruction onto cultural treasures, like the University Library at Louvain, burned by German troops. In World War II, as Nazi officials looted art across Europe, the Allied armies assembled "Monuments Men," architects and art historians working with French and Italian curators, who raced to protect cultural treasures from destruction and targeting. The 1954 Hague Convention protects these precious resources in theory, but in wartime, conservation often falls to a low priority behind survival. In Bamiyan, Iraq, the Taliban blew up medieval statues of the Buddha in 2001 as religious cleansing, while the Islamic State (ISIS) in Syria looted ancient archeological sites and sold the unearthed items illicitly to finance its activities.
>
> Corine Wegener, the cultural heritage preservation officer at the Smithsonian, also an army reservist who served with the 352nd Civil Affairs Command in Baghdad, works to help Iraqi and Syrian museum professionals save their treasures. Working with a coalition of museums and the U.S. Institute of Peace, the Smithsonian runs workshops on emergency conservation, like freezing water-damaged papers, and provides the materials like plastic sheeting and braces to secure immovable mosaics and statuary with sandbags. Archaeologists who run the seasonal sites are also trained to involve local workers in the discoveries and their importance to the area's heritage—not just for tourism and jobs but also a link to a shared past and a patrimony belonging to the people who live there. The U.S. military, recognizing the value of protecting sites, documents, and artwork in good community relations, has developed procedures to avoid unnecessary damage, and the United Nations Educational, Scientific and Cultural Organization (UNESCO) has issued a handbook for military protection of cultural property.

sabotaged by Ba'athists, Arif's brother, General Abdul Rahman Arif, took over control of the state. The 1967 War, in which Israel humiliated Egypt, struck a serious blow to Nasser's prestige and allowed the Ba'athists to reorganize themselves in secret. In 1968, a faction of Ba'athist officers, led by Ahmed Hassan al-Bakr, removed Arif from power and established their regime.

Ba'athist Iraq

In the hands of Hassan al-Bakr and hid chief lieutenant, Saddam Hussein, Ba'athism took on the characteristics of a fascist, authoritarian state, led by a small circle of men from Tikrit. Modernization and reform were to be accomplished in a secular, state-driven economy, buttressed by a powerful army and one-party, ethno-nationalist government. These plans were made possible by the oil boom of the 1970s, during which money flowed into Iraq, raising living standards and paying for massive infrastructure and social programs. Rather than bring in guest workers, as other Gulf states chose to do, Iraq created its own middle class through education and enlistment of women. As in Gaddafi's Libya, "state feminism" urged women to play their part in the revolution by producing large families, as well as participating in education and the economy, and offered them the social welfare net of childcare and subsidy to make that possible. Additionally, women in the public sphere were accessible for indoctrination through mandatory literacy programs and exposure to the Ba'athist ideology. In 1979, suspicious of Hassan al-Bakr's overtures to Ba'athists in Syria, Saddam Hussein forced him to retire and took over the country, cementing his power with a purge of the party that killed hundreds of officials and their families.

With the support of the United States, Hussein began a war with Revolutionary Iran in 1980. Over the next eight years, the war would lead to the deaths of 150,000–340,000 Iraqis. The length of the war strained the mandatory conscription system for men, so volunteer service for women began in 1986, with all-women units formed as a challenge to Iran's use of women volunteers. Women were also allowed to join the Ba'athist Militia, which operated as a home guard and political counterbalance to the army. Women during the war usually served as medical personnel, drove trucks, and replaced men in noncombat jobs. The large losses also meant that thousands of women became widows. "The Time of Deportations" started in 1987, as Hussein, suspicious of non-Arab, non-Sunni minorities, turned on Shia and Persians, as well as the Kurds. Reaching back into Ottoman records, Ba'athist bureaucrats identified those whose families had asked for exemption from military service on the grounds of non-Arab background and forced them to leave the country. The Kurds were the target of the "Anfal," a military terror campaign against their region (see Kurd entry). Overall, Hussein's genocidal rampage killed and displaced more than 400,000 people.

The First Gulf War and Sanctions

In 1990, Iraq's economy was burdened by the huge amounts Hussein had borrowed to fight his wars in the 1980s. Neighboring Kuwait owned $30 billion of the debts, and both refused to forgive or renegotiate it, and also would not lower oil production to raise the value of Iraq's reserves. In response, and convinced that the United States would not intervene, Hussein invaded Kuwait in August 1990. When UN sanctions against Iraq failed to force a withdrawal, a Coalition of the United States and its allies quickly ejected Iraqi troops from Kuwait and, after a one-month air campaign that devastated Iraq's infrastructure, launched a ground invasion. After surrendering, and signing terms promising to give up chemical warfare and allow the Kurds a measure of autonomy, Hussein was allowed to stay in place.

After the war, Hussein turned on the remaining minority groups in Iraq, many of whom had been encouraged by the Americans to rise up against the government. He also impinged on the no-fly zone protecting the Kurds and gave indications that he was still developing weapons of mass destruction in defiance of the surrender conditions. As a result, the United Nations and the United States did not lift the sanctions, and Iraq suffered economic devastation. While the elite continued to live lavishly, common people, especially women, suffered significantly, with tens of thousands starving until the 1996 UN proposal for an oil-for-food program was accepted in 1996.

During this period, Hussein theatrically embraced Islam, commissioning a Koran written in his own blood and instituting elements of Sharia Law. Education and social welfare infrastructure collapsed, with illiteracy soaring from 8 percent in 1991 to 45 percent in 2003. Women, who had made up 23 percent of the workforce in 1991, were pushed out of jobs by underemployed men, and the percentage was down to 10 percent in 1997. Some women found they had to marry in order to get food or not be a burden on their families, and conservative social mores restricted their dress and public presence. In 2000, Hussein's son Uday arrested 300 prostitutes and pimps, publicly executing them as a message of both government authority and harsh social discipline. The secret police, and members of the Ba'athist elite, were allowed to carry out torture, rape, and murder against dissenters or indulge in personal grudges, terrorizing the population.

Hussein remained belligerent through punitive airstrikes in the late 1990s, and it was well known that his regime abused its people and continued to violate the terms of the peace. The United States had invaded Afghanistan in 2001 in response to the 9/11 attacks, and encouraged by Vladimir Putin, an influential group of politicians in the George W. Bush administration, some of whom had worked with his father's presidency in the early 1990s, were convinced that Iraq was planning attacks on the United States as part of an "axis of evil" with Iran and North Korea and had weapons of mass destruction (WMDs) to carry them out. Part of the argument for a second American invasion of Iraq was a Huntingtonian clash-of-cultures ideology that Iraqis hated the American way of life and freedom and that their women were in need of rescue from Islamic subjugation and oppression. The United States contacted members of the diaspora Iraqi population, many of whom had resettled in the Arab community of Dearborn, Michigan, and funded "Women for a Free Iraq" to advise and coordinate American efforts.

The 21st Century

This second Gulf War began as a three-week campaign in March 2003, quickly toppling Hussein and subduing the Iraqi army. Precision munitions struck at government buildings and Hussein's palace in an attempt to preserve infrastructure, which was already in extremely poor shape. Regional, ethnic, and sectarian conflict exploded in the wake of Hussein's removal, with the victorious invaders in the middle of a developing civil war. In an attempt to remove Ba'athist elements from the government and civil service, the Americans and their Coalition allies conducted a mass removal of bureaucrats and military officers, which shredded the experienced system of delivering services and guaranteeing security. This not only removed women from jobs, as party membership was mandatory for most positions, but many of the male workers ejected turned their expertise to crime. Male frustration at powerlessness and sudden poverty found outlets in looting, honor killings, kidnappings, and rapes, with more than 2,000 women reported missing by 2006.

Committed to establishing a government in which women would play a significant role as peacemakers and national builders, the U.S. Government disbursed $10 million to seven organizations, all begun in the United States, as the Women and Democracy Initiative. These organizations sought to provide resources for women to become political candidates, take part in the drafting of a new constitution, and improve their ability to participate as full citizens. President Bush addressed this in a speech to Iraqis on International Women's Day, and First Lady Laura Bush brought guests from Iraqi women's groups to the State of the Union in 2004. Many of the originators of these policies had good intentions, but this feminism from above had difficulty taking root when Iraqi women struggled with everyday life with intermittent power, unsafe streets, and no jobs as foreign companies with contracts undertook rebuilding without including Iraqis. Diaspora women, who had been away from Iraq for decades, regarded the women living there as backward, while they were seen as unappreciative of the hardships suffered under the 13 years of sanctions or the things Iraqi women had achieved before those hard times.

In each iteration of the new Iraqi government, women have been allotted quotas for seats, usually 25 percent. However, those chosen or elected have a difficult time being included in the planning meetings that drafted the constitution and important policy. For example, the Iraqi Governing Council issued Declaration 137, repealing the family code in operation since 1968 and placing women under Sharia Law. This was never approved by Paul Bremer, the American envoy, but similar initiatives appeared in the constitution, forbidding laws to contradict Islam and mandating conservative social policy, such as requiring women to have the permission of a male relative to get a passport. Women officials have suffered intimidation and threats, with some murdered, like Lame'a Abed Khadawi, if their demands threatened male authority. It has been more acceptable for women to do charity work, filling in for missing social services by feeding hospital patients or caring for the elderly.

With the appearance of Al-Qaeda women operatives in 2005, coalition troops needed to use their limited female personnel to search travelers at checkpoints rather than inflame local feelings. To augment this, "Daughters of Iraq," many of them widows of slain policeman, trained as volunteer security officers. Unlike Afghanistan, where there have been large-scale efforts to recruit women into the police and the military, Iraq struggles with large numbers of unemployed men, delaying until 2009–2010 programs to add women to these institutions. To the present, this has been limited to larger cities, and the proportions of women to men extremely small, with an average class of 1,000 police cadets containing 50 or fewer women. High pay is an attractive reason to join, but widespread violence, refusal of women's authority, and threats to recruits' families lead many to drop out. The military has been slightly more successful, moving women from civilian support jobs into similar uniformed trades.

The Shia, majority population in Iraq, has formed militias to defend itself and, as of 2016, begun including women. In the Hashd al-Shaabi, at least 3,000 women have been trained to use weapons and stand guard, as well as do the cooking, media, and medical tasks of the group. According to leaders, the presence of enthusiastic women shames men who would otherwise remain at home to join in rather than be outdone.

Al-Qaeda's branch in Iraq, which has tried to subvert U.S. efforts to stabilize the government, launched attacks on Shia sites and populations in an attempt to incite violence between Sunnis and Shiites. Captured documents suggest that there were intense, generationally based debates between Mullah Omar and al-Zawahiri over the legitimacy of using women to conduct bombings. Al-Zawahiri's position won out, and the first woman suicide attack, conducted by a woman in men's clothing, took place against a group of police recruits at Tal Afar in 2005. This was followed by the appearance of Muriel Degauque, a Belgian woman radicalized in Europe, who followed her husband to Iraq and rammed a Kia car bomb into an American military convoy. It is likely that Al-Qaeda was running female training camps in Jalalabad and Kandahar and hoped to inflame sentiments when security forces searched and suspected local women of being bombers. Between 2003 and 2008, Al-Qaeda carried out 1,715 attacks, 51 of them executed by women. Of suicide bombings, women were one-third of the perpetrators. In a particularly striking incident, two women, one of them probably with Down syndrome, detonated a bomb in Baghdad, which killed 73 people.

Although no longer living under the Ba'athist regime of Saddam Hussein, Iraqi women have seen a regression of their rights and continued instability in their ability to conduct normal life. For some, this is reason to join a nongovernmental organization (NGO) program and work for peaceful change, risk running for office to take part in the political process, or take up arms as a militia member or extremist operative.

Further Reading

Addario, Lynsey. "Jihad's Women." *The New York Times*, October 20, 2001. http://www.nytimes.com/2001/10/21/magazine/jihad-s-women.html.

Al-Ali, Nadje, and Nicola Pratt. *What Kind of Liberation?: Women and the Occupation of Iraq.* Berkeley: University of California Press, 2010.

Al-Ali, Nadje, and Nicola Pratt. "Women in Iraq: Beyond the Rhetoric." *Middle East Report*, no. 239 (2006): 18–23. doi:10.2307/25164724.

Al-Ali, Nadje, and Nicola Pratt, eds. *Women and War in the Middle East.* London: Zed Books, 2009.

Binkovitz, Leah. "Q+A: How to Save the Arts in Times of War." *Smithsonian.com*, January 24, 2013. https://www.smithsonianmag.com/smithsonian-institution/qa-how-to-save-the-arts-in-times-of-war-5506188/.

Coleman, Isobel. "Women, Islam, and the New Iraq." *Foreign Affairs* 85, no. 1 (2006): 24–38. doi:10.2307/20031840.

Dickey, Christopher. "Women of Al Qaeda." *Newsweek*, May 25, 2013. http://www.newsweek.com/women-al-qaeda-113757.

Efrati, Noga. *Women in Iraq: Past Meets Present.* New York: Columbia University Press, 2012.

Graham-Brown, Sarah. *Sanctioning Saddam: The Politics of Intervention in Iraq.* London: I.B. Tauris, 1999.

Hartmann, Margaret. "How ISIS Is Destroying Ancient Art in Iraq and Syria." *Daily Intelligencer*, March 6, 2015. http://nymag.com/daily/intelligencer/2015/03/isis-destroys-ancient-art.html.

Ismael, Jacqueline S., and Shereen T. Ismael. "Living through War, Sanctions and Occupation: The Voices of Iraqi Women." *International Journal of Contemporary Iraqi Studies* 2, no. 3 (2009): 409–24. doi:10.1386/ijcis.2.3.409_1.

Stone, Jennie, and Katherine Pattillo. "Al-Qaeda's Use of Female Suicide Bombers in Iraq: A Case Study." In *Women, Gender and Terrorism*, edited by Laura Sjoberg and Caron Gentry, 159–75. Athens: University of Georgia Press, 2011.

"U.S. Committee of the Blue Shield." *Uscbs.org*. https://uscbs.org/index.html.

Von Knop, Katharina. "The Multifaceted Roles of Women inside al-Qaeda." *Journal of National Defense Studies*, no. 6 (May 2008): 139–62.

Zuhur, Sherifa D. *Iraq, Women's Empowerment and Public Policy.* Carlisle, PA: Letort Paper Series, Army War College, 2006.

Ireland

Background

The roots of conflict in Ireland were sown in the 12th century, when Norman lords under King Henry II of England invaded Ireland at the request of the deposed King of Leinster, then stayed to claim land. This mix of Gaelic lords and Normans was further complicated in the Elizabeth and Jacobean periods as first Protestant Church of England settlers arrived, followed by a program of "plantation" of Scottish Calvinist colonists encouraged by James I. Ireland played a significant part in the English Civil War, supporting Charles I, and suffered harsh treatment and occupation from Oliver Cromwell's troops, including the capture of Dublin and the Sieges of Drogheda and Wexford, where Parliamentary troops sacked the towns, killing thousands of inhabitants. Irish Catholics sided with James II in 1688 against William and Mary and, after his loss at the Battle of the Boyne in 1690, were subject to punitive and draconian penal laws imposed by the British monarchy, meant to cripple the ability of Irish people to resist British rule. By the 18th century, disenfranchisement vis the penal laws, and the effects of their economic restrictions on inheritance meant that 15 percent of the population who were Protestant and English-speaking, ruled over a majority of 85 percent who were Catholic and largely Gaelic speakers.

The British regarded Ireland as both a testing ground for their colonial policy and a potentially dangerous backdoor for their enemies, usually the French, to attack the British Isles. In 1798, the winds of the French Revolution stirred a widespread bid for independence, led by Theobald Wolfe Tone, in which armed Irish people rose in expectation of help from the French fleet to overthrow the royal government. Women played a crucial role in the rising as members of the United Irish, transporting arms, arranging logistics, and guarding camps. The French were intercepted by the British Navy, and when the Irish fought, it was a bloody loss of 30,000 lives in three months, with more

> **Women, Truth, and Reconciliation**
>
> Nuala O'Loan, 26, a law professor waiting to attend a talk at her university at Ulster Polytechnic Jordanstown, looked at her watch: 12.40 pm. The next thing she knew, it was 1 pm, the room was filled with debris from an Irish Republican Army (IRA) bombing, and she was miscarrying her first child. This tragic experience informed the next 20 years O'Loan taught in Northern Ireland, including serving as a "lay visitor," empowered to see any person held in police custody. After the 1999 Police Act, requiring an Ombudsman to be hired as auditor, Secretary of State for Northern Ireland Mo Mowlam recalled O'Loan, acting as a consumer advocate, forcing the power company to return 9 million pounds. Appointed to the position, O'Loan sparked immediate protest—she was English-born but devoutly Catholic, married to a Member of Parliament (MP) who stood for Irish reunification, and whose impoverished childhood made her a fierce champion against injustice.
>
> In her seven-year term, O'Loan took on the Royal Ulster Constabulary (RUC), which meant receiving up to 400 complaints a day of corruption going back to the apex of the Troubles in the 1960s. Her report on the Omagh bombing, finding that the RUC ignored warnings and conducted a shoddy investigation, caused police officials to demand her removal. Instead, even under death threats to her family, she kept digging, into the murder of Raymond McCord, a civil rights activist, and Robert Hamill, whom a mob beat to death while the RUC stood by. In particular, she uncovered the practice of using informers against the IRA whose crimes the RUC covered up to get information. Since 2007, she has been the UN envoy to Timor-Leste and a life peer. When she left, 85 percent of police thought that they had been treated fairly by her office, a remarkable accomplishment.

executed for treason by the authorities. Women supported both strains of Irish nationalism emerging from this disaster in the early 19th century—armed force, as advocated by the Young Ireland movement, and the campaign for political reform led by Daniel O'Connell.

Potatoes, a monocrop on which the Irish food supply was dependent, began to fail in 1845 as the result of a fungal blight. Over the next three years, the lack of any social safety net cast hundreds of thousands into deeper poverty and starvation, while landlords continued to export grain elsewhere and restrict fishing. Nearly a million Irish people died, with a million more emigrating to Canada, the United States, and Australia, where they formed a distinct and proud diaspora population with strong ties to their country of origin. Within a generation, many of these emigrants were in positions of power politically and within the police and military forces of their adopted countries. Some emigrants, arriving during the Mexican-American or Civil War, went directly into the army, where they learned valuable military skills and gained access to weapons that they intended to use to free Ireland from British rule.

Women and Irish Nationalism

Back in Ireland, educated and upper-class women were at the forefront of the Gaelic revival, championing the rediscovery of Irish folk culture in the form of songs, mythology, and folktales, highlighting the heroes of Celtic sagas like Maeve of the Cattle Raid of Cooley and Brigid. Lady Augusta Gregory and Jane, Lady Wilde (Oscar Wilde's mother) were members of this group. Wishing to take a more aggressive stance, women like Constance Markievicz joined Sinn Fein and the Daughters of Ireland in the early 20th century, which often overlapped with women's suffrage campaigning. In 1909, Markievicz was a cofounder of a paramilitary scouting club for Irish boys, the Fianna Eireann, modeled on the Boy Scouts and the ancient Irish heroic brotherhoods. Members of this group usually migrated to the Irish Volunteers and the Irish Republican Brotherhood and took part in violent clashes with the police and the British Army. Women and their access to private homes and social networks were crucial to gun running and the covert transmission of intelligence and commands.

On the brink of achieving some measure of Home Rule in 1914, under the negotiations of John Redmond with the British government, Ireland joined Britain in waging war against Germany and Austria-Hungary in World War I, with 180,000 volunteers enlisting in Irish regiments for service in France. To support them, women on the Irish home front acted similarly to those in England—forming Red Cross groups, raising money, and sending morale-boosting letters and gifts. Irish nationalists, however, were quickly disillusioned by the carnage of the war, and their faith waned that participation would earn independence. In 1916, the Irish Volunteers and Irish Republican Brotherhood seized the Dublin Post Office, with units including Markievicz, Helena Molony, and other women in arms. After a week, the British Army suppressed the rising, executing many of its male leaders. A few women, like artist Grace Gifford, with fiances in prison awaiting execution for the rising, convinced the authorities to let them marry hours before the sentence was carried out, living the rest of their lives as widows of the movement.

In the 1918 elections, in which some women could vote, Sinn Fein won a majority of Irish seats in the London Parliament, including Markievicz, who became the first woman elected to the House of Commons, although Sinn Fein members of parliament (MPs) refused to be seated and instead proclaimed their own parliament, the Dail Eireann, in 1919. The British sent in security forces, recruited from demobilized World War I veterans and called the "Black and Tans" for their salvaged uniforms, who were immediately in violent conflict with the Irish Republican Army (IRA), evolved from the old Volunteers and the Brotherhood. When the British agreed to a partition of Ireland in 1922, keeping the northern six counties as Ulster, with the rest becoming independent, a second round of fighting broke out between those accepting the treaty and those who demanded full unification. As vicious as the fighting had been between the Black and Tans and the IRA, the 1922–1923 civil war killed far more Irish people. Women were rarely the active guerrillas but were vital sources of information, acted as lures and lookouts, and would undertake "hen patrols" to spot enemy lookouts and flush them out by banging garbage can lids or pots and pans.

Women and "the Troubles"

The Republic of Ireland and Northern Ireland settled into an uneasy coexistence in the 1930s. During World War II, Ireland remained neutral, despite overtures from Nazi Germany, and thousands of Irish workers, including many women, flooded into northern English cities to work in wartime manufacturing jobs left empty by the massive manpower draft. In the Republic, women held a traditionally restrictive place in a conservative social order upheld by the influence of the Catholic Church, with severe restrictions on divorce and contraception and harsh social and legal punishments for perceived sexual deviance and illegitimate births. In the urban centers of Ulster, however, the 1950s saw a hardening of neighborhood boundaries, with areas becoming distinctly Protestant or Catholic, marked with wall murals and flags denoting their population's political allegiance. Through gerrymandering and other repressive tactics, including housing and employment discrimination, Protestants in the North kept a firm grip on economic and political power over Catholics. Ahead of the 1964 elections, Ian Paisley, a Presbyterian minister and politician, known for his incendiary sermons, called on Protestants and the Royal Ulster Constabulary (RUC) to march on the offices of Sinn Fein's representatives in Belfast and remove the Tricolor flag, hung there against laws forbidding the display of symbols that could incite breach of the peace. Officers, cheered on by Protestants, smashed up the offices and seized the flag, while brawling with Irish Catholic Republicans, resulting in 30 hospitalizations and escalating tensions between the communities.

Catholics in the North turned to tactics being used by the American Civil Rights Movement and pioneered by Gandhi in India—marches, passive resistance, and demonstrations involving women and children. However, the IRA was back, too, with arms and personnel recruited from the Republic of Ireland, able to move back across the border to safety at will. The RUC unleashed its counterinsurgency unit, the B-Specials, which had worked against the IRA since the 1920s. Empowered by the Tory Edward Heath government in London, the RUC used tear gas, beatings, and intimidation to quell disorder, and elements of the British Army were sent to monitor their behavior. Originally seen as protection from the RUC, the British troops quickly responded to IRA nail bombs and rioting with bullets and widespread internment of suspected IRA agents. On January 30, 1972, in Derry, a march of 10,000–15,000 peaceful protesters encountered military roadblocks, triggering young IRA sympathizers in the crowd to begin throwing rocks at soldiers in position on top of neighboring buildings. In less than 15 minutes, the march deteriorated into brawling and panic as the soldiers opened fire, killing 26 people.

For the next 27 years, the IRA and its offshoot, the Provisional Irish Republican Army (PIRA), waged a violent campaign of terrorist acts to achieve Irish reunification, while the RUC and British military, joined by Ulster paramilitary groups like the Ulster Defense Association (UDA) and Ulster Volunteer Force (UVF), countered with their own acts of aggression. Young women, radicalized in segregated neighborhoods, joined or supported paramilitary groups, becoming especially valuable as men went to prison or died. The IRA, which received training from the Palestine Liberation Organization (PLO) and other organizations that utilized women, found that women made excellent, patient snipers and bomb makers and that when dressed in the height of 1970s' fashion, a pair of platform sandals could conceal half a pound of explosives from counterinsurgency security forces not yet used to searching or suspecting woman.

The wave of women IRA operators included the Price Sisters, Marian and Dolours, who set off a car bomb at the Old Bailey in London in 1973, injuring 200 people, and Evelyn Glenholmes, who escaped capture after the bombing of the Irish Guards barracks in Chelsea by fleeing to the Republic of Ireland, which refused to extradite her to the North in the 1980s, citing errors in the warrants. Dr. Rose Dugdale, an English heiress, joined the PIRA after being radicalized by lover Walter Heaton and a trip to Cuba and turned against her wealthy family. She engineered an operation that stole 19 Old Master paintings, using knowledge gained from her unwitting father, an insurance executive at Lloyd's of London. Marion Coyle kidnapped a Dutch industrialist and attempted to ransom him for Dugdale's release from prison but failed. In 1985, Ella O'Dwyer and Martina Anderson, already seasoned guerrillas, were arrested with Patrick Magee, who had engineered the Brighton Hotel bombing. The unrest and carnage of the 1970s in Northern Ireland displaced as many as 60,000 people, the largest involuntary movement since the end of World War II.

Many of these women, like Mairead Farrell, went to the Armagh Gaol after being sentenced for participation in bombings and violent protests. Refused the status of political prisoners, they refused to wear prison clothes and engaged in hunger strikes and blanket protests in concert with male IRA prisoners like Bobby Sands. The prison authorities responded to the women's refusal to wear clothes or use toilet facilities by allowing their wing of the prison to deteriorate into fetid and horrific conditions as punishment. The women earned the respect of men in the IRA by refusing to back down and undergoing extreme physical and psychological abuse in prison.

Since 1944, the RUC had hired and trained women to act as police officers, especially to handle and interview women and children, expanding their duties to traffic and shoplifting, and eventually investigating domestic and child abuse. The women were not allowed to have guns and often resented that the men would hand off cases of spousal battery or child neglect they did not want to spend time on. The work culture of the RUC was also one in which women, to be accepted, either leaned into the "ladylike" appearance and behavior expected of them, which allowed them to ignore the brutality and corruption, or became "one of the boys" and were silent bystanders rather than be excluded. Elements of the British Army sent to Norther Ireland included women, who, unlike those serving elsewhere, carried weapons, even though they were assigned noncombat logistics and support duties.

Protestant women in the North were the wives, sisters, daughters, and friends of Loyalist militia members, if rarely allowed to be active participants. They smuggled weapons, sometimes in baby carriages, provided an underground network of medical care, and were summoned for cleanup of sites where torture and murders took place. They formed a vital system of smuggling material into prisons, as well as communicating between imprisoned members of the organizations. A community cookbook issued by one of the groups, and compiled by the women, included several pages of gallows humor on household hints for bloodstain removal. In one of the few occasions they acted with direct violence, it was the beating to death of Ann Ogilvy in 1974, who was having an affair with a married man, and the wronged wife assembled a group to retaliate and enforce social norms.

Into the 1990s, the IRA and PIRA used women to carry out attacks, with Geraldine Ferrity driving a car bomb to the site in County Tyrone, where its detonation killed Albert Cooper, an Ulster Defense Force member, and the women who, like the Tamil Tigers, used false pregnancy padding to disguise explosive belts to attack the Belfast airport. By 1994, however, things in Ireland were changing significantly. Membership in the EU since 1973 had done little for the Republic up to that point, but a wave of foreign investment sparked a construction boom and creation of jobs in light industry, which relieved the poverty and underemployment that had fueled so much of the anger and involvement in extremist politics. Bombings at Canary Wharf in 1996 and at Omagh in 1998 by the IRA were widely reviled for causing civilian deaths, signaling a change in public support for the campaign, including U2 denouncing

Ireland

the cause from the stage of a concert. The tide had turned against both violent ends of the political spectrum, and negotiators, including diplomats from the United States, began work on the Good Friday Agreement for ceasefire.

The 21st Century

The agreement, which was negotiated with representatives of the Northern Irish Women's Committee at the table and completed at a time when both the British secretary of state for Northern Ireland (Mo Mowlam) and the Republic's minister of state (Liz O'Donnell) were women, effected an immediate relaxation of the strained way of life practiced for nearly 30 years as people sorted through how to move forward. Nongovernmental organizations (NGOs) that had been working on community building emerged as a venue where women from both sides could slowly work on finding their common causes in abatement of poverty, improving quality of life, and gaining political representation, although these groups rejected automatic assumption of commonality as women in favor of "rooting" relationships over time and meaningful work. Adding women to the committees arranging for the routes of provocative Ulster Loyalist and Republican parade marches cut down on the deliberate baiting and removed them as a yearly flashpoint for violence, while the concerted pressure applied by women, like the McCartney Sisters, trying to get justice for their PIRA-slain brother, changed the narrative of heroic freedom fighters to the more realistic admission that the tactics and alliances with criminals had been the tools of cowards and psychopaths. Ongoing investigations into the practice of the RUC protecting criminal informants and police brutality continue and reach back into the 1960s.

The 1998 agreement included the release of hundreds of prisoners, many of them serving long sentences for bombings and killings. This remains a very sore point among victims and their families, who resent seeing Martina Anderson and Evelyn Glenholmes as political representatives and on committees to advocate for peace. Many women identified with Northern Irish militia groups remain convinced that the IRA is being rewarded for bad acts, and that they have been sold out by the political process, their Protestant culture more under siege than ever.

Women in Northern Ireland are able to join the British armed forces and have followed, with the exception of units posted to the North, the same integration and trade restrictions as their peers from Scotland, England, and Wales. The Republic of Ireland has allowed women to enlist for all trades since their admission in 1979, including special operations and rangers. The Irish Defense Force sends missions as UN Peacekeepers, including to Cyprus, the Israeli–Syrian border, and the India–Pakistan border, which have included women. Currently, women make up 5.7 percent of the total force. Ireland has positioned itself as a champion of United Nations Security Council Resolution

(UNSCR) 1325, sending Anne Anderson to the UN Human Rights Council (2013–2015) and the UN Women Executive Board and naming Nuala O'Loan as a special envoy for the promotion of women in peacemaking. The PIRA remains active and, in 2010, bombed MI5 headquarters in Northern Ireland, making it necessary for both the security forces and the peacemakers to continue their work.

Further Reading

Ashe, Fidelma. "Re-envisioning Masculinities in the Context of Conflict Transformation: The Gender Politics of Demilitarizing Northern Irish Society." In *Gendered Wars, Gendered Memories: Feminist Conversations on War, Genocide and Political Violence*, edited by Ayse Gul Altinay and Andrea Peto, 228–42. London: Routledge, 2016.

Bloom, Mia. *Bombshell: The Many Faces of Women Terrorists*. London: Hurst, 2011.

Brewer, John D. "Hercules, Hippolyte and the Amazons—Or Policewomen in the RUC." *The British Journal of Sociology* 42, no. 2 (1991): 231–47. doi:10.2307/590369.

Cockburn, Cynthia. *The Space between Us: Negotiating Gender and National Identities in Conflict*. London: Zed Books, 1998.

Corcoran, Mary S. *Out of Order: The Political Imprisonment of Women in Northern Ireland, 1972–98*. Devon, UK: Willan Publishing, 2006.

Hattenstone, Simon. "The Monday Interview: Nuala O'Loan." *The Guardian*, March 10, 2002. https://www.theguardian.com/uk/2002/mar/11/northernireland.simonhattenstone.

Hoewer, Melanie. "UN Resolution 1325 in Ireland: Limitations and Opportunities of the International Framework on Women, Peace and Security." *Irish Political Studies* 28, no. 3 (2013): 450–68.

Horgan, John. *Divided We Stand: The Strategy and Psychology of Ireland's Dissident Terrorists*. Oxford: Oxford University Press, 2013.

Kaufman, Joyce P., and Kristen P. Williams. *Women at War, Women Building Peace: Challenging Gender Norms*. Boulder, CO: Lynne Rienner Publishers, Inc., 2013.

MacDonald, Eileen. *Shoot the Women First*. London: Arrow Books, 1992.

Mcevoy, Sandra. "Loyalist Women Paramilitaries in Northern Ireland: Beginning a Feminist Conversation about Conflict Resolution." *Security Studies* 18, no. 2 (2009): 262–86. doi:10.1080/09636410902900095.

Sweeney, Joanne. "Nuala O'Loan: 'The Truth Does Set People Free'." *The Irish News*, January 14, 2017. https://www.irishnews.com/lifestyle/2017/01/14/news/nuala-o-loan-the-truth-does-set-people-free—879081/.

Ward, Margaret. "Gender, Citizenship, and the Future of the Northern Ireland Peace Process." *Éire-Ireland* 41, no. 1 (2006): 262–83. doi:10.1353/eir.2006.0012.

Israel

Background

Old Testament tradition offers a number of examples of women who used violence or participated in military operations to protect the Jewish people. Rahab the Harlot assisted Joshua as he and his men scouted the city of Jericho, and in return, she and her family were protected when the city fell. In the *Book of Judges*, Deborah, the prophet and judge, accompanies her general, Barak, and his troops to fight a neighboring Canaanite, Sisera. She prophesies, however, that the victory will belong to a woman. Sisera encountered a local woman, Jael, who, after offering him the hospitality of her tent, waited for him to become sleepy and then drove a tent peg through his head with a hammer. In a similar episode, the Assyrian general Holofernes laid siege to the city of Bethulia by cutting off its water supply and demanded that Judith, a beautiful widow, come to his tent. Judith plied him with wine, and when he was drunk and unconscious, cut off his head and displayed it to his troops, demoralizing them and breaking the siege. Queen Esther, using diplomacy and charm, saved diaspora Jews in the Persian Empire by convincing her husband the emperor to allow them to defend themselves from the genocidal machinations of Haman, an event that is celebrated as the holiday of Purim.

The men and women living in the shtetls of Eastern Europe drew inspiration from warlike Jews as a defense against the harassment of their neighbors and violent pogroms from the Russian authorities. Embracing Zionism, the drive to acquire a Jewish homeland in Palestine, and the prospect of gender equality being debated in the late 19th century, waves of these settlers emigrated to the Middle East beginning in the 1880s. Sometimes working side by side with Muslim neighbors, the settlers began ambitious irrigation and land reclamation projects, founding kibbutz, or communal farms. As the population increased, however, land purchases from absentee Ottoman landlords began to threaten the peasants who perceived that the Jewish population was increasing and organizing. During

> **Military Motherhood**
>
> On May 16, 2015, the Israeli Air Force Facebook page posted a photo for Mother's Day. In previous years, the page had shown photos of women in uniform with their children—in 2014, the chosen shot was of a pilot scooping up her pink-clad toddler in a smiling embrace. The 2015 photo, however, was of the chin to waist of a combat pilot, seated comfortably, and, with an unbuttoned blouse and pulled up white undershirt, nursing her child. Comments were overwhelmingly supportive and positive, praising the anonymous woman for combining defense of the state and nurturing of the child, although critics used the post to accuse the Israeli Air Force (IAF) of attempting to put a deceptively warm face on militarism. The positive reaction likely reflects both the higher acceptance of breastfeeding of newborns in Israel and the shift away from a bifurcated "men as soldiers, women as mothers" idea of national service.
>
> By contrast, in 2012, American Sergeant Terran Echegoyen-McCabe and Staff Sergeant Christina Luna, serving at Fairchild Air Base, participated in a photo shoot meant for the base organization Mom2Mom. They expected the photo, of them nursing their children, in their utility uniforms, to be used in the base health center along with other photos on the theme of family wellness. The photographer posted them to social media and created a storm of criticism, with responses charging that it was a disgrace to the uniform. Although the U.S. military mandates opportunities for women to breastfeed or pump, it also restricts activities in uniform, and the public has a far more critical view of both public breastfeeding and the integration of military women. Both women were reprimanded for using the uniform for "campaigning," a rule usually applied to wearing the uniform to endorse a product or a political candidate.

World War I, the British negotiated with the Sheriff of Mecca and his family, promising them autonomy, as well as promulgating a pair of documents that alarmed the Arab population. The first, the Sykes-Picot agreement of 1916, planned to place Palestine under a joint British–French administration, while the Balfour Declaration of 1917 promised Zionists a homeland in Palestine. Under this structure, Jews emigrated in larger numbers, fleeing the aftermath of the Bolshevik Revolution, as well as rising fascism in Europe.

From the beginning, kibbutzim organized for defense and included women in their armed guards and emergency response teams. Bar Giora, organized in 1907, evolved by 1909 into the Hashomer, or "Watchmen," who patrolled on

Israel

Women members of an Israeli Defense Force Honor Guard welcome U.S. secretary of defense Robert Gates to Tel Aviv in 2007, shortly after women served in combat in the Second Lebanon War in 2006. Conscripted along with men for national service, IDF women increasingly serve in combat roles and on the front lines of national security. (U.S. Department of Defense)

horseback and whose membership included Manya Shochat and Rachel Yanait. As hostilities escalated, separate groups coalesced into the Haganah (Defense), which drew additional members from youth organizations and may have had a membership of as much as 40 percent women. Two of these women, Devorah Drachler and Sarah Chizik, died fighting at Tel Hai. Between 1936 and 1938, Arabs revolted against the British Mandate, demanding an end to Jewish emigration and more political autonomy. The British Army suppressed the revolt but, in the ensuing violence, had to allow an expansion of Haganah activities as the Jews operated patrols and built up caches of arms.

World War II and the War of Independence

In 1939, as the situation in Europe disintegrated, the British issued the White Paper, a draft document that reiterated a commitment to a Jewish homeland but limited emigration and the ability to buy land, terms rejected by Arabs and Jews. When war broke out, Jews chose a strategy in which they would aid the British in fighting fascism in Europe and against a possible invasion of the Middle East but continue to fight for their homes in Palestine. The Haganah spun off two major armed groups, the Palmach, in 1941 (Strike Force), which had about 16 percent women, and the paramilitary Irgun, a highly disciplined group of about 1,600, 400 of them women, which had been founded in 1929 to conduct attacks on Arabs and, in the late 1930s, smuggle Jews into Palestine against the quotas set by the British. The British worked with Palmach against Vichy French forces in North Africa but banned the organization in 1942, pushing it underground. The British preferred that Jews enlist in Jewish Brigades authorized by Churchill in 1944 or that women sign up for the Auxiliary Territorial Service (ATS). At least 4,000 women served in the ATS, with an additional 900 in the Women's Auxiliary Air Force. This offered access to further training, weapons, and passage into Europe, where many of the volunteers hoped that they could locate family members who had survived the Holocaust.

In the aftermath of World War II, demobilized Jewish soldiers, some of whom had set up cells in Europe to investigate and assassinate Nazi officials, as well as arrange the transport of refugees to Palestine, rejoined Irgun and the Palmach, turning their expertise against the British. Irgun, in 1946, bombed the King David Hotel in Jerusalem, the headquarters of the British Mandate administration, escalating the conflict and inflaming opinions in Britain about the possibility that the British could regain control. Following the establishment of the state of Israel in 1947, women fought in the ensuing War of Independence, especially in the Battle for the Roads, in which convoys of soldiers, medics, and supplies had to cross hostile territory. Women fought as armed combatants until a woman member of Haganah died at Sheikh Jarrah on the border of east and west Jerusalem in 1948, after which the organization withdrew women from frontline combat and into support roles.

Women and the IDF

David Ben-Gurion, the first prime minister of Israel, oversaw the implementation of the 1949 Security Service Law, which created the Israel Defense Force (IDF), staffed with a core of career professionals but manned through male conscription of two-year tours and yearly reserve obligation to age 50. Ben-Gurion, well aware of women's contribution as fighters, needed the support of conservative religious parties and believed that for the future of the nation, women's duty was to be mothers of soldiers and settlers of the territory gained in 1948. The IDF eagerly took up the exaggerated masculine image of the kibbutz pioneer settler, tanned from outdoor work and muscular from manual labor, as a refutation of stereotypes of Jews as bookish, weak, or retiring, a macho vision that left little room for women. For women, who were also conscripted, but for shorter periods and with deferments, an auxiliary, Hel

Nashim, or CHEN, was organized on the model of the British ATS and used for support and educational tasks, especially projects assimilating new emigrants and teaching them Hebrew. CHEN, the acronym of the force, means "charm" in Hebrew, and the women were given instruction in cosmetics and proper decorum. Conservative religious women and those who wished to leave the military to marry or give birth were allowed to leave or granted deferment and were only liable for reserve duty until they had a child.

In the Six-Day War of 1967, women, including medical personnel called up from the reserve, supported the combat troops but were not allowed near the front lines. Golda Meir, who became prime minister in 1969, justified the exclusion by reiterating the great privilege of bearing children and building the Israel of the Future. Meir balanced a difficult leadership style of being both decisive and forceful with the affectionate and protective mien of the nation's mother, earning her the sobriquet "strongest man" in the cabinet. She approved of the Mossad plan to retaliate against the murder of Israeli athletes at the 1972 Olympics and was commander-in-chief of the IDF during the 1973 Yom Kippur War. Of the 4,000 Israelis who died in the war, only 3 were women, who had illegally stayed at the front after being ordered to evacuate. During the First Lebanon War in 1982 the IDF allowed women soldiers across the border during the day, in order to provide a "touch of home" and raise the morale of the troops through their presence, so long as the army returned them to Israel before dark. The First Intifada took place from 1987 to 1993 in the West Bank, which the IDF, as a matter of policy, considered under the authority of civilians in the Ministry of Defense and did not classify the uprising as combat, thus allowing women soldiers who did consider that they had been on the front lines and experienced the same danger as men.

Women who wished to contribute to the military found conscription frustrating and limiting. The IDF has a "tooth to tail" or combat to support ratio of 1:20, requiring large numbers of supply, logistics, medical, training, and administrative personnel. Combat soldiers, though, have a special cachet in Israeli society, often parlaying this respect and admiration into success in their civilian careers via networks built in the IDF or with employers who prefer to recruit from the military. Women fulfilled important educational functions, especially with emigrants, but in cases where they were instructors for weapons systems like tanks, their lack of field experience undermined their credibility no matter how thorough their mechanical or technical knowledge. Women who failed courses were usually assigned to secretarial pools, where commanders tried to be assigned the most attractive women and treated them as coffee-fetching receptionists. In the 1980s, only one-third of conscripts were women, and in comparison to 80 percent of men, only 15 percent of women finished their term of service.

The commander of the CHEN, Brigadier General Israela Oron, lobbied to have authority over women soldiers transferred to their functional commander, rather than resting with a CHEN supervisory officer, increasing direct accountability and mainstreaming the women into their units, while CHEN continued to advocate for women's issues and provide oversight. The 1991 Gulf War was an anomaly in Israeli military experience, as the IDF contributed no troops. Instead, as SCUD tactical ballistic missiles from Iraq triggered alarms, nurses and women involved in civil defense rushed to hospitals, leaving their men and children sealed up in their homes. Authorities noted the frustration of men with their inaction and a spike in incidents of domestic violence.

21st-Century Changes

Alice Miller, a 22-year-old Jewish emigrant from South Africa, where she had already acquired a pilot's license, applied for IDF flight training during her term of conscription in 1994. She was rejected on the grounds that women, serving shorter tours, would not be worth the investment of specialty training. Miller appealed this decision and won but ultimately did not meet the qualifications set by the IDF. Defying expectations that she would not be worth the investment, Miller stayed in the IDF for a decade as an aeronautical engineer before marrying the son of an Indian Air Force officer. Because of these discussions, and changes in the civilian work world, the Knesset recognized sexual harassment as a crime in 1998 and passed legislation that year opening all military trades to women. CHEN dissolved in 2001, with its commander moving into being an advisor to the chief of staff on women's issues. More women entered the pilot training pipeline, with the first combat navigator graduating in 1998, then the first combat pilot in 2001. Meanwhile, the border police and anti-chemical weapons units admitted women and two women died in the line of duty, Hani Abramov in 2001 and Keren Ya'akobi shot at the Tomb of the Patriarchs in 2002.

The Caracal battalion was organized in 2004 to be a mixed-gender unit and was named after the Negev desert cat because of the animal's ferocity and lack of sexual dimorphism and assigned the number 33 commemorating the women killed in the 1948 War of Independence. With 60 percent women, the unit serves along the border with Egypt and has produced Lieutenant Noy, the first women to command a sniper patrol, as well as Eleanor Joseph, the first Arab woman to serve in an IDF combat job. A second mixed unit, the Lions of Jordan, came into being in 2014 and is deployed near the Jordanian border. It had the first women battalion commander, Major Oshrat Bachar, now a lieutenant colonel. Women served in combat in the 2006 Second Lebanon War, including Sergeant Major Keren Tendler, the only female casualty of the war, who died with the rest of her crew when a Hezbollah rocket hit her helicopter. The IDF spokesperson was, for the first time, a woman, Brigadier General Miri Regev, who subsequently won election to the Knesset as a member of Likud and has served as acting prime minister while Netanyahu was on foreign visits in 2017.

The IDF is anxious to include the religiously observant in military service, with parallel programs for orthodox men and women that allow them access to gender-segregated bases, kosher food, and time for prayer and observances. Men who refuse to serve with women have raised the ire of IDF women soldiers, who feel it undermines their integration and disadvantages them. For conservative religious women, the Garin program allows about 80 women a year to serve their period of conscription under chaperonage, with regular visits from their teachers. In a related initiative begun in 2015, the IDF hopes to solve its shortage of software engineers and cyber warriors by recruiting these women to undergo university curriculum, for which the military will pay 80 percent in exchange for an extra year and a half of service.

The image of Israeli women, especially in uniform with weapons, has been a potent sexual signal around the world since the 1920s. In 1948, the popular magazine *Bamahane* (In the Camp) printed a photo of Ziva Arbel, a Palmach member, drinking from a pitcher after being in the field. The caption asked "who is jealous of the pitcher?" and a popular singer rushed out a recording of "I Wish I Was a Pitcher." During the First Lebanon War, the same magazine offered photos of CHEN women putting up window boxes, smiling at the reader and suggesting that anywhere they were had to be safe and like home. This veered into the overtly sexual in 2007, when, at the behest of the Israeli consulate in New York, the IDF volunteered a group of women for a *Maxim* magazine photo spread called "Chosen Ones" in order to raise recognition and support for Israel. One of the women, a military fitness instructor, is Gal Gadot, now an actress playing Wonder Woman. Women politicians in the Knesset were angered by the shoot and labeled it as exploitative and demeaning to women.

Further Reading

Ahronheim, Anna. "IDF Opens New Track for Religious Women in Cyber Defense Directorate." *Jerusalem Post*, October 3, 2017. http://www.jpost.com/Israel-News/IDF-opens-new-track-for-religious-women-in-Cyber-Defense-Directorate-506622.

Berger, Eva, and Dorit Naaman. "Combat Cuties: Photographs of Israeli Women Soldiers in the Press since the 2006 Lebanon War." *Media, War & Conflict* 4, no. 3 (2011): 269–86. doi:10.1177/1750635211420630.

Berkovitch, Nitza. "Motherhood as a National Mission: The Construction of Womanhood in the Legal Discourse in Israel." *Women's Studies International Forum* 20, no. 5–6 (1997): 605–19. doi:10.1016/s0277-5395(97)00055-1.

Bloon, Anne. "Israel: The Longest War." In *Female Soldiers—Combatants or Noncombatants? Historical and Contemporary Perspectives*, edited by Nancy Loring Goldman, 137–62. London: Praeger, 1982.

Brownfield-Stein, Chava. *Fantazyah shel medinah: tatslume hayalot Tsahal ve-Erotizatsyah shel ha-Militarizm ha-Ezrahi be-Yisrael*. Tel Aviv: Resling, 2012.

"Chosen Ones: Israeli Defense Forces." *Maxim*, September 13, 2007. https://www.maxim.com/women/chosen-ones-israeli-defense-forces.

Dlugosz, Idalia. "Mothers or Warriors? Women Combat Soldiers in the Face of Gender Stereotypes in the Israel Defense Forces." Master's thesis, Leiden University, 2014.

Eran-Jona, Meytal. "Married to the Military: Military-Family Relations in the Israel Defense Forces." *Armed Forces & Society* 37, no. 1 (2010): 19–41. doi:10.1177/0095327x10379729.

Eran-Jona, Meytal, and Manon Andres. "Organizational Culture and Military Families: The Case of Combat Officers in the Israeli Defense Force." In *Military Families and War in the 21st Century: Comparative Perspectives*, edited by Rene Moelker, 43–56. London: Routledge, 2013.

Gagnon, Madeleine. *Women in a World at War: Seven Dispatches from the Front*. Burnaby, BC: Talonbooks, 2003.

Gal, Reuven. "Israel: Still Waiting in the Wings." In *The Postmodern Military: Armed Forces after the Cold War*, edited by Charles Moskos, 224–41. Oxford: Oxford University Press, 2000.

Greenberg, Hanan. "Female Officer to Command Sniper Platoon." *Ynetnews*, June 29, 2011. https://www.ynetnews.com/articles/0,7340,L-4089028,00.html.

Izraeli, Dafina. "Gendering Military Service in the Israel Defense Force." In *A Soldier and a Woman: Sexual Integration in the Military*, edited by Gerard DeGroot and Corinna Peniston-Bird, 256–74. London: Longman, 2000.

Jacoby, Tami Amanda. "Fighting in the Feminine: The Dilemmas of Combat Women in Israel." In *Gender, War, and Militarism: Feminist Perspectives*, edited by Laura Sjoberg, 80–90. London: Praeger, 2010.

Jorgensen, Connie. "Women, Revolution and Israel." In *Women and Revolution in Africa, Asia and the New World*, edited by Mary Ann Tetrault, 272–97. Columbia: University of South Carolina Press, 1994.

Kelly, Amita. "Breast-Feeding in Uniform: Brave or Brazen?" *NPR*, June 5, 2012. www.npr.org/2012/06/05/154344798/breastfeeding-in-uniform-brave-or-brazen.

Klein, Uta. "Gender Perspective of Civil-Military Relations in Israeli Society." In *Proceedings of the Challenge of Continuity, Change and the Military, ISA RC01*, edited by Gerhard Kummel, 201–10. Strausberg: Sozialwissenschaftliches Institut der Bundeswehr, 2001.

Klein, Uta. " 'Our Best Boys': The Making of Masculinity in Israeli Society." In *Male Roles, Masculinity and Violence*, edited by Ingeborg Brienes, Robert Connell, and Ingrid Eide, 163–80. Paris: UNESCO, 2000.

Klein, Yael. "Israel Air Force in a Special Mother's Day Tribute." *Jerusalem Online*, May 16, 2015. www.jerusalemonline.com/news/politics-and-military/military/israel-air-force-in-a-special-mothers-day-tribute-13376.

Lebel, Udi. "Localization of Bereavement: Bereaved Families, Economic Discourse and the Hierarchy of Israeli Casualties." In *Advances in Military Sociology: Essays in Honor of George C. Moskos*, edited by Guiseppi Caforio, 11–42. Bingley, England: Emerald Publishing, 2009.

Lomsky-Feder, Edna, and Eyal Ben-Ari. *The Military and Militarism in Israeli Society*. Albany: State University of New York Press, 1999.

Maman, Daniel, Eyal Ben-Ari, and Zeev Rosenhek, eds. *Military, State, and Society in Israel: Theoretical and Comparative Perspectives*. New Brunswick, NJ: Transaction Publishers, 2001.

Rosman-Stollman, Elishiva. "Women of Valor: The Garin Program and the Israel Defense Forces." *Israel Studies* 14, no. 2 (Summer 2009): 158–77.

Sasson-Levy, Orna. "Constructing Identities at the Margins: Masculinities and Citizenship in the Israeli Army." *The Sociological Quarterly* 43, no. 3 (2002): 357–83. doi:10.1111/j.1533-8525.2002.tb00053.x.

Schiff, Zeev. *A History of the Israeli Army (1870–1974)*. San Francisco, CA: Straight Arrow Books, 1974.

Yuval-Davis, Nira. "Front and Rear: The Sexual Division of Labor in the Israeli Army." In *Women, State, and Ideology: Studies from Africa and Asia*, edited by Haleh Afshar, 186–204. Albany: State University of New York Press, 1987.

Italy

Background

The conservative, Catholic kingdoms of pre-Risorgimento Italy had no tradition of military women, as the *carbonari* secret revolutionary societies were all-male, and the restrictive social mores confined elite women to discussions of political reform rather than armed intervention to achieve them. When Giuseppe Garibaldi returned from Latin America to lead his Redshirts against the Bourbons of southern Italy, he brought his fiery Brazilian guerrilla wife Anita, but she died of malaria and complications from pregnancy in 1849, and the movement quickly became limited to male participation. Unification in 1870 led to some improvements in the legal and educational status of women, but their leadership roles were as school administrators and nurses, although some activists, like Benito Mussolini's mother, applied their teaching to the radical goals of bringing literacy and political consciousness to the peasantry.

During World War I, Italy called upon women to replace men in the fields and factories and for middle-class women to take on public jobs like telegraphy, being ticket takers on public transportation, and running military relief work for soldiers and their families. Countess Lina Cavazza founded the Central Bureau of News, which routed letters and messages to soldiers' families and kept them informed about the progress of the war, while the women's organization Pro Patria founded and maintained a home for wounded soldiers, the Casa del Soldato. The Italian Red Cross soon had 600 nurses working in the war zone, some of whom volunteered their own skin for grafts on the wounded.

In 1919, in the wake of World War I, the Italian Parliament passed a law, 1176, which barred women from military and police service. The empowerment and liberation women found in working during the war was not acceptable, only the *Associazione Madri e Vedove dei Caduti in Guerra* role of grieving widows and mothers. The nascent Fascist Party, taking power in 1923, adhered

> **The Rome Statute**
>
> Dissatisfied by provisions in existing international law about war crimes and genocide, jurists and representatives from more than 200 nongovernmental organizations (NGOs) gathered in Rome in June–July 1998 to formulate a statute defining specific illegal actions taking place during war between states or as part of intrastate conflict, or in the aftermath of or opportunity created by such events. One of the most significant changes to existing Geneva Convention protections was the shift of orientation from crimes against the family or against a woman's honor and her community to recognition of rape and torture as a violent crime against an individual. Rape, torture, medical experimentation, sexual slavery, forced pregnancy, prostitution, "disappearances," human trafficking, use of human shields, and targeting of refugees are crimes specifically lobbied for inclusion by NGOs focused on the rights of women and children in conflict zones. Additional provisions advise the court to select judges with concern for gender representation and special expertise on gendered crimes, and mandates witness protection and privacy measures lacking in previous tribunals.
>
> The statute passed 120-7, with the United States, Israel, and China known to vote no, although President Bill Clinton later signed the law in December 2001. With the ratification of the statute by 60 countries, it went into effect on July 1, 2002. Critics point to continued problems, like light sentences served concurrently in prisons more comfortable than the offenders' homes and the exclusion of homosexuality as a protected category under "gender." Additionally, at the urging of the Vatican, the law carefully defined forced pregnancy so that it could not be construed to affect national laws on abortion. Despite these limitations, the Rome Statute remains a recourse for women whose countries are unable or unwilling to prosecute gender-based war crimes.

to rigid gender roles typical of subsequent fascist movements in Spain and Germany. Women's place was at home, as the mother of a large family of sons who would be soldiers for the nation, and although fascist doctrine called women to a "sacred duty to defend" Italy, they could best do so as obedient housewives, leaving politics and work to men who needed full employment and recovery from Italy's humiliation at Versailles.

Once Italy entered World War II, anti-fascist women, many of whom had been living carefully on the margins of fascist society, began to engage as partisans and members of the resistance, joining men in sabotage, smuggling, destruction of infrastructure, kidnappings, and maintaining communication networks. Two Communist-affiliated women, Filomena Luciani (who was elected to Parliament in 1946) and Leonilda Iatti, founded the Union of Italian Women (UDI) to organize partisans and political agents during the war. Among the fascists, manpower losses and the increasingly untenable position of Mussolini in 1944 led to the creation of a women's military auxiliary, which enlisted 6,000 women to perform noncombat tasks like signals, clerical work, and hospital aides, although some were seconded to more elite assignments like the *volpi argentate* (silver fox) intelligence unit. These women, who have only recently begun to talk about their experiences because of the anti-fascist taboo for the last 60 years, say that they joined out of a sense of duty to serve the nation and anger at those who wanted to give up on the war. More than 300 of these women died in service, from disease, air raids, and partisan activity.

The 1948 postwar Italian constitution declared that women enjoy legal and social equality with men, but it would not be until 1963 that a new law opened all public jobs in the civil service bureaucracy to women, and at that time, physical requirements for the police were set deliberately to exclude them. Italy relied on mass male conscription to fill out its Cold War army, an unpopular rite of young manhood, but one which supplied a sufficient reserve that women would never be needed. Few women were pressing to be included in military service, as the left regarded the military as oppressive, while Catholic Women's Organizations stressed that women should devote themselves to children and family.

Surprisingly, one armed branch of the government did want women. In 1959, the national police created a special women's auxiliary, seeing that women were better equipped to handle women prisoners in the jails, investigate sensitive domestic crimes, and deal with incidents involving children. This, along with the difficulty in recruiting men who would accept the civil service pay and restrictions, led to a rapid feminization of the police services. In 1981, the demilitarization of the police allowed women access to the mainstream organization, and by 1992, 10 percent of Italian police were women, with an increasing number of excellent recruits coming from pools of women applicants. The police actively marketed themselves to women as a career *because* the police were far more likely to use weapons or see action-packed operations than the military peacekeepers on deployment before the 1990s.

During the Cold War, the Italian military slowly earned the trust and respect of the domestic population working with local authorities on disaster relief, whether earthquake, flood, or forest fires, as well as undertaking UN Peacekeeping missions. Article 11 of the 1946 constitution rejects wars of aggression and commits Italy to diplomatic and military activity to keep and restore peace. During this period, the Italian military developed a deeply ingrained vision of itself as especially fit for this duty because of their friendly, helpful character and lack of the negative imperial baggage on the scale of the British or French. Italian soldiers engaged in what would now be called reconstruction activities —running hospitals, building schools, digging wells, and other projects to improve the lives of the local population. These actions received the praise and approval of John Paul II, which improved the standing of the military in the eyes of many conservative Italians.

1981–Present

In 1977, Parliament passed a law lifting all restrictions on women in public and private employment. In practice, however, the military dealt with women applicants by simply rejecting their bids, and the women invariably gave up after deadlines had passed for the year's academy or training classes. However, in 1981, Diadora Bussani, a young woman from Trieste, submitted her application to the Livorno Naval Academy. It was summarily returned. She filed an appeal with the Tuscan Regional Court, which sided with her, and passed the case to Rome, where the Council of State overturned their decision and refused to admit her. She and her lawyers forwarded the paperwork to the European Court of Justice in 1982, where the judges condemned Italy's decision but did not order her admission. Bussani gave up on her dream of being a naval officer, although the U.S. Navy, hearing about the case, conferred an honorary enlistment in the Sixth Fleet. She had, however, set in motion a sea change to Italian policy.

The end of the Cold War, and the reorientation of defense priorities away from the defunct Soviet Union, raised questions about the role of Italy's forces in the new strategic landscape. Peacekeeping in the Balkans was very different than the experiences of previous troops in Lebanon and Egypt, where they had largely enforced an agreed-upon policy or border, not forcibly separated combatants or intervened in an ongoing conflict. This was increasingly no job for conscripts, who dreaded their service, and whose voting families were not happy to have them in harm's way.

In response to this situation, the Ministry of Defense opened the Sabatini Barracks outside of Rome for a 36-hour experiment in 1992: 29 women, chosen from a pool of applicants, experienced life as a military recruit, including a training exercise, briefings, and familiarization with weapons and vehicles. A dozen of the women were sufficiently impressed with the possibilities of a military career that they formed the National Association of Women Soldier Aspirants (ANANDOS), a group that quickly swelled to 600 members with a newsletter, meetings, and lobbying team. Over the next seven years, the Ministry of Defense used ANANDOS as a focus group to develop a law and follow-on policies for integrating women into the Italian armed forces.

The women were very clear that they would refuse any auxiliary women's branch and wanted amalgamation into the regular forces. The new law, which had landslide support in Parliament with a vote of 592-9, began the process of admitting women to the academies in 2000, as noncommissioned officers (NCOs) in 2001 and as enlisted volunteers in 2002, in parallel with phasing out male conscription by 2005. The original intention had been to limit women to noncombat roles, but a 2000 European Court of Justice case mooted all limitations except the special physical parameters required for the carabinieri riot police, special forces, and service on submarines. Having accomplished its purpose, ANANDOS disbanded in 2004, turning over representation of Italy's military women to the Gruppo Donna Soldate (GDS), which works as an advisory body to the Ministry of Defense.

The addition of women has burnished the legitimacy and public profile of the Italian Peacekeeping force, which remains a key asset in Italy's strategic vision. Mixed-gender peacekeepers signal the modernity and values of the nation, cement Italy's value as an ally and member of NATO and the European Union, and Italy can offer special expertise in training police forces and combating insidious 21st-century threats like transnational smuggling, extremism, trafficking, and exploitation of antiquities. In particular, Italy runs a UN school in Turin for training and building police forces. Men and women peacekeepers offer similar reasons for enlisting: a desire to serve other people, a craving for career offering excitement and patriotic feelings for Italy, and a drive that has taken them to multiple rotations in Iraq and Afghanistan.

Women in the Italian forces receive the generous pronatal benefits of civilian workers, along with special efforts to keep military parents together and plan deployments to be less disruptive to families with young children. The military realized that men no longer have spouses who subordinate their careers to a husband's, or who have time for traditional military wives' support activities, with the situation exacerbated among married or partnered military women. When the unit is one like the elite Alpine Regiment, drawn from the whole country and stationed in north, this has caused problems of isolation, lack of family support, and stress of separation. By contrast, the Sassari Regiment, recruited entirely from Sardinia, allows its soldiers to take advantage of their multigenerational local networks of family and friends for help during deployments.

In 2016, only 4.3 percent of the Italian forces were women, still one of the lowest in NATO. Using the current personnel pipeline, the Ministry of Defense predicts the first woman brigadier general will make rank in 2026, and they are exploring measures to increase recruiting. However, the pension system reports that even in the 21st century, very few women work a continuous 40 years, without many hitting a 20-year stretch either. Italy's shrinking population demographics raise questions about how to change this trend to encourage women to join the military and sustain defense and peacekeeping programs.

Further Reading

Askin, Kelly. *War Crimes against Women: Prosecution in International War Crimes Tribunals*. The Hague: Martinus Nijhoff, 1997.

Byron, Christine. *War Crimes and Crimes against Humanity in the Rome Statute of the International Criminal Court*. Manchester: Manchester University Press, 2009.

Caforio, Giuseppe, and Marina Nuciari. "Italy and Its Military: Towards a New Deal." In *Military and Society in 21st Century Europe: A Comparative Analysis*, edited by Jurgen Kuhlmann and Jean Callaghan, 259–82. Piscataway, NJ: Transaction, 2000.

De Guttry, Andrea, Emanuele Sommario, and Lijiang Zhu, eds. *China's and Italy's Participation in Peacekeeping Operations: Existing Models, Emerging Challenges*. Lanham, MD: Lexington Books, 2014.

Ilari, Virgilio. "Penelope's Web: Female Military Service in Italy, Debates and Draft Proposals 1945–1992." In *Women Soldiers: Images and Realities*, edited by Elisabetta Addis, Valeria Russo, and Lorenza Sebesta, 150–61. New York: St. Martin's Press, 1994.

Lehr-Lehnardt, Rana. "One Small Step for Women: Female-Friendly Provisions in the Rome Statute of the International Criminal Court." *Brigham Young University Journal of Public Law* 16, no. 2 (March 1, 2002): 317–54.

Miglietta, Guglielmo Luigi. "The Italian Army and Society: From Separation to a Relationship of Trust." Master's thesis, United States Army War College, 2005.

Nuciari, Marina. "Italy: A Military for What?" In *The Postmodern Military: Armed Forces after the Cold War*, edited by Charles Moskos, John Allen Williams, and David R. Segal, 137–55. Oxford: Oxford University Press, 2000.

Nuciari, Marina, and Guido Sertario. "Military Families and Deployments Abroad in Italy: In Search of Adequate Answers for a New Issue." In *Advances in Military Sociology: Essays in Honor of Charles C. Moskos*, edited by Giuseppe Caforio, 263–80. Bingley, UK: Emerald, 2008.

Obradovic, Lana. *Gender Integration in NATO Military Forces*. Burlington, VT: Ashgate Publishing Group, 2014.

Paoletti, Ciro. *A Military History of Italy*. Westport, CT: Praeger Security International, 2008.

Schiavo, Gianluca. "The Italian Civil War in the Memories of Female Fascist Soldiers." In *Gendered Wars, Gendered Memories: Feminist Conversations on War, Genocide and Political Violence*, edited by Ayse Gul Altınay and Andrea Peto, 135–44. London: Routledge, 2016.

Schwegman, Marjan. "Amazons for Garibaldi: Women Warriors and the Making of the Hero of Two Worlds." *Modern Italy* 15, no. 4 (November 2010): 417–32. doi:10.1080/13532944.2010.506293.

Japan

Background

Although Japan's premodern history yields early women clan leaders, warrior women, and family members of samurai, held up in popular culture and artwork as models of feminine virtues, there was little presence of women in formal military structures until World War II. Interest in women's historical leadership, sparked by the small number of male heirs in the contemporary imperial family, led to the discovery of Yamato-era ancient female clan rulers and powerful wives of emperors and local nobles. During the Heian period, women like Tomoe Gozen and Hojo Masako were influential as the wives of military conquerors and Shogun, and women of the samurai class were expected to train with swords and staffs, although only expected to use them in the protection of their households. Women with this background like Yamakawa Futaba took part in the conservative armed resistance of samurai to the Meiji Restoration in 1868, with survivors becoming upper-class advocates for women's education and role in the opening of modern Japan.

Working-class and peasant women were vital to the industrialization of the country, working in agriculture and in the silk textile mills, although they generally left employment to marry and have children. Demands on Japan's workforce from the Russo-Japanese War and World War I were not sufficient to drive demand for women's participation, but the militarization of Japan in the 1930s saw the formation of voluntary associations like the Greater Japan National Defense Women's Association, under the supervision of the military, to support and encourage male soldiers with care packages, rallies, and donations, and the war itself led to the employment of more than 4 million Japanese women in civilian industry by 1944. In the last days of the war, Japanese preparations for invasion included rallying civilian militia in Okinawa who were trained to fight to the death against American soldiers. Had the United States

> **Military Bases**
>
> The 1995 rape of a 12-year-old Okinawan girl by U.S. military personnel, and the crass statement by Admiral Richard Macke, commander of the U.S. forces in the Pacific, that the accused should have hired a prostitute instead, crystalized decades of resistance on the part of the Okinawans to the enormous American military presence on their island since 1945. Already traumatized by fighting in World War II, and the loss of population to fighting and as "comfort women," Okinawans subsequently saw the best land seized for the 39 U.S. installations built on the strategic island. During the Korean and Vietnam Wars, the bases were well-known "R&R" rest and recreation locations for men rotating out of combat to drink, visit prostitutes, and take advantage of the strong U.S. dollar, leading to a pervasive expectation that local women were sexual commodities on whom they could take out frustrations and aggression.
>
> Since the return of Japanese control of the land in 1972, Okinawans, especially the post-1995 organization Okinawa Women Act against Military Violence, have demanded accountability for the more than 120 reported rapes and adjustments to the Status of Force Agreement with the United States that would support mixed-race children resulting from fraternization of local women and U.S. personnel, push for more prosecution of crimes against Okinawan women, and provide economic development alternatives to clubs and brothels. The network of bases continue to house 30,000 American service people and 22,000 civilians, with ongoing protests and conflicts often at odds with the Japanese government's desire for cordial relations with the United States.

mounted a full invasion, it is likely that they would have encountered large numbers of armed women, children, and elderly people.

In a far darker involvement of women, the Japanese military expanded its official military brothels, which employed Japanese prostitutes, to a system of kidnapping, coercing, and luring women in their colonies and wartime possessions, including Korea, China, the Philippines, and Burma to be "comfort women," a horrific life of rape, abuse, and forced service to the Imperial Japanese Army. Estimates range from 20,000 to 400,000 women involved, many of whom were permanently injured or rendered sterile by their treatment and who faced stigma and ostracism from their families and countries at the end of the war. Japan's continued wrestling with the issue of acknowledgment and compensation, whether through private charity or official government policy, remains a major point of conflict with its regional neighbors.

By 1940, pressure on the male population of Japan to serve in the military required that women move into roles as factory workers, civil defense volunteers and, like these high school students, members of the Home Defense Force. Here, they train with rifles in anticipation of repelling an invasion of the Home Islands. (Pix Inc./ The LIFE Picture Collection/Getty Images)

Postwar Japan and the Cold War

Representatives of the U.S. military, headed by General Douglas MacArthur, insisted on a social and economic reorganization of Japan as part of the unconditional surrender in 1945. Along with redefining the powers of the Emperor, the new constitution formalized in 1946 granted women the right to vote, established gender equality before the law, and barred Japan from having an offensive military. The parts of the document involving women were drafted by two Americans, Beate Sirota and Eleanor Hadley, in Japan to act as consultants on the cultural and economic changes MacArthur wished to undertake. Under these restrictions, Japan formed a National Police Reserve in 1950, then steadily upgraded this to the Self-Defense Force (SDF) by 1954. An Army Nursing Corps was founded in 1952.

The further integration of women into the Japanese military has followed three major motivations. The first is a desire on the part of the public to have a sharp delineation between the SDF and the previous Imperial Army. As the military was reconstituted, even the terminology was changed to avoid suggestions of aggressive militarism, and veterans of World War II were discouraged from associating themselves with the new personnel. SDF personnel are infrequently seen in uniform by the public and never as official representatives of their service at controversial sites like the Yasukuni Shrine. The presence of women in the military serves as a reassurance that the contemporary SDF is protective, nonaggressive, and integrated into Japanese society. Ironically, the SDF presents itself to men as a peaceful, rational, and cooperative alternative to a stereotype of corporate salarymen as individualistic, aggressive, and combative figures. Promotional materials for children featuring cartoon characters like Prince Pickles and Miss Parsley reinforce through the "cute" aesthetic the distinctly unwarlike goals of the SDF.

The second major theme is that the inclusion of women is a sign of Japan's modernity and role as a global leader in social and technological innovation. One of the arguments used in 1968 for the founding of the Women's Army Corps to provide communications, intelligence, and supply capabilities was that technology and Japan's well-funded and extremely well-equipped force would allow the mitigation of women's lesser physical strength through their application of attention to detail and organizational skill to sophisticated machines. A desire to parallel U.S. military organization and not appear behind European social development led to exchanges of women personnel with the U.S. Women's Army Corps school in the 1960s, followed by swift recognition of UN declarations like Convention on the Elimination of All Forms of Discrimination against Women (CEDAW) and United Nations Security Council Resolution (UNSCR) 1325 on the status of women.

Third, the Japanese economy of the 1960s–1990s offered little incentive for men to join the military, especially one which downplayed traditional military masculinization in favor of humility and public service. Women, especially those seeking an alternative to corporate jobs and the stability of government employment during recession, form a necessary recruiting pool. Some women join the SDF because of a family connection, or because they are disappointed in their exam scores for the police academy or university, but an increasing number cite a desire to take part in meaningful work protecting the country. The National Defense Medical College graduated women for the first time in 1991 and the National Defense Academy in 1992, although there were complaints from male students that the ban on physical punishment that accompanied women's enrollment and the remodeling of their dormitories privileged their classes over previous students. By 1991, 80 percent of military jobs were open to Japanese women, and 61,000 were serving in the three branches (land, sea, and air) of the SDF.

The Japanese Constitution and regulations governing the SDF guarantee Japanese women equal treatment and opportunity, although this is shaped by and interpreted by a society that is still very traditional. The military expects and allows women to resign to be married or when they have families, and since 1993, Japanese labor laws have allowed women to take menstruation leave on the job (although women increasingly use birth control pills, legal since 1999, to mitigate medically difficult periods rather than take leave). Recruiters emphasize to families that military service is an excellent opportunity for young women to mature away from home in a safe environment, with the SDF serving to develop characteristics of the ideal "good wife, wise mother" even if they choose to serve only a short term of enlistment.

In 1991, the Japanese government's interpretation of their constitutional limitations restricted participation in the First Gulf War to financial support of the coalition and reconstruction work, leading to diplomatic bruised feeling when left out of thanks from Kuwait and charges of "checkbook diplomacy." Possibly as a refutation of this, Japan sent peacekeepers to the UN mission in Cambodia in 1992–1993, followed by deployments to Mozambique and the Golan Heights, where women SDF members served as peacekeepers for the first time. These peacekeepers, however, participated under strict conditions: a cease fire had to already be in place, the country being patrolled had to agree to their presence, the peacekeepers must keep strict neutrality, and weapons could only be used for self-protection. This, combined with their response to the 1995 Kobe-Awaji earthquakes in Japan, and their work with police after the Tokyo subway attacks, earned the SDF respect and international recognition as a professional force capable of delivering humanitarian emergency management and disaster relief. This was a significant change in public opinion about an organization sometimes described in the Japanese media as "zeikin dorobo" (tax thieves) and "hikagemono" (social outcasts).

Women and Antinuclear Activism

As the only country on which a nuclear weapon has been used, Japan and its citizens have a unique relationship with nuclear power and nuclear weapons. Forbidden by their constitution from researching or possessing nuclear weapons, Japan nonetheless has multiple nuclear power generating plants. As early as 1946, protest groups organized around support for residents of Hiroshima were attempting to publicize the horrific damage of the nuclear blasts, and in 1954, Japanese women began petitions against nuclear testing in response to the irradiation of a Japanese fishermen on the *Lucky Dragon* by U.S. tests at Bikini Island.

In 1955 *Gensuikyo* (Japan Council against Atomic and Hydrogen Bombs) formed, although its association with the Japanese Communist Party was sufficiently provocative in the Cold War that socialists, liberals, and many women's organizations founded the rival *Gensuikin* (Japan Congress against Atomic and Hydrogen Bombs) in 1965. Although both advocated for a ban on nuclear weapons, *Gensuikyo* went further with links to the *anpo-toso* (anti-treaty with the United States) movement and anti-militarism, especially during the Vietnam War. After earthquakes have threatened Japan's nuclear power generation, most recently in 2011 at Fukushima, the movement has been revitalized to include advocacy of a total ban on the use of nuclear materials for weapons or power. The grassroots organizing and protesting has often been led by women who frequently point to their roles as citizens, mothers, and community elders as a reason they have a duty to protect the country from further nuclear depredation.

Japan and the 21st Century

On September 11, 2001, Japan lost 20 citizens in the attacks on the World Trade Center. Quickly, the Japanese parliament enacted the Anti-Terrorism Special Measures Law so that SDF personnel and police could actively protect U.S. bases in Japan, as they would otherwise be limited to responding after the fact. In addition, the Maritime Self-Defense Force sent ships to the Arabian Sea to be used as logistical support to U.S. coalition actions in the region, a significant departure from their participation in the First Gulf War and a move toward more direct participation in military affairs. Critics of the move suggested that the government was using the crisis as a reason to further militarize and inventing "gai-atsu" (foreign pressure) and shame from 1991 to further their goals.

Although Japan sent peacekeepers to East Timor in 2002, a deployment that included women, its focus shifted from the United Nations to Japan's treaty relationship with the United States, sending teams to Samawa, Iraq in 2004 as a Reconstruction and Support Group. This required the parliament to pass the Humanitarian Relief and Iraq Reconstruction Special Measures Law to again abrogate the restrictions in Article 9 of the Constitution and debate was particularly sharp because of the dangerous nature of the region and the deaths of two Japanese diplomats in Tikrit shortly before the group deployed. The kidnapping of journalists and aid workers and the murder of a Japanese backpacker further alarmed the Japanese public about the dangers to their troops, who were guarded by Australian soldiers as they did their work building infrastructure and establishing clean water supplies. Publicity photos from the Japanese Ministry highlighted the presence of Japanese military women, who made up 10 percent of the personnel, usually interacting with smiling local children over donated educational supplies, and coverage of the experience stressed the safety of the soldiers and the relief they brought to the Iraqi people. By the time the teams withdrew in 2008, the action was deeply unpopular with the Japanese public, and a court had ruled their deployment partially unconstitutional.

Beginning in 1993 with the first peacekeeping missions overseas, the SDFs realized that they needed support services for both the deployed troops and their families where none had existed before. The programs implemented included continuous support services on the U.S. model of "family readiness" extending from predeployment through return, with special emphasis on keeping families informed and aware of their loved ones' activities, underwriting phone calls, computer access and free shipping of packages, and family counseling. Additionally, members of the public were encouraged to partake in a "yellow handkerchief" campaign to show support, with some women's clubs making little felt frogs (in Japanese, the words for "frog" and "return" are similar) to send with soldiers for luck. However, there is still significant stigmatization of mental health issues in Japanese society, and military doctors were unprepared for the rise in symptoms among not just troops but their families as well in response to deployments and natural disasters.

Public reaction was drastically different, however, when the SDF responded to natural disasters, sending first responders to earthquakes in 2009 and 2010, as well as adding women to the crews of escort naval vessels and patrol helicopters who undertook this work. The 2011 earthquake, at 9.0 on the Richter scale, one of the largest recorded in Japanese history, also spawned a tsunami and major damage to the Fukushima Nuclear Power Plant. Although local police and emergency crews train for such events, the sheer scale of the destruction required the centralized command structure and communication network that the SDF could provide, so they mobilized more than 115,000 troops. In the ensuing days, the SDF rescued 19,000 people, delivered relief supplies, restored airport and port operations, and conducted searches for 4,000 missing and 16,000 dead people. SDF leaders especially complimented the work of women soldiers in the delicate and highly personal work of door-to-door contact, discovery of corpses, and notification of families, which allowed the SDF access to people's homes and personal information in ways less available to male personnel.

Japan continues to wrestle with the role of its military and the acceptable limitations to its use. In 2015, the government lifted a self-imposed ban of arms sales, entering into bidding for projects ranging from submarines to search and rescue aircraft, and political discussion continues about how and under what aegis peacekeepers and emergency response crews should be used. Three hundred and fifty Japanese Peacekeepers doing infrastructure work in South Sudan in 2016 arrived with permission from the Japanese government to bear arms to protect themselves, UN workers, and local civilians, marking the first time Japanese soldiers have been given leave to return fire since 1945.

These developments and the 2010 National Defense Program Guidelines planning for a "dynamic defense force" fundamentally changed the circumstances under which the SDFs constructed themselves and recruited women into their ranks. Currently, women may not serve in the infantry, tanks, reconnaissance, flight squadrons, engineering, anti-tank helicopters, chemical reconnaissance, tunnel warfare, or submarine career fields, but the Japanese government has set targets to raise the participation of women in open fields to 9 percent (currently 6 percent) by 2030. Japan's neighbors have accepted their humanitarian activity but still bear deep resentment of the country's behavior in World War II, and the unresolved questions of compensation for "comfort women," political visits to shrines that are the burial places of convicted war criminals, and the way in which Japan educates its students about its military history. Japan's post-1945 army and its inclusion of women are so entwined with values of nonaggression, defense, and national service that changes to these roles and escalating conflict with regional actors like North Korea or China may signal a need for significant evaluation of why, how, and who wears Japan's uniform.

Further Reading

Cockburn, Cynthia. *Antimilitarism: Political and Gender Dynamics of Peace Movements*. Basingstoke: Palgrave Macmillan, 2012.

Frühstück, Sabine. *Uneasy Warriors: Gender, Memory, and Popular Culture in the Japanese Army*. Berkeley: University of California Press, 2007.

Hadley, Eleanor M., and Patricia Hagan Kuwayama. *Memoir of a Trustbuster: A Lifelong Adventure with Japan*. Honolulu: University of Hawaii Press, 2003.

Havens, Thomas R. H. *Valley of Darkness: The Japanese People and World War Two*. New York: University Press of America, 1986.

Katahara, Eiichi. "Japan: From Containment to Normalization." In *Coercion and Governance: The Declining Political Role of the Military in Asia*, edited by Muthiah Alagapper, 69–91. Stanford: Stanford University Press, 2001.

Kawano, Hitoshi, and Atsuko Fukura. "Family Support and the Japan Self-Defense Forces: Challenges and Developing New Programs." In *Military Families and War in the 21st Century*, edited by Rene Moelker, Manon Andres, Gary Bowen, and Philippe Manigart, 302–18. London: Routledge, 2015.

Kirk, Gwyn, and Carolyn Bowen Francis. "Redefining Security: Women Challenge U.S. Military Policy and Practice in East Asia." *Berkeley Journal of Gender, Law & Justice* 15, no. 1 (September 2013): 229–71.

Midford, Paul. "Japan's Response to Terror: Dispatching the Self-Defense Force to the Arabian Sea." *Asian Survey* 43, no. 2 (2003): 329–51.

Oriki, Ryoichi. "The Role of Self-Defense Force in Responding to the Great East Japan Earthquake." Speech, The NIDS International Symposium on Security Affairs, Japan, Tokyo, 2011. www.nids.mod.go.jp/english/event/symposium/pdf/2011/e_01.pdf.

Pons, Philippe. "Japanese Troops Find New Legitimacy through Disaster Work." *The Guardian*, May 17, 2011. https://www.theguardian.com/world/2011/may/17/japan-earthquake-army-identity-pons.

Sato, Fumika. "A Camouflaged Military: Japan's Self-Defense Force and Globalized Gender Mainstreaming." *Asia-Pacific Journal*, 3rd ser., 10, no. 36 (August 28, 2012): 1–23.

Takazato, Suzuyo. "Report from Okinawa: Long-Term U.S. Military Presence and Violence against Women." *Canadian Woman Studies/Les Cahiers de la Femme* 19, no. 4 (2000): 42–47.

Tanaka, Yuki. *Japan's Comfort Women: Sexual Slavery and Prostitution during World War II and the US Occupation*. London: Routledge, 2002.

Wiegand, Karl L. "Japan: Cautious Utilization." In *Female Soldiers: Combatants or Non-Combatants? Historical and Contemporary Perspectives*, edited by Nancy Loring Goldman, 179–88. Westport, CT: Greenwood Press, 1982.

Korea

Background

The mountainous nation of Korea has long posed a challenge to neighbors who wished to conquer it. In Korean mythology, its first people were the descendent of the sun deity and a bear that had been transformed into a woman at Mount Paektu. In the early history of Korea, there were Queens of the Silla Dynasty, which ruled until 918 AD, and records of women clan heads, but this declined significantly after the full adoption of Confucianism. The Neo-Confucian policies of the Yi Dynasty (1392–1910) almost entirely confined women to roles as mothers and dutiful wives. In 1898, wealthy widows formed the Korean Women's Rights Organization to lobby for increased legal status for women and the establishment of girls' schools. These efforts were short lived and suppressed by the Japanese in the annexation of Korea in 1910.

When anti-Japanese resistance broke out in the 1930s, women accompanied guerrillas as support troops, although it was rare to find them organized as fighting units or bearing arms. The period of World War II in Korea also saw the forced recruitment of thousands of Korean women as "comfort women" by the Japanese Army, which used them as prostitutes. Those military men who had experience in the conflict, often trained by Chinese or Soviet soldiers, formed the core of the new armies in North and South Korea. Women who had been abused by the Japanese often attempted to hide their background because of conservative Confucian family norms or, if unable to return to society, moved into working in the sex trade attached to South Korean and American military bases after 1948.

North Korea

In 1945, with Soviets occupying the northern part of Korea above the 38th parallel, the United Nations created a plan to oversee elections and the eventual

> **Espionage**
>
> At Kuala Lumpur International Airport in Malaysia, two women grabbed Kim Jong-nam, the estranged half-bother of North Korean leader Kim Jong-un, spraying a lethal nerve agent in his face. He would die soon after en route to the hospital. Apprehended later, the two turned out to be North Koreans traveling on forged passports, one purportedly from Vietnam. It is likely that the women were part of an elite espionage unit, recruited and trained to operate as honey traps and saboteurs. In 1987, Kim Hyon-hee planted a bomb on Korean Air 858, killing 115 people, while in 2008, Won Jeong-hwa posed as a defector and infiltrated South Korean military circles to gain military information. During debriefings in captivity, the women revealed that they had been recruited as children on the basis of their beauty and athleticism, then trained for years at a remote spy school where they learned martial arts, languages, and familiarity with the luxuries like popular music, credit cards, and food delicacies they were likely to encounter outside North Korea. They knew that their families were hostages to their good behavior and that they had likely been executed for the women's failure to complete their missions.
>
> Since the 1970s, North Koreans have used women to lure Japanese nationals into kidnappings, while others served as sexual enticements for business to reveal industrial secrets. Children the women had were often used as blackmail and hostages. More recently, North Korea has adapted to the Internet, with specially trained women posting on social media and dating platforms to gain access to businesses and government offices. It is almost certain that the waitresses at North Korean restaurants in China are members of this trained cadre.

return of governance to the Korean people. The failure of this plan led to the Cold War creation of separate governments in 1948, with the North backed by the Soviet Union. In June 1950, North Korea invaded the South, starting the Korean War (1950–1953), a disastrous decision that cost more than 500,000 North Korean lives, including many civilian women and children and left swaths of the country in ruins.

The founder of the North Korean regime, Kim Il-sung declared a radical program of "Chollima" (Flying Horse) economic policy, stressing liberation through the labor of nation building. With the loss of so many men in the fighting, women were necessary in the workforce and expected to leave their families to promised socialized housework and childrearing done in government-supplied nurseries, kitchens, and laundries. Kim Il-sung's first wife, Kim Jong-suk, had been a 16-year-old peasant when she joined the anti-Japanese guerrillas and bore four children between being held as a prisoner by the Japanese, foraging for food, and living in exile in Soviet territory. After her death in 1949 from childbirth and complication of tuberculosis, she was honored as the mother of the nation as well as a fierce fighter, with a museum devoted to her rifle. The North Korean regime expected similar commitment of its women as mothers to rebuild the population, workers to produce economically, and armed soldiers to defend it from enemies. The 1955 signature policy of Juche, or self-reliance, in which Marxist-Leninism acquired aspects of personality cult in devotion to Kim Il-sung, also locked North Korea into decades of austerity and poverty for most of the population.

Despite propaganda that stressed the equality of citizens, few women rose to positions of authority within the government. One exception was Ho Jong-suk, the feminist daughter of Communist Party leader Ho Hon, who was also celebrated as an anti-Japanese guerrilla. Chon Ho-suk served as a Supreme Court justice and member of the Assembly and was trusted to meet international delegations. Her husband, Choe Chang-ik, ran afoul of Kim Il-sung, and she divorced him before his fall during a political purge in 1960. Confucian values of obedience, hierarchy, and deference to men, including avoidance of divorce, permeated the regime despite the end of the family lineage book system and Kim Il-sung's vocal support for women's rights. Families of dissidents, especially their mothers, were blamed for raising insufficiently revolutionary children and were usually punished for defections or acting against the regime.

Throughout the Cold War, North Korea conscripted all of its young men for 10-year stints in the military and expected them to be celibate throughout. Women could volunteer to serve in the armed forces, although numbers are not available about those who did. It is likely that they were assigned to civilian work and expected to care for their parents closer to home. In the 1970s, North Korea promoted birth control, which has yielded much smaller families. This medical advance did not translate into availability of safe maternity hospitals, drugs for sexually transmitted disease, or skilled medical care, so the life expectancy of North Korean women has been around 66, 12 years less than counterparts in South Korea.

The death of Kim Il-sung in 1994, along with the end of Soviet support, precipitated a crisis within the regime. Between 1991 and 1996, the economy contracted 30 percent, followed by devastating floods and a famine that may have killed 330,000 people. During the crisis, women were expected to forage for food and often ate last or the least palatable edibles like tree bark. Nongovernmental organizations (NGOs) reported that as many as 42 percent of North Korean children suffered from malnutrition and that women were shifting to favoring daughters in the sex selection of their children because girls ate less and were more docile. Kim Jong-il (d. 2011) and Kim Jong-un have changed the regime by transitioning into apparatchik capitalism, scaling down the rations issued to the population, and expecting small-scale private business to rebuild the economy while the elite enjoy material comfort. This has led to women entering the black market as producers of foodstuff and home-assembled consumer goods.

These developments have made service in the North Korean military more attractive to women. Military units frequently have their own food supply in the form of rabbit breeding or catfish ponds and offer priority access to imported goods. As of 2003, the shortage of men for conscription, because of famine, demographic decline, and evasion, led to a scaling down of physical requirements to age 16 and a minimum 4'9" height. Women defectors to South Korea, who outnumber men 3:1, report that military units may now be 10 percent women, and Kim Jong-un has been photographed with women fighter pilots he calls "flowers of the sky" and combat units like the coastal antiaircraft battalions. In early 2018, Kim Jong-un named his sister, Kim Yo-Jong, to head the intelligence service, continuing a practice of North Korean leaders to favor their close female relatives as confidants and advisers, although some have fallen afoul of the leader and been violently purged. Kim Yo-Jong subsequently represented her brother's regime at the 2017 Winter Olympics in Pyeong-Chang, South Korea. The fragile economy and posture as a belligerent make it likely that North Korea will become increasingly dependent on the use of women in its armed forces.

South Korea

The partition of Korea in 1948 also created a South Korean Nation under Syngman Rhee, which has defined itself politically and economically in opposition to North Korea. Helen Kim (Kim Hwal-lan), founder of *The Korea Times*, and a PhD from Columbia University, represented South Korea at the UN General Assembly, helping achieve international recognition for the new nation. Other women veterans of the anti-Japanese fighting held positions in the Ministry of Health or Education. The 1950 outbreak of the Korean War caused the government to upgrade 500 women recruited as a high school auxiliary program into uniformed support personnel to allow the maximum number of men to go into combat. These women were mostly demobilized at the cease-fire in 1953, but the authorities recognized the utility of women soldiers and founded the Army Women's Training Center in 1955. The center produced small numbers of women who served in auxiliary women's units for each branch of the South Korean armed forces, particularly in medical roles.

Under Park Chung-hee, president from 1963 to 1979, South Korea underwent a militarized and rapid industrialization and Cold War positioning as a key U.S. ally. This required universal male conscription for 26-month tours and the obedience and cooperation of the civilian population to work in regimented industry, go without consumer goods that were intended for export, and adhere to economic frugality. In many ways, although men carried out the military duties, the austere economic restrictions, rice export, and repression of dissent were felt keenly by women, who largely remained in the home. Additionally, women were asked to contribute to the success of the country by practicing birth control, a program that has now reduced South Korean fertility to 1.187 children per woman, one of the lowest in the world.

As part of their commitment to the United States, South Korea sent 300,000 soldiers a year to fight in Vietnam from 1965 to 1973, including small numbers of military women working as nurses, psy-ops officers, clerks, and communications personnel. As of 1969, eight women had undergone airborne training but were never deployed as combat troops. An all-woman special warfare unit formed in 1975 was likely used for intelligence gathering and guarding women prisoners. A 1973 law allowing some male conscripts to be diverted into needed industrial work was quickly used by wealthy families to keep their sons out of the fighting, a move that has sparked resentment ever since.

In 1971, the United States considered reducing the large number of American troops in South Korea, which the government regarded as a serious threat to the stability of the Korean peninsula. As a negotiating tactic, the South Korean government agreed American demands for a "clean up campaign" of the camp towns around U.S. bases, which were rife with sex workers, bars, and illicit businesses. For the first time, the authorities had to take responsibility for and reckon with the effect of bases on the civilian population. Since this program, the Korea Special Tourist Association, a department of the government, has licensed sex workers and supervised their medical treatment, as well as offered classes and indoctrination to make them better ambassadors to the Americans and advocates of South Korean national security. Despite this government intervention, their lives are still ones of poverty, violence, and marginalization, especially for those who have mixed-race children.

In 1988, in response to a new Equal Employment Law, the South Korean Supreme Court ruled that women could no longer be dismissed from the military for marrying or becoming pregnant, both of which had been used to limit the career participation of women. Activists at the time were also campaigning for changes to the conservative family laws instituted in the 1950s, which preserved primogeniture of sons in inheritance and allowed prior military service to be used as employment criteria, a condition that shut women out of corporate jobs. This push also achieved the availability of public nurseries for working mothers in 1990. In response to this, the military ended separate auxiliary services for women, amalgamating them with the mainstream army, navy, or air force. The new president, Kim Young-sam (1993–1997), the first civilian leader in decades, proceeded with plans to globalize South Korea's administration and democratize the military, including fully integrating women.

South Korean nurses accompanied troops to the Gulf War in 1991, and six were assigned in peacekeeping units in the Western Sahara in 1994. Women assigned to the training commands began acting as instructors and drill sergeants, a cultural friction that succeeded because of the South Korean military's existing emphasis on obedience and hierarchy. A 1995 film, "A Woman Platoon Leader," which screened widely and to popular acclaim, documented the work of one such instructor, who tempered her authority with nurturing encouragement and was portrayed as an "elder sister," which fit within acceptable parameters of women's social power. In quick succession, South Korea promoted its first woman colonel in the army (1997), first woman to command an infantry company (1997) and commander of a training center (1998). Women personnel were allowed on battleships for the first time in 2003. Opening the military academies to women in 1997–1999, with quotas of 10 percent of the class, has allowed the services to choose extremely competitive candidates possessed of higher grades than male hopefuls, with the 2012 Air Force Academy incoming class selecting 12 women from 822 applicants. This approach led to Hwang Gun-jeong graduating as first in the Air Force Academy's class. In 2010, colleges in South Korea opened their Reserve Officers Training Corps (ROTC) detachments to women, which will add another pathway to commissions.

Despite this rapid transformation, the South Korean military remains highly gendered and traditional. The presence of North Korea and the potential for war allow critics to point to the time needed to bring women recruits up to physical fitness and the fear that women will not stand up to the kind of brutal, infantry combat expected of a repeated, large-scale North Korean invasion. A generational conflict exists among senior women, who were not allowed to marry or have children and younger women who are demanding childcare and flexible work schedules to deal with their families. Women are generally held to stricter curfew hours and housing on bases and required to wear skirts and high-heeled shoes when men are in more utilitarian uniforms. Popular representations of military life, like the popular show "Youth Report," involve conscript men competing to have visits from their mothers (who arrive in traditional Korean dress with care packages of food) and bawdy tests within units to win time with their girlfriends. Women soldiers have been featured on the program, but rarely win, avoiding the problem of showing their parents or sexual partners.

The success of the birth control campaign of the 1970s means that South Korea is now in a position to need more high-quality soldiers than it can consistently find through conscription. Young women, frustrated by their continued exclusion from the executive ranks of corporations, and the 6.2 percent unemployment rate for ages 25–29, may find the military to be an attractive prospect. National defense plans set a target of increasing the percentage of women and reached 5.5 percent in 2014. Brigadier General Yang Jung-suk, a nursing officer, became the highest ranking woman at that grade with her promotion in 2014, offering ambitious women the hope that they can also find career satisfaction in the South Korean military.

Further Reading

An, Tai-Sung. *North Korea: A Political Handbook*. Wilmington, DE: Scholarly Resources, 1983.
Brooke, James. "As North Korean Men Turn to Business, Women Join the Army." *The New York Times*, August 16, 2003. http://www.nytimes.com/2003/08/17/world/as-north-korean-men-turn-to-business-women-join-the-army.html.
Hassig, Ralph C., and Kong Dan Oh. *The Hidden People of North Korea: Everyday Life in the Hermit Kingdom*. Lanham, MA: Rowman & Littlefield, 2015.
Hong, Doo-Seung. "Women in the South Korean Military." In *Proceedings of the Challenge of Continuity, Change and the Military, ISA RC01*, edited by Gerhard Kummel, 123–42. Strausberg: Sozialwissenschaftliches Institut der Bundeswehr, 2001.
Jung, Kyungja, and Bronwen Dalton. "Rhetoric versus Reality for the Women of North Korea: Mothers of the Revolution." *Asian Survey* 46, no. 5 (2006): 741–60. doi:10.1525/as.2006.46.5.741.
Khor, Samantha. "How North Korea's Female Spies Are Handpicked and Trained to Kill." *SAYS.com*, February 16, 2017. http://says.com/my/news/how-north-korea-s-female-spies-and-assassins-are-recruited-and-trained.
Kwon, Insook. "Militarism in My Heart: Militarization of Women's Consciousness and Culture in South Korea." PhD dissertation, Clark University, 2000.
Lee, Dongmyung. "Integration of Women into Combat Units in the Republic of Korea Army." Master's thesis, Command and General Staff College, Ft. Leavenworth, Kansas, 2014.
MacDonald, Eileen. *Shoot the Women First*. London: Arrow Books, 1992.
Moon, Katharine H. S. *Sex among Allies: Military Prostitution in U.S.-Korea Relations*. New York: Columbia University Press, 1997.
Moon, Katharine H. S. "South Korean Movements against Militarized Sexual Labor." *Asian Survey* 39, no. 2 (1999): 310–27. doi:10.1525/as.1999.39.2.01p0440a.
Moon, Seungsook. "Beyond Equality versus Difference: Professional Women Soldiers in the South Korean Army." *Social Politics: International Studies in Gender, State & Society* 9, no. 2 (Summer 2002): 212–47. doi:10.1093/sp/9.2.212.
Moon, Seungsook. *Militarized modernity and Gendered Citizenship in South Korea*. Durham, NC: Duke University Press, 2007.
Moon, Seungsook. "Trouble with Conscription, Entertaining Soldiers." *Men and Masculinities* 8, no. 1 (2005): 64–92. doi:10.1177/1097184x04268800.
Myong-song, Kim. "Kim Jong-un Puts Sister in Charge of State Security." The Chosun Ilbo (English Edition): Daily News from Korea—North Korea, January 25,

2018. http://english.chosun.com/site/data/html_dir/2018/01/25/2018012501295.html.

Olsen, Edward. "The Societal Role of the ROK Armed Forces." In *The Armed Forces in Contemporary Asian Societies*, edited by Edward Olsen and Stephen Jurika, 87–103. Boulder, CO: Westview, 1986.

Park, Kyung Ae. "Women and Revolution in South and North Korea." In *Women and Revolution in Asia, Africa and the New World*, edited by Mary Ann Tetrault, 161–91. Columbia: University of South Carolina Press, 1994.

Smith, Hazel. *North Korea: Markets and Military Rule*. Cambridge: Cambridge University Press, 2015.

Suh, Dae-Sook. *Kim Il Sung: The North Korean Leader*. New York: Columbia University Press, 1988.

Willacy, Mark. "Exclusive: My Life as a North Korean Super Spy." *ABC News*, April 10, 2013. http://www.abc.net.au/news/2013-04-10/my-life-as-a-north-korean-super-spy3a-exclusive/4621358.

Winn, Gregory F. T. "North Korea: A Garrison State." In *The Armed Forces in Contemporary Asian Societies*, edited by Edward Olsen and Stephen Jurika, 104–22. Boulder, CO: Westview, 1986.

Kurds

Background

Claiming land that currently exists within the borders of modern Turkey, Iran, Iraq, and Syria, 30–45 million Kurds are currently the largest ethnic group in the world without its own country. Possibly descended from the nomadic Medes, the Kurds appear as tribal people in medieval records, and their fighting prowess led to both conflict with dominant empires in the region as well as military service to the Safavids, Seljuk Turks, and Ottomans as fierce auxiliary cavalry. Kurdish society was traditionally patriarchal, but the structure of authority by chieftain families allowed for extraordinary women to lead intellectually and militarily. In the 17th-century Jewish community of Iraqi Kurds, Asenath Barzani, a rabbi's daughter, had an extraordinary marriage contract that exempted her from housework so that she could concentrate on Torah and legal studies, later taking over her husband's yeshiva in Mosul. Another woman, Xanzad, was the chieftain of Harit and Soran and led her clan on lucrative raids into Iran. During the Crimean War of the 19th century, Fatma the Black commanded Kurdish cavalry for the Ottoman Empire against the Russians. Minority groups within the Kurds, such as the Yezedi, have had powerful women leaders like Meyan Xatun (1913–1957) well into the 20th century. In 1880, a powerful Kurdish leader, Sheik Ubeydullah, attempted to demand a separate homeland from the Ottoman Empire but was crushed and sent into exile.

World War I, which broke up the Ottoman Empire into new countries and European-run mandates, originally seemed advantageous to the Kurds, who were promised their own land under early treaty arrangements. Instead, they were divided into subjects of the new rulers of Iraq, Iran, Syria, and Turkey. Adile Xanim, a woman Kurdish chief of the Jaf tribe, who ran her own courts and markets in northern Iran, reminded the British that she had saved their soldiers in World War I and expected them to honor their promises. Instead, the British supported the rulers they had installed and used force to put down

> **Angel of Kobane**
>
> In the fall of 2014, a photo ricocheted around social media, accompanied by celebrations of "amazons," "badass women," and "combat cuties." A young woman in fatigues and holding a gun smiles directly at the camera while she flashes a V for victory sign. The men behind her seem disheveled, tired, and shambolic, while she is confident and defiant. The photo, taken at a swearing-in ceremony for home guard soldiers in the northern Syrian town of Kobane, turned up days later on a Kurdish blog, after which the *Slemani Times* tweeted it out to moderate attention, including a response from the Islamic State (ISIS) that they had killed her, accompanied by a photoshopped shot of a man holding a woman's severed head. Journalist Pawan Durani forwarded the photo, adding the claim that the woman was named "Rehana" and that she was a sniper with 100 kills. This racked up more than 5,000 likes, fueled by the mysterious armed beauty and concerns for her safety.
>
> Swedish reporter Carl Drott was there at the swearing-in ceremony and corrected the story: "Rehana" was a volunteer with little training, patrolling the city to relieve the women actually doing the fighting, and she was a former law student from Aleppo who joined the fight after ISIS killed her father. Why was the image so attractive? The public, learning about ISIS's horrific and retrograde treatment of women, relished the idea of a young woman taking violent revenge on them, defying the stereotype of a helpless victim and adding the insult of the rumor that ISIS believed they would be denied entrance to Paradise if slain by a woman. The construction of "Rehana" and her sniper kills fulfilled a Western fantasy of resistance and charisma that proved to be powerful, wishful thinking and propaganda.

Kurdish uprisings. This situation, of being trapped between great powers, persisted into the 1970s, with the United States intervening to first support Kurd independence when advantageous and then shifting support to Iraq at the outbreak of the Iran–Iraq War.

The PKK and Turkey

In response to discrimination against Kurds and a continued desire for their own state, Abdullah Ocalan founded the Partiya Karkeren Kurdistan (PKK), or Kurdish Worker's Party, in 1978, along with an inner circle that included Sakine Cansiz, and emerged from intellectual student activist circles in Ankara. Because of its Marxist orientation, evident in the "worker's" party name, women were part of PKK ideology from the beginning, and political education included the "double oppression" of patriarchy and Turkish discrimination. Ocalan added to this his own experience seeing a sister sold into marriage against her will to arrive at *Jineology*, or science of women, in which a country's freedom can only be measured by the liberation of its women. Against a background of traditional Kurdish tribalism, this was a startling development.

After 1984, armed actions by the PKK against the Turkish state created a cycle of reprisals and repressions, which escalated violence and divided the Kurdish community. Turkish towns hired Kurdish guards to protect them from the PKK. When the PKK attacked, they were harming fellow Kurds along with Turks and their property, as well as bringing down government attention on the whole population, including bans on the Kurdish language, imprisonment, and economic discrimination. Sakine Cansiz spent 1980–1991 in a Turkish prison, before being released and regrouping women's units in PKK training camps in Lebanon. Leyla Zana, a Kurdish activist and politician, was elected to the Turkish parliament in 1991 but was arrested and imprisoned after appending a Kurdish oath to her swearing in, in defiance of the language ban. While in jail, she was awarded the 1995 Andrei Sakharov Prize for free thought. During the escalation of violence between the PKK and the Turkish military, women comprised at least 30 percent of PKK forces and conducted 11 of the 15 successful suicide attacks before 2000, producing mixed and single-gender units from their training camps in the Qandil Mountains of Iraq.

Turkey succeeded in having the United States and the European Union (EU) declare the PKK a terrorist group, and it was with Central Intelligence Agency's (CIA) assistance that Abdullah Ocalan was captured in Kenya and imprisoned by the Turkish government in 1999. Since then, Ocalan has urged the PKK to turn its ambitions to acquiring protections as a minority group, rather than a separatist homeland, and pursuing these goals via elections. The Peace and Democracy Party, restructured into the Democratic Regions Party in 2014, requires at least 40 percent of its candidates to be women, and as of 2016, it had successfully placed 23 Kurdish women in the Turkish parliament. Despite these positive developments, Kurds, especially poorly educated women who have migrated to urban areas, struggle under language bans and ethnic prejudice. In 2013, Sakine Cansiz, the founding mother of the PKK, and two other Kurdish activist women were murdered at the Paris Kurdish Information Center, and it is not known if this was possibly an act by the Turkish government or an inter-PKK factional power struggle.

Iraq and the Anfal

The Kurdish population of Iraq resisted the authority of the central government with the armed Peshmerga, meaning "those who confront death." Far more male-dominated than the PKK, the Peshmerga have nevertheless included women, like Margaret George Shello, who joined at age 20 in 1960 and commanded Peshmerga guerrillas at the Battle of the Zawita Valley before her death in 1969, possibly at the hands of a spurned suitor, more likely assassinated by a rival Kurdish faction or by the Iraqi army. Leyla Qasim, a Kurdish student leader, led a failed assassination attempt on Saddam Hussein in 1974 and was executed by the Ba'athist regime as she sang the Kurdish anthem on the scaffold. With the withdrawal of U.S. support for the Kurds during the Iran–Iraq War, the Iraqi government moved to eliminate the Kurds and other minority populations, like the Chaldeans and Assyrians as a threat.

In 1987, Ali Hassan al-Majid, soon to be nicknamed "Chemical Ali," a cousin of Saddam Hussein, and newly promoted to secretary of the Northern Bureau of the Ba'athist Party, began an anti-insurgent campaign announced as "Anfal," or the "spoils of war" named in the eighth Sura of the Koran. This clearly marked the targets—all ethnic minorities, some of whom were not Muslim—as outsiders and unwanted interlopers in Iraqi state. Over the next six and a half months, the Iraqi army destroyed more than 4,000 villages, murdered men and boys, herded the surviving women and children into camps where they were starved and tortured, and in Halabja, used poison gas as a tool of genocide. A conservative estimate is of 180,000 dead, with tens of thousands more permanently disabled or sickened by gas. The deaths of so many men left their widows and dependents in legal limbo, illiterate and stranded without papers or family connections in refugee camps. The 1991 First Gulf War, and the usefulness of the Kurds to the United States, led to the creation of a safe, "no fly" zone in northern Iraq to shelter the Kurdish population.

This zone has, since 1991, developed into a "de facto" Kurdish state within Iraq. Women within the Kurdistan Regional Government have taken up crucial administrative jobs, as judges, within the police force, and running infrastructure like the airport. With support from the Kurdish diaspora population in Europe and the United States, Kurdish women demanded laws in 2000 against honor killings, forced marriages, domestic violence, and discrimination against girls in education, although it is unknown how well these are enforced outside of population centers. The diaspora organizes itself for representation through the Kurdish National Congress, which, as of 2013, is cochaired by German-educated Nilufer Koc.

Syria

In the wake of the Syrian Civil War, a coalition of Kurds, Turks, Syrians, and Arabs has declared an autonomous region under the 2014 Constitution of Rojava. Because of substantial influence and support from the PKK, the constitution contains significant advances for women—establishment of women's houses in cities under Rojava control to shield abused and trafficked women, banning of child marriage and honor crimes, and a requirement for every institution to be headed by a coequal man and woman. In contrast to the position of women under the Assad government, and the horrifically repressive policies of the Islamic State (ISIS) toward women, this is a major change.

Women serve not only in the People's Defense Force (YPG) but also in single-gender Women's Detachments (YPJ), liberating towns from the Syrian government as well as defending them from ISIS, like, Meysa Abdo, a woman YPG commander, responsible for the city of Kobane. Women Peshmerga in Iraq have also engaged ISIS, as it spread in their direction, but the currently more traditional Peshmerga have restricted women to support functions rather than frontline combat. Yazidi minority women have come to Rojava-controlled areas to fight, especially after YPG forces aided the escape of thousands of Yazidis trapped by ISIS on Mount Sinai. It is likely, despite the fundamental conservatism of Kurdish society, that as the Syrian Civil War continues, and until ISIS is defeated, women from the PKK, Peshmerga, and other Kurdish subgroups will take up arms to defend themselves and their lands, whether out of jineology or self-preservation.

Further Reading

Aydin, Aysegul, and Cem Emrence. *Zones of Rebellion: Kurdish Insurgents and the Turkish State.* Ithaca, NY: Cornell University Press, 2015.

BBC Trending. "Who Is the 'Angel of Kobane'?" BBC News, November 3, 2014. Accessed December 11, 2017. http://www.bbc.com/news/blogs-trending-29853513.

Bengio, Ofra. "Game Changers: Kurdish Women in Peace and War." *Middle East Journal* 70, no. 1 (2016): 30–46. doi:10.3751/70.1.12.

Brownfield-Stein, Chava. "Gender and Visual Representations of Women Combatants." In *The Palgrave International Handbook of Gender and the Military*, edited by Rachel Woodward and Claire Duncanson, 475–91. London: Palgrave, 2017.

Dirik, Dilar. "Western Fascination with 'Badass' Kurdish Women." October 29, 2014. Accessed December 11, 2017. http://www.aljazeera.com/indepth/opinion/2014/10/western-fascination-with-badas-2014102112410527736.html.

Düzgün, Meral. "Jineology." *Journal of Middle East Women's Studies* 12, no. 2 (2016): 284–87. doi:10.1215/15525864-3507749.

Hardi, Choman. *Gendered Experiences of Genocide: Anfal Survivors in Kurdistan-Iraq.* Burlington, VT: Ashgate, 2010.

Jwaideh, Wadie. *The Kurdish National Movement: Its Origins and Development.* Syracuse, NY: Syracuse University Press, 2006.

Kharel, Gopi Chandra. "Kurdish Female Fighter Rehana Dead or Alive? Kobani Warrior Gains Fame for Killing 100 ISIS Militants." *International Business Times*, India Edition, October 16, 2014. Accessed December 11, 2017.

http://www.ibtimes.co.in/kurdish-female-fighter-rehena-dead-alive-kobani-warrior-gains-fame-killing-100-isis-militants-611546.

Kuloglu-Karsli, Ceyda. "Coping Strategies of the Kurdish Women towards Deprivation Situations after the Conflict-Induced Internal Displacement in Turkey." *International Journal of Business and Social Research* 3, no. 5 (May 2013): 158–67.

Neurink, Judit. "No Frontline Deployment for Female Kurdish Troops." Rudaw.net, September 28, 2014. Accessed December 11, 2017. http://www.rudaw.net/english/kurdistan/28092014.

Salih, Mohammed A. "Young Women Find Liberation as Guerrillas." Global Information Network, March 19, 2007.

Salih, Mohammed A. "Meet the Badass Women Fighting the Islamic State." *Foreign Policy*, September 12, 2014. Accessed December 11, 2017. http://foreignpolicy.com/2014/09/12/meet-the-badass-women-fighting-the-islamic-state/.

Yildiz, Guney. "Kurdish PKK Co-Founder Sakine Cansiz Shot Dead in Paris." BBC, January 10, 2013. http://www.bbc.com/news/world-europe-20968375.

Liberia

Background

The modern nation of Liberia came into existence as the resettlement project of American abolitionists and black nationalists, centered on the American Colonization Society, who believed that the best way to undermine slavery in the United States and offer a future to free black people was to start colonies in Africa. Additionally, slaveholders wanted to remove free black people from slave-holding states to reduce the chances of rebellion or political challenges. Between 1822 and 1867, 13,000 people immigrated to Liberia, which declared independence in 1847, and achieved recognition as a sovereign nation. Unfortunately, the newly arrived colonists were interlopers in an area already populated by the Krahn and Grio people, who did not want their Western-style government or their Christianity. Anglo-Liberians, the descendants of the colonists, controlled resources and political office until the 1970s, when minorities began demanding power-sharing and access to the wealth generated by resources and foreign investment.

In 1980, Master Sergeant Samuel Doe, a member of the Krahn minority, overthrew the president of Liberia, William Tolbert, in a bloody coup. Wanting to keep Liberia a Cold War ally, the United States supported Doe, although his new regime quickly became more repressive and undemocratic than its predecessor. In 1985, a failed assassination led by demoted General Thomas Quiwonkpa triggered persecution of Gio and Mano people in the Nimba area of the country. This tyranny, in its turn, encouraged Charles Taylor, who had been ejected from Doe's government for embezzlement, using support from neighboring countries like Cote d'Ivoire and with the backing of expatriate Gios, Manos, and Anglo-Liberians, invaded in 1989. This armed insurgency reached Monrovia, the capital, in 1990, capturing and executing Doe. For the next seven years, at least seven factions fought to control Liberia, creating one of Africa's most vicious civil wars.

> ### Postconflict Leadership
>
> In November 2005, Ellen Johnson Sirleaf became the first women elected to the presidency of an African nation, inheriting leadership of a country racked by civil war for a generation. Born in 1938, Sirleaf married in 1956, following her husband to the United States, where she had four children, and attended Harvard University, where she earned a master's in public administration. She later divorced her husband for abuse and returned to Liberia, where she served in the cabinet of William Tolbert as minister of finance (1979–1980) before Tolbert's assassination and the government's overthrow by Samuel Doe. Sirleaf defied Doe and was elected to Parliament in 1985 but was forced to flee the country, working for The World Bank, Citibank, and the United Nations. In her UN post, she investigated the genocide in Rwanda.
>
> Although she was unsuccessful in challenging Charles Taylor for the presidency in 1997, she won in 2005, after his forced resignation. Liberian women played a huge role in her election, driving voter registration, arranging for coverage of market stall jobs so that women could go to the polls, and offering endorsement from women-led organizations active during the civil war as peacemakers. As president, Sirleaf has endorsed mandatory primary education, freedom of information, and a Truth and Reconciliation Commission, and in 2011, she was awarded the Nobel Peace Prize along with Leymah Gbowee and Tawakkol Karman. In 2017, barred constitutionally from running for a third term, Sirleaf retired from the presidency and was succeeded by Senator George Weah, a former sports celebrity, whom she had defeated in the 2005 election.

Civil War

Few people in Liberia could remain unaffected by the war. Conservative estimates are of 200,000 killed, and more than half of the population experienced dislocation from their homes at least once by the fighting. A sample population interviewed by doctors suggests that 48 percent of all women in Liberia experienced some form of sexual violence during the period of the civil war. The chaotic nature of the factions' alliances with one another and shifting areas of control added to the violence and the damage to civilians. Fighters pressed children into service, often forcing them to rape and kill family members and supplying them with drugs, with some groups having an estimated 10 percent of their soldiers under age 15. Conditioning them to violence often took the form of flouting social taboos in harming elders, pregnant women, and authority

During the Liberian Civil War, women defied clear categorization as coerced victims, civilians, or perpetrators, as they were forced into armed groups via kidnapping as sex slaves, or joined out of a willingness to loot or take revenge. Some of the women formed their own all-female militias, perpetuating the cycle of violence and creating more participants in the conflict. (Alvaro Canovas/Paris Match via Getty Images)

figures. In 1992, Taylor's National Patriotic Front of Liberia's (NPFL) soldiers ambushed and murdered Catholic nuns, an escalation of taboo breaking into international outrage.

Women were both victims and participants in the fighting, blurring the lines between combatants and noncombatants as they experienced assault and kidnapping, and then also joined in the activities of the group that coerced them. Among the fighters, having a "harem" of women signaled status, with the women reassigned as the men died or were demoted in the group's hierarchy. The women performed support duties like cooking and acquiring food while being expected to be sexually available on demand, leading to rapes, sexually transmitted disease (STD) epidemics, and injuries from forced penetration. Pregnant women, especially those who had been circumcised, had a very difficult time giving birth without adult expertise, sometimes suffering debilitating fistulas. The women sometimes joined groups of their own volition, seeking the luxury goods looted by the fighters, protection, or because their families had been killed or scattered as refugees.

Some of the women took up arms themselves, forming all-women units as well as operating alongside the men. Leaders usually considered that the presence of women made the men more aggressive, as they would be afraid to look cowardly or lose status in front of a female audience. The career of Col. Black Diamond, a doctor's daughter, typifies this blurred spectrum of victim and perpetrator: Raped by men from a faction led by Taylor, she joined a unit of Liberians United for Reconciliation and Democracy (LURD), rising to Colonel and cultivating an iconic image with black leather, an AK-47, and a beret while engaging in attacks that continued the cycle of violence on civilians as well as armed enemies.

Through the actions of a peacekeeping force from the Economic Community of West African States, which was criticized for siding with factions instead of intervening to stop the fighting, and the tireless activism of a network of Liberian women, who pressed for a cease-fire and elections, voting was held in 1997 under the supervision of Ruth Sando Perry. Taylor won the election, after which he purged the army and set up an anti-terrorism unit and police force, which acted as his personal enforcers, through whom he conducted illicit trade in conflict diamonds and intervened in the civil war raging in Sierra Leone. In 1999, this sparked a rebellion and second civil war, as forces united against Taylor seized two-thirds of the country and laid siege to Monrovia. In 2003, with pressure from the advancing rebels, indictments for war crimes in Sierra Leone, a second powerful wave of women organizing as Women of Liberia Mass Action for Peace, and international censure, Taylor resigned and left for exile in Nigeria, from which he was extradited to The Hague for trial. The subsequent 2005 elections were notable for the large-scale participation of women as well as the efforts made to offer open and fair polling.

The 21st Century

Two waves of disarmament, demobilization, and reintegration (DDR) programs occurred in Liberia, after the 1997 elections and then again in 2005 as part of the Truth and Reconciliation program. In contrast to Sierra Leone, the DDR process incorporated UNSCR 1325 and specifically considered the needs of women. In both cases, women participated and completed programs at a far lower rate than they had been present in the armed conflict. Planners of DDR programs were deeply concerned with male idleness as a threat to social order and prioritized this over dealing with women, who faced multiple obstacles to access, including poor dissemination of information to illiterate or remote audiences, lack of childcare, distance necessary to travel to available programs, embarrassment about medical problems, and stigma from their families. Some UN observers, in an effort to discourage Liberians from "benefits syndrome" dependency, questioned women about their actions to such a degree that they were discouraged from enrolling in programs and steered toward more general programs assuming they had been victims rather than the more hazy but accurate "women associated with fighting forces" (WAFF) categorization. While

UNICEF offered guidelines for programs affecting children, no organization shaped programming for women.

Although DDR programs ended in 2009, Liberia remains a difficult place for women, with a life expectancy of 48 years and high rates of women in poverty. The long-lasting civil war disrupted agricultural cycles and landholding, while lack of maintenance allowed the jungle to reclaim roads. The actions of the rebel groups deliberately shattered family and community bonds, creating challenges in restoring the traditional means by which women conducted business and participated in labor exchanges to build houses, secure credit, or undertake other large projects. Some women combatants like Julia Rambo, who built up a chain of bars, or Martina Johnson, who parlayed her military leadership into heading security at the Monrovia Airport, have prospered in the postconflict world. Many more, like Black Diamond, find themselves unemployable and estranged from their families, and without the medical care, vocational skills or reintegration needed to participate in the nation's peaceful future.

Further Reading

Adams, Melinda. "Liberia's Election of Ellen Johnson-Sirleaf and Women's Executive Leadership in Africa." *Politics & Gender* 4, no. 3 (September 2008): 475–84. doi:10.1017/s1743923x0800038x.

Cain, Kenneth L. "The Rape of Dinah: Human Rights, Civil War in Liberia, and Evil Triumphant." *Human Rights Quarterly* 21, no. 2 (1999): 265–307. doi:10.1353/hrq.1999.0022.

Christoffersen, Karin. "Disarming and Re-Integrating Female Ex-Combatants: A Case Study of the Gender Mainstreaming of DDR in Liberia." Master's thesis, University of Oslo, 2010.

Cooper, Helene. *Madame President: The Extraordinary Journey of Ellen Johnson Sirleaf*. New York: Simon & Schuster, 2017.

Liberian Women Peacemakers: Fighting for the Right to Be Seen, Heard, and Counted. Trenton, NJ: Africa World Press, 2004.

Norwegian Nobel Committee. "The Nobel Peace Prize for 2011." News release, October 7, 2011. https://www.nobelprize.org/nobel_prizes/peace/laureates/2011/press.html.

Pray the Devil Back to Hell. DVD. Directed by Gini Reticker. Produced by Abigail Disney. Amherst, MA: Balcony Releases, 2008.

Swiss, Shana. "Violence against Women during the Liberian Civil Conflict." *Journal of the American Medical Association* 279, no. 8 (1998): 625–29. doi:10.1001/jama.279.8.625.

Utas, Mats. "Victimcy, Girlfriending, Soldiering: Tactic Agency in a Young Woman's Social Navigation of the Liberian War Zone." *Anthropological Quarterly* 78, no. 2 (2005): 403–30. doi:10.1353/anq.2005.0032.

Libya

Background

As a traditional tribal society ruled by an Italian colonial administration, Libyan women had little role in public life, although like many adherents of Sunni Islam, Libyans acknowledge and admired the political skill and military actions of Aisha, the wife of Muhammad and daughter of Abu Bakr. Even under the first independent government, the monarchy of King Idris (1951–1969), women remained firmly in a private sphere of the "haouch" or patriarchal family, bound by their male relative's honor code, despite 1963 laws on compulsory education and women's suffrage.

Jamahiriya and Gaddafi

In the first nine years of Muammar Gaddafi's new government, women were the subject of legislation protecting mothers and calling for more participation from women in civil life, largely as a refutation of colonialism, but received little practical support. In 1977, as part of his declaration of *Jamahiriya*, or "state of the masses," Gaddafi implemented significant changes to bring about a state where women, rather than being an appendage of a male relative, could choose their own way. Along with training school for driving and subsidized day care, one of those paths was to join in the Jamahiriya's army of the people. Early steps included required in-school, biweekly sessions of hand-to-hand fighting instruction for girls aged 15–18 and locally available training on a volunteer basis for older women. Gaddafi refuted criticisms of this new policy by insisting that the threat posed by the United States and Israel required the full participation of the nation's population.

In 1979, Libya opened the Women's Military Academy (WMA) in Tripoli, training enlisted soldiers in a three-month program and officers in a two-year cycle, meant to educate volunteers in "science, awareness, culture and revolution." After 1981, the staff of the school were majority women, almost all former graduates. Each year's class enrolled around 800 students, 10 percent of whom were foreigners, usually from Syria, Lebanon, or Palestine. In 1987, Gaddafi opened the military's senior military schools, including those for pilots, to graduates of the WMA. Women who completed this program served in integrated military units or in the educational system, often choosing posts near their family home.

As early as 1981, an elite cadre, *al-Rahibat al-Thawriyat*, or the "Revolutionary Nuns," emerged from this pool of women soldiers. Those who joined had to be virgins and took vows of chastity to devote themselves to the nation and to Gaddafi personally. As Gaddafi lost confidence in his East German personal guards, he began choosing Revolutionary Nuns for additional training as his security force, and they completely replaced his male bodyguards by the early 1990s. While Gaddafi argued that this entourage of women was an example of his regime's modernity, critics argued that he chose them because assassins were less likely to shoot at women or as a measure of pure showmanship.

When they appeared with Gaddafi, the women guards wore Western-style fatigues with makeup and elaborately styled hair, frequently drawing comment in coverage of his state visits. Although commonly derided as decorative, the guards were present at a 1998 ambush of Gaddafi's motorcade in Dirnah, where one died from gunshot wounds while shielding him, and in 2006, the guards refused to be disarmed by Nigerian Security Forces during a visit to Abia, requiring the Nigerian president to intervene and allow them to keep their weapons. Since 2011, women have come forward to report that they were pressured into joining, sometimes to save their brothers from criminal prosecution, or by their families to secure special favors, and that Gaddafi, his sons, and his inner circle raped at least five women members of his guard. When Gaddafi and his family fled Tripoli in August 2011, the Revolutionary Nuns did not accompany him, and some of those who remained behind asserted that loyalist soldiers raped them and forced them to execute rebels.

Post-2011 Libya

Gaddafi's investment in women's education and participation in public life may have contributed significantly to his downfall. Many women took active part in the overthrow of his regime, whether taking to the streets in protest or working as delegates in the coalition councils planning for a post-Gaddafi nation. Although there is no official record of their numbers or participation, women's charity groups like *Byte Mawada* collected money used to run refugee camps, negotiate for the purchase of weapons, and smuggle supplies to the battlefield. The group Free Women of Misrata organized and staffed field kitchens, feeding thousands of displaced Libyans and soldiers engaged in the fight.

Necessity broke down remaining taboos, like nurses restricted to sex-segregated hospital wards, and women expected these gains to carry forward into the new regime.

Tragically, this has not, as of 2017, been realized. From nearly a third of seats in the planning councils being held by women, only one remained in 2012. Polygamy, which had been functionally illegal under Gaddafi, returned in 2013, along with a reduction to 10 percent in the number of seats allotted to women in the national governing body. Concerns for personal safety have driven women from their prerevolution jobs in the police, military, and education fields although the new government has not formally dismissed them. The concept of women, especially as an educated elite, serving on an equal footing in the military, seems to be irrevocably tarnished by association with Gaddafi's sponsorship, and it seems unlikely that the conservative Islamic government now in control of Libya will allow them to return to the status held under his regime. It is unknown how many women remain in the Libyan military, which is estimated to contain approximately 35,000 people in 2017.

Further Reading

Coughlin, Kathryn. "Women, War and the Veil: Muslim Women in Resistance and Combat." In *A Soldier and a Woman: Sexual Integration in the Military*, edited by Gerard DeGroot and Corinna Peniston-Bird, 223–39. London: Pearson, 2000.

Fetouri, Mustafa. "Women Face Setbacks in New Libya." Al-Monitor, March 23, 2015. http://www.al-monitor.com/pulse/originals/2015/03/libya-women-murder-situation-gaddafi-regime-militias.html.

Graeff-Wassink, Maria. "The Militarization of Women and 'Feminism' in Libya." In *Women Soldiers: Images and Realities*, edited by Elisabetta Addis, Valeria Russo, and Lorenza Sebesta, 137–49. New York: St. Martin's Press, 1994.

Graeff-Wassink, Maria. *Women at Arms: Is Ghadafi a Feminist?* London: Darf Publishers, 1994.

Micallef, Mark. "Gaddafi 'Raped' His Female Bodyguards." *Times of Malta*, August 28, 2011. https://www.timesofmalta.com/articles/view/20110828/local/Gaddafi-raped-his-female-bodyguards.382085.

Rogers, Amanda. "Revolutionary Nuns or Totalitarian Pawns: Evaluating Libyan State Feminism after Mu'ammar al-Gaddafi." In *Women's Movements in Post-Arab Spring North Africa*, edited by Fatima Sadiqi, 177–93. New York: Palgrave Macmillan, 2016.

Stephen, Chris, Irina Kalashnikova, and David Smith. "Libyan Women: It's Our Revolution Too." September 16, 2011. https://www.theguardian.com/world/2011/sep/16/libyan-women-our-revolution-too.

Nepal

Background

The Himalayan nation of Nepal was unified under a dynasty of Gorkha kings who conquered the disparate tribal people living there in 1769. These kings reached an accommodation with the British East India Company and the British Empire but were overshadowed by a dynasty of ambitious prime ministers, the Ranas, who assumed control in 1846. Under the Ranas, Nepal's people were aggressively placed into a Hindu system of class and caste, which stratified inequality and created a small aristocratic group of landowners, and a much larger population of rural peasants. In opposition to this, Communist and Congress parties formed in exile in India and worked to establish representation and development for Nepalese people. In 1951, the Gorkha dynasty took back control of government, eventually responding to demands from the opposition and beginning the "panchayat" system, in which a thin veneer of democracy belied the authoritarian monarchy. It took until 1990 to force the king to allow a real parliament and restrict his power to that of a constitutional monarch, but the legislature was quickly mired in dysfunction.

A profound urban-rural divide made it difficult for politicians in Kathmandu to connect with the needs of Nepalese people in remote villages, where unemployment was extremely high, and most of the people were semiliterate and undereducated. Traditional practices like high dowries, corruption, inaccessible school fees, and abuse by landlords stymied improvements and social mobility. The already high inequality was then exacerbated by tensions between castes and tribal groups. Women suffered disproportionately from these problems, as they married as very young women, were less likely to be literate, and remained behind while large numbers of Nepalese men followed migratory seasonal work away from home. Ostracism of widows and toleration of alcoholism and domestic violence, with little recourse for women to leave, made life extremely difficult. Additionally, in 1991, neighboring Bhutan ejected

> **Propaganda**
>
> To communicate their ideology and gain support from the rural and often semi-literate population of villages, the Maoist insurgents of the People's War created cultural units, including the Madhya Samana Battalion, in which 1,500 full-time artists formulated, rehearsed, and presented songs, skits, and dance routines. Nepal's people have a long history of using festival and ceremonial songs to critique authority and to surreptitiously pass antiauthoritarian messages against landowners and the monarchy. The cultural units built on this, tailoring lyrics to reflect current events and recent outrages by the police or the army, with actors re-creating the torture and deaths of guerrilla heroes. Some of the songs feature lyrics like "wake up farmer/your right has been ravaged" and "without a gun on the shoulder/good days won't come for the poor." Maoist stoicism features in plays like "After Understanding," which make fun of the sentimentality in traditional folk stories and ask that people put their emotions aside to be effective soldiers.
>
> Political rallies in Nepal draw people from distant villages, so hearing a single speech is a poor use of travel or work time. Cultural units provide hours of entertainment and indoctrination between appearances by speakers and can be adjusted on the spot to reflect the material presented. Sometimes, hecklers in the audience shout "dance, dance!" displaying a clear preference for the vehicle they prefer—dense political jargon or topical skits. Cassette and CD recordings of the revolutionary songs, usually issued in runs of 1,000, are sold to help finance guerrilla operations. With the end of the war, these functions have been folded into the responsibilities of the Young Communists League and the All-Women's Association of Nepal (Revolutionary), which use similar tactics for anti-alcohol and domestic violence campaigns.

more than 100,000 people of Nepali descent, leaving them living in seven refugee camps in Nepal, a situation that put considerable stress on the economy and social system.

People's War

In 1996, the Communist Party of Nepal-Maoist launched an insurgent war against the government. Their 40-point list of demands included the end of the monarchy, land redistribution, egalitarianism, and rural economic development. Their strategy for achieving victory was, at the outset, to begin in rural regions, establish alternative "pro-people" institutions in place of the government, and eventually encircle the few cities. Their early military actions were attacks on police garrisons, where they seized weapons and upgraded their arsenal from knives and homemade weapons to rifles and pistols. The capitol was so far out of touch with the people that they missed the insurgency developing around them. When the police finally launched a response in 1998, the Kilo Sierra II plan, it was a brutal and sweeping attempt at suppression. Instead of rooting out the rebels, the indiscriminate arrests, torture, harassment, and deaths alienated the population further. In April 2001, the People's Liberation Army (PLA), with assistance and training from some sympathizers with experience in the Indian army, conducted a series of attacks over five days, which killed 70 policemen. This shock brought the government to the negotiating table, but talks quickly collapsed.

Holding her rifle, a Maoist guerrilla in Nepal's civil war watches a training exercise in 2005. Women, disproportionately affected by Nepal's poverty and authoritarian government, formed as much as 30 percent of the Maoist forces, shattering religious and gendered traditions with their armed participation in the 10-year conflict. (STR/AFP/Getty Images)

At the royal palace in Kathmandu, a bizarre episode unfolded in June 2001. Crown Prince Dipendra, probably angry that his parents were preventing him from marrying the woman of his choice, attacked his family while under the influence of alcohol and drugs. Twenty-one people died, including the king and queen, and Dipendra then shot himself. The king's surviving brother, Gyanendra, was crowned days later. Up to this point, the PLA had avoided engaging with the Royal Nepalese Army, thinking them a ceremonial force. In many ways, this was true, as they had not fought a major war since conflict with Tibet in 1982, and their recent experience had been as paid UN peacekeepers. In the chaos following the massacre, the PLA attacked the army at Goraki in November 2001, capturing a huge cache of weapons and ammunition.

King Gyanendra, cognizant of 9/11 and the ways that the United States was framing global terrorism, immediately labeled the PLA as a terrorist group and issued a Terrorist and Disruptive Acts Order (TADO), allowing the army and police to conduct shoot to kill operations and sweeps for suspected members of the PLA. Devi Khadka, who refused to sign a fraudulent death certificate for her brother, who had died in police custody, was raped by policemen and beaten. Bindi Chaulagai, pregnant when picked up as a suspected PLA member, was beaten so badly that she miscarried and died. These women's stories, repeated by cultural education units of the PLA, brought in sympathy and recruits. For the next four years, the PLA and the government of Nepal clashed in a series of small but high-casualty engagements as the PLA hit police outposts, banks, and government buildings, retaining control of the rural road network.

Shifting Goals

In 2005, the PLA abruptly shifted tactics. After casualties estimated at 13,000, neither side was in a position to achieve their aims. The PLA had frightened the urban middle class with tactics like bombing a bus, killing 40 people. The government's army, meanwhile, had received $29 million in aid from the United States to buy weapons and night-vision scopes and undergo counterinsurgency training. In return, the army, hoping to be posted to lucrative peacekeeping jobs, offered to deploy to Afghanistan, but the United States asked that they concentrate on the crisis in their own nation. The PLA leaders softened their doctrinaire Maoism and appeared on TV as legitimate political actors, advocating for a bourgeois democratic republic. For international non-governmental organizations (NGOs), already horrified by the harsh tactics of the authorities and impressed by the disciplined and gender-mixed PLA camps they had toured, an end to the conflict now seemed possible.

King Gyanendra then overplayed his hand, dismissing parliament and attempting to rule on the authoritarian and militarized basis the last four years had built up. Instead, the PLA seized the opportunity to rally seven political parties together to demand new elections through waves of strikes and marches. The king folded, and in 2007 elections, Maoists won 82 seats and were named to five cabinet positions. Immediately, the new prime minister, a member of the Congress party, lifted the label of "terrorist" applied to the PLA. In subsequent elections in 2008, the Maoists won a landslide.

Building a Future

Suspicious of the solidity of their political success, the PLA converted its youth wing into the Young Communist League, held in reserve as a pool of potential protesters and guerrillas. For the rest of the insurgents, the PLA agreed to have the United Nations monitor the demobilization, disarmament, and reintegration (DDR) process. Around 19,603 combatants came to seven camps and 21 satellite offices to turn in weapons and decide their futures. During this process, the United Nations estimated that 20–30 percent of the combatants were women. The Nepalese army agreed to accept 6,500 ex-PLA members, but only 1,442 agreed to join their former opponent, none of them women. A few women who had acted as "barefoot doctors" or combat medics for the PLA were hired by the National Police as rural health workers. The rest of the PLA accepted cash retirement packages, tiered to their rank, and at the lowest level, representing several years of income. Many PLA members resented the prospect of "rehabilitation," seeing it as a punishment or a waste of time to learn vocational skills with little realistic market for them. NGOs feared that the cash would quickly be blown on alcohol or luxury goods, but studies afterward found that two-thirds of the recipients built homes, sent their children to school, or started small businesses. For women, the DDR process offered a chance to break into new areas of employment like driving a three-wheeled tug taxi or operating a tea kiosk, both of which had been unthinkable before the war.

Problems did not magically go away. Nepal remains a poor, developing country. PLA couples who met and married during the war find that their mixed-tribal and mixed-caste marriages are not acceptable to their families, forcing some to move to new settlements. Women who became pregnant and left their children for fostering with villagers had difficulty locating and reclaiming them. Domestic violence and alcoholism, although the targets of campaigns by the Maoist-affiliated All-Women's Association of Nepal (Revolutionary), remain high. In 2015, an association of PLA veterans met to draft demands for memorials to their fallen comrades, an official history, and provisions for the many disabled survivors of the conflict. The new parliament allots one-third of the seats to women, but many rural people believe that the Maoists have sold out to urban interests and will not follow through on their promises.

A traditional way out of poverty in Nepal for men has been to earn a place with the Gurkha regiments of the British army, which selects 300 every year from more than 15,000 applicants, based on strict physical criteria. The Indian army and the Singapore Police Force also recruit from the Nepalese male population. Those selected serve in an elite British unit, receive a salary that is very high in comparison to Nepalese jobs, a guaranteed place for 15 years, and a British passport, which also applies to their wives and children. For 200 years, Gurkhas have built a reputation as loyal and ferocious soldiers and retired to Nepal as local patrons and decision makers. Beginning in 2007, the British army will consider women applicants, in compliance with British laws forbidding sexual discrimination in the military. Reporters observing the yearly competitions noticed a large number of women who had been PLA fighters. Women who do not make the selection cut have other opportunities. Pabin Rai, the daughter of a Gurkha, used her status as a British passport holder to travel to the United Kingdom and enlist in the British army, earning even more than those in Gurkha regiments. The Gurkha "brand" is so potent around the world that a contracting company recruits male and female security workers for Gulf clients and, recently, a cruise line that specifically requested women personnel.

Further Reading

Acharya, Avidit Raj. "The Maoist Insurgency in Nepal and the Political Economy of Violence." *SSRN Electronic Journal* (2009). doi:10.2139/ssrn.1603750.

Cottle, Drew, and Angela Keys. "The Maoist Conflict in Nepal: A Himalayan Perdition?" *Australian Journal of International Affairs* 61, no. 2 (2007): 168–74. doi:10.1080/10357710701358337.

Devkota, Bhimsen, and Edwin Van Teijlingen. "Demystifying the Maoist Barefoot Doctors of Nepal." *Medicine, Conflict and Survival* 26, no. 2 (2010): 108–23. doi:10.1080/13623699.2010.491382.

Eichler, Maya. *Gender and Private Security in Global Politics*. New York: Oxford University Press, 2015.

Gautam, Shobha, Amrita Banskota, and Rita Manchanda. "Where There Are No Men: Women in the Maoist Insurgency in Nepal." In *Women, War and Peace in South Asia: Beyond Victimhood to Agency*, edited by Rita Manchanda, 214–51. Thousand Oaks, CA: Sage, 2001.

Gobyn, Winne. "From War to Peace: The Nepalese Maoist's Strategic and Ideological Thinking." *Studies in Conflict & Terrorism* 32, no. 5 (2009): 420–38. doi:10.1080/10576100902831578.

Hutt, Michael. *Himalayan Peoples War: Nepal's Maoist Rebellion*. London: Hurst & Company, 2004.

Lawoti, Mahendra, and Anup K. Pahari. *The Maoist Insurgency in Nepal: Revolution in the Twenty-First Century*. London: Routledge, 2012.

Manchanda, Rita. "Maoist Insurgency in Nepal." *Cultural Dynamics* 16, no. 2–3 (2004): 237–58. doi:10.1177/0921374004047750.

McDougall, Dan. "First Female Gurkhas Start Their Training." *Telegraph*, July 29, 2007. http://www.telegraph.co.uk/news/worldnews/1558844/First-female-Gurkhas-start-their-training.html.

Nayak, Nihar. "The Maoist Movement in Nepal and Its Tactical Digressions: A Study of Strategic Revolutionary Phases, and Future Implications." *Strategic Analysis* 31, no. 6 (2007): 915–42. doi:10.1080/09700160701740488.

Nepal, Mani, Alok K. Bohara, and Kishore Gawande. "More Inequality, More Killings: The Maoist Insurgency in Nepal." *American Journal of Political Science* 55, no. 4 (2011): 886–906. doi:10.1111/j.1540-5907.2011.00529.x.

Newar, Naresh. "Women after War." *Nepali Times*, December 8, 2006. http://nepalitimes.com/news.php?id=12936#.WnXF2qinHIU.

Subedi, Dambaru B. "Conflict, Combatants, and Cash: Economic Reintegration and Livelihoods of Ex-Combatants in Nepal." *World Development* 59 (July 2014): 238–50. doi:10.1016/j.worlddev.2014.01.025.

Thapa, Ganga B., and Jan Sharma. "From Insurgency to Democracy: The Challenges of Peace and Democracy-Building in Nepal." *International Political Science Review* 30, no. 2 (2009): 205–19. doi:10.1177/0192512109102437.

Yadav, Punam Kumari. *Social Transformation in Post-Conflict Nepal: A Gender Perspective*. Basingstoke, England: Taylor & Francis Ltd, 2016.

New Zealand

Background

New Zealand was settled a generation after Australia, and the two countries developed differently in their social, political, and military trajectories. When the first colonization parties landed in the 1830s, the indigenous Maori people had already acquired muskets, which they used in intertribal warfare and then to defend themselves from the British. One of the first armed confrontations was the kidnapping of Jacky Guard's wife and children, survivors of a shipwreck in 1834. The British army felt honor bound to rescue civilian noncombatants and used excessive violence to find and free them. The military effectiveness of the Maori won the respect of the British, who classified them as a "martial race" and yielded treaties different from those with other indigenous people, as well as interest in enlisting them in the military. Settlers to New Zealand tended to emigrate as families and were highly engaged in Victorian middle-class activism, which they imported to their new home, including campaigns for women's suffrage. In 1893, New Zealand became the first nation in the world to offer universal female voting, including both European and Maori women.

New Zealand's first overseas deployment of troops was to the Boer War in 1899, to which 6,500 men were so motivated to volunteer that the first two contingents paid their own way. Women echoed the excitement, forming troops of "Khaki Girls" to raise money and undertake local work like collecting medical supplies, knitting, and practicing drill. Professional nurses accompanied the soldiers as part of the newly established Royal New Zealand Nurse Corps. In World War I, to which New Zealand sent 103,000 men, 550 women nurses from the upgraded New Zealand Army Nursing Service served in Egypt, Salonika, and Great Britain. Ten of them died when their ship, the HMT *Marquette*, sank after being torpedoed off the coast of Egypt in October 1915. Women on the home front of World War I included Maori women's groups to specially address the needs of Maori soldiers for ceremonial objects as well as the care packages of cigarettes, chocolates, and small luxuries collected for everyone in uniform. The New Zealand branch of the Women's League for Peace and Freedom had campaigned against the war and spent the war years advocating for the rights of conscientious objectors and support for war widows and orphans. The nursing corps was delayed in demobilization because of the 1918 flu pandemic, in which they served the civilian and military population.

World War II and the Cold War

Seeing the clouds gathering in Europe, three nurses, led by Rene Mary Shadbolt, volunteered to treat members of the International Brigades in the Spanish Civil War, traveling there in 1937. World War II prompted the military to scale up its involvement of women. Along with 602 nurses in the Pacific theater serving on ships, women became liable for industrial conscription in 1942. Each military service formed a women's auxiliary: the air force under Wing Officer Frances Kaine in 1941 (3,746 women), the navy under Director Ruth Herrick, and the army under Lt. Colonel Vida Jowett, both in 1942. All of the women were used for noncombat jobs, including clerical, communications, signals, and intelligence tasks. Additionally, General Bernard Freyberg created a series of New Zealand Clubs in Cairo, Rome, and London, hosted by young women, known as "Tuis," who were chaperoned by his wife, Barbara, and who offered morale and welfare services like hospital visits, parties, and letter writing. In 1942, they were absorbed into the army as the Women's Auxiliary Army Corps (Welfare Division). Thirty-six WAACs and 30 nurses not demobilized at the end of the war continued to serve in the Occupation of Japan until 1947 as part of "Jayforce," New Zealand's contingent.

Mutinies and manpower shortages made keeping the women's separate services necessary throughout the Cold War, despite mandatory 18-month male conscription from 1949 to 1972. Two nurses served in the Korean War, one a flight nurse on the medical evacuation route from South Korea to Japan, and nurses supported the military contingents in the Malayan Emergency (1949–1964) and New Zealand's controversial participation in the Vietnam War (1964–1972). During this period, the armed forces were exempt from the Equal Pay Act applicable to civilians, receiving 85 percent of a man wage, and left the service when they got married or became pregnant. In response to lobbying by the women's movement, military women received small arms training for self-defense, beginning in the 1970s, and in 1977, the separate women's services were all amalgamated into the army, air force, or navy, with the byproduct that men were now eligible for military nursing jobs. As of that year, 21 of 85 trades were open to women, expanded to noncombat pilots in 1988, and ship crews in 1989 after trials run in 1986 on the HMNZS *Monowai* to test the abilities of women to do the jobs and military facilities to accommodate them.

The 21st Century

The 1990s saw an increase in women MPs in the New Zealand parliament, to 30 percent in 1993. The greater representation of women in politics and the civilian workforce caused the military to review its policies to stay competitive as a recruiter and employer. A government working group recommended women in combat jobs as soon as possible. Although this was not achieved fully until 2000, women in the 1998 peacekeeping force in Bosnia were part of a battalion of artillery. Currently, 17 percent of New Zealand Defense Force are women, one of the highest in NATO.

Further Reading

McGibbon, Ian Callum. *New Zealand and the Korean War*. Auckland: Oxford University Press, 1996.

McGibbon, I. C., and Paul Goldstone. *The Oxford Companion to New Zealand Military History*. Auckland: Oxford University Press, 2000.

Smith, Philippa Mein. *A Concise History of New Zealand*. Port Melbourne, Victoria: Cambridge University Press, 2012.

Nigeria

Background

In the early 19th century, the British established a sphere of influence in West Africa, which touched on the coast of what is today Nigeria. The interior was controlled by the Hausa, Fulani, Yoruba, and Igbo people, with whom the British traded for palm oil, cocoa, and groundnuts via trading companies. In 1861, British gunboats seized Lagos, establishing a formal British foothold. The Berlin Conference of 1885 issued international recognition of Britain's possession as part of the larger Scramble for Africa, and this status allowed for the formation of the Royal Niger Company in 1886. The company, which existed until 1900, was always at a disadvantage relative to the French and German national protectorates in neighboring regions of West Africa, and the British state stepped in to completely annex Nigeria as a protectorate in 1901 and then as a colony in 1914. At every stage, this was an imperial venture over disparate people, disconnected ethnically and geographically from one another but under British educational systems, laws, and cultural hegemony.

In general, the British worked well with the majority-Muslim emirs of the Hausa and Fulani north, whose authoritarian style of control meshed with the British need for reliable sources of men and materials. The Igbo and Yoruba of the South and East were predominately a mix of Christian converts and indigenous animists, whose economy based on trading networks and decentralized power tended to result in the growth of a professional, Western-educated middle class who increasingly embraced nationalism. In 1862, the British raised the Nigerian Constabulary from primarily Hausa soldiers and Igbo officers in order to have an armed internal police force and border security. Nigerians served the British army in World War I, fighting in Africa as well as working as support troops on the Western Front. Nigerian nationalists were incensed that India leveraged steps toward independence from their wartime sacrifices while African colonies had not. In World War II, soldiers from

Nigeria fought in the 82nd (West Africa) Division in Burma under British command, returning with expertise that would help the country form the Nigerian Regiment in 1956 in preparation for further independence from Great Britain. Under the economic agreements between the colony and mother country, Nigerian women bore the brunt of scarce consumer products and a lowered standard of wartime living.

Gaining independence in 1960 as a federation of four states, Nigeria quickly formalized the creation of a navy (1958) and air force (1964) to compliment the Nigerian Regiment expanded into the national army. The discovery of oil in 1956 exacerbated tensions between the four regions of the country and the ethnic groups within them, over sharing the oil wealth as well as distribution of power in the parliament and the persecution and exclusion of the minority groups. In January 1966, Igbo army officers assassinated the prime minister and staged a coup, only to be thrown out by a counter coup led by General Johnson Aguiyi-Ironsi, who dissolved the federal structure of the country in favor of a central government, a move almost immediately reversed by a coup in July 1966. The Biafran region, including the oil city Port Harcourt, with a majority Igbo population, seceded, sparking the 1967–1970 Nigerian Civil War.

Civil War and Reintegration

Over the next three years, the national government fought to retain Biafra, while the Igbo organized an armed resistance. At least two women serving in the national army, Captains E. Onyejiaka and M. Nzerogu, defected to the Biafran side and took up commissions as majors. From the outset, women played vital roles in supply, intelligence, transportation, and casualty care, but as the fighting became more desperate, militias of shotgun-wielding women and mixed-gender units of Biafrans operated in the field. As part of their suppression strategy, along with air strikes, the national government blockaded Port Harcourt, creating a famine in which between 500,000 and 2 million Biafrans died of starvation, cementing the image of skeletal African children in the minds of Western aid donors and humanitarian organizations. Doctors without Borders, in fact, was founded in 1971 to handle the consequences of the brutal conflict. The secessionists surrendered in 1970, and the region was reabsorbed under a policy of "no victor, no vanquished," with Nzerogu and Onyejiaka returning to their former ranks in the military. While UNICEF stepped in to do relief work for the many orphaned, injured, and malnourished children, disarmament, demobilization, and reintegration (DDR) in the aftermath of the war almost entirely overlooked women, except for a few token prosecutions of national soldiers for rape.

From 1970 to 1999, Nigeria underwent a continual series of coups and countercoups, each resulting in the dismissal and exclusion of bureaucrats, soldiers, and politicians with affiliation to the losing groups. Regardless of their religious or ethnic orientation, the rhetoric of coup plotters often excoriated women as being at fault for the nation's economic and social ills—by hoarding food, supporting the emerging feminist movement, undermining traditions, and being bad mothers or sexually promiscuous. Although subject to the waves of professional purges, women continued to serve in the Nigerian armed forces as directly commissioned officers, almost always in the medical and support services, like Major General Aderonke Kale, the first woman to make general officer rank, a psychiatrist, who became the armed forces' chief medical officer in 1994 and served until her retirement in 1997.

The 21st Century

In 2002–2003, women played a vital role in protests in the delta region against the oil industry. The oil boom in the delta created not just pollution and sunken farms in a "death economy," but the attendant social ills of a region where multinational companies held locals to menial labor and an injection of cash badly disrupted traditional social bonds and conflict resolution, as well. Beginning in July, women and their allies, often activist grandsons, seized the Texaco/Chevron export facilities, the Escravos terminal, and 12 more drilling and work sites. Using nonviolent protest, which included the women stripping naked, a traditional rebuke by older women, to shame men who remained on the job, they shut down production and demanded restitution, protection of the environment, and participation in negotiations with the companies. This quickly took on international dimensions with alliance to Greenpeace, condemnation of the U.S. "Coalition of the Willing" to invade Iraq, and presence with other indigenous environmental protesters at the Cancun WTO meeting. Pressure from the Niger Delta Women for Justice was sufficient to keep Nigeria out of the U.S. alliance and Second Gulf War. Plans for the Nigerian and possibly the U.S. military to suppress the protesters and regain control of the terminals were scrapped because of the savvy use of the surrounding mangrove swamps and difficult terrain by the activists to protect themselves.

President Goodluck Jonathan, as a signature policy of his administration, opened the Nigerian Defense Academy to women for the first time in 2011, for both the standard noncombat course and, most significantly, for a cadre of 20 women in the combat course. Quickly nicknamed Jonathan's Queens, the women excelled in their four years of training, winning the gold naval award and silver army and air force awards. Of the six slots allotted to the Nigerian military at the U.S. Military Academy, West Point, two women from the class were chosen to represent the country. In 2011, Blessing Liman became the first woman pilot in the Nigerian Air Force, following many women who work in civil and commercial aviation. In 2012, Rear Admiral Itunu Hotonu became the first woman of general officer rank in the navy, which she had joined as an engineer in 1985 after being turned down by the army because of policies barring women from that specialty. Additionally, women appear frequently in combat roles in Nollywood action films and adventure novels in the vein of Tom Clancy, perhaps signaling a public mainstreaming of the idea of women serving in frontline military jobs. The new 2017 defense policy, however, seems poised to close combat jobs to women, largely driven by complaints from conservative Muslims.

In April 2014, the Congregation of the People of Tradition for Proselytism and Jihad, or Boko Haram, an Islamic extremist group from northern Nigeria, attacked the Federal Government Girls' College in Chibok, where students were taking national exams. They kidnapped 279 girls, who were subsequently forced to convert and married off to Boko Haram fighters, as the organization believed that women should not be in school. Aside from the Chibok students, as many as 600 other women and children may have been abducted from other towns. Some of the girls escaped, and their testimony of abuse and rape drew international attention in the form of a global hashtag #BringBackOurGirls and raised $400 million. Through the efforts of the Nigerian military, 84 of the girls have been found or their bodies identified, with some returning pregnant or having given birth. As of 2018, 195 of the Chibok girls, along with hundreds of others, remain captive or missing. Authorities believe that because of the global publicity, the surviving girls are especially valuable hostages to Boko Haram's leadership and will be used to their advantage in some future negotiation.

Further Reading

Comolli, Virginia. "The Regional Problem of Boko Haram." *Survival* 57, no. 4 (2015): 109–17. doi:10.1080/00396338.2015.1068560.

Dennis, Carolyne. "Women and the State in Nigeria: The Case of the Federal Military Government, 1984–1985." In *Women, State and Ideology: Studies from Africa and Asia*, edited by Haleh Afshar, 13–27. Albany: State University of New York Press, 1987.

Doghor, Tessa. "Military Stops Admission of Female Cadets." *Business Day: News You Can Trust*, November 13, 2017. https://www.businessdayonline.com/military-stops-admission-combatant-female-cadets/.

Ehikioya, Augustine. "From the Villa- Enter Jonathan's Queens." *Nation Nigeria*, October 17, 2016. http://thenationonlineng.net/villa-enter-jonathans-queens/.

Falola, Toyin, and Bukola Oyeniyi. *Nigeria*. Santa Barbara, CA: ABC-CLIO, 2015.

Lawrance, Benjamin N. "Boko Haram, Refugee Mimesis, and the Archive of Contemporary Gender-Based Violence." *Radical History Review* 126, no. 126 (2016): 159–70. doi:10.1215/01636545-3594505.

Matfess, Hilary. *Women and the War on Boko Haram*. London: Zed Books, 2017.

Ojeleye, Olukunle. *The Politics of Post-War Demobilisation and Reintegration in Nigeria.* Farnham, England: Ashgate, 2010.

Turner, Terisa E., and Leigh S. Brownhill. "Why Women Are at War with Chevron: Nigerian Subsistence Struggles against the International Oil Industry." *Journal of Asian and African Studies* 39, no. 1–2 (2004): 63–93. doi:10.1177/0021909604048251.

Norway

Background

Norway's rugged geography and rural economy of fishing and farming are the traditional foundation of a belief in a national character prizing egalitarian common sense and community responsibilities. Although women remained legal minors until 1840, it was common for them to run family businesses, manage and work rural farms, and control family resources while men were away for long periods, a status recognized by Mary Wollstonecraft in her 1759 visit. Craft and trade acts in the 1840s legalized women-run businesses, and the mass emigration of the 19th century highlighted the role of women left behind while male family members staked claims in America or participated in a remittance economy, sending money back to Norway. The status of women was the centerpiece of Ibsen's provocative play, *A Doll's House*, which pushed for the 1890 end of coverture marriage and women's suffrage, which was fully achieved in 1913.

Norway was neutral in World War I, although its continued trade relationship with Great Britain made Norwegian ships targets for German U-boats, at a cost of half the fleet and 2,000 sailors, further raising the responsibilities of the women in coastal towns who increasingly took on the jobs to which the men never returned. Norway opened civil defense and some administrative and medical military jobs to women in 1938 in recognition of rising international tensions. During the German occupation of Norway, women played a key role in the Resistance, performing sabotage, refusing as teachers to take part in the Nazi-dictated curriculum, smuggling Jews and downed Allied pilots to safety, and undertaking coast watching and acts of political defiance. More than 4,000 women were imprisoned in Norway for anti-Nazi activity, although memories of the Resistance tend to focus on the *gutta da skaven* (lads in the snow) activities of male guerrillas.

> **Peacekeeping**
>
> In 2014, UN Secretary-General Ban Ki-moon appointed Norwegian Major General Kristin Lund as force commander, United Nations Peacekeeping Force in Cyprus (UNFICYP). Lund (b. 1958) joined the army in 1979 and served as a transport officer in Norway's deployment of peacekeepers to Lebanon in 1986, where she noticed that checkpoints with female soldiers could search civilians in a culturally sensitive way, finding more weapons and saving lives. She also deployed as part of Norway's North Atlantic Treaty Organization (NATO) contribution to Operation Desert Shield, Balkan Peacekeeping and International Security Assistance Forces (ISAF) in Afghanistan, and as part of the United Nations Protection Force (UNPROFOR) in Croatia and Bosnia. In Norway, she did staff work as chief of staff for the Norwegian Home Guard and Department of Veteran's Affairs.
>
> As force commander in Cyprus, Lund oversaw the work of 1,000 people, as the island's Greek and Turkish population began a new round of unification talks. Lund appreciated that her tenure would affect both the Cypriots and the image of women in security and peacekeeping and reflect the Norwegian value of equality. When meeting with the public, Lund sought out older women, as they had been most opposed to reunification in recent voting, to be sure she understood their concerns. In 2017, she was appointed head of mission for the UN Truce Supervision Organization and has worked with the Nordic Women Mediation Network to promote the inclusion of women and indigenous people in the earliest stages of treaty and peacebuilding efforts.

Postwar

The postwar reconstruction of the Norwegian military excluded women until reservists were included in 1959. The base of the Norwegian military was a large pool of conscripted men, who regarded their national service as a rite of passage and a representation of cheerful, tough outdoorsmen, even to the point that the image most associated with them was a man on skis. After Norway joined NATO in 1949, and then began engaging in UN Peacekeeping missions in 1964, this orientation of the military was a poor match for both engagements in Lebanon, Egypt, and the Congo and Norway's pride in a national commitment to equality and the improvement of the status of women. After a series of laws between 1977 and 1984 gradually expanding women's access to service, 1985 marked full occupational equality in the Norwegian military for women, although only men continued to be liable for conscription. Norway sent a field hospital to aid the United States in the First Gulf War, which met public perceptions of Norway's role as a humanitarian provider, but the addition of the armed Coast Guard ship KNM *Andenes* marked a turn toward more aggressive deployments, including dispatching fighter planes to Operation Allied Force in Bosnia and committing to join NATO's Immediate Reaction Force.

This new interest in peacekeeping and deployment was a poor fit for an army largely made of conscripts expecting to guard their homeland on skis, leading the country to study modernization and a more diverse armed force. In 1995, Solveig Krey took command of a submarine as the first woman in command of a Norwegian navy vessel. Norway's political leaders believe that participating in overseas engagements earns them credibility in diplomacy and in their relationship with larger NATO partners, and they tie service with international organizations to promotion to senior officer ranks. More than 8,000 Norwegians have served in Iraq and Afghanistan since 2001, gaining a reputation as a relevant, solid ally, although the public was shocked by the improvised explosive device (IED) deaths of 4 soldiers in 2010. In 2012, the troops in Afghanistan were led by Col. Ingrid Gjerde, the first Norwegian woman to hold a combat command. Mixed-gender units have shown themselves better able to interact with local civilians, changing the dynamic for women in traditional societies and modeling assertive roles. Since 1985, Norway has initiated 198 programs to encourage women to volunteer for the military and set ambitious targets to increase their number, although by 2016 only 10.7 percent were women.

A representative case study is the presence of women in Norway's peacekeeping contingent in southern Lebanon, which began in 1978 with women present as medical support personnel, but after 1985 evolved to include armed women staffing checkpoints and going on patrol. After a short time in tents outside of the town, peacekeepers moved into abandoned houses, putting them into close contact with the local population, many of whom were women who took jobs with the soldiers as translators and clerical workers. The Lebanese were used to women in military roles from the conflict, and the demographics of the local population were heavy with single mothers and widows because of the loss of men to flight or deaths in the war. Those men who were in the area respected the uniform and showed no difficulties with obeying Norwegian women peacekeepers, even being relieved at checkpoints that their women relatives accompanying them would not be harassed or abused, while Lebanese women were comfortable having coffee and bringing issues to women personnel.

In 1992, Major General Lars Eric Wahlgren of Sweden took over the detachment and demanded that women be returned to support roles after more than a decade of experience in combat jobs. Although Norway insisted the women obey the UN commander despite their national laws, the Norwegian women undertook a media campaign that highlighted their good service and the peacekeeping career of Maj. Britt Brestrup, who served in Lebanon, the Golan Heights, and the border zone of Iraq and Kuwait, who pointed out that Norwegian men used to egalitarian Scandinavia had far more problems relating to sequestered, traditional societies of women than Norwegian women ever had compelling compliance from Muslim men.

The Norwegian public, which cherished this image of their soldiers as the "good boys next door," were shocked when *Alfa Magazine* published an expose of Norway's elite Telemark Battalion in Afghanistan. The unit, which has 12 women in its 500 strong ranks, gave interviews expressing that war was "better than sex," showed reporters vehicles on which they had painted symbols associated with Norse mythology and warrior culture (and white power movements), and seemed to embody a rejection of Norwegian contemporary values in their aggression. Officers quickly painted over the symbols and apologized, but the negative perception remains. Partially in response to fears that the forces are too dominated by male culture, Parliament passed a law mandating that as of summer 2016, women are available for conscription along with men, allowing the nation to choose the best 8,000–10,000 to serve each year from an enlarged pool of 60,000 young people. Reaction to this new national service obligation remains to be seen, but few young people expressed reservations about mixed-gender training and most welcomed the opportunity.

Further Reading

Carvalho, Benjamin De, and Iver B. Neumann. *Small State Status Seeking: Norway's Quest for International Standing*. Abingdon, England: Routledge, 2015.

Dyvik, Synne L. " 'Valhalla Rising': Gender, Embodiment and Experience in Military Memoirs." *Security Dialogue* 47, no. 2 (2016): 133–50. doi:10.1177/0967010615615730.

"Farewell Statement by Outgoing UNFICYP Force Commander, Major General Kristin Lund." United Nations Peacekeeping Force in Cyprus, July 28, 2016. https://unficyp.unmissions.org/farewell-statement-outgoing-unficyp-force-commander-major-general-kristin-lund.

Faure, Gaëlle. "The First Woman to Lead a U.N. Peacekeeping Mission." *News Deeply: Women and Girls*, July 11, 2017. https://www.newsdeeply.com/womenandgirls/articles/2017/07/11/the-first-woman-to-lead-a-u-n-peacekeeping-mission.

Haaland, Torunn Laugen. "Friendly War Fighters and Invisible Women: Perceptions of Gender and Masculinities in the Norwegian Armed Forces on Missions Abroad." In *Making Gender, Making War: Violence, Military and Peacekeeping Practices*, edited by Annica Kronsell and Erika Svedberg, 80–94. London: Routledge, 2011.

Haaland, Torunn Laugen. "Participation in Peace Support Operations for Small Countries: The Case of Norway." *International Peacekeeping* 14, no. 4 (August 2007): 493–509. doi:10.1080/13533310701427777.

Karame, Kari H. "Military Women in Peace Operations: Experiences of the Norwegian Battalion in UNFIL, 1978–1998." In *Women and International Peacekeeping*, edited by Louise Olsson and Torren L. Tryggestad, 85–96. London: Frank Cass, 2001.

Peace Research Institute Oslo. "Nordic Women Mediators (NWM)." PRIO. Accessed November 9, 2017. https://www.prio.org/Projects/Project/?x=1725.

Rones, Nina. "Norwegian Defence Tradition: An Obstacle to Increased Participation by Women?" In *Military Women: The Achilles Heel in Defence Politics?* edited by Frank Bruntland Steder, 53–82. Oslo: Abstrakt Forlag, 2015.

Rones, Nina, Kari Fasting, and Claire Duncanson. "Theorizing Military Masculinities and National Identities: The Norwegian Experience." In *The Palgrave International Handbook of Gender and the Military*, edited by Rachel Woodward, 145–62. London: Palgrave Macmillan, 2017.

Pakistan

Background

In 1932, the Muslim League, headed by Mohammad Ali Jinnah, the future founder of Pakistan, issued a resolution affirming its commitment to women's rights. When partition came in 1947, Jinnah's sister, Fatima Jinnah, a dentist, and Begum Ra'ana, the wife of Prime Minister Liaqat Ali Khan and a trained economist, wanted to raise the opportunities available to women in the new nation. In the immediate circumstances, they saw thousands of refugees from India in need of services and in many cases reluctant to seek medical help from male doctors after spending their lives in purdah, or seclusion from male nonfamily members. Begum Ra'ana founded a volunteer medical service, which she convinced the Pakistan army to absorb as a women's unit of the medical corps. In 1949, she started the Pakistan army's Women's National Guard, with herself as its brigadier general. At the same time, the navy opened a naval reserve for women. In both organizations, women served noncombat support functions, usually medical, educational, and clerical.

The Family Law Ordinance of 1961 moved Pakistan toward a more modern, secular vision of women's rights, establishing procedures for marriage, divorce, and prosecution of sexual offenses, which moved away from traditional tribal and religious judgment. The administration of Zulfikar Ali Bhutto (1970–1977) expanded opportunities for employment in the civil service and foreign service and included gender equality in the constitution. In rural courts, however, judges were still following traditional mores.

General Zia, who seized control of the government in 1977, reversed many of these changes as he oriented the regime as a "return to Islam." Women in civil service and on television were required to cover themselves modestly and appear only in programs directly relevant to women and were withdrawn from foreign service. The 1979 Zina Ordinance reclassified many

> **Families of Prisoners of War**
>
> Following findings by the British House of Lords that the preemptive detention of terrorism suspects in prisons was unlawful, Parliament passed the 2005 Prevention of Terrorism Act, allowing for Control Orders restricting suspects the home secretary "reasonably believed" a threat to their homes for house arrest or severely restrictive curfews. Because many of these men lived with extended families, this quickly affected the women and children in their households, many of whom had come to Britain from countries like Jordan, Pakistan, and Afghanistan, and who followed traditional and conservative social customs mandating their modesty and separation from public life. The Control Orders' restrictions, which included forbidding the suspect to handle money or meet any unauthorized visitors, threw substantial family responsibilities onto women who had few skills to navigate British life and who often did not speak English. The children could be denied Internet access needed for school and were the victims of bullies and isolation imposed by the watch on their homes.
>
> As many of the prisoners had been tortured in the countries they fled as refugees to Britain, or who suffered debilitating injuries and depression in prison before 2005, the Control Orders prevented their proper medical and psychiatric treatment, which also deeply affected the women, some of whom developed mental illnesses of their own from the stress. The right of authorities to raid and search the home at any time added to an atmosphere to continual vulnerability and fear. In 2011, Control Orders were superseded by the Terrorism Prevention and Investigation Measures (TPIM), which allowed for more extensive electronic monitoring, although critics see this as a high-tech rebranding of the same preemptive imprisonment and restriction of liberty.

crimes as private matters, with the result that rapes were considered adultery, with punishments administered to women. Zia, a key American ally in the fight against the Soviets in Afghanistan, positioned his conservatism as a refutation of Western corruption and Communism. After Zia's death in a plane crash in 1998, Benazir Bhutto, the daughter of Zulfikar Ali Bhutto, and an outspoken, British-educated advocate for women's rights, became prime minister. Lacking support in the legislature, she was unable to change the laws Zia had put into place and instead had to promote opportunities for women through a Women's Ministry and in 1989 the establishment of the First Women Bank to provide support and financing for women starting businesses.

Among the many problems Bhutto faced in office were a resurging Taliban and domestic rebellion from the Muttahida Qaumi Movement (MQM), a minority population of Urdu-speaking immigrants to Karachi. Drawn from the urban middle class, and largely rejecting Islamist constraints on women, MQM was able to mobilize 7,500 women, whose presence at protests lent legitimacy to their demands. Military and police operations against the MQM stoked an escalation in violence, with 2,095 dead in Karachi by 1995. Women participated in the movement's kidnappings and assassinations, and witnesses report that they have tortured prisoners, as well as acting as lookouts, couriers, and smugglers. As men are arrested and killed, women take up more responsibility for mobilizing marches, usually appearing at the front has human shields, and taking responsibility for collecting bodies from the authorities after incidents of violence. Clashes between the MQM and the government continued in 2017.

Benazir Bhutto (1953–2007), daughter of Prime Minister Zulfikar Ali Bhutto, became the first woman elected to lead a Muslim majority nation when she served as prime minister of Pakistan from 1988–1990 and 1993–1996. Bhutto struggled with corruption, conservative religious opposition and hostility from the military, and in December 2007, she was assassinated while campaigning for her Pakistan People's Party. (AFP/Getty Images)

21st Century

Even during conservative Islamist governments, women continued to serve in the military medical service. In 2002, Major General Shahida Malik, a doctor, became the first woman to earn that rank, followed by Dr. Shahida Badshah. Because of the possibility of encountering acts of terrorism, women in the

Pakistani military began receiving limited combat training in 2004 but were still barred from active participation, which might place them in harm's way. Women in the early 2000s gained admission to the Naval Academy and graduated into jobs in logistics, education, and administration, but never on a warship or submarine. Women cadets from the army's academy appeared on the roster of ceremonial guards at Jinnah's tomb in 2006, a major departure from traditional practice, but one which his sister's actions made possible.

Somewhat surprisingly, the Pakistan air force admitted women to pilot training in 2003, with the first graduates earning their wings in 2006. Along with women qualified to fly transports and helicopters, some have been assigned to F-7s, a fighter airframe. Flight Officer Marium Mukhtar, flying an F-7 in 2015, crashed with her copilot and died. Because she had lost the chance to bail out at proper altitude in order to pilot the aircraft away from a populated area, she was hailed as a martyr. She received a military funeral, and the state TV channel made a movie of her life, *Ek Thi Marium* (2016).

Under the presidency of Asif Zardari, Benazir Bhutto's widower, laws passed in 2010 making sexual harassment and acid attacks a crime, as well as rewriting the procedures for prosecuting rape to include DNA evidence. Several women served in high-profile cabinet jobs, including Hina Rabbani Khar, the foreign minister, and Nargis Sethi, the first woman defense minister. In 2013, 24 women from the medical corps and computer support offices graduated from the paratrooper course. Within the police force, women have served as sky marshals since 9/11, and the force includes women in high-risk jobs like the bomb disposal unit.

This expansion of military trades for women is tied to the recent trend by the global jihadi movement of using women as operatives. In 2011, three women suicide bombers, one known to be from Tehrik-e-Taliban, detonated themselves in public spaces. Others have been intercepted before they could execute their plans. Having women at checkpoints, as security guards, and in the criminal justice system is vital to preventing and controlling this new threat.

Further Reading

Abbas, Zaffar. "Pakistan Gets Women Combat Pilots." BBC News, March 30, 2006. http://news.bbc.co.uk/2/hi/4861666.stm.

Brittain, Victoria. *The Meaning of Waiting: Tales from the War on Terror*. London: Oberon Books, 2010.

Brittain, Victoria. *Shadow Lives: The Forgotten Women of the War on Terror*. London: Pluto Press, 2013.

Cohen, Stephen Philip. "The Role of the Military in Contemporary Pakistan." In *The Armed Forces in Contemporary Asian Societies*, edited by Edward Olsen and Stephen Jurika, 285–308. Boulder, CO: Westview Press, 1986.

Desk, Web. "Flying Officer Mariam Mukhtar Dies in F-7 Jet Crash." *Nation*, November 24, 2015. https://nation.com.pk/24-Nov-2015/flying-officer-mariam-mukhtar-dies-in-f-7-jet-crash.

Gagnon, Madeleine. *Women in a World at War: Seven Dispatches from the Front*. Burnaby, BC: Talonbooks, 2003.

Haroon, Anis. "'They Use Us and Others Abuse Us': Women in the MQM Conflict." In *Women, War and Peace in South Asia: Beyond Victimhood to Agency*, edited by Rita Manchanda, 177–213. Thousand Oaks, CA: Sage, 2001.

Jafar, Afshan. "Women, Islam, and the State in Pakistan." *Gender Issues* 22, no. 1 (2005): 35–55. doi:10.1007/s12147-005-0009-z.

Jamal, Amina. "Feminist 'Selves' and Feminism's 'Others': Feminist Representations of Jamaat-e-Islami Women in Pakistan." *Feminist Review* 81, no. 1 (2005): 52–73. doi:10.1057/palgrave.fr.9400239.

Noor, Saba. "Women Suicide Bombers: An Emerging Security Challenge for Pakistan." *CTTA: Counter-Terrorism Trends and Analysis* 3, no. 11 (November 2011): 1–3.

"Pakistan Army: First Female Paratroopers Make History." *Express Tribune*, July 14, 2013. https://tribune.com.pk/story/576801/pakistan-army-first-female-paratroopers-make-history/.

Papanek, Hanna. "Purdah in Pakistan: Seclusion and Modern Occupations for Women." *Journal of Marriage and the Family* 33, no. 3 (1971): 517. doi:10.2307/349849.

Rizvi, Hasan-Askari. *Military, State and Society in Pakistan*. London: Palgrave Macmillan, 2014.

Zedner, Lucia. "Preventative Justice or Pre-Punishment? The Case of Control Orders." *Current Legal Problems* 60, no. 1 (2007): 174–203.

Palestine

Background

Ottoman sultan Abdul Hamid II's decision to allow emigration from Zionists in eastern Europe disrupted the lives of the Arab Muslims and Christians in Palestine. As settlers moved in and bought land from absentee landlords in Istanbul, which they terraformed with irrigation and reclamation projects, the earlier inhabitants found themselves squeezed out of the labor market and the changing society. These tensions accelerated during World War I, when the British issued promises, including the Balfour Declaration and Sykes-Picot Agreement, which threatened traditional allegiances and the future of Palestine as a Muslim-majority area. The British, with Jewish help, put down the 1936 Arab Revolt against this wave of change, and in 1947, the creation of the nation of Israel changed life forever. Neighboring Islamic countries declared war immediately, and in the ensuing fighting, Israel gained considerably more territory than the original UN plan. For the 520,000–800,000 Palestinians who fled, and found that they could not, or did not, want to return to their homes, this was al-Nakba, the disaster.

Egyptian leader Abdul Nasser created the Palestine Liberation Organization (PLO) in 1964, but it was quickly taken over by Yasser Arafat and other diaspora Palestinians, who had founded the nationalist movement Fatah in 1959. Having lived in exile for more than a decade, Palestinians in Jordan had created an extensive state within a state, one so threatening to the Jordanian government that in September 1970, the Jordanian army conducted a purge and ejected the PLO and its adherents, along refugees. The presence of Palestinians also exacerbated tensions and led to the Lebanese Civil War (1975–1990).

The PLO leadership retreated to Tunisia, much to the resentment of the hundreds of thousands of people living in camps, which had become their permanent residences. PLO-affiliated groups executed the massacre of Jewish athletes at the 1972 Munich Olympics, as well as hijackings and bombings. In

> **Children and War**
>
> Licensed by the Palestinian Authority (PA), the al-Aqsa TV network run by Hamas premiered a startling children's program in 2007. "Tomorrow's Pioneers" featured a young, hijab-wearing host, Saraa Barhoum, who took calls from children and acted in skits with a cast of costumed animal characters. Barhoum encouraged children to prepare to fight for Palestine and celebrated martyrdom. The character Farfour the Mouse was killed on air by an actor playing an Israeli interrogator, Nahoul the Bee died from lack of access to a hospital, and Assoud the Rabbit was a casualty in a rocket attack. Nassur the Bear survived to the end of the show's run in 2009. The producer of the show insisted that these experiences were common to Palestinian children and that the show helped them cope with everyday life under Israeli occupation. The show received scathing criticism for its use of cartoons and children to encourage terrorism and anti-Semitism, and the Disney Company demanded Farfour, who bore a striking resemblance to Mickey Mouse, to be discontinued.
>
> Although the show ended production, episodes air on Middle Eastern TV stations and are available on the Internet. Barhoum, the niece of a Hamas spokesman, has cultivated a singing career and makes music videos continuing to celebrate martyrs and the actions of Hamas. Israeli Educational TV attempted to counter this programming with a show developed with the U.S. Children's Television Workshop, about a street where Arabs and Israelis coexist, including segments designed by child psychologists to help viewers process trauma. Some members of the PA felt that the show damaged their cause by reaching out to children with hateful rhetoric, and the PA took the show off the air shortly before the station passed out of their control in 2009.

1970, Leila Khaled, of the Popular Front for the Liberation of Palestine, twice hijacked airplanes, once carrying on the explosives in her bra, startling the passengers and crew that it was the diminutive woman in the white pantsuit who was in charge and not the man with the machine gun. Bilal Mugrabi, in the process of hijacking a bus in Lebanon, chose to blow it up when it was boarded by Israeli soldiers. Women fighting in the Lebanese war, like Loula Abboud, led units that ambushed Israeli patrols.

First Intifada

In 1987, Palestinians began the First Intifada, or uprising, in response to an incident in which an Israeli truck struck a car in the Jabalia refugee camp,

Palestine 217

Leila Khaled, the first woman to hijack an airliner, and a member of the Popular Front for the Liberation of Palestine, smiles down on the West Bank from a mural on Bethlehem's Apartheid Wall. Khaled, who has since renounced violence, was elected to the Palestinian National Council. (Ian Walton/Getty Images)

killing four. For the next six years, Palestinians engaged in a full spectrum of resistance activities, from throwing Molotov cocktails to refusing to pay taxes. From the beginning the ability to carry out this uprising rested on the cooperation of Palestinian women who established a parallel economy, donated blood, produced and smuggled food, and refused to buy goods from Israeli vendors. The Israel Defense Forces (IDF) lost considerable international goodwill through its repressive response, using 80,000 soldiers and engaging in tactics like breaking bones and using tear gas on protesters. The Likud Party in Israel believed that it could weaken the PLO by promoting alternative groups among the Palestinians, especially the one that would evolve into Hamas, and it began to gain ground in local councils.

This did not temper the intifada, but it did have an effect on the women. Hamas, as an Islamist organization, discouraged women from direct action. One of the founders of the PLO, Khalil al-Wazir, put his wife, Um Jihad, in charge of disbursing funds to the families of martyrs, a significant position of power, but after his death in 1988, she agreed with the increasingly dominant voices insisting that the role of women was to be the domestic support of the movement, and the mothers of martyrs, although women continued to march in the front of demonstrations as human shields.

The 1993 Oslo Accords, which ended the intifada and established the Palestinian Authority as a government entity, also created a large bureaucracy including women. In the 21st century, this has evolved to employ women as police officers, 3 percent of the 30,000 strong force, and 400 women in Yasser Arafat's Presidential Guard of 16,000 members. High unemployment has made it attractive for women to have these jobs, although some groups believe that the Palestinian Authority is too collaborationist. In 2014, having also received training from Jordan and the United States to be more professional and effective, the Presidential Guard trained 22 women in a commando course. The PLO's spokeswoman during the Oslo process, Hanan Ashrawi, offered a modern face to the party, but as the conditions of the accord collapsed in the 1990s, Ashrawi also faded from political prominence.

Second Intifada

Ariel Sharon made a provocative visit to the Temple Mount in 2000, sparking a second intifada by the Palestinians, met with responding force by the IDF. In August 2001, in retaliation for the deaths of two Hamas commanders, a male suicide bomber detonated a nail bomb at a Sbarro pizza restaurant, striking at dinner time and killing 15 people, some of them children, wounding an additional 130. The bomber's handler, who had scouted the location, and delivered him to the site, was Ahlam al-Tamimi, a 20-year-old Jordanian-born journalist and student, whose westernized appearance allowed her to pass unnoticed in Jerusalem. The brutality of this attack shocked the international community as graphic pictures of the casualties appeared in the media.

As Hamas took the aggressive lead in planning and executing bombings and attacks, leaving Fatah appearing weak, Arafat gave a speech in January 2002, offering the idea that women might also join the struggle directly as *shahida* martyrs, an "army of roses." It is unlikely that Arafat anticipated women would answer his call immediately. The same month, Wisal Idris, a young woman medic for the Red Crescent, used her ambulance to transport a bomb, which she detonated at Jaffa Road in central Jerusalem, killing 2 and wounding 100 people. Her funeral became a huge Fatah event, and Saddam Hussein placed a plaque in Baghdad commemorating her act.

In February 2002, Darine Abu Aisha, acting in the name of Hamas, made a suicide video and then detonated a bomb at a Jerusalem checkpoint. The spiritual leader of Hamas, Sheikh Ahmed Yassin, who had been adamantly against women's participation, issued a fatwa allowing women to undertake direct action and outlined that they would receive the same benefits of martyrdom as men. They would be restored to health and beauty in paradise, and they would be able to recommend 70 people to Allah to gain entry as well. Over the next year, two more women performed suicide bombings. Between 2002 and 2009, along with acting as lookouts, fund-raisers, smugglers, and recruiters, women attempted 96 suicide attacks, completing 8.

Motivations

This large pool of women, many in Israel's HaSharon prison, has been studied extensively by criminologists, psychologists, and security analysts seeking an explanation for the increasing presence of women in violent terrorist acts. Palestinian society is conservative and collective, with women's identity grounded in her family, and preserving the family's honor. At all points of their lives, these women are monitored by men, from their fathers to their husbands to their sons, with few alternatives to an early marriage, large family, and constrained life in crowded and dangerous Palestinian camps, which have evolved into sprawling shantytowns. While violence is a defining feature of Palestinian men's identity, women usually define themselves and are defined by their motherhood. In the vocabulary of sociology, women are doubly oppressed, by being part of a minority population, as well as a woman in a deeply restrictive patriarchal society. In court, one man explained that his woman bombing partner had no knowledge of the plan, telling the judge that women have "half a brain."

Why, then, are there women suicide bombers? Studies almost always discount the same kind of radicalization in the ideology of extremist Islam that men evidence in suicide videos. Women tend to describe themselves as being more disciplined and devoted and better than Israeli or Western women, who are spoiled, weak, and selfish, while they are making the ultimate sacrifice. One of the possibilities offered is that the women have been manipulated, sometimes catfished, on the Internet. Some of the women resent that their handlers demand that they surrender all of their personal valuables and money to them before going on the mission and that they experience rushed and cursory rituals of departure, like the videotaping. Another possibility is that the women feel as if their martyrdom is redeeming them or their families or getting revenge for the death of a loved one. Wisal Idris had been divorced by her husband for infertility, while Darine Abu Aisha's father, a contractor, had been ostracized by his community for working with the Israelis. Being searched or harassed at a checkpoint may be so socially devastating to a culture that prizes modesty that death is the only outlet. Because of the celebrity status offered to bombers who carry out their missions, featured on posters, trinkets, and videos, and known to the whole population, the appeal may be exciting and meaningful to women whose futures are constrained by economic depression and poor marital prospects.

In a single month, November 2006, two women detonated suicide bombs. One, Marwa Masoud, was a young student, acting on November 6, while on November 23, Fatima Omar Al-Najar, a grandmother of 53, blew herself up. Mariam Farhat, the mother of three men who committed suicide bombings, is widely admired and won election as a representative of Hamas. Suicide bombers are the "smart bombs of the poor," able to detonate as circumstances offer, and women suicide bombers can infiltrate public spaces in a different way than men. Regardless of their motivation, there seems to be no sign of a reduction in the frequency of their appearances in terrorism, and in the repertoire of Palestinian resistance.

Further Reading

Berko, Anat, and Edna Erez. "Gender, Palestinian Women, and Terrorism: Women's Liberation or Oppression?" *Studies in Conflict & Terrorism* 30, no. 6 (2007): 493–519. doi:10.1080/10576100701329550.

Bloom, Mia. *Bombshell: The Many Faces of Women Terrorists*. London: Hurst, 2011.

Brown, Katherine. "Blinded by the Explosion? Security and Resistance in Muslim Women's Suicide Terrorism." In *Women, Gender and Terrorism*, edited by Laura Sjoberg, Grace Cooke, and Stacy Reiter Neal, 194–226. Athens: University of Georgia Press, 2011.

Davis, Joyce. *Martyrs: Innocence, Vengeance and Despair in the Middle East*. New York: Palgrave Macmillan, 2004.

Gagnon, Madeleine. *Women in a World at War: Seven Dispatches from the Front*. Burnaby, BC: Talonbooks, 2003.

Gelvin, James L. *The Modern Middle East: A History*. New York: Oxford University Press, 2016.

Kaufman, Joyce P., and Kristen P. Williams. *Women at War, Women Building Peace: Challenging Gender Norms*. Boulder, CO: Lynne Rienner Publishers, Inc., 2013.

MacDonald, Eileen. *Shoot the Women First*. London: Arrow Books, 1992.

Mayer, Tamar. *Women and the Israeli Occupation: The Politics of Change*. London: Routledge, 1994.

Naaman, Dorit. "Brides of Palestine/Angels of Death: Media, Gender, and Performance in the Case of the Palestinian Female Suicide Bombers." *Signs: Journal of Women in Culture and Society* 32, no. 4 (2007): 933–55. doi:10.1086/512624.

Nissenbaum, Dion. "Hamas TV's Child Star Says She's Ready for Martyrdom." McClatchy's, August 14, 2007. http://www.mcclatchydc.com/news/nation-world/world/article24468043.html.

Peteet, Julie M. *Gender in Crisis: Women in the Palestinian Resistance Movement*. New York: Columbia University Press, 1992.

Schweitzer, Yoram. "Palestinian Female Suicide Bombers: Virtuous Heroines or Damaged Goods?" In *Female Terrorism and Militancy: Agency, Utility and Organization*, edited by Cindy Ness, 131–45. London: Routledge, 2008.

Sjoberg, Laura, and Caron E. Gentry. *Mothers, Monsters, Whores: Women's Violence in Global Politics*. London: Zed Books, 2013.

Victor, Barbara. *Army of Roses: Inside the World of Palestinian Women Suicide Bombers*. London: Constable, 2004.

Philippines

Background

Islam reached the Philippine islands in the 13th century, where, along with tribal religions, it became the predominant faith until Spanish explorers claimed and colonized the land in the 16th century, imposing Catholicism as the official church. Women took prominent roles in resisting the Spanish and are remembered in popular culture as heroines. Gabriela Silang, whose husband was assassinated during his attempt to use the British presence during the Seven Years' War to eject Spain, took over his troops, and she was executed after her capture in 1763. Gregoria de Jesus founded the women's division of the Katipunan, or anti-Spanish independence movement in 1896, and Salud Algabre, as a Sakdalista, led a 1935 protest against landlordism and corruption. The prevailing image of Philippine women, however, was the idealized Maria Clara, fictional heroine of the popular nationalist novel *Noli Me Tangere* by Jose Rizal, which assigned women to be chaste and docile and guard their honor while men achieved independence.

The Spanish-American War in 1898 ejected the Spanish from their longtime colony but replaced them with an American administration rather than independence. In the ensuing fighting between the Americans and the forces led by Emilio Aguinaldo, women were not combatants but were treated with great brutality by the Americans if suspected of aiding the rebels. Aguinaldo surrendered to the Americans in 1901, but the Moro people of Mindanao did not accept the treaty. The Moros, a significant Muslim majority, had made the Bates Treaty with the Americans in 1898, staying out of the conflict in exchange for autonomy. This was abrogated, triggering a guerrilla war lasting until 1913. In this case, Moro women fought as combatants, alarming American soldiers who had, after their violent counterinsurgency tactics had been condemned in the United States, been ordered not to fire on women. The numbers are unknown, but they were enough to inspire a popular song, "If a Lady's Wearing

> **Humanitarian Operations**
>
> Beginning in the 1990s, major humanitarian relief organizations like Oxfam and the International Committee of the Red Cross began studying specific ways in which women interacted with relief programs. Subsequently, they published guides meant to shape planning and execution of aid operations in ways that ensured women access to resources like food distribution and medical care and encouraged their participation in stabilization efforts. Along with recommendations that organizations keep and monitor disaggregated statistics by age, gender, and family status (widows, heads of household, and separated minor children), they offered insights into why and how help must be extended in culturally acceptable ways that take into account the special circumstances of women in conflicts.
>
> Women left to protect family property may be targeted because they are loved ones of combatants, or are unarmed, and they may not have papers or ownership documents in their own names. Medical personnel should include women and those with expertise in gynecology and female genital mutilation (FGM), if that is part of the area's customs, and strict privacy and confidentiality should be offered. Childcare should be provided so that women can queue for food, participate in food-for-work programs and other services, and their toilet, cooking, and foraging (for firewood, food, and water) areas should be well lit and protected. Checkpoints and curfews should be enforced in ways that do not invite authorities to harass, demand bribes from, or constrain women unnecessarily and information should be provided in ways designed to reach those with low literacy or keeping traditional seclusion. These efforts, included in planning and offering services to refugees and people displaced by conflict, can help mitigate disproportionate burdens on women affected by 21st-century war.

Pantaloons." Women in the 1930s campaigned for suffrage, which was granted in 1937, and against the growing power of landlords who had transitioned from paternal management of the land into sharecropping capitalists, to the detriment of their tenants. Some were active in the Communist Party of the Philippines, founded in 1938.

The Huks

The Japanese invaded the Philippines in 1941, prompting many activists to set aside their ultimate aims of nationalism, independence from the United

States, or communist economic reform, in order to resist. The Hukbalahap, or People's Anti-Japanese Liberation Army, or the "Huks," was extremely successful. Women most frequently acted as couriers and intelligence gatherers and maintained supply relationship with villages, while the Huks retreated into the jungle, but in 1942, a raiding party led by Felipa Culala ("Dayang Dayang") swept into Mandili to rescue prisoners held there and then ambushed a party of collaborating police and Japanese soldiers. The Huks were partners of the United States in liberating the Philippines, especially rescuing American soldiers held in Japanese prison camps in Luzon.

The Huks were very disillusioned by the postwar retention of elite collaborators in the new, independent government and reconstituted their units as an explicitly communist resistance to exploitation and economic inequality. The Huks attempted to model their political ideals in their guerrilla structure, contracting civil marriages (sometimes polygamous ones because of a first wife remaining in the barrio) and the women rejecting conventional femininity in favor of a rifle and ambushes. Edward Lansdale, the U.S. military's expert on counterinsurgency, aided the Philippine government in suppressing the Huks through psychological operations and rehabilitating Huk prisoners. In the case of women like Remedios Gomez, seen by the press as the "Joan of Arc of the Philippines," this took the form of elaborate makeovers and restoration of proper womanliness, sometimes through Cinderella-style weddings attended by high Catholic Church officials and the president, Ramon Magsaysay. In a particularly cruel tactic, the Philippine army made it a point to find and seize the Huks' children, calling them "Hucklings," and place them with politically reliable families. Through these means, the Huks were defeated by 1957, and they faded away, although some of their women leaders were sought out by women in the 1970s feminist movement as speakers and role models.

The New People's Army (1969–present)

The causes for which the Huks fought had not seen significant improvement in the 1960s. Younger activists, influenced by the Cultural Revolution in China, revived the revolution in Luzon as a Maoist movement, rather than the Marxism of the Huks, and began a protracted "people's war" against the government. Taking Maoist military theory as its model, the New People's Army (NPA) included armed women combatants, popularly called *amazonas*, after the mythological Amazons, and ebbed and flowed with the degree of government pressure and provocation. Never receiving substantial support from an external sponsor like the Chinese, the NPA depended on capturing government arms and equipment, and through extortion of businesses. Women in the NPA often took advantage of the Philippines's traditional gender roles and negotiated in public with the military, where they were treated with more deference, but they were also the subject of vicious torture, including rape, with many military interrogators convinced that skin moles were a sign of Communist sympathies and a reason to strip search and assault women prisoners. The Maoist orientation of the NPA only went so far against ingrained expectations, and few women acted as leaders, although they insisted on community programs like the ones that offered vocational training to sex workers after the closure of Subic Bay Naval Base and Clark Air Force Base by the American military in 1991. Currently, the NPA is active, with about 10,000 members, and is considered a terrorist organization by the Philippine government and the United States.

The Mindanao National Liberation Front (1969–1996)

The Moro people, a substantial Islamic population, were increasingly pushed out of their traditional living areas and culturally marginalized by waves of post–World War II Catholic settlers, including businessmen with private armies who began exploitative and extractive industry on Moro land, almost always with government approval. The Mindanao National Liberation Front's (MNLF) orientation, although majority Muslim, is nationalist and secessionist rather than sectarian, putting it at odds with the Moro Islamic Liberation Front (MILF). Fighting began in 1972 against the Marcos regime, and lasted until 1996, killing approximately 100,000 people and displacing 500,000 more. Part of the escalation and violence was that not only did the Philippine army attempt to suppress the MNLF, but local Catholics also formed militias, called "Ilaga,"or rats, and both provoked and retaliated. Women were active in the MNLF, forming the Subong Bangsa Bai as a women's division, which not only fought as combatants but also provided medics, intelligence, and community education. The Bangsamoro Women's Committee operated as a funding arm, collecting alms and food for the guerrillas.

Government reforms under Corazon Aquino successfully addressed some of the MNLF's demands, enough that the movement declined in relation to its rivals, and its leaders were amenable to cease-fire talks in 1996. As part of this amnesty, many women left the movement to attend college, start families, or retire from political activism. Giobay Diocolano left the MNLF, earned a university degree, and returned as the founder of a nongovernmental organization (NGO) meant to rebuild communities after the fighting. As part of an extraordinary rehabilitation agreement, the Philippine military offered ex-MNLF fighters 5,750 slots in the army, and 1,500 in the national police force, with fighters allowed to assign their slot to a family member proxy. Twenty-eight women, 11 of them proxies for their fathers or brothers, accepted the offer. This has been most successful in the police force, which had recently opened women's and children's desks to investigate domestic violence and child neglect, as the army placed almost all of the MNLF women in desk jobs.

The Moro Islamic Liberation Front (1969–2014)

Just as young activists became interested in the Chinese Cultural Revolution, others looked to religion, with larger numbers of Muslims from Mindanao performing the Hajj to Mecca and encountering transnational Islamic political leaders. The founding of the MILF was sparked by the Jabidah massacre, in which the Philippine army murdered 29 Muslim recruits it was training. The original orientation of the movement, which was predominantly nationalist, changed in the late 1980s with the arrival of battle-hardened mujahideen from Afghanistan, who also connected the MILF to Al-Qaeda through Osama bin Laden's brother in law, Mohammed Jamal Khalifa, and his businesses in the Philippines. With significant diaspora funding and international jihadi goals, the MILF posed a significant threat to the Philippine military, with major battles at their Camp Abubakar in 2000 and at the Buliok Complex in 2003.

The MILF chose to engage in talks with the government, arriving at an agreement in 2014, which began a demobilization and disarmament process. The MILF used large numbers of male child soldiers, and although the presence of women was necessary to support operations, and women were seen in arms, the organization hides the identities and the roles of women. NGOs operating in the aftermath have been careful to frame their programs as community oriented, not ex-combatant oriented, so to include women who were certainly involved in the fighting. The agreement for the cease-fire included increased regional autonomy, in which several prominent women, like Sandra Siman and Zenadia Bubong, both married to former MNLF commanders (which makes it likely they were also members of the movement), have won election to local and regional political office.

The MILF spawned several splinter groups, which refused to honor the cease-fire, including the Abu Sayyaf group, which is explicitly Wahhabi and associated itself with the Islamic State (ISIL). It was responsible for the kidnapping and beheading of tourists, and the bombing of the SuperFerry 14, which sank and drowned 100 people in Manila Bay. It is likely that just as Al-Qaeda and ISIS began to use women as bombers and armed agents, continued fighting with the Philippine military will result in these groups using women in more public armed roles.

The Philippine Armed Forces

The Women's Auxiliary of the Philippine army was formed in 1963, and was limited to no more than 1 percent of the total personnel of the military. A similar cap, of 5 percent, applied to the National Police. The women who volunteered performed noncombat and medical duties, as well as ceremonial guard posts, for which the most beautiful and tallest candidates were selected. Uniforms and grooming standards emphasized their femininity and distance from combat, although all received training with the M-16 and Colt 45 pistol acknowledging the reality of the ongoing guerrilla conflicts. In 1976, they received permission to marry and remain in the service, so long as they had been in for five years, a period later reduced to three. Misconduct, including premarital sex or pregnancy, was ground for dismissal from the military. The military's participation in the end of the Marcos government and the election of Corazon Aquino was rewarded with a substantial pay raise in 1987, which, in also applying to women, made the army a desirable job.

Republic Act 7192 of 1993 opened all military trades to women, partially in recognition that their everyday work was on the front line of a multithreat insurgency. Women have served in special counterinsurgency (COIN) units and in educational teams sent to villages to represent the government. In 1999, the Philippine Military Academy admitted its first women students, capping the percentage at 5 percent while new barracks and other facilities can be built to accommodate them and changing the minimum height requirement from 5'4" to 5'2". The academy, long a source of social mobility and access to a network of prominent alumni, is a significant step toward women gaining the same political and economic advantage as male officers in their careers, and in their postservice lives. Arlene de la Cruz, graduating in 1999, was the top-rated cadet of her class, winning the ceremonial presidential saber. The first nonmedical general officer from the women's division was Ramon Gao in 2011, a personnel specialist, followed by Lina Sarmiento of the Philippine National Police. In 2013, the Philippines dispatched its first woman-led peacekeeping mission to Haiti, under Captain Luzviminda Camacho, also the first woman to command one of their naval vessels, the BRP *Manuel Gomez*. The prominent role of the military in Philippine politics, and the continued conflict with extremist groups, suggests that women will expand their roles in counterinsurgency and probably increase in number.

Further Reading

Advincula-Lopez, Leslie. "Military Educational Institutions and Their Role in the Reproduction of Inequality in the Philippines." In *Advances in Military Sociology: Essays in Honor of Charles C. Moskos*, edited by Guiseppe Cafforio, 307–25. Bingley, England: Emerald Publishing, 2009.

Berry, William E. "The Changing Role of the Philippine Military during Martial Law and the Implications for the Future." In *The Armed Forces in Contemporary Asian Societies*, edited by Edward Olsen and Stephen Jurika, 215–40. Boulder, CO: Westview Press, 1986.

Bertrand, Jacques. "Peace and Conflict in the Southern Philippines: Why the 1996 Peace Agreement Is Fragile." *Pacific Affairs* 73, no. 1 (2000): 37–54. doi:10.2307/2672283.

Hall, Rosalie Arcala. "Whose Job, What Job? Security Sector Performance in a Local Communist Frontline in Central Philippines." In *Advances in Military Sociology: Essays in Honor of Charles C. Moskos*, edited by Guiseppe Cafforio, 403–31. Bingley, England: Emerald Publishing, 2009.

Hall, Rosalie Arcala, and Julian Smith. "Women in Combat: Both Spoilers and Enablers of Peace." *Diplomat*, February 15, 2016. thediplomat.com/2016/02/women-in-combat-both-spoilers-and-enablers-of-peace/.

Hedström, Jenny, and Thiyumi Senarathna. *Women in Conflict and Peace*. Stockholm: International IDEA, 2015.

Hilsdon, Anne-Marie. *Madonnas and Martyrs: Militarism and Violence in the Philippines*. London: Allen & Unwin, 1995.

Lanzona, Vina. *Amazons of the Huk Rebellion: Gender, Sex, and Revolution in the Philippines*. Quezon City, Philippines: Ateneo de Manila University, 2012.

Licklider, Roy E. *New Armies from Old: Merging Competing Militaries after Civil Wars*. Washington, DC: Georgetown University Press, 2014.

Lindsey-Curtet, Charlotte, Florence Holst-Roness, and Letitia Anderson. *Addressing the Needs of Women Affected by Armed Conflict: An ICRC Guidance Document*. Geneva: ICRC, 2007.

Majul, Cesar Adib. *The Contemporary Muslim Movement in the Philippines*. Berkeley, CA: Mizan Press, 1985.

Mangosing, Frances. "PH Sends First Female Officer to Lead UN Peace-Keeping Mission." *Inquirer Global Nation*, October 28, 2013. globalnation.inquirer.net/88849/ph-sends-first-female-officer-to-lead-un-peace-keeping-mission.

O'Connell, Helen. *Women and Conflict*. Oxford, England: Oxfam International, 1993.

"Philippine Army Has First Female General." ABS-CBN News, April 6, 2011. news.abs-cbn.com/nation/04/07/11/philippine-army-has-first-female-general.

Selochan, Viberto. *The Military, the State, and Development in Asia and the Pacific*. Boulder, CO: Westview Press, 1991.

Tan, Andrew T. H. *A Handbook of Terrorism and Insurgency in Southeast Asia*. Cheltenham, England: Edward Elgar, 2009.

Ward, Jeanne, and Beth Vann. "Gender-Based Violence in Refugee Settings." *Lancet* 360, no. 1 (2002): 13–14. doi:10.1016/s0140-6736(02)11802-2.

Poland

Background

During the period of Poland's occupation by its Russian, German, and Austrian neighbors (1772–1918), resistance to foreign rule attracted the support of and depended on the participation of Polish women. Because of the decentralized nature of the uprisings, individual women could raise troops from their estates or join underground political networks. Those who chose to take up arms, like Captain Emilia Plater of the 1830 November Uprising, wore uniforms, organized and equipped local regiments, and accepted ranks. Their life stories were central to the Polish underground and diaspora's romantic nationalism, celebrating heroic sacrifice and resistance to oppression. In 1863, Maria Piotrowiczowa, from a wealthy landowning family, raised troops to fight the Russians in another uprising and was hacked to death by Cossacks. The ghastly circumstances of her death scandalized Polish patriots, who officially banned women from combat service, although women continued to join disguised in men's clothing. Nonmilitary women were instrumental in organizing and sustaining the hidden Polish educational system, which preserved the Polish language and sent well-qualified students like Marie Curie to European universities in evasion of restrictions imposed by the Russians.

In the years leading up to World War I, Polish women joined and participated in organizations like the Combat Wing of the Polish Socialist Party, which undertook violent action to agitate for national independence, including assassinations and bombings, with some setting up and running covert munitions and explosive factories. The chaos and confusion of the war allowed sub-rosa Polish groups to emerge and join the conflict, often with women as officers and soldiers. A Polish Legion, with an auxiliary Women's Intelligence Service, fought as part of the Austro-Hungarian Army in hopes of getting training and concessions after the war, while others attached themselves to the German Imperial forces for the same purpose. Marshal Josip Pilsudski formed

> **Girl Scouting**
>
> The Boy and Girl Scout movements retain significant elements of their founding relationship to the armed forces. Lord Baden-Powell created the Boy Scouts in 1908, in the wake of his experiences with subpar Boer War conscripts, and saw the organization as a way to improve the pool of British manpower. Although the Girl Guides, established in parallel, were never as explicitly paramilitary, the Polish iterations of both organizations were vital parts of Polish nationalism, guerrilla units, and military training. Between 1910 and 1918, scouting was illegal in Russian and German sections of Poland and operated as an underground network by Andrzej Markowski and his wife Olga Drahonowska-Malkowska, officers in the Polish Military Union, who ran training camps and children's homes for those orphaned or stranded by World War I. During the 1930s, girl scouting and its leadership were deeply intertwined with *Przysposobienie Wojskowe Kobiet* or Female Military Training to prepare girls to assist as auxiliaries.
>
> In 1939, Nazis and Soviets invading Poland targeted Boy Scouts as potential threats, along with military cadets, but largely overlooked the existence of the Girl Scouts, many of whom were absorbed into the "grey ranks" of the Polish Home Army, under the command of leaders like Anna Zawadzka (1919–2004). The postwar Communist government dissolved the organization in 1950, replacing it with a "Scout and Guide Organization" modeled on the Soviet Young Pioneers, but scouting survived underground and in the diaspora population. In the 1980s, as one of the few organizations allowed some independence, a revival attracted 3 million members and had leaders allied with the Solidarity movement. Today, Polish Girl Scouting is intensely nationalistic and cognizant of its heroic past, with an oath that includes serving the Homeland, and its events and rituals, like wreath laying and celebrations closely tied to the military.

the Polish Military Organization as an independent force, which accepted women like Maria Wittek, to both act as frontline combatants and serve as support troops, while the Voluntary Legion of Women and People's Militia's existed to raise supplies and undertake local functions. These groups continued to fight until 1922, pushing back the Ukranians and Russians and establishing the borders of the newly re-created Polish nation.

Unusually for a postwar civilian population, Poland did not expect women to return to domesticity. Women gained suffrage in Poland in 1918, and women veterans of World War I and the independence movement held jobs as physical education teachers, scout leaders, and social service workers, from which they advocated for voluntary training programs. Throughout the 1920s and 1930s, the Female Military Training Program ran nongovernmental, voluntary summer camps and classes for thousands of women to teach them first aid, shooting, emergency management and driving, radio, and self-defense skills, in parallel with the mandatory conscription demanded of Polish men. In 1938, with war looming in Europe, the government authorized Maria Wittek to form an official Women's Auxiliary tasked with crewing antiaircraft guns and working in communications, signals intelligence, and sentry duties.

World War II and the Cold War

The 1939 invasion of Poland by both the Germans and the Soviets proved this planning fortuitous. The occupying forces made a point to target and eliminate the Polish army, its cadets and male organizations, like the Rifleman's Clubs, which could be threatening, but largely ignored women. These prepared women moved into the Polish Home Army, often in positions of command, eventually numbering at least 22 percent of the force. In recognition that they were full combatants, rather than an auxiliary, the Home Army sent Elzbieta Zawadzka to London to petition the government-in-exile for an official proclamation of their status. Zawadzka, already a commando with the *Cichociemni* (Silent Unseen), trained as a parachutist while there and returned in 1943 with approval for Polish women to have the same rights and responsibilities as male soldiers. The Home Army's courier network was under the command of Wanda Kraszewska-Ancerewicz and had agents across occupied Poland and Western Europe, while other women did the equally dangerous work of destroying infrastructure, assassinating Nazi officials, and harassing the regime with propaganda and acts of public defiance. In the Warsaw Uprising of 1944, women were significant in the planning and execution of the operations, with more than 2,000 captured by the Germans, and, unusually, treated as prisoners of war rather than partisans.

The Communist government of postwar Poland wanted to eliminate any rivals for power or groups that might challenge their authority and cracked down on many wartime fighters who had no links to the new regime. Wittek and Zawadzka were imprisoned and forced into menial jobs, and women largely written out of the history sanctioned and taught by the party, even though this was in contrast to the official policy of gender equality before the law. Instead, the emphasis was on "Mother Poland" being defended by large, Warsaw Pact armies, and that women's role was to sacrifice sons for the cause, not derail trains and throw grenades themselves. In the 1980s, women workers and union leaders at the Gdansk Shipyards, like Anna Walentynowicz, formed the backbone of the growing Solidarity movement in opposition to the government, although Lech Walesa was its most recognizable leader to allies in the West. In 1988, in need of specialized personnel to augment male professionals and conscripts, the Polish military allowed women to join as medical officers.

The 21st Century

After 1989 and the severing of links to the Soviet Union and the Warsaw Pact, Poland followed a similar path to Hungary, requesting admission to NATO and accepting guidance about the inclusion of more women. President Lech Walesa promoted Maria Wittek to brigadier general in 1991 and then Zawadzka as a rehabilitation and apology for their persecution under communism. As of 2017, these are the highest ranks earned by women in the Polish armed forces. In 1999, the same year Poland sent an assault battalion to serve in NATO's operations in Bosnia, the government formed a Council on Women, which recommended full integration of women and immediate opening of military academies to mixed-gender classes. In tandem, Poland also phased out military conscription for men, concluding the transition in 2009, although reserving the right to call up men for military service in national emergencies and requiring women with medical or veterinary expertise to register for similar call-up in extreme situations. Under this new restructuring, women are not barred from any career field, although they may be withdrawn from situations in which they could be affected by biohazards, radiation, noise damage, or prolonged periods underground.

In 2016, only 5 percent of Poland's military were women, in contrast to Hungary's rapid inclusion of women into the ranks. Women have gained political traction in Poland's parliament through the implementation of soft quotas by participating parties in 2001 and legal election quotas (based on those of Scandinavian countries) in 2010, but the military does not present an attractive career option to most women. The small number of women in the Polish military are often deployed to Polish UN Peacekeeping detachments, which specialize in military police and special operations functions. One explanation for this slow evolution in Poland, despite their long history of capable military women, is that they consider their purpose to still be as a mass-military bulwark against Russia and prize numbers and infantry capabilities over the specialties that other nations have used to recruit women. As an attempt to present a welcoming face to potential recruits, the military has offered self-defense classes for women in more than 30 Polish cities and maintains close links to the Catholic Church and its social support organizations.

Further Reading

Fuszara, Malgorzata. "Poland: A Success Story? Political History of Introducing Gender Quota in Post-Communist Poland." *Teorija in Praksa* 54, no. 2 (2017): 317.

Gorecki, J. *Stones for the Rampart: The Story of Two Lads in the Polish Underground Movement*. London: Polish Boy Scouts' and Girl Guides' Association, 1945.

Grzebalska, Weronika, and Andrea Peto. "Militarizing the Nation: Gender Politics of the Warsaw Uprising." In *Gendered Wars, Gendered Memories: Feminist Conversations on War, Genocide and Political Violence*, edited by Ayse Gul Altınay and Andrea Peto, 121–33. New York: Routledge, 2016.

Gzyl, Karol. "The Polish Scouting and Guiding Association (ZHP) / English Summary." Związek Harcerstwa Polskiego, January 12, 2015. Accessed December 19, 2017. https://zhp.pl/serwis/en/.

Hauser, Ewa, Barbara Heyns, and Jane Mansbudge. "Feminism in the Interstices of Politics and Culture: Poland in Transition." In *Gender, Politics and Post-Communism: Reflections from Eastern Europe and the Former Soviet Union*, edited by Nanette Funk and Magda Mueller, 257–73. New York: Routledge, 1993.

"Information for Our Polish Member Organization." World Association of Girl Guides and Girl Scouts. Accessed December 19, 2017. https://www.wagggs.org/en/our-world/europe-region/member-organizations/Poland/.

Karkoszka, Andrzej. "Defense Reform in Poland 1989–2000." In *Post-Cold War Defense Reform: Lessons Learned in Europe and the United States*, edited by Istvan Gyarmati and Theodor Winkler, 165–88. Washington, DC: Brassey's, 2002.

Krwawicz, M. Ney. "Women Soldiers of the Polish Home Army." 2002. Accessed December 10, 2017. http://www.polishresistance-ak.org/12%20Article.htm.

Obradovic, Lana. *Gender Integration in NATO Military Forces*. Burlington, VT: Ashgate Publishing Group, 2014.

Penn, Shana. *Solidarity's Secret: The Women Who Defeated Communism in Poland*. Ann Arbor: University of Michigan Press, 2008.

Sinczuch, Marcin, Marian Kloczkowski, and Mariusz Wachowicz. "Polish Military Forces in Peacekeeping Missions and Military Operations Other Than War: Experiences after 2000." In *Advances in Military Sociology: Essays in Honor of Charles C. Moskos*, edited by Guiseppe Caforio, 157–71. Bingley, England: Emerald Publishing, 2009.

Zawadzka, Anna. *Dzieje harcerstwa zenskiego w Polsce w latach 1911–1948/49*. Warszawa: Harcerskie Biuro Wydawnicze Horyzonty, 2004.

Russia

Background

Among the Russian nation's earliest founders is St. Olga of Kiev, who, before she was canonized by the Orthodox Church for helping to introduce Christianity to the Slavs, defeated her enemies by getting them drunk and locking them in a sauna that she subsequently torched. Later in her campaign to establish her sons and grandsons as rulers of the Rus, she ended a siege by demanding a tribute of pigeons, to which her troops attached flaming straw and released back to their nests within the town. In the 18th century, Peter the Great's wife Catherine accompanied him on his military campaigns, while Catherine II's carefully cultivated relationship with the Imperial Guards allowed her to overthrow her husband, Peter III, in 1763.

During the Napoleonic invasion of Russia, peasant partisans engaged in the scorched earth tactics, which stranded the French in 1812, with women particularly feared for their viciousness. Among the uniformed military, one woman, Nadezhda Durova, served in male disguise as a cavalry officer and recorded her memoirs as *The Cavalry Maiden* (1836). Women were active in the revolutionary movement, as the wives and daughters of Decembrist officers sent into exile in Siberia, as well as joining in the more radical anarchist and Marxist movements. In 1878, Vera Zasulich attempted to assassinate the governor of St. Petersburg, beginning a wave of targeted terror attacks against government and royal figures. In the 1905 Russian Revolution, women were prominent in the trade unions and professional groups of teachers, medical workers, and reformers demanding change, as well as in the crowds of peasant marchers.

World War I

The demands placed on the Russian population by World War I could only be met by conscripting men and encouraging women to take their places in the

> **Suicide Bombers: The Chechen Black Widows**
>
> In June 2002, Khava Barayeva drove a truck full of explosives into a barracks building at a Russian base in Chechnya, becoming the first of the suicide bombers dubbed "Black Widows" by the Russian media. Nineteen women wearing explosives died during the Dubrovka Theater hostage crisis in 2002, most of them having expressed to family and friends that they intended to self-detonate. Since 2002, at least 50 percent of suicide bombings carried out in Turkey, Chechnya, and Sri Lanka involve women, with Chechen bombings having a high female participation rate of 81 percent. Although Russian journalists have suggested that the women were duped, coerced, or used as pawns, this does not seem to be the case.
>
> Studies of the video statements left by the women, and interviews with their families, strongly point to a desire for revenge for the deaths of a loved one or harsh treatment by the Russian authorities, a desire to be of service to their people, perhaps even to earn women status through proof that they could carry out a violent action or shame men into political action. Most of the women involved have some familial link to networks of jihadis and have adopted Wahhabi Islam, including the non-native hijab form of dress. While women are absent from the command level of Chechen terrorism, their ability to pass unsearched and unremarked allows for a deadlier selection of target and additional horror at the violence coming from female hands.

factories, fields, and heavy industrial works, with middle-class women taking on roles as managers and inspectors. Just as they had in the Crimean War, women, including members of the imperial family, volunteered as nurses and hospital workers, a role that fit neatly with the image of women as helpers and nurturers in support of military men. In the desperate need for manpower, women's detachments of volunteers were recruited as Red Cross drivers, telephone operators, and clerical workers.

In 1914, Maria "Yashka" Bochkareva, with the permission of Nicholas II, joined the Russian Second Army and distinguished herself as an noncommissioned officer (NCO) and rescued wounded men under fire. In 1917, with the support of General Brusilov and the Orthodox Church, she proposed that the Provisional Government allow her to form an all-woman battalion. From 2,000 volunteers, 300 made it through harsh training to form the First Russian Women's Battalion of Death, which went into battle at Smorgen, Lithuania, capturing 200 prisoners and outperforming the regular troops, who were drunk and poorly motivated. Princess E. M. Shakhovskaya and E. P.

Formed late in WWI under the Provisional Government, the soldiers of the 1st Russian Women's Battalion of Death stand with their bayonets after completing harsh basic training under Maria Bochkareva. Many of these women fought in the White Army against the Bolsheviks in the Russian Civil War, including Bochkareva, who was executed by the Soviet secret police in 1920. (George Rinhart/Corbis via Getty Images)

Samsonova volunteered and were accepted as military pilots. To prevent the operation of independent women's units raised by individual patrons, subsequent groups, like the Third Kuban Women's Shock Battalion, were absorbed by the Provisional army. Elements of these units defended the Winter Palace against Bolshevik troops, which also had large numbers of women. The Provisional Government offered positions to women in the Ministry of Social Welfare and was debating changes to the Russian civil code enfranchising women when the Bolsheviks seized power late in 1917.

The Bolsheviks had little time for feminism or women's rights separated from class warfare. British suffragette Emmeline Pankhurst had visited the Russian women's units in 1917 but was derided as "bourgeois" and an agent of the British monarchy. During the Civil War, women acted as Bolshevik political commissars and fought as a female infantry unit against Poland in 1920. During the 1920s, "New Soviet Women" entered engineering, hard sciences, and laboring trades in unprecedented numbers, along with encouragement to take leadership positions in youth groups, gun clubs, and sports. In 1925, a new law allowed for universal conscription, but in practice, this applied only to men.

Stalinism's crash industrialization program required women to drive tractors, lay bricks, weld steel, and mine coal alongside men, as well as participate in traditional peasant agriculture.

World War II

In 1939, the Universal Military Duty Law reaffirmed the ability of the Soviet state to conscript men and women and specifically required the registration of women with medical and technical skills. Few women served in the Soviet-Finnish War of 1939, but with the Nazi invasion of 1940, the Red Army mobilized 800,000 women (8 percent of the total force) along with tens of thousands of volunteers for civilian labor battalions. Unlike British and American planners, who had to contend with public opinion and squeamishness about women pulling the trigger of a gun, Stalin could mandate the combat availability of women.

Drawing from the popular flying clubs, Maria Raskova organized Aviation Group 122, which included the 586th Fighters and the 588th Night Bombers, who flew open cockpit Po-2 biplanes. At the tremendous cost of 27 percent casualties, the women pilots terrorized German soldiers, who gave them the nickname the "Night Witches." Women also proved to be excellent snipers, like Lyudmila Pavlichenko, whose tour of the United States under the sponsorship of Eleanor Roosevelt featured press conferences at which the young Russian woman, immortalized in a song by Woody Guthrie, laughed at questions about her cosmetics choices when she wanted to discuss her 309 kills. Mariya Oktyabrskaya and Aleksandra Boiko both raised money and bought their own T-34 tanks (one named "Front Line Female Comrade"), which they commanded with Stalin's approval and male crews. Partisans operating as irregular troops usually included women, who were treated especially harshly by Nazis when captured or killed.

At the end of the war, despite having earned 91 decorations as Heroes of the Soviet Union, and 100,000 women awarded medals for heroism, most were demobilized into noncombat jobs like air traffic control, parachute packing, and clerical work. Some women managed to stay in flight instruction and test piloting but were usually forced out and not allowed into civil aviation places with the national airline, Aeroflot. As an unusual exception, background as civilian pilots and skydivers created a pipeline for the Soviet space program, producing Svetlana Savitskaya (1982, Salyut 7), Yelena Kondakova (1994/1997), and Elena Serova (2014).

The Cold War—Present

Facing the effects of massive losses during World War II, the Soviet Union aggressively promoted pronatalist policies for women, prioritizing motherhood and rebuilding the population over women's wartime advances in the economy and discouraging birth control and abortion. Planners were particularly concerned with the comparative fertility of non-Slavic, Islamic women from the Soviet Republics and feared being outnumbered. Women had little representation in the Politburo outside of gendered ministries, although they had more seats in regional Soviets and continued to work in the professions, especially chemistry and engineering, at a higher rate than their Western counterparts. The proper role of women, aside from a greatly reduced number of noncombat support roles in the Red Army and the intelligence services, was as mothers willing to sacrifice their sons.

This ethos began to fail in the 1970s under the strain of Soviet rhetoric losing ground to the Western women's movement and the enduring shortages of consumer goods and labor-saving devices. Women who bore the brunt of shopping, cooking, line-standing, and child-rearing were increasingly disillusioned with the "second shift" after full-time jobs. The 1979 invasion of Afghanistan strained the ability of male conscripts and their families to deal with prolonged warfare without the acknowledgment and community support that has existed in World War II. Afghan veterans, known as "Zinky Boys," as a play on Russians as "men of steel" and on the zinc coffins secretly hustled back into Russia on night trains to hide losses, were a far cry from the "New Soviet Men" who defeated Hitler.

After the collapse of Communism, the Russian military languished under Yeltsin, downsizing from 3.4 to 2.3 million, with many leaving to join privatized businesses. Those who stayed complained of the terrible pay, decrepit housing, and low social status accorded to military personnel. Around 1990, the Russian military forces had only 10,000 women. In 1992, to fill in critical gaps, women were encouraged to volunteer as contract soldiers, drawing interest from the wives of remaining officers already living in remote garrison towns. Young men actively evaded their 18 months of conscript service, modeling themselves after the gangsters and oligarchs of the new economy rather than defenders of the motherland.

Chechnya, a mountainous, tribal region of the Caucasus, declared independence in 1991. Because the region sits astride crucial oil pipeline routes and access to the Caspian Sea, the government invaded to restore control in 1994. The Chechens responded with a grueling guerrilla campaign, including suicide bombings, hostage taking, and ambushes. As casualties mounted, the Soldiers' Mothers Association, founded in 1989 to protest the Afghan War and assist its veterans, criticized the ongoing abuse of recruits, pervasive and violent hazing, and high fatalities. The Russians ended the war in 1996, withdrawing and leaving the Chechen Republic independent and quickly shifting to Islamist control.

Circumstances were very different in 1999, when insurgents from Chechnya invaded Dagestan. Russian president Vladimir Putin, who rose to power from the state's security forces, would not rely on conscripts for a military response in the 11-year war that followed. More than 100,000 women now serve as contract soldiers, with more in the Federal Security Service (FSB) augmenting male agents. The use of career military and special forces allowed Putin to engage the Chechens far more aggressively than conscripts were willing to do, or was palatable to the public, as demonstrated in the ruthless actions sacrificing hostages at the Beslan school and the Dubrovka Theater, as well as the many human rights abuses reported in Grozny.

Putin's personal image is one of exaggerated machismo, and he is frequently photographed performing traditionally masculine activities like judo, riding on horseback, or shirtless. This carries over into the restored morale and reputation of the Russian military as aggressive and red blooded, despite the far greater presence of women in the forces. The government subsidizes women's groups that, unlike the Soldiers' Mothers, cooperate with the state, and this encouraged Afghan veterans' families to sue Svetlana Alexievich, the historian who collected oral histories of the "Zinky Boys," as defamatory and defeatist. Although many Russian women soldiers saw combat in Chechnya, the official policy is that they serve noncombat roles and are frequently presented as submissive and sexy. A media profile of Olga Maltseva, a battalion commander, stressed that at home, Maltseva's nonmilitary husband was the head of the family, despite her warfighting expertise. Other rituals, like Miss Russian Army beauty pageants, are meant to keep women in their place as well as encourage men to volunteer to work with them. Russia's population demographic makes it difficult to sustain the large military forces that currently exist. Political debates about conscripting women, as well as accepting them as military volunteers, have stalled, but the many potential threats in Russia's borderlands may soon force further consideration.

Further Reading

Alexievich, Svetlana. *Zinky Boys: The Record of a Lost Soviet Generation*. London: Chatto & Windus/Random Century Group, 1992.

Alexievich, Svetlana, Keith Hammond, and Ludmila Lezhneva. "'I Am Loath to Recall': Russian Women Soldiers in WWII." *Women's Studies Quarterly* 23, no. 3–4 (1995): 78–84.

Bigg, Claire. "Russia: Army Puts on a Pretty Face." Radio Free Europe/Radio Liberty, April 8, 2008. www.rferl.org/a/1059432.html.

Bloom, Mia. "Death Becomes Her: The Changing Nature of Women's Role in Terror." *Conflict & Security* 11, no. 1 (Winter 2010): 91–98. doi:10.1017/s1049096510000703.

Bloom, Mia. *Dying to Kill: The Allure of Suicide Terror*. New York: Columbia University Press, 2007.

Campbell, D'Ann. "Women in Combat: The World War II Experience in the United States, Great Britain, Germany, and the Soviet Union." *Journal of Military History* 57, no. 2 (1993): 301–23. doi:10.2307/2944060.
Cottam, Kazimiera Janina. *Women in Air War: The Eastern Front of World War II.* Newburyport, MA: Focus Publishing, 1998.
Eichler, Maya. "Militarized Masculinities in International Relations." *Brown Journal of World Affairs* 21, no. 1 (2014): 81–93.
Eichler, Maya. *Militarizing Men: Gender, Conscription, and War in Post-Soviet Russia.* Stanford, CA: Stanford University Press, 2012.
Griesse, Anne Eliot, and Richard Stiles. "Russia: Revolution and War." In *Female Soldiers: Combatants or Noncombatants?* edited by Nancy Loring Goldman, 61–84. Westport, CT: Greenwood Press, 1982.
Hamilton, V. Lee, David R. Segal, Mady W. Segal, Robert D. Caplan, Richard Price, and Amiram Vinokur. "How Downsizing the Russian Military Affects Officers and Their Wives (1995–1997, Russian Federation)." *ICPSR Data Holdings* (December 23, 2011). doi:10.3886/icpsr30542.v1.
Krylova, Anna. *Soviet Women in Combat: A History of Violence on the Eastern Front.* Cambridge: Cambridge University Press, 2014.
Mathers, Jennifer. "Women in the Russian Armed Forces: A Marriage of Convenience?" *Minerva* 18, no. 3–4 (2000): 135–48.
Nechemias, Carol. "Women and Politics in Post-Soviet Russia: Where Are the Women?" In *Women in the Politics of Postcommunist Eastern Europe*, edited by Marilyn Rueschemeyer, 8–35. New York: M.E. Sharpe, 1998.
Novikova, Irina. "Soviet and Post-Soviet Masculinities: After Men's Wars in Women's Memories." In *Male Roles, Masculinities, and Violence*, edited by Ingeborg Breines, Robert Connell, and Ingrid Eide, 117–30. Paris: UNESCO, 2000.
Pennington, Reina. " 'Do Not Speak of the Services You Rendered': Women Veterans of Aviation in the Soviet Union." In *A Soldier and a Woman: Sexual Integration in the Military*, edited by Gerard DeGroot and Corinna Peniston-Bird, 152–74. London: Longman Publishing, 2000.
Speckhard, Anne, and Khapta Akhmedova. "Black Widows: The Chechen Female Suicide Terrorists." In *Female Suicide Bombers: Dying for Equality?* edited by Yoram Schweitzer, 63–80. Tel Aviv, Israel: Jaffee Center Publication, 2006.
Stoff, Laurie. "'They Fought for Russia': Female Soldiers of the First World War." In *A Soldier and a Woman: Sexual Integration in the Military*, edited by Gerard DeGroot and Corinna Peniston-Bird, 66–82. London: Routledge, 2017.

Sierra Leone

Background

Like Liberia, Sierra Leone was founded as a resettlement colony for freed slaves. The British government needed a place for the thousands of former slaves their armies had freed and who had fought as Loyalists during the American Revolution, especially after the failure of settlements in Nova Scotia and the pressure of the presence of free black people in London, and carved out a piece of West Africa for this purpose in 1787. After 1807, when Britain outlawed the slave trade, thousand more former slaves were sent to the area, exacerbating tensions with both neighboring indigenous people and the slave traders who continued to operate in the region. Throughout the 19th century, the British favored westernized, Christian settlers, replicating British educational and legal systems and allowing domestic slavery and a restrictive apprenticeship process, which continually angered the indigenous people on whom these were applied.

Sierra Leone became a colony (the city of Freetown) and protectorate (the more populous hinterland) in 1924, followed by the granting of a monopoly on mining granted to DeBeers Company in 1935. A new constitution in 1951 brought colony and protectorate together, although this exacerbated tensions between the descendants of settlers and the majority Temne and Mende people. After independence in 1961, parliamentary government survived until 1967, when the prime minister, Sir Albert Margai, was perceived to be favoring the Mende people over the carefully balanced political alliance built by his half brother Sir Milton Margai, the first prime minister (d. 1964), and used increasingly authoritarian means to hold on to power and promote his political party. In the 1967 elections, the opposition party won a majority, triggering a military coup that removed Siaka Stevens, the putative prime minister. A rival military faction then staged a countercoup and restored Stevens to power. The erosion of political norms allowed Stevens to create a

> **Fictionalized Women in Conflict**
>
> A run-down brothel in the eastern Congo serves as a refuge for women, a trade station for diamond and coltan miners, and R&R club for government soldiers and rebel insurgents, all under the stern watch of Mother Nandi, who carefully negotiates a violent world of war crimes and exploitation. Lynn Nottage, inspired by Bertolt Brecht's play *Mother Courage* (1939), spent a Guggenheim Fellowship in Uganda and Kenya, visiting camps for displaced women and men being deradicalized from the Lord's Resistance Army. These interviews inspired the play, *Ruined*, which won the Pulitzer Prize for Drama in 2009, an unusual honor for a play with no American characters or references to American life.
>
> "Ruined" in Nottage's use can be the devastation of the land for commodities or the war crimes against women, including rape and enslavement. Two of the characters, Salima and Sophie, were kidnapped and sexually abused by rebel soldiers, then rejected by their families as disgraced. Sophie, additionally, has been so injured after being raped with bayonets and stick that she has constant infections and can no longer have sex without an expensive treatment in an inaccessible big city. Nottage presents the ways in which all of the women attempt to retain control of their bodies and their personal agency as the brothel endures visits from the government troops as well as their insurgent enemies and hosts the mining company agent whose foreign cash drives fighting over the resources in the ground. Nottage has subsequently won the 2017 Pulitzer for drama with her work, *Sweat*, about working-class American women in Pennsylvania.

single-party state, cemented by a 1978 new constitution and ruthless purges of enemies within the bureaucracy and the military. This lasted until 1991, when Stevens's successor, Major General Joseph Momoh, failed to deliver on reforms or anticorruption policy. The Revolutionary United Front (RUF), with help from Liberia's Charles Taylor, attacked, igniting an 11-year civil war.

Women had played little role in the parliamentary politics of Sierra Leone up to the outbreak of the war, although elite women held tribal chieftainships and were active in the educational institutions, and the everyday agricultural and market transactions of women formed the economic foundation of the country. Women typically married much older men, often in polygamous arrangements, and their dowries represented an important transfer of wealth. Women tended to have regular income streams through farming and trading, separate from their husbands, with which they maintained the household and which they could use to divorce. In rural areas, secret societies of women kept a monopoly on sexual and reproductive knowledge, conducting rituals that marked adulthood and status to girls. Young men, blocked from marriage and lucrative places in the civil service and education by their elders, formed a pool of potential angry and frustrated combatants.

Civil War

The long war involved not just the RUF, and the Sierra Leone army, but also Executive Outcomes, a South African mercenary company, another military coup under the Armed Forces Revolutionary Council, and peacekeepers from Economic Community of West African States Monitoring Group (ECOMOG) and the United Nations. Adding to the chaos, factions fought to possession of areas with lucrative resources like gold and diamonds, which they could easily sell to buy arms or luxury goods, and which they could force the civilian population to produce for them. It was not unusual for members of the military to become "sobels"—soldiers in the daytime, rebels at night, when there were opportunities for looting and extortion. In response, some areas fielded protective militias to defend themselves from all sides. Depending on the faction, women made up between 10 and 50 percent of the armed fighters, with a majority taking active part in operations and attending cross-border training in neighboring countries like Burkina Faso. Some women joined the groups willingly, even moving from the prewar army or police into a faction, while others were the victims of kidnapping or coercion for food and protection. Women might be attached to a male fighter, their status rapidly cycling with his, or take on status of their own as commanders like Adama "Cut-hand" Toronka of the RUF, who originated the practice of amputating prisoners' limbs as a terror mechanism. Theoretically, the RUF had a women's auxiliary that provided a matching woman counterpart for each male commander, but this was rarely fully staffed.

Attempts to end the conflict foundered on regional tensions and interfaction mistrust, as the UN commander accused Nigeria of working with the RUF to mine diamonds and the RUF seizing arms and equipment from peacekeepers. In 2000, however, the intervention of Guinea in the form of bombing raids on rebel camps, combined with the Chechnya-won expertise of Russian attack helicopters added to the UN contingent and reinforced by a British force that had originally been sent only to evacuate foreign nationals, tipped the advantage to the government of Sierra Leone and brought all of the factions to the negotiating table in 2002. In the previous 11 years, more than 50,000 people were killed, 70 percent of the schools had been destroyed, and, due to the pacification policies of the government, at least half of the population had been dislocated from their homes at least once.

The 21st Century

Disarmament, demobilization, and reintegration (DDR) programs faced the challenge of demobilizing, disarming, and reintegrating 75,000 combatants at 70 decentralized camps. Of the total participants, only 7 percent were women, and of the 6,845 children, 8 percent were girls. From the start, the programs overclassified women as victims and abductees rather than participants and armed combatants and framed a return to normalcy in terms of disarming men. One of the incentives for coming to a program was the $300 reward for a weapon, which caused men to take guns from women fighters, subsequently lessening the women's ability to claim entry to needed DDR services. Vocational training channeled women into gendered and oversaturated occupations like hairdressing and cloth dyeing, which would not support them independently, and the war had destroyed the traditional networks of trade and family land holdings, which could be used for credit and rebuilding. Some women refused to join DDR programs out of suspicion of the official photos and identification issued, or because they had sexually transmitted diseases (STDs) or genital trauma and were alienated by the doctors. Planners assumed most of the program members would be young men, so they failed to provide segregated toilets or medical treatment rooms, deterring women from seeking aid. Women who had been "bush wives" and subsequently had children, or who had formed sexual relationships with peacekeeping troops, and who do not want the children, or have been rejected by their families because of the children, face unemployment and social stigma, some turning to prostitution.

The current government of Sierra Leone has attempted to reintegrate former fighters. The new Sierra Leone army, which the British have helped to train, has absorbed thousands of ex-RUF members, including "Cut-hand" Adama, although she is a rare female exception in a male-dominated force. Other women ex-combatants have hired on with military contractors as support personnel for operations in Afghanistan, another avenue where the majority of Sierra Leone employees are men. The newly reconstructed Sierra Leone police force has a special unit for Family Support to combat domestic violence, and the laws have been altered to remove legal disadvantages of illegitimate children and speed the adoption process. More than a decade of war significantly upended women's lives, with peace offering few of the mitigations available to men.

Further Reading

Coulter, Chris. *Bush Wives and Girl Soldiers: Women's Lives through War and Peace in Sierra Leone*. Ithaca, NY: Cornell University Press, 2009.

Denov, Myriam. "Girl Soldiers and Human Rights: Lessons from Angola, Mozambique, Sierra Leone and Northern Uganda." *International Journal of Human Rights* 12, no. 5 (2008): 813–36. doi:10.1080/13642980802396903.

MacKenzie, Megan H. *Female Soldiers in Sierra Leone: Sex, Security, and Post-Conflict Development.* New York: New York University Press, 2016.
MacKenzie, Megan H. "Securitization and Desecuritization: Female Soldiers and the Reconstruction of Women in Post-Conflict Sierra Leone." *Security Studies* 18 (2009): 241–61. doi:10.18574/nyu/9780814761373.003.0005.
McKay, Susan. "Girls as 'Weapons of Terror' in Northern Uganda and Sierra Leonean Rebel Fighting Forces." *Studies in Conflict & Terrorism* 28, no. 5 (2005): 385–97. doi:10.1080/10576100500180253.
McKay, Susan. "Reconstructing Fragile Lives: Girls' Social Reintegration in Northern Uganda and Sierra Leone." *Gender & Development* 12, no. 3 (2004): 19–30. doi:10.1080/13552070412331332280.
McKay, Susan R., and Dyan E. Mazurana. *Where Are the Girls? Girls in Fighting Forces in Northern Uganda, Sierra Leone and Mozambique: Their Lives during and after War.* Toronto: CNIB, 2006.
Shepler, Susan. "Postwar Trajectories for Girls Associated with the Fighting in Sierra Leone." In *Gender, War and Militarism: Feminist Perspectives*, edited by Laura Sjoberg and Sandra Via, 91–101. Santa Barbara, CA: Praeger, 2010.
Thomas, Kevin J. A. *Contract Workers, Risk, and the War in Iraq: Sierra Leonean Labor Migrants at US Military Bases.* Montreal: McGill-Queens University Press, 2017.

South Africa

Background

In order to better serve as a trade depot and supply stop for their ships coming from Java, the 17th-century Dutch colonized South Africa with rural farmers, later derisively called "Boers," who remained isolated and traditionally Calvinist, away from changes in modern Europe. The Napoleonic Wars caused Dutch territories to pass into British possession, sparking cultural and legal clashes between a modernizing and increasingly antislavery British Empire and Dutch-originated Afrikaans settlers with patriarchal dominion over large *kraal* farms of wives, African slaves, and children. Those unwilling to live under British laws undertook the Great Trek north to establish their own states in the Transvaal and Orange Free State, provoking conflict with the Zulu people of that region and, after the discovery of gold and diamonds in the late 19th century, with the British.

Although women did not serve in uniform in the Zulu Wars or the Boer Wars, Boer women were expected to help defend their frontier homesteads, and British women followed their troops as wives, camp followers, and laundresses. In the Second Boer War, British general Lord Baden-Powell considered women and children so vital to the Boer commando operations that he established "concentration camps" into which 115,000 civilians could be separated from the combatants, denying them food and information, and giving the British hostages. As many as 28,000 died in the camps from disease and poor nutrition, causing international outrage and raising sympathy for the Boer cause, and creating the powerful symbol of suffering Afrikaans womanhood that the apartheid government would use to inspire protective and militaristic response from South African white men. After the Union of South Africa was founded in 1910, Afrikaners retained their grip on power although now a minority when combined with the British population, by threatening to withhold military support to the British Empire. This threat was a powerful one, as South Africa sent troops and supplies to World Wars I and II, including women nurses, drivers, and signal operators and vital materials like industrial diamonds, rubber, and palm oil.

Cold War and Apartheid

South Africa achieved independence from Britain in 1931 but remained part of the Commonwealth until forced out in 1961. One of the major points of friction had been the desire of the Afrikaans population to continue to restrict black land ownership and formalize a racial segregation system privileging the white minority. In 1948, the election of the National Party to power allowed the creation of the *Apartheid* regime, which brutally restricted nonwhite South Africans' civil rights, economic mobility, and standard of living, confining them to separate living spaces, educational systems, and exclusion from political power.

In this system, the South African military and police were a reflection of and enforcer of the white social order, with the military having significant political power. Military leaders insisted on conscripted national service by white men to ensure a large reserve force in the face of anti-apartheid movements seeking arms and aid from the Soviet Union and neighboring states' wars of decolonization flowing over the border. By 1971, male conscription alone was unable to meet the demands of South Africa's defense in expectation of an enemy's "total onslaught," although politicians who were afraid it would signal defeatism refused to consider anything but voluntary service for women. Previously, women had been military auxiliary nurses, and worked in the arms industry, but served mainly as home front supporters and highly publicized reasons for white men to feel protective of the nation. President P. W. Botha authorized the recruitment of "Botha's babies," women who would be trained for traditionally gendered communications, medical and clerical jobs to free up men for combat duty, and in 1985, established the South African Army Women's College to graduate 500 students a year.

In contrast, the resistance movement of the African National Congress (ANC) and other anti-apartheid groups was founded with the liberation and equality of women as a core tenant. In the ANC's armed wing, *Umkhonto we Sizwe*, or Spear of the Nation (MK), women like Thandi Modise and Jackie Sedibe trained side by side with men, often under the instruction of revolutionary advisers from Cuba or the Soviet Union. Women formed the backbone of the logistical supply of the movement, smuggling weapons and food, collecting intelligence, and organizing mass demonstrations against police brutality and restrictions confining nonwhite people to segregated townships. Some women committed themselves to peaceful means of protest, but others, including Winnie Mandela, argued the righteousness of moral violence, even retaliation against collaborators, was the only way to bring down the apartheid system.

Women activists were particularly adept at internationalizing boycotts and protests against South Africa, putting economic pressure on the regime.

Amalgamation and Integration

Under the leadership of F. W. de Klerk in 1990, South African began a process of dismantling apartheid and sharing governance, beginning with the decriminalization of the ANC and then the release of Nelson Mandela from prison. Among the many issues to be addressed was the downsizing of the military, the establishment of civilian control over it, and the integration of MK, Kwa Zulu, Azanian People's Liberation Army, and Inkatha Freedom Party soldiers into one national force. To build a common society united by shared institutions, this process took into account not just race but also gender, with targeted retention and recruitment goals to make the force better reflect South African society. With the drastic reorientation of the force's purpose to one of defense and peacekeeping rather than counterinsurgency and domestic repression, advocates argue that the inclusion of women also makes a more effective force through good community relations. The first woman promoted to the rank of general officer (now a major general) was Jackie Sedibe, the former head of MK communications branch, and wife of ANC political leader Joe Modise. As of 2011, women make up 26 percent of the South African military, with many seeing it as a desirable civil service job with prestige and potential for promotion.

Guidelines issued in 1997 opened all ranks and occupational specialties to women, including combat positions, with an estimate that 20 percent of women in 2016 were in combat jobs. This is a sea change from a military that feared that even the prospect of including women spelled defeatism and that the image of wounded or captured women would demoralize the population. Women continue to struggle with problems like lack of equipment and uniforms made for them and with perceptions that they received preferential treatment. As the South African Defense Force (SADF) undertakes peacekeeping operations in the Sudan, they make special effort to recruit women, in the hopes of increasing their ability to interact with the civilian population and handle issues like human trafficking and rape.

Additionally, paramilitary groups like the Black Mambas recruit women to do antipoaching work under military discipline and training. The women, who protect Kruger National Park, operate 21-day patrols into the veldt, spotting injured animals and illegal hunters, both at considerable risk to themselves. In a society where violence against women remains common, visible role models of military, police, and paramilitary women are an important signal to young women. Like their uniformed colleagues, the women serve as a reminder and symbol of South Africa's transformation from the rigid apartheid regime to one that draws strength from its diverse population and natural resources.

Further Reading

Boje, John. *An Imperfect Occupation: Enduring the South African War.* Urbana: University of Illinois Press, 2015.

Cilliers, Jakkie, and Lindy Heinecken. "South Africa: Emerging from a Time Warp." In *The Postmodern Military: Armed Forces after the Cold War*, edited by Charles Moskos, John Allen Williams, and David R. Segal, 242–64. New York: Oxford University Press, 2000.

Cock, Jacklyn. "Women and the Military: Implications for Demilitarization in the 1990s in South Africa." *Gender & Society* 8, no. 2 (June 1994): 152–69. doi:10.1177/089124394008002002.

Gans, Andrew, and Kenneth Jones. "Lynn Nottage's 'Ruined' Wins Pulitzer Prize for Drama." *Playbill*, April 20, 2009. http://www.playbill.com/article/lynn-nottages-ruined-wins-pulitzer-prize-for-drama-com-160117#.

Gener, Randy. "In Defense of 'Ruined': 5 Elements That Shape Lynn Nottage's Masterwork." *American Theater*, September 2010, 118–23.

Goyanes, Christina. "These Badass Women Are Taking on Poachers—and Winning." Nationalgeographic.com, October 12, 2017. https://www.nationalgeographic.com/adventure/destinations/africa/south-africa/black-mambas-anti-poaching-wildlife-rhino-team/.

Heinecken, Lindy. "Transitions and Transformation in Gender Relations in the South African Military: From Support in Warfare to Valued Peacekeepers." In *The Palgrave International Handbook of Gender and the Military*, edited by Rachel Woodward and Claire Duncanson, 355–68. London: Palgrave, 2017.

Leslie, Anita. *Train to Nowhere: One Woman's War, Ambulance Driver, Reporter, Liberator.* London: Bloomsbury, 2018.

Morris, Patricia. "Women, Resistance and the Use of Force in South Africa." In *Women and the Use of Military Force*, edited by Ruth Howe and Michael Stevenson, 185–203. London: Lynne Rienner Publishers, 1993.

Nottage, Lynn. *Ruined.* London: Nick Hern Books, 2012.

Steyn, J. J. "The Changing Face of South Africa's Military Forces." Master's thesis, U.S. Army War College, Carlisle, PA, 2001.

Unterhalter, Elaine. "Women Soldiers and White Unity in Apartheid South Africa." In *Images of Women in Peace and War*, edited by Sharon Macdonald, Pat Holden, and Shirley Ardener, 100–20. Madison: University of Wisconsin Press, 1987.

Van der Waag, Ian. *A Military History of Modern South Africa.* London: Grub Street, 2018.

Sri Lanka

Background

The island nation of Sri Lanka, previously called Ceylon, became a Portuguese and then Dutch colony after European discovery in 1505. The minority Tamil population, which converted to Christianity, or added Christian practices to their Hinduism, became favored for posts in the bureaucracy, much to the resentment of the Buddhist-majority Sinhalese. The British took over Ceylon after the Napoleonic Wars, importing tens of thousands more Tamil from southern India as indentured laborers for their tea plantations, enlarging the population and exacerbating ethnic tensions with their overt favoritism. In 1948, when the island gained independence, the Sinhalese renamed it Sri Lanka and began using their political majority to strip the Tamils of resources and power. In 1956, they imposed a Sinhala-language-only policy for official documents and employment and set quota pushing Tamils out of universities, civil services, and licensed professions. Throughout the 1960s, Tamils organized nonviolent protests and attempted to work politically, but violence flared when the Tamils achieved enough representation in Parliament to demand change.

Civil War

In order to compete for votes, Sinhalese parties became more intransigent toward the Tamils, while resistance parties began to form to take more violent action in achieving a separate Tamil state. Some of the parties, like the PLOTE (People's Liberation Organization of Tamil Eelam) and EPRLF (Eelam People's Revolutionary Liberation Front), drew from the proliferation of Marxist-Leninist guerrilla groups of the 1970s, but the eventual survivor of their brutal trials by firefighting the Sinhalese state and each other was the LTTE, or Liberation Tigers of Tamil Eelam. Velupillai Prabhakaran founded the group in

> **Child Soldiers**
>
> Insurgent groups often use children as lookouts, couriers, soldiers, and even suicide bombers, choosing this strategy because children are malleable, easier to control than adults, and in many situations, less suspected by an enemy of carrying contraband or posing a threat. Child soldiers, defined as anyone under the age of 18 engaged in armed conflict, are both kidnapped and conscripted into action but may also be attracted to an armed group for food, adventure, the attention of a charismatic leader, or access to luxury goods. Some groups, like the Liberation Tigers of Tamil Eelam (LTTE), ran orphanages, from which they created their Tamil Leopard units. Reintegrating child soldiers is difficult, as their communities and parents may be dead, or unwilling to take them back, and their social and emotional development has been warped by brutalization and deprivation.
>
> Niromi de Soyza (a chosen pen name) offers an account of her time in the Tamil Tigers at the point they began arming women, but before their launch of suicide bombings, joining at age 17 in rebellion against the strictures of caste and religion applied to her by an upper middle-class professional family and in response to recruitment techniques in the schools using handsome young men and appeals to emotional patriotism. Her shock at the violence, intergroup squabbles, and primitive living conditions led her to resign and rejoin her family in 1988. Unusually, the LTTE forbade sexual contact among their soldiers, so she did not experience rape or abuse, and her family both welcomed her back and had the means to send her to a rehabilitative boarding school and then emigrate to Australia. Her account has been criticized by Sinhalese as romanticizing the struggle as a propaganda tool for Tamils and by some Tamils as being a fabricated autobiography.

1972, advocating for preservation of a pure Tamil language and culture in a separatist enclave in the northeast portion of the island, and gained notoriety in 1975 for assassinating the mayor of Jaffna outside a Hindu temple.

In response to these acts of political terrorism, the Sinhalese-majority government enacted the Prevention of Terrorism Act in 1979, allowing the military and police to arrest and detain for 18 months anyone suspected of acts of "disharmony," which covered any protest or dissent. This was followed by Emergency Regulation 15A, which gave permission for the disposal of bodies without autopsy, identification, or report, essentially giving the authorities carte blanche to kidnap, murder, and hide the evidence, leading to a wave of disappearances and terror.

Throughout the conflict, women played a prominent role in the majority government. Sirimavo Bandaranaike became the world's first woman prime minister in 1960, pledging to honor the political agenda of her husband, S.W.R.D Bandaranaike, assassinated in 1959 after enacting the Sinhala-only language policy. The couple's daughter, Chandrika Kumaratunga, was elected to the prime ministership and then the presidency in 1994 after the assassination of her husband, a prominent actor, by a Marxist extremist. As she ascended to higher office, her mother resumed the position of prime minister. Both women leveraged their connection to martyred men, claiming the mantle of authority as "mothers of the nation" and instruments of their husbands' will to end the conflict.

The government also formed volunteer women's auxiliaries to all of its services' branches, beginning in 1972 with the air force. In 1979, the army created the Sri Lanka Army Women's Corps, modeled on the British Auxiliary Territorial Service (ATS), to cope with the increased demand the conflict placed on the Sri Lankan authorities, although, true to its ATS origins and the training of the first recruits in Great Britain, it restricted the women to support duties to free up men for combat by undertaking jobs like air traffic control, electronic warfare, nursing, law, and finance. In the 2000s, they organized all-women police units in order to more effectively deal with women prisoners and search women who might be LTTE agents at roadblocks and in public spaces.

In 1983, the LTTE ambushed and killed 13 government soldiers. The government responded by displaying their mutilated bodies and encouraging "riots" in response. These mob actions of "Black July" took the form of allowing Sinhalese hit squads to rampage through the civilian property of Tamils, some even armed with lists of targets and their valuable property. The LTTE, which had been weakened by the loss of supporters to disappearances and torture, opened their organization to women. Unlike their Marxist-Leninist Tamil rival groups, whose ideology built women into participation from the start, the LTTE had to retrofit women into their vision of a pure Tamil culture. As women occupied a distinctly subordinate position as obedient daughters, wives, and mothers in the traditions the LTTE sought to save, LTTE's shift produced a distinctive form of women's participation in armed conflict, first as "Freedom Birds" of the propaganda and information-gathering arm and then as active combatants. During the early 1980s, the LTTE received training and aid from other insurgent groups like the Provisional Irish Republican Army (PIRA) and Palestine Liberation Organization (PLO), who used women as agents, demonstrating the utility of including them in the group's operations.

Prabhakaran took the traditional womanly virtues of modesty, charm, coyness, and fear and transformed them into courage, confidence, and thirst for liberation, grafted to the submissive *thatkodai* self-sacrifice of martyrdom. The government's targeting of the entire Tamil population, with special humiliations and assaults of women, offered fertile recruiting grounds. Women who had been stripped naked in front of their towns, raped, or maimed were offered a way to restore their dignity and get revenge on their tormentors. The LTTE encouraged women to join them as friend groups and structured their camps as families, strictly forbidding sexual contact or romantic flirtations, although they often used attractive young men to recruit in girls' schools. Calling one another "brother" and "sister," the recruits lived under rigid restrictions, from their proscribed braided hairstyles to their scheduled rounds of instruction, physical activity, and local service to the civilian population. In order to avoid being raped after capture, all LTTE soldiers wore a cyanide capsule around their necks as a mark of devotion and pride. After Prabhakaran himself married in 1984, LTTE women were allowed to marry after the age of 35 if they acquired the permission of their commanders, although afterward, they were expected to put aside their unisex fatigues for traditional Tamil saris and downshift to support roles. In a traumatized society where most had seen violence, the LTTE offered an opportunity for women to break from caste and gender restrictions in defense of their homes, an offer that proved so attractive that eventually 30 percent of the LTTE were women.

By 1987, the LTTE were one of the most brutal and effective terrorist organizations in the world, not just attacking government buildings and officials but also turning on Tamils who were seen as insufficiently supportive of the cause and attacking Sinhalese Buddhist temples and concentrations of civilians in marketplaces. The government of India, aware that LTTE was training among Tamils in southern India, sent peacekeepers to Sri Lanka in 1987 in an attempt to achieve a peaceful end to the conflict, but this devolved over the next three years into fighting between the LTTE and the Indian army, which used airstrikes against Tamil-held areas, killing large numbers of civilians and spilling over into deaths of Sinhalese. In 1990, the Sri Lankan government insisted that India withdraw. In this escalation of firepower, the LTTE shifted into tactics that came to define the rest of its existence: the Black Tiger suicide bombers, many of whom were women.

Accepting this tactic as a natural evolution of self-sacrifice, and wearing C-4 suicide vests designed by Prabhakaran, Black Tigers unleashed devastating attacks in India and Sri Lanka. The most spectacular of these was the 1991 assassination of Rajiv Gandhi, the prime minister of India, by a woman code-named Dhanu, who disguised the explosives she carried as a false pregnancy bump. Admiring her beauty, Gandhi disregarded warnings from a woman police bodyguard with a casual, "Relax, baby," seconds before Dhanu detonated her bomb, killing 16 people, including Gandhi. Black Tigers used the pregnancy ruse frequently, including a bomber who infiltrated a Sinhalese military compound posing as the wife of an officer on her way to a medical appointment. Other attacks took the form of "Sea Tigers" crashing speedboats into military troops' carriers and ultralight aircraft into more than half of the Sri Lankan national airline's inventory of planes.

Wearing their strictly prescribed modest braids, women of the "Tamil Tigers" drill with their weapons in Sri Lanka in 1996. Under their fatigue tops, they all carry cyanide capsules to use for suicide in the event of capture, in order to avoid rape and torture by their captors. (Cyril LE TOURNEUR/Gamma-Rapho via Getty Images)

During the planning of suicide operations, women volunteered, often so many that names had to be drawn from a lottery tambola. Women scarred or maimed in previous operations especially prized the chance to die rather than live in a postconflict world where they would be devalued because of their disability. Those chosen enjoyed a rare chance to meet Prabhakaran and his senior circle of advisors for dinner, after which he took the extraordinary step of washing the dishes, a move that dramatically humbled a high-ranking man before women. After their deaths, the LTTE celebrated them on Heroes' Day, with coordinated public relations campaigns of murals, posters, books, and films, which further drove recruitment. Although the reality was that suicide bombers wore three dog tags to make sure their body parts could be identified and the LTTE credited, the Tigers thoroughly glamorized women suicide bombers and used their ability to move through society while attracting less suspicion.

Postconflict Disarmament, Demobilization, and Reintegration

The government's response to decades of conflict was to accelerate their use of force. In 2009, Prabhakaran, his wife, and sons were caught and killed in an ambush, significantly crippling the LTTE, which had centered around his cult of personality and had few leaders who could exert his authority effectively. Although few women served as high-level leaders, the government targeted midlevel cadre commanders extensively and undermined the ability of the Tigers to carry out their operations. After 26 years of warfare, the Sri Lankan government declared victory and began a disarmament, demobilization, and reintegration (DDR) 6+1 program (educational, psychosocial, vocational, cultural, spiritual, recreational, and community facets) designed in consultation with the United Nations and the Red Cross, although the military reserved the right to overrule any part of the plan that interfered with their suppression of resistance. This plan, like all of the previous attempts at cease-fires, had been negotiated without the presence or input of Tamil women.

Despite the presence of large numbers of women among the LTTE, DDR plans have concentrated on serving male combatants. Former fighters were housed in segregated camps, with men participating in carefully orchestrated sporting events against Sinhalese teams as an attempt to bring the communities together. Because the LTTE never attempted to change the role of women in mainstream Tamil society, men have had a far easier time transitioning into civilian work, while women cannot transfer their skills to self-sufficient employment. Just as they feared, those with scars cannot offer dowries high enough to attract a respectable husband, and the disabled have few supports for independent living. The military's approach to this has been to allow supervised courting between camps of demobilized fighters, crowned by mass weddings attended by Bollywood stars and political VIPs. This is a plan that holds little appeal for women who joined the Tigers in the first place to change their role in traditional society.

As of 2010, 70,000 people had died in the Sri Lankan civil war, with a further 700,000 displaced and 60,000 missing. The diaspora population of Tamils, as they were during the fighting, continue to be a major source of charitable support for LTTE personnel. Within communities, the Sri Lankan army has exacerbated tensions by destroying LTTE memorials to their suicide bombers and has made few concessions to the Tamil minority. The LTTE demonstrated that women can be successfully mobilized and used in sustained terrorist operations without losing diaspora or community support. The poorly handled DDR process and unresolved problems between the Tamil and Sinhalese populations offer no guarantee that the peace will continue or that the women will return to their traditional place.

Further Reading

Alison, Miranda. " 'In the War Front, We Never Think That We Are Women': Women, Gender and the Liberation Tamil Tigers of Eelam." In *Women, Gender and Terrorism*, edited by Laura Sjoberg and Caron Gentry, 131–58. Athens: University of Georgia Press, 2011.

Ann, Adele. *Women Fighters of Liberation Tigers.* London: LTTE International Secretariat, 1993.
Bloom, Mia. *Bombshell: Women and Terrorism.* Philadelphia: University of Pennsylvania Press, 2011.
Coomaraswamy, Radhika. "Violence, Armed Conflict and the Community." In *Women in Post-Independence Sri Lanka,* compiled by Swarna Jayaweera, 79–98. London: Sage, 2001.
Gagnon, Madeleine. *Women in a World at War: Seven Dispatches from the Front.* Vancouver, BC: Talonbooks, 2003.
Gunawardena, Arjuna. "Female Black Tigers: A Different Breed of Cat?" In *Female Suicide Bombers: Dying for Equality?* edited by Yoram Schweitzer, 81–90. Tel Aviv, Israel: Jaffee Center, 2006.
Haviland, Charles. "Sri Lanka Mass Wedding for Former Tamil Rebels." BBC News, June 14, 2010. Accessed December 12, 2017. http://www.bbc.com/news/10308540.
"International Laws and Child Rights." Child Soldiers International. Accessed December 17, 2017. https://www.child-soldiers.org/.
Jordan, Kim, and Miriam Denov. "Birds of Freedom? Perspectives on Female Emancipation and Sri Lanka's Liberation Tigers of Tamil Eelam." *International Journal of Women's Studies* 9, no. 1 (September 2007): 42–62.
Krishnan, Sonny Inbaraj. "The Transition of Teenage Girls and Young Women from Ex-Combatants to Civilian Life." *Intervention* 9, no. 2 (2011): 137–44. doi:10.1097/wtf.0b013e328348dffb.
Mazurana, Dyan, and Susan McKay. "Child Soldiers; What about the Girls?" *Bulletin of the Atomic Scientists* 57, no. 5 (September 1, 2001): 30–35. doi:10.2968/057005010.
Perry, Alex. "How Sri Lanka's Rebels Build a Suicide Bomber." *Time,* May 12, 2006. Accessed December 12, 2017. http://content.time.com/time/world/article/0,8599,1193862,00.html.
Rajasingham-Senanayake, Darini. "Ambivalent Empowerment: The Tragedy of Tamil Women in Conflict." In *Women, War and Peace in South Asia: Beyond Victimhood to Agency,* edited by Rita Manchanda, 102–30. London: Sage, 2001.
Rajasingham-Senanayake, Darini. "Sri Lanka: Transformation of Legitimate Violence and Civil-Military Relations." In *Coercion and Governance: The Declining Political Role of the Military in Asia,* edited by Muthiah Alagappa, 294–316 Stanford, CA: Stanford University Press, 2001.
Schulenkorf, Nico. "Bridging the Divide: The Role of Sport Events in Contributing to Social Development between Disparate Communities." *European Journal of Tourism Research* 3, no. 2 (2010): 127–31.
Somasundaram, Daya. "Child Soldiers: Understanding the Context." *British Medical Journal* 324, no. 7348 (May 25, 2002): 1268–71. doi:10.1136/bmj.324.7348.1268.

Soyza, Niromi De. *Tamil Tigress*. London: Allen & Unwin, 2016.
Stack-O'Connor, Alisa. "Lions, Tigers, and Freedom Birds: How and Why the Liberation Tigers of Tamil Eelam Employs Women." *Terrorism and Political Violence* 19, no. 1 (2007): 43–63. doi:10.1080/09546550601054642.

Sweden

Background

Sweden is proud of its long tradition of strong, independent women, from the rights of Viking women to inherit property and head family business through the interpretation of medieval church laws to allow widows and unmarried women to give testimony, own property, and represent themselves in court proceedings, and married women acting in proxy for their husbands enjoyed his legal status. At the elite level, the Swedes prized the actions of women like Blanda of Varena and Kristina Gyllenstierna, who defended the country from invaders. During the 18th century, enlightened law codes expanded primary public education to the boys and girls of every Swedish Lutheran parish, allowed women members of guilds to vote for them, and offered a resettlement program for unmarried mothers in an attempt to deter infanticide. Women were also regarded as an asset of the army, with men allowed to bring their families to do camp work, cooking, and nursing until banned in 1798, after which only professional women sutlers could follow the troops. During the 18th century, there were at least four documented cases of women in men's clothing serving in the Swedish military as soldiers.

After losing Finland to Russia in 1809, Sweden's military status declined significantly, and after fighting to enforce the union with Norway in 1813, the country declared its neutrality in the wars of the 19th century and World Wars I and II. For self-defense and in case of public emergencies, Sweden fielded an all-male army but found it difficult to pay for their arms and equipment. In 1924, Swedish branch of the Lotta Svard women's organization raised money to pay for the training time needed, and throughout the interwar period, women provided field kitchen, nursing volunteers, and sewing and knitting of hats, socks, and gloves and opened morale canteens. Additionally, the Swedish Blue Star, an organization dominated by women, offered fund-raising and volunteers for the care of military animals like horses, mules, and dogs. During

World War II, the Swedish army called up a large number of men for border and coast-watching duty, requiring women to step into civilian jobs and noncombat auxiliary roles like signals, command, motor corps and control, and clerical work and free up more than 100,000 men for service.

Cold War

Sweden's postwar policies, especially during the 1960s, created the "Folkhemmet," or social welfare state, which offered women opportunity and equality in the workplace, as well as generous maternity benefits and access to higher education and childcare. The Swedes, who did not join NATO, were stuck between U.S. demands to position nuclear submarines in Swedish waters in order to fire on the Soviet Union and a public that was increasingly anti-militarist and especially incensed by the Vietnam War. Ultimately, Sweden received secret guarantees for defense assistance from the United States, including investment and technical help with the Saab 37 Viggen aircraft, but the military and the practice of conscription for men had suffered a blow in public opinion. In 1977, a parliamentary report concluded that noncombat jobs should be opened to Swedish women, leading to informational "summer camp" recruiting fairs, and in 1989, a declaration that all occupations in the Swedish military were to be open to women.

During the 2000s, Sweden made a deliberate choice to approach gender integration, along with the transition to an all-volunteer force, from a position of improving operational effectiveness. Peacekeeping missions in the Congo brought into sharp relief the reality that dealing with women refugees, human trafficking and societies that would not allow male peacekeepers access to private space, and adding women helped rather than hindered military operations. Under the guidance of Charlotte Isaksson, the first senior gender adviser to the Swedish military, there were field exercises based on interactions with Balkan displaced people and the 2012 establishment of the Nordic Center for Gender in Military Operations outside of Stockholm. In Afghanistan, Swedish peacekeepers put these lessons to use with an experiment, Operation Juliet, with both single-gender and mixed-gender engagement teams, concluding that mixed-gender teams offered the highest flexibility and utility. This approach allowed them to support parallel *tribal* jurgas (traditional, consensus-building conferences for men) while women met in *shuras* and pleased the more traditional military planners who had resisted change on the grounds that women might subtract rather than add value. The country's trade unions, which represent soldiers and officers, were active in the retrofit of the Swedish naval fleet in preparation for women's inclusion, mandating changes already in place in civilian workspaces.

Despite the care taken in Sweden's gender integration of their military, there have been problems in both the small details that make gender mainstreaming run more smoothly and the remaining gulfs in work culture. Women found that the equipment the military issued them was just the smallest men's size, or that anything retooled for them was labeled "odd sized," and that the issued bath towels were not large enough to cover above and below the waist when using barracks showers. In more pressing complaints, Swedish training materials to combat sexual harassment offer instructions to young women to report and just refuse bad actions from colleagues and superiors, a statement that women point out is extremely difficult for subordinates to do. There is resentment of stated principles of valuing women in the armed forces and Swedish egalitarianism as a national character trait while excusing harassment as a bad habit picked up abroad, or an outlier. In recent surveys, 31 percent of Swedish women military personnel reported experiencing sexual discrimination, although more commonly of hostile work environments than assault or quid pro quo threats.

As of 2016, women comprised 8.3 percent of Sweden's armed forces. Their current strategic planning sees including women, and more of them, as a "natural" progression, and one that enhances their ability to conduct peacekeeping missions, a cornerstone of their diplomatic prestige and national image. The next decade of evolution in the all-volunteer force will see increased competition from civilian employers, and a need for the military to offer excellent recruits reasons beyond what they can get in a civilian occupation with Sweden's existing social welfare state.

Further Reading

Björkdahl, Annika. "Swedish Norm Entrepreneurship in the UN." *International Peacekeeping* 14, no. 4 (August 2007): 538–52. doi:10.1080/13533310701427959.

Eduards, Maude. "What Does a Bath Towel Have to Do with Security Policy: Gender Trouble in the Swedish Armed Forces." In *Making Gender, Making War: Violence, Military and Peacekeeping Practices*, edited by Annica Kronsell and Erika Svedberg, 65–79. London: Routledge, 2011.

Egnell, Robert, Petter Hojem, and Hannes Berts. *Gender, Military Effectiveness, and Organizational Change: The Swedish Model*. London: Palgrave Macmillan, 2014.

Estrada, Armando X., and Anders W. Berggren. "Sexual Harassment and Its Impact for Women Officers and Cadets in the Swedish Armed Forces." *Military Psychology* 21, no. 2 (2009): 162–85. doi:10.1080/08995600902768727.

Tornqvist, Kurt. "Sweden: The Neutral Nation." In *Female Soldiers—Combatants or Noncombatants: Historical and Contemporary Perspectives*, edited by Nancy Loring Goldman, 203–14. London: Praeger, 1982.

Turkey

Background

During the Ottoman period, women played no official role in the highly organized military of the empire, although high-ranking women in the Ottoman court, like the mothers and favored consorts of the sultans, might influence foreign policy or promote particular commanders and officials, as Suleiman the Magnificent's wife Roxelana, the Hurrem Sultan, did during his reign in the 16th century. The Ottoman military, which owed its loyalty directly to the sultan, slid from the most fearsome users of musketry in Europe to being quickly eclipsed as the gunpowder revolution took hold among its enemies. In the late 19th century, reform-minded officers with experience as attachés in European countries looked to modernize both the empire and their profession through education and westernization, which included undertaking critical examinations of the legal and educational status of women similar to the debates going on in Europe. In 1908, a group of military officers, the Young Turks, seized power and ended the absolute monarchy of the sultan, transferred the loyalty of the military to the state rather than to its ruler, and insisted on reforms like mandatory primary education for boys and girls and the founding of a women's university in 1915. By World War I, there was a thriving women's press of specialty newspapers and magazines and a variety of social organizations that represented women's interests and reflected the growing modernization of the urban middle class.

During the Balkan Wars and World War I, Ottoman women of the middle and upper class organized to support the military with fund-raising and Red Crescent volunteer work and support for military widows and orphans through the Committee of the Society for National Defense, which had at least 4,000 members in 1914. In 1917, the army Women's Worker Battalions replaced men in the factories and fields and even accompanied the army as logistical support and created the stereotype of "Sgt. Fatma" and her laden pack animal. More educated women stepped into work as post office clerks, telegraph and telephone operators, and secretaries. The war, and the subsequent dismantling of the Ottoman Empire, affected women significantly, as the dislocation of hundreds of thousands of refugees uprooted people from their homes and sent them into new nations with few resources or infrastructure to assist them, while the survivors of brutal campaigns against the Armenian and Assyrian minorities struggled to emigrate or blend in with the local population.

Ataturk and State Feminism

The modern Turkish nation emerged from this chaos and conflict, under the leadership of one of the Young Turk generals, Mustafa Kemal, who was elected as the first president in 1923 and given the title Ataturk, or "Father of the Turks," in 1934. His political program, Kemalism, was one of secular modernization, with women and the military playing crucial roles in the transformation of the country. Halide Edib, a woman activist, novelist, and journalist, earned the rank of sergeant in the nascent national army as an organizer and fiery orator against the occupation of Turkey by Greek and British troops, working closely with Ataturk until 1926. Ataturk surrounded himself with educated, westernized women, marrying Latife Uşaklıgil, who had studied law at the Sorbonne and who exercised great influence on the reforms introduced affecting women. Kemalism embraced state feminism, in which women owed a duty to the nation to be educated and to become productive citizens and mothers. Suffrage was attained in 1934 (although women had been write-in candidates voted in by men since 1923), polygamy banned, and veiling discouraged, although Ataturk himself never dared to outlaw it. In an effort to display the advancements made by women in the 1920s, the state sponsored Miss Turkey contests, sending winners to European competitions as a matter of national pride.

The military, too, was to be a harbinger of modernity and foundation of the state. The Ottoman Empire promoted a phrase, "Every Turkish man is born a soldier," as a reference to their origins as nomadic warrior people, but Ataturk genuinely meant that "every Turk is born a soldier," including women in the nationalist effort. In 1927, the first census made it possible to transition from the millet system of collecting recruits by quota from individual ethnic groups to conscription and mandatory national service for all men. During conscript military service, and for career officers, the military was meant to be apolitical, secular, and a vehicle for assimilation and education. In 1929, Turkey introduced a Latin script, which had to be taught to both the illiterate and those used to the Arabic writing system used previously, and the teaching was done in the army as well as by a corps of women teachers sent out to villages with chalkboards.

These ideas came together in the person of Ataturk's adopted daughter Sabiha Gokcen, one of eight orphans he took in after the war. To comply with

Turkey

the new surname law, he offered her the last name "Gokcen," which means "pertaining to the sky," and she quickly lived up to this image by joining the Turkish bird flying society and then taking glider and parachute courses in the Soviet Union. Back in Turkey, she enrolled in the air academy as its first and only woman student in 1935 and was so small that a special training plane with closer pedals had to be made available. She then joined an air force regiment for tactical school in Eskişehir, serving with uniformed pilots. In 1937, she became the first woman combat pilot attached to a national army (earlier Russian women had not been to a formal academy and did not serve in official units) when she served in the month-long bombing campaign against Kurdish rebels in Dersim. When she asked Ataturk for permission to participate, he insisted that she take along one of his pistols to shoot herself rather than be captured and abused by tribal men. In 1938, as a goodwill tour, she flew to all of the Balkan capitals to demonstrate Turkish aerial mastery and the regime's advantages for women. Gokcen urged Ataturk to fully integrate women into the military, but he refused to intervene and sent her to petition the commander of the air force, who refused. As the only woman in the Turkish air force, she was the chief instructor at the academy until 1954, where, among hundreds of men, she trained four other women as civilian pilots, and she retired from flying in 1964. In 1952, as Turkey sent troops to the Korean War as a member of the United Nations, she volunteered as a pilot but was refused because of UN regulations forbidding women in combat roles.

Turkey remained neutral in World War II and quickly joined NATO in 1952. Since then, NATO and alliance with the United States have been a defining element of the Turkish military, with U.S. bases infusing money into the local and national economy, and throughout the Cold War, involving Turkey in plans that would have sent troops to tie up 30 Warsaw Pact divisions in the Black Sea region in the event of a NATO-Soviet War. In 1955, a group of women noticed that admission to military academies was for "Turkish students" and, after the military attempted to clarify it as "male Turkish students," challenged the written regulation in court, where they won. After these women graduated successfully, with Second Lieutenant Leman Altincekic becoming the first female jet aircraft pilot and Second Lieutenant Şenay Ciper Gunay the first female jet combat pilot, the military, representing a fundamentally still conservative and male-dominated culture, changed the policy in the early 1960s, shutting women out until 1992.

Since the 1950s, the Turkish military has fulfilled Ataturk's vision of the professional force as a reliable guarantor of secular democracy. On three occasions, 1960, 1971, and 1980, the officer corps has launched coups against governments that have veered, in the view of the military, too far into corruption, Islamism, or financial irresponsibility, with civilian control restored by new elections within a few years. However, during those periods of martial law, the military has imprisoned and tortured dissidents, often targeting women who did not fit within conservative gender roles and using sexual humiliation and assault. Along with NATO responsibilities, Turkey has maintained a large conscript army, both to keep up with the capabilities of Greece, its enemy in Cyprus (although Greece is also a NATO member), and to serve as a process of nationalistic education for young men. The Army Mutual Assistance Fund, established to finance pensions for career soldiers, is one of the most profitable investments in the country, with seats on the boards of companies and social service organizations, and the affinity groups created by time in the military are a major means of social mobility for men who serve.

In 1992, under Prime Minister Suleyman Demirel and the True Path Party, the Turkish military began an upgrade and modernization, beginning with the readmission of women to military academies. Under Demirel's successor, Turkey's only woman prime minister, Tansu Ciller, the overhaul involved transitioning from a mass force meant to face Soviet divisions into a flexible response to Kurdistan Workers' Party's (PKK) insurgent attacks, weapon of mass destruction (WMD) threats, defending energy security, and deterring extremism. Critics of Ciller locate the expansion of military response to the Kurds as a distraction from the 1994 financial crisis and a desire to be a Turkish "Iron Lady" in the model of Margaret Thatcher's role in the Falklands War. Although out of office in 1996 under a cloud of corruption charges, her election was a watershed in the public visibility of professional, Western-educated, and assertive women, and her work with the military signaled that there was potential for further women's participation.

The 21st Century

The counterinsurgency against the PKK, however, had changed the experience of Turkish conscripts to one far more dangerous than Cold War garrison time. Since 1984, more than 6,200 men have been killed in military operations, with thousands more wounded and disabled. The stress of repeated deployments has stressed career soldiers and their families, while men have increasingly attempted to evade conscription, despite the social stigma that accompanies being granted a pink "rotten report" excusing one from service. As of 2016, only 2 percent of the Turkish military is women, and they serve under significant restrictions from combat jobs, postings on submarines, or in areas of high risk. The Turkish military remains very traditional, with 80 percent of career soldiers married and commanders' wives expected to be the "mother of the military family" responsible for the garrison's social services and charity work. Meanwhile, women from Turkey's ethnic groups, like the Abkhazian, have left the country to fight as guerrillas in conflict between post-Soviet states in the Caucasus.

The prime ministership of Recep Tayyip Erdogan, beginning in 2003, has seen a significant rebalancing of the civil military relationship in Turkey. Laws requiring punishments for honor crimes against women and defining harassment have improved women's legal status, likely as a continued move toward possible European Union's (EU) admission, but it is unclear how they are enforced in rural regions or how they apply to the military. Erdogan's suspicion of the armed forces, which have stood in opposition to many of his overtly religious policies, has led to purges since 2008, including the prosecution of the 2010 "Sledgehammer" plot organized by former senior officers against the government. In 2016, a military coup attempt failed, leading to the dismissal and imprisonment of hundreds of soldiers and significant changes to the command structure and personnel of the forces, although it is not apparent how this will affect the small number of women currently serving.

Further Reading

Aberal, Burge. "Silencing Sexual Violence and Vulnerability: Women's Narratives of Incarceration during the 1980–83 Military Junta in Turkey." In *Gendered Wars, Gendered Memories: Feminist Conversations on War, Genocide and Political Violence*, edited by Ayse Gul Altınay and Andrea Peto, 93–108. London: Routledge, 2016.

Altınay, Ayse Gul. *The Myth of the Military-Nation: Militarism, Gender, and Education in Turkey*. New York: Palgrave Macmillan, 2006.

Biri, Alp, Annica Kronsell, and Erika Svedberg. "The 'Rotten Report' and the Reproduction of Masculinity, Nation and Security in Turkey." In *Making Gender, Making War: Violence, Military and Peacekeeping Practices*, 95–109. New York: Routledge, 2011.

Coughlin, Katheryn M. "Women, War and the Veil: Muslim Women in Resistance and Combat." In *A Soldier and a Woman: Sexual Integration in the Military*, edited by Gerard DeGroot, and Corinna Peniston-Bird, 223–39. New York: Longman, 2000.

Dogan, Setenay Nil. "We Left Our Skirts to Men as We Went to the Front: The Participation of Abkhazian Women from Turkey in the Abkhazian War." In *Gendered Wars, Gendered Memories: Feminist Conversations on War, Genocide and Political Violence*, edited by Ayse Gul Altınay and Andrea Peto, 145–58. London: Routledge, 2016.

Feroz, Ahmad. *The Making of Modern Turkey*. London: Routledge, 2015.

Grigoriadis, Ioannis. *Trials of Europeanization: Turkish Political Culture and the European Union*. New York: Palgrave Macmillan, 2009.

Kandiyoti, Deniz, ed. *Fragments of Culture: The Everyday of Modern Turkey*. London: I.B. Tauris, 2006.

Karaosmanoglu, Ali L., and Mustafa Kibaroglu. "Defense Reform in Turkey." In *Post-Cold War Defense Reform: Lessons Learned in Europe and the United*

States, edited by Istvan Gyarmati and Theodor Winkler, 135–64. Washington, DC: Brassey's, 2002.

Mango, Andrew. *The Turks Today*. New York: Overlook Press, 2006.

Metinsoy, Elif Mahir. *Ottoman Women during World War I: Everyday Experiences, Politics, and Conflict*. Cambridge: Cambridge University Press, 2017.

Narli, Nilufer. "EU Harmonization Reforms, Democratization and a New Modality of Civil-Military Relations in Turkey." In *Advances in Military Sociology: Essays in Honor of Charles C. Moskos*, edited by Guiseppi Caforio, 433–72. Bingley, England: Emerald Publishing, 2008.

Saktanber, Ayse. *Living Islam: Women, Religion and the Politicization of Culture in Turkey*. London: I.B. Tauris, 2002.

Yaroglu, Kadei, Yavuz Ercil, Unsal Sigri, Gary Bowen, and Philippe Manigart. "Family Support Systems in the Turkish Military." In *Military Families and War in the 21st Century*, edited by Rene Moelker and Manon Andres, 278–301. London: Routledge, 2013.

United Arab Emirates

Background

The United Arab Emirates (UAE) federated in 1971, joining seven disparate kingdoms recently enriched by large-scale oil production. This economic boom instigated rapid social change, as the council comprised of the emirates' rulers chose to spend on infrastructure, education, and the creation of an expensive and cutting-edge military. In the last decade, the council has allowed more input from the people of the emirates, determined to cultivate a sustainable system of government. However, much of the workforce of the UAE consists of guest workers, who make up 85 percent of the 10 million population. Foreigners cannot be employed in the civil service or serve in the military, creating a significant problem for a country whose wealth removes the economic incentives its people have to join.

In 2014, the UAE mandated conscription of young men up to the age of 30, who must serve 9 months if they have completed high school and 24 months if they have not. For those who choose the military as a career, most officers are subsequently sent to one of the West's prestigious schools, like West Point, Sandhurst, or St. Cyr. These measures, though, have not succeeded in providing enough personnel for national security, causing the UAE to choose an unusual path for a conservative country committed to Sharia law.

Recruiting and Retaining Women in the 21st Century

The Khawlah bint al-Azwar school in Abu Dhabi was founded in 1990 and named for the Islamic warrior woman who led troops against the Byzantine Empire in the Battle of Yarmouk in 636 CE. Under its commanding officer, Colonel Afrah Al-Saeed Al-Falasi, women who volunteer undergo six months' training programs in groups of 150 to prepare them for work in the General Staff. The curriculum is challenging, with 30 percent dropping out in each class, but the school is structured with 7 am to 3 pm weekday meetings and on-site childcare to retain the women who can do the academic and physical work. The school makes special provision to protect women who use the school as an opportunity to leave marriages, preventing contact with abusive family. For women from the less wealthy parts of the federation, the military is an opportunity for social mobility, a high salary, and an adventurous job. Interestingly, older Emiratis are more supportive than the millennial generation toward the school and women soldiers, citing their deference to the royal family who founded it and the necessity in having native-born subjects protect the country.

Women graduates who undergo additional training in protective security and martial arts form a special guard for female members of the royal families, and important guests, including a visit by Camilla, Duchess of Cornwall, which was covered extensively by the press. In UN Peacekeeping missions to Somalia, Kosovo, and Afghanistan, women graduates have provided stability and humanitarian functions. A team of nine women from the school, accompanied by three Emirati male officers, climbed Mt. Everest in 2016. Emirati women currently form 20 percent of the diplomatic corps, with female ambassadors in Sweden and Spain. Women also hold highly paid positions in finance and civil service as judges and prosecutors. Most strikingly, four women have completed training to fly the country's fleet of F-16 fighters. One of them, Maj. Mariam Al-Mansouri, 35, a 2008 graduate, qualified in 2014 and has since flown sorties against ISIL.

Further Reading

Al-Oraimi, Suaad Zayad. "Defying the Prohibited Arena: Women in the UAE Military." In *Women in the Military and in Armed Conflict*, edited by Gerhard Kimmel and Helene Carreiras, 129–60. Strausberg, Germany: SOWI, 2008.

Rugh, Andrea. *The Political Culture of Leadership in the United Arab Emirates*. London: Palgrave Macmillan, 2015.

"UAE Women Prove Competency in Military." *Gulf News*, July 8, 2012. http://gulfnews.com/news/uae/general/uae-women-prove-competency-in-military-1.1045873.

"UAE's Female Fighter Pilot Leads Airstrikes against ISIL." *National*, September 24, 2014. https://www.thenational.ae/uae/government/uae-s-female-fighter-pilot-leads-airstrikes-against-isil-1.235550.

"Woman Who Reached for the Skies . . ." *National*, June 9, 2014. https://www.thenational.ae/uae/government/woman-who-reached-for-the-skies-1.586232.

United States

Background

Within the confines of 18th-century warfare, women took part on both sides of the American Revolution. As patriots, they had been the backbone of boycotts against British trade since the 1760s, and in the war, cut off from European manufactured goods, had to create an economy from homespun, local agriculture, and small-scale manufacturing. A few women, like Mary Ludwig Hays, "Molly Pitcher," stepped into male roles on the battlefield as men fell, with Hays joining a gun crew to keep the cannons firing at the Battle of Monmouth. Others, like Deborah Sampson, enlisted in the military disguised as men, with Sampson able to keep up her deception until she was badly wounded. On the loyalist side, women organized supply efforts and raised enough money to buy the loyalist navy a privateer ship, the *Fair American*. With men in both the Tory and Patriot armies gone for extended campaigns, and the men in militias faced with the risk of crippling injury or death, women had to take over the management of family farms, businesses, and land. This recognized responsibility clashed with the conservative course of the resulting political settlement, as the Constitution removed the right to vote from women who had enjoyed that right as property owners in some of the states, like New Jersey, and the prevailing sense was that women made excellent "republican mothers" raising citizens but not participating in political public life.

In the War of 1812, Lucy Brewer, in male clothing, served in the crew of the USS *Constitution* (despite navy regulations of 1802, 1841, and 1881 forbidding women on military ships), while First Lady Dolley Madison organized the evacuation of the White House as British troops approached, her cool head saving precious documents and artwork from the looting and burning of the Executive Mansion. Sarah Borginnis/Brewer probably accompanied the armies of Zachary Taylor in the Seminole Wars, but she joined the military record as a laundress, camp follower, nurse, and fighter during the Mexican-American

> **Equipment Design**
>
> Amid the discomforts of deployment to Iraq and Afghanistan, military women have found that their protective gear, including body armor, just does not fit very well, causing bruises at the hips, banging against knees, and providing the most coverage in places where their most vulnerable areas are not located. In 2012, the Human System Integration Project at Aberdeen Proving Grounds, Maryland, began reevaluating how the U.S. military designs, tests, and issues its mission critical equipment to a physically diverse population of users when the standard is not an average male. Their findings, of 50 issues unique to women users, would not surprise crash test labs, which have been required to use a fifth percentile female form since 2011. The military, however, has issued small-sized versions of equipment designed for men, resulting in higher fatigue, injury, and inefficient operations.
>
> New standards, applied to gear that will likely be issued in 2019, take into account women's narrow shoulders, shorter torsos, and the location of their ovaries in design of the "groin plate" meant to shield men's testicles. Additional features include a notch at the back of body armor to accommodate a bun or ponytail, darts to assure a snug fit to body armor, and lighter weight material to provide protection without unnecessary effort to carry. Additionally, the lab issues guidelines for the design of vehicles and weapons systems with the goal of making sure that seating, operation, and repair are able to be undertaken by people of a wide spectrum of physical size and shape without risking fatigue or accidents from awkward use.

War in 1846. Tirelessly, she provided nursing care, food, and encouragement during battles and defended a cannon even after being wounded by a sword blow. She received a military pension and after her death was breveted a colonel for burial in a military cemetery in California.

During the American Civil War, both the public and the government were unprepared for the realities of 19th-century mass mobilization. Receiving news that the Union armies lacked the ability to care for their wounded using the traditional system of regimental surgeons, Clara Barton, the first woman to work as a clerk in the federal patent office, and Dorothea Dix, a well-known activist for mental health care, organized a sanitary commission and nursing service along the lines of Florence Nightingale's work in the Crimean War. Dr. Mary Walker and Dr. Elizabeth Blackwell, two of the very few women with medical degrees at the time, joined as medical personnel and worked in the hospitals and surgery tents along with 6,000 other women who signed on to be nurses.

Capt. Kerry Kane, USAF pilot, checks her F-15 before taking off from Turkey to patrol Iraq's no-fly zone in 1998. The 1993 directive officially admitting women pilots to combat missions put women like Kane in the cockpit to serve in Iraq, Kosovo, Libya, and Afghanistan. (U.S. Air Force)

Through her work, Walker was awarded the Congressional Medal of Honor, only to have it rescinded by Congress in a reclassification of the award in 1917 (President Carter restored it in 1977). Barton remained in government service after the war, heading the graves commission that located, catalogued, and memorialized the tens of thousands of military dead left behind on battlefields and in prison camps. Confederate women also acted as nurses but without the overarching administration organized by the Union.

Women on both sides used their social access to work as spies and intelligence agents, with the Confederates hearing from socialite Rose O'Neal Greenhow and Mary Surratt, whose boardinghouse was the center of a courier network, and the place where her son plotted Lincoln's assassination with John Wilkes Booth. In Richmond, Elizabeth Van Lew, who had freed her family's enslaved people at her father's death, worked with former slave Mary Elizabeth Bowser to report on the Confederate leadership. Harriet Tubman, the Moses of the Underground Railroad, worked as a nurse for the Union army and convinced Captain James Montgomery to give her command of a raiding party of 150 African American soldiers. On a single night in 1863, she used her knowledge of the Combahee River plantations to attack the property of leading South Carolina secessionists, freed 750 enslaved people, and encouraged hundreds more to escape. As in previous conflicts, women donned men's clothing to enlist on both sides. It is likely that as many as 400 did so, and 5 were present at the Battle of Gettysburg.

The next major deployment of American troops was to the Spanish-American War in 1898. Annie Oakley, the star of Wild Bill Hickok's western extravaganza, offered President McKinley a squad of 50 lady sharpshooters, but her offer was officially declined. Instead, recognizing that the tropical environment of Cuba was likely to be as deadly as the Spanish, the army hired Dr. Anita Newcomb McGee as assistant surgeon general in order to find and employ 1,500 nurses as contract workers. Following the war, the army created the army nurse corps in 1901 and the navy its own service in 1908. Significantly, these women were not in the military, but temporary and separate employees of it, despite their highly regarded contributions.

World Wars I and II

While World War I raged in Europe, American military planners considered the massive manpower requirements of any U.S. participation. The secretary of the navy, knowing that his branch would need substantial numbers of clerks, telephone and telegraph operators, and typists, had military lawyers investigate the definition of the word "yeoman" in navy regulations. Finding that it could be stretched to include women, in 1916, he authorized the recruitment of hundreds of women and put them to work in Washington, D.C., offices. General Pershing, deploying to France, called for a similar pool of French-speaking "hello girls" to operate telephone exchanges for the military in Europe and found them in the upper-class women whose education included tours of Europe and years of French conversation practice.

In addition to these new uses of women's skills, 21,460 nurses provided medical support in U.S. hospitals and in field clearing stations near the front lines in Europe. Volunteers with the YWCA offered morale-raising activities and rehabilitation in hospitals, while American women at home adapted to rationing of meat, wheat, and fat and responded to calls to grow their own vegetables, buy war bonds, and cheerfully send their men off to fight. African American women were allowed to join the nursing corps but were held back from overseas deployment, a restriction that benefited the black community during the 1918 flu epidemic. While overloaded public health systems struggled to recall doctors and nurses from Europe, African American communities had the services of expert men and women whose race kept them from working at white facilities. At the end of the war, the military demobilized all of its women employees except a small corps of nurses, although, fearing a wave of pacifism from women, created a position of public relations liaison and staffed it with Anita Phipps, who established links to women's clubs and patriotic organizations benefiting the armed forces.

New Deal programs of the 1930s employed large numbers of women, from the actors and writers of the Works Progress Administration (WPA) to the "She-She-She" women-only projects designed in parallel to the male-only CCC conservation and environmental camps. As war loomed, however, only men were required to register for selective service and, after 1941, drafted to fight America's two-front war in Europe and the Pacific. Representative Edith Nourse Rogers (R-MA), who had pushed for veteran's care in the interwar years, introduced a 1941 bill to create women's military corps, mindful that at the end of World War I, the women had been only contract employees and ineligible for benefits offered to male veterans. Southern congressmen especially derided this idea, joined by General George Patton, who ridiculed petticoat soldiers and the abandonment of children and home. Generals Eisenhower and Marshall, however, saw how dependent ally Great Britain was on the use of women to keep their war efforts functioning, and the disciplined skills the women brought to the fight. Aided by Marshall, Rogers reintroduced a bill in 1942, which passed and brought separate women's corps into legal existence.

The army had the Women's Army Corps (WAC), the marines the U.S. Marine Corps Women's Reserve (USMCWR), the Coast Guard Women's Reserve (SPARS), and the navy's Women Accepted for Volunteer Emergency Service (WAVES). Carefully selected women headed these services, like Oveta Culp Hobby, a media executive and wife of a Texas governor at the WAC, and Wellesley College president Mildred McAfee at the WAVES. Congress and military planners argued about the details of women's uniforms and whether they could possibly supply feminine undergarments in standardized form. The army turned the problem over to manufacturers experienced in men's suits, while the navy sought out the women's wear expertise of Mainbocher of New York. In all cases, and in all field environments, the women had to remain feminine and conservative in their clothing. Women's colleges provided sites for boot camps with adequate facilities, and with the help of Mary McLeod Bethune, the services recruited African American women from historically black colleges and universities (HBCUs) to work in segregated divisions. Over their initial objections, the military found that the women excelled at discrete projects like the secret LORAN navigation system, in the Manhattan Project, and translating sensitive material as linguists, codebreakers, and intelligence analysts.

Like their colleagues in British intelligence, the Office of Strategic Services, a precursor to the Central Intelligence Agency (CIA), found that women blended into occupied Europe with far more ease than men and used volunteers like

Virginia Hall to conduct intelligence gathering, sabotage, and guerrilla operations. Nurses followed immediately after combat troops, with Nurse Frances Slanger, stepping onto the Normandy beachhead only hours after it had been established by D-day landings. Slanger, a Polish Jewish refugee from World War I, died when Germans shelled her field hospital in 1944. In the Philippines, 80 nurses stayed behind at Corregidor and were prisoners of war under horrific conditions, while military nurses trapped in Bastogne at the Battle of the Bulge carried on under heavy fire. In 1943, a planeload of 13 nurses en route to the front in Italy crashed in Albania, after which the women and 13 male survivors made their way on foot 800 miles to safety in Italy. In the civilian workforce, tens of thousands of women followed the example of Rosie the Riveter and learned the heavy industrial trades of welding, casting steel, and operating heavy equipment.

Jacqueline Cochran and Nancy Harkness Love, advocates for women in aviation before the war, pressed the government to accept the services of female pilots to ferry aircraft from their manufacturers in order to spare trained manpower for combat. The resulting Women Airforce Service Pilots (WASP) and Women's Auxiliary Ferrying Squadron (WAFS), operating as civilian contractors, flew 60 million miles and cost 38 women their lives in accidents. Their practical green trousers saw them ejected from New York restaurants for indecency and arrested after a crash landing in Georgia by a sheriff who could only categorize women in work clothes as vagrants and prostitutes. Demobilized in 1944, the women campaigned until 1977 for recognition of their work and until 2016 for the right to be buried in military cemeteries. Their difficulty in being recognized during the war was exacerbated by a vicious slander campaign that surfaced in 1943, claiming that military women were sexually voracious deviants who had joined to seduce men or lesbians who intended to wreck decent American society. First Lady Eleanor Roosevelt, a staunch promoter of minorities in the armed services, publicly denounced the accusations and blamed them on Nazi propaganda agents, although this was entirely domestic pushback on the expanding role of women by that point in the war.

The Cold War

This public feeling, and the turn against the Soviet Union in the nascent Cold War, led to the majority of the 350,000 women serving in World War II to be demobilized at the end of the conflict. Ironically, as the Russians and Chinese were dismissing their women from armed services, the stereotype remained of terrifying Communist Amazons whose rejection of domestic life symbolized opposition to freedom and capitalism. Only 6,500 American women remained by 1947, mostly in medical capacities. Because of Rogers's efforts in 1942, women veterans were eligible for the G.I. Bill, and those who pursued college degrees using it completed their programs at a rate of 19.5 percent, higher than men's 15 percent. In 1948, responding to the threats ongoing in Eastern Europe and the Occupation of Japan, Senator Margaret Chase Smith (R-ME) introduced the Women's Armed Service Integration Act, making the women's corps permanent and legal elements of their parent services, although with severe caps of 2 percent of the total force (with women officers limited to 10 percent of the total women and promotable no higher than O-5) and in only noncombat trades.

American participation in the Korean War led to the deployment of 500 nurses, who worked in large military hospitals in Japan, as well as in the Mobile Army Surgical Hospitals located close to the front, and popularized in American consciousness by the long-running TV show, *M*A*S*H*. Major Genevieve Smith was the first of 14 women flight nurses who died in Korea in plane crashes while retrieving and transporting wounded personnel. In 1956, the American advisors to Vietnam took a small number of nurses with them, and women medical personnel took part in humanitarian operations in the 1958 Lebanon crisis, the 1962 Iranian earthquake, and the 1965 intervention in the Dominican Republic. Nonmedical women established themselves as experts in specialty fields like air traffic control, becoming so vital to their commands that superiors refused to remove them. General Curtis LeMay, a staunch opponent of women's presence in his Strategic Air Command, never knew that the best tower traffic controller at Maxwell Air Force Base in the 1950s was a woman, as care was taken to hide her (and her voice) from him during his visits. The 1964 Civil Rights Act, aimed at reducing racial discrimination, also opened the federal service to challenge by women demanding equal treatment, and President Lyndon Johnson supported eliminating the caps to promotion and force size in 1967.

Escalation of American forces in Vietnam caused women to take on jobs that, although noncombat, moved them closer to combat operations. Major Norma Archer, a photo operations analyst, started giving the morning briefings at Seventh Air Force Headquarters because of her expertise in film. Military intelligence made extensive use of women, employing 1,200 as interpreters, image analysts, and clerks, while the services relied on 6,000 women for traditional medical roles as nurses. Without computers, running the war required large numbers of secretaries, stenographers, filers, and typists, jobs that the army believed could be done better by women, freeing men to carry rifles. At least 600 women officers and enlisted deployed to Vietnam for the air force and 500 for the WAC.

Many of these women were African Americans, who, since World War II, had found that despite its many problems, the standardized pay and promotion scales of the armed forces offered better opportunities than the civilian workforce. The Tet Offensive in 1968 placed women, relegated to rear areas, under direct fire, offering a test of their coolness and ability to work under combat conditions. Flight Nurse Lt. Jane Lombardi at Da Nang loaded a plane full of wounded men while dodging bullets, earning the recognition of a bronze star for her courage. Like their male colleagues, military women returning from Vietnam received a mixed welcome, with commenters on the left insisting that women had no business helping the war machine and on the right demanding that women remain in traditional domestic roles.

The deep unpopularity of the draft, and the Vietnam War, forced the armed services to review their recruiting and personnel policies in the early 1970s. In congressional hearings, Representative Emanuel Celler (D-NY) insisted that "war is death's feast, it is enough that men attend," but in the reality of transitioning to an all-volunteer force, removing women from the equation was impossible. Women entered the ranks of military chaplains, campus Reserve Officer Training Corps (ROTC) programs, and aviation training, with the navy pinning wings on women pilots in 1974. Lifting caps on promotion in 1967 also allowed women to rise to eligibility for general officer rank, with the first, Brigadier Generals Anna Mae Hays of the Army Nurse Corps and Elizabeth P. Hoisington of the WAC promoted in 1970, followed quickly by Jeanne M. Holm of the air force and Alene B. Duerk of the navy in 1971. These changes highlighted the ways in which military policy had not kept up with social changes, as women who became pregnant or who married a man with children (even if the stepchildren were adults) had to leave the military, and women were prevented from living in post housing if married to a civilian spouse, since the man could not be counted as a dependent. The dependent policy changed in 1973, and the federal court case *Crawford v. Cushman* reversed the no-child rules in 1976.

Relative détente with the Soviets in the 1970s made the inclusion of women more palatable to the American public, and it was pushed by the growing number of powerful women in Congress, including Patricia Schroeder (D-CO), Barbara Boxer (D-CA), and Beverly Byron (D-MD) with positions on the Armed Services Committees. This was also the high-water mark for support of the Equal Rights Amendment, with people assuming that its passage would expose women to conscription obligations alongside American men. Congress required that the military academies open to women in 1976, followed by the coast guard in 1977 and women's service on noncombat ships in 1978 and in missile crews in 1979. Critics pointed to the widely held belief that a unit with more than 35 percent women would suffer a drastic reduction in effectiveness, and the military used the 1977 European REFORGER wargame to test this hypothesis. They found, surprisingly, that not only was effectiveness not reduced, but in some units, their capabilities also increased with a large number of women present. In 1978, the separate women's services were amalgamated into their parent service, with combined promotion lists and identical rank structures and badges.

Many expected that Ronald Reagan would reverse these changes as part of his commitment to traditional family values, but he and his defense advisors wanted women as part of the reescalated Cold War military forces. In 1983,

100 women served in the invasion of Granada, Operation Urgent Fury, as military police, intelligence officers, and transport pilots. Patrolling Libya in 1986, women flying K-135 refueling tankers technically qualified for combat air medals, especially because tankers made more accessible targets than the faster fighter planes they refueled, but all of the crew awards were disqualified rather than allowing women to have them. This blurry line between combat and noncombat trades was increasingly difficult to maintain in the face of modern, multidomain warfare. Operation Just Cause, the 1989 invasion of Panama to remove General Manuel Noriega from power, was another example of the problem. Women pilots and military police reported for deployment, only to be sent home because of combat exclusion rules but then were hastily recalled because their units could not function at reduced strength. Captain Linda Bray, an MP, led her unit to secure a police dog kennel but, finding it guarded by armed troops, engaged in a successful gun battle, making her the commander of American male soldiers in combat.

In the brief moment between the invasion of Panama and the First Gulf War, women experienced vicious pushback for their expanded military presence. Women who sued gained entry to the private military colleges, Virginia Military Institute (VMI) and the Citadel, but experienced harassment and abuse, as well as public disapproval. A navy pilot's convention, Tailhook, in Las Vegas featured a hallway of drunken officers who groped civilian women and military colleagues, causing a huge scandal when Lt. Paula Coughlin officially complained. Critics of women in the military used this as proof that women could never be accepted and would not have been assaulted if they were in their proper roles and not present at a male-oriented event. Others, ironically, pointed out that this debunked the idea that men would be so chivalrous to women that they hesitated in combat. Instead, the men had harmed the women without hesitation and prioritized protecting other men from responsibility. The Navy Investigative Service's report failed to satisfy Assistant Secretary of the Navy Barbara Pope, who felt it did not hold senior leaders responsible and placed responsibility on low-ranking enlisted men. Additionally, its author, Rear Admiral Duvall Williams, told Pope that many navy women personnel were strippers and hookers. A second investigation, handled by the Office of Inspector General, led to the reorganization of the investigative service and the discipline of 14 admirals and 300 male pilots. Conservatives claimed that the investigation was a liberal use of political correctness to destroy military culture.

The First Gulf War

The U.S.-led coalition invasion of Iraq in 1991 involved the deployment of 41,000 women, who made up 7 percent of the total force. Fears of widespread fraternization, women refusing to leave their families, and combat breakdowns did not materialize, although support organizations had to recalibrate their male-oriented family materials from "while dad is away" to include mom and to aid women in developing family support plans. Saudi Arabia, site of most of the American staging areas, required strict modesty from military women, a requirement that chafed women and their male colleagues. Of the 149 deaths in the Gulf War, 15 were women, which did not spark the expected outcry from the American public. Specialist Melissa Rathbun-Nealy became a prisoner of war when her convoy became lost, and, with three male colleagues, was held by Iraqis for 33 days. Rathbun-Nealy reported good treatment from her captors, despite rumors exaggerated by the army, in order to inflame other soldiers, that she had been tortured and sexually assaulted. Major Rhonda Cornum, a surgeon, was the only other woman prisoner during the war, captured when her helicopter crashed. Cornum, who retired in 2012 as a brigadier general, was sexually assaulted and subjected to a mock execution as part of her interrogation, but she has insisted that this was traumatic but survivable and did not hinder her from acting as the senior officer among the prisoners and remaining focused on resistance.

The American public processed this new expansion of women's roles via two films in the 1990s. *Courage under Fire* (1996) saw Meg Ryan as a military helicopter pilot, nominated to receive the Congressional Medal of Honor, and revealed over the course of the film to be an effective and honorable leader, despite resistance from men in her unit. *G.I. Jane* (1997), in which Demi Moore integrates the navy's elite SEAL team, stressed that the female character had to physically match and desexualize herself by shaving her head and becoming "one of the guys" to earn her place. In the actual military, the navy, challenged in court to justify the exclusion of women from specific trades, opened 20,000 more jobs to women, and all of the services started putting women in the pipeline for combat aircraft in 1993. Women in the 1990s deployed to Somalia (1,000), Haiti (1,200), Bosnia (15,000), and Kosovo (8,000, including combat pilots). In the former Yugoslavia, confronted with fighting that had included genocide and the large-scale sexual exploitation of women, female military personnel were vital in policing and conducting operations in areas where men could not interact or go.

However, problems persisted in the military's handling of sexual harassment and treatment of homosexuality. In 1996, it was discovered that 12 drill instructors at Aberdeen, Maryland, were coercing recruits under their authority into sexual contact. At Fort Leonard Wood, another large training facility, three more men were charged with sexually exploiting trainees under their command. These cases forced the military to refine its regulations on fraternization and offer sexual harassment training and a whistle-blower's hotline. Meanwhile, public acceptance of same-sex relationships was outpacing military regulations. Since World War II, the military had feared effeminate gay men and suspected that military women were lesbians, ejecting those found to be gay with dishonorable discharges and sometimes courts-martial and prison terms. In 1992, Congress enacted an absolute ban on homosexuals serving, but the Clinton administration issued an executive order forbidding recruiters and military authorities from asking about an individual's sexual orientation. Quickly nicknamed "don't ask, don't tell" (DADT), the policy allowed military personnel to join and continue to serve if willing to keep their personal lives secret, a restriction that increasingly insulted and frustrated gay military personnel who wanted the same recognition and support for their families as those offered to straight people. Two lesbian women, Col. Margarethe Cammermeyer and Major Margaret Witt were instrumental in challenging the ban and DADT policy in court. The ban was rescinded by congressional action in 2011.

The 21st Century

On September 11, 2001, women military personnel and civilian contractors were among those killed in the attack on the Pentagon, with the medical staff of the complex shifting from routine support into a full triage department. Three women in medical support roles deployed in November 2001 with the first U.S. forces to Afghanistan, followed by far larger numbers in full invasions of Afghanistan and Iraq, averaging 12 percent of the total force. Captain Allison Black, navigator on a Special Operations AC-130H gunship, called down fire on Taliban, much to the surprise of Afghan men, who began calling her the "angel of death" after hearing her voice on their radios demanding surrender. In ground operations, women were increasingly meeting the qualifications for the prized Combat Action Badge while in technically noncombat trades. In 2005, Leigh Ann Hester, MP, earned a silver star for combat bravery, followed by Monica Lin Brown, who faced enemy fire to retrieve wounded comrades in 2007. In 2009, the Marine Corps assigned women marines, as Female Engagement Teams in Afghanistan, and the Lioness Program in Iraq, to accompany infantry patrols and build rapport with local women whose traditional customs prevented them from being in contact with male strangers. These women, whose ability to search other women for potential threats, and collect intelligence, were still under noncombat rules, despite doing dangerous jobs on the front lines of the war.

If these actions showed that women were highly capable, other scenarios offered a far darker view of both the public's ideas of military women and the dangers of assuming that women were automatically moral paragons. In 2003, Private Jessica Lynch was a clerk for a support company when her convoy ran into an ambush. Injured, she became a prisoner, one of the first women missing in Iraq. A rescue mission, filmed live, retrieved her from the hospital where she had been treated, and hastily generated books and a TV movie heralded her rescue from the hands of ill-intentioned enemies. In reality, Lynch had been treated properly, given medical attention and carefully protected by Iraqi personnel at great risk to themselves. Another woman, an African American from the same unit, Specialist Shoshana Johnson, was also injured in the fighting and held for weeks but received a fraction of the interest. Critics suggested that Lynch fit the narrative of appealing damsel in distress.

At Abu Ghraib in Iraq, one of 16 prisons under the command of General Janis Karpinski, a reserve officer called up for the conflict, whistle-blowers revealed that guards, many of them reservists, subjected prisoners to interrogations consisting of sexual humiliation and torture and that they had photographed themselves while conducting these sessions, including dragging a prisoner on a dog leash. Americans were especially shocked that three of the perpetrators were young women, Lynndie England, Sabrina Harman, and Megan Ambuhl, whose soap opera–like relationship with their male coworkers became the focus of the ensuing investigation of their conduct. While all of the women involved in Abu Ghraib were disciplined for their actions, military intelligence does find it advantageous to recruit and train women interrogators, using the conservative religious beliefs of Islamic male prisoners toward women to increase their feelings of humiliation and powerlessness when under the authority of women.

Women have consistently advanced in their respective service to occupy positions of command on combat vessels, over combat troops, and in charge of major operations. In 2011, Major General Margaret Woodward, promoted to command AFRICOM, which usually deals with humanitarian and stabilization operations, because of her experience in logistics, became responsible for the 11-day air campaign Operation Odyssey Dawn against Libya. Army officer Ann E. Dunwoody reached four-star rank in 2008, followed by Janet C. Wolfenbarger, who became the air force's first woman four-star general in 2012. Navy four-star admiral Michelle Howard was promoted to her rank in 2014.

The political prestige and gravitas accorded male veterans is slowly accruing to women, with female veterans running for state and national legislative office. In 2013, Rep. Tulsi Gabbard, a major in the Hawaii National Guard, took her seat in the House of Representatives, while in 2016, Tammy Duckworth was elected to the Senate from Illinois. An army helicopter pilot in Iraq, Duckworth underwent double amputation after being shot down and was transferred to the Illinois National Guard, from which she retired as a lieutenant colonel in 2014. Lt. Col. (ret.) Amy McGrath, the first woman marine to fly an F-18 in combat, is poised to run in 2018 for a House seat representing Kentucky.

The presence of so many women, and the need to retain them, has caused major reorganization of family support services. Although military personnel enjoy traditional activities like the formal service balls, units recognize that spouses are often working full-time and are unavailable to undertake the social and charitable roles that the wives of commanders performed a generation ago. In 2012, *Military Spouse* magazine, which has reoriented itself to cater to the changed family dynamic of the 21st century, named Jeremy Hilton as their spouse of the year. Hilton, whose wife is an air force lieutenant colonel, retired from the navy to be a stay-at-home parent for the couple's disabled daughter. As a high-profile spokesperson for military families, Hilton has made it a point to expose the problems of moving frequently during a military career and finding services for a child with special needs.

In November 2012, four women, Col. Ellen Haring, Major Mary Jennings Hegar, Captain Zoe Bedell, and Command Master Sergeant Janice Baldwin, joined by the American Civil Liberties Union (ACLU), filed a suit contending that the ban on women in combat, and its effect on their ability to be promoted without combat experience, violated their Fifth Amendment rights. Rather than contest the suit, the Obama administration announced in 2013 that it would open all trades to women, with full expansion to be complete in 2016. Submarine service on Virginia-class vessels welcomed women in 2015, while other all-male bastions, like the army expert infantryman course, graduated six women in 2016, and the marine infantry officer course produced a woman graduate in 2017.

Women serving in the U.S. military continue to encounter problems with the health care system being oriented to male care and the restrictions imposed by federal bans on funds spent for abortion. As a result, an American military woman must seek care at a civilian hospital, which is easy near Western European bases, but far more complicated in areas of the United States and in conservative areas of deployment in the Middle East and Africa. Despite extensive training programs undertaken after Tailhook and Aberdeen, domestic violence, sexual harassment, and assault remain significant problems in the military. While civilian American women have 6:1 likelihood of being the victim of unwanted sexual contact or coercion, military women are at 3:1. Senior officers like General Jeffrey Sinclair, in 2014, have been court-martialed for illegal relationships with junior officers, possessing pornography and adultery.

The United States' long wars in Iraq and Afghanistan made clear both the necessity of allowing women in its military branches and the many problems still to be worked out in their utilization. Women have yet to be commander in chief in the United States, or secretary of defense (although three women have been secretaries of the air force), and the language of military planning and operations is still highly gendered in a world of measuring one nation's missiles against another's.

Further Reading

Addis, Elisabetta, ed. *Women Soldiers: Images and Realities*. New York: Macmillan, 1994.

Alfonso, Kristal L. M. *Femme Fatale: An Examination of the Role of Women in Combat and the Policy Implications*. Maxwell AFB, AL: Air University Press, 2012.

Barkalow, Carol, and Andrea Raab. *In the Men's House: An Inside Account of Life in the Army by One of West Point's First Female Graduates*. New York: Berkley Books, 1992.

Campbell, Dann. "Women in Combat: The World War II Experience in the United States, Great Britain, Germany, and the Soviet Union." *Journal of Military History* 57, no. 2 (1993): 301–23. doi:10.2307/2944060.

DeGroot, Gerard, and Corinna Peniston-Bird. *A Soldier and a Woman: Sexual Integration in the Military*. Harlow, England: Longman, 2000.

Elshtain, Jean Bethke, and Sheila Tobias, eds. *Women, Militarism, and War: Essays in History, Politics, and Social Theory*. Savage, MD: Rowman and Littlefield, 1990.

Fenner, Lorry M. "'Either You Need These Women or You Do Not': Informing the Debate on Military Service and Citizenship." *Gender Issues* 16, no. 3 (1998): 5–32. doi:10.1007/s12147-998-0020-2.

Godfrey, Phoebe. "'I Was One of the Better Interrogators': Gender Performativity, Identity Transformation and the Female Military Intelligence Officer in the Iraq War." In *Gender and Conflict since 1914*, edited by Ana Carden-Coyne, 154–70. London: Palgrave, 2012.

Hertz, Rosanna. "Guarding against Women? Responses of Military Men and Their Wives to Gender Integration." *Journal of Contemporary Ethnography* 25, no. 2 (1996): 251–84. doi:10.1177/089124196025002004.

Holm, Jeanne. *Women in the Military: An Unfinished Revolution*. Novato, CA: Presidio Press, 1992.

Jaafari, Joseph. "The Pentagon Is Finally Designing Combat Gear for Women." *Motherboard*, March 7, 2016. https://motherboard.vice.com/en_us/article/qkjkpm/pentagon-egg-freezing-military-women-combat.

King, Anthony. "Here's Why Women in Combat Will Work." *War on the Rocks*, December 4, 2014. https://warontherocks.com/2014/12/heres-why-women-in-combat-will-work/.

Monahan, Evelyn, and Rosemary Neidel-Greenlee. *A Few Good Women: America's Military Women from World War I to the Wars in Iraq and Afghanistan*. New York: Anchor Books, 2011.

Nanos, Janelle. "Armor All: New Body Armor Design Issued for Women in the Military." *Boston*, September 26, 2013. http://www.bostonmagazine.com/news/2013/09/26/new-body-armor-women-military/.

Nantais, Cynthia, and Martha Lee. "Women in the United States Military: Protectors or Protected? The Case of Prisoner of War Melissa Rathbun-Nealy." *Journal of Gender Studies* 8, no. 2 (July 1999): 181–91.

Obradovic, Lana. *Gender Integration in NATO Military Forces*. Burlington, VT: Ashgate Publishing Group, 2014.

Quntar, Salam Al, Katharyn Hanson, Brian I. Daniels, and Corine Wegener. "Responding to a Cultural Heritage Crisis: The Example of the Safeguarding the Heritage of Syria and Iraq Project." *Near Eastern Archaeology* 78, no. 3 (2015): 154–69. doi:10.5615/neareastarch.78.3.0154.

Ritchie, Elspeth Cameron, and Anne L. Naclerio. *Women at War*. Oxford: Oxford University Press, 2016.

Savage-Knepshield, Pamela A., Jeffrey Thomas, Kristin Schweitzer, Richard Kozycki, and David Hullinger. "Designing Military Systems for Women in Combat." *Military Medicine* 181, no. 1S (2016): 44–49. doi:10.7205/milmed-d-15-00203.

Simon, Rita J. *Women in the Military*. New Brunswick, NJ: Transaction Publishers, 2001.

Sjoberg, Laura, and Caron E. Gentry. *Mothers, Monsters, Whores: Women's Violence in Global Politics*. London: Zed Books, 2013.

Skaine, Rosemarie. *Women at War: Gender Issues of Americans in Combat*. Jefferson, NC: McFarland & Company, 1999.

Snyder, R. Claire. "The Citizen-Soldier Tradition and Gender Integration of the U.S. Military." *Armed Forces & Society* 29, no. 2 (2003): 185–204. doi:10.1177/0095327x0302900203.

Soderbergh, Peter A. *Women Marines in the Korean War Era*. Westport, CT: Praeger, 1994.

Stachowitsch, Saskia. "Military Gender Integration and Foreign Policy in the United States: A Feminist International Relations Perspective." *Security Dialogue* 43, no. 4 (2012): 305–21. doi:10.1177/0967010612451482.

Stiehm, Judith Hicks. *Arms and the Enlisted Woman*. Philadelphia, PA: Temple University Press, 1989.

Stiehm, Judith Hicks. *It's Our Military, Too! Women and the U.S. Military*. Philadelphia, PA: Temple University Press, 1996.

Weinstein, Laurie Lee, and Christie C. White. *Wives and Warriors: Women and the Military in the United States and Canada*. Westport, CT: Bergin & Garvey, 1997.

Yuhl, Stephanie E. "Militarized US Women from the Wars in Iraq and Afghanistan: Citizenship, Homelessness and the Construction of Public Memory in a Time of War." In *Gendered Wars, Gendered Memories: Feminist Conversations on War, Genocide and Political Violence*, edited by Ayse Gul Altinay and Andrea Peto, 159–78. London: Routledge, 2016.

Vietnam

Background

Traditional Vietnamese society was a mix of practical social mores, which allowed women to take on the necessary duties of agriculture and village life, overlaid by the Confucian ethics imposed by the conquest of the country by the powerful Chinese empires to the north, who possessed Vietnam as a client state or colony for hundreds of years. This layered culture expected women to do brutal labor but be uncomplainingly patient, loyal, and self-sacrificing under the authority of their fathers, husbands, and sons. This was the norm when French colonial forces arrived in the mid-19th century and established French Indochina. French innovations included education for the middle and upper class, including women, which sent Vietnamese intellectuals to learn medicine, philosophy, and politics at the Sorbonne. The French regarded this as part of their duty as colonial masters, offering their civilizing mission of the French language, the Enlightenment, and Catholicism to people. They lauded exemplary pupils, until those pupils took their new knowledge and became revolutionaries.

In 1930, the Indochinese Communist Party founded a Women's Union, which Ho Chi Minh praised by pointing out that "women are half the people." Like many anti-colonial resistance movements, the Vietnamese critique of France found it useful to use the vocabulary of gender, painting a picture of the deep inequalities of men and women and highlighting the social constraints placed on women by traditional society. Although some revolutionaries genuinely wanted women's liberation, many more were couching their own feelings of resentment, powerlessness, and exploitation in the frame of wrongs done to women, rather than prioritizing doing anything about it. The French had no such difficulty recognizing women as a threat and arrested women activists like their male counterparts, although on one occasion in the 1930s, the police, intending to humiliate their woman prisoner, ordered her to strip for a search in the public street. The women nearby formed a crowd, and in solidarity, stripped off their clothes as

> **Historical Women as Role Models**
>
> In 40 AD, Imperial Han China ruled Vietnam as a province, imposing cultural assimilation and deference to the occupiers' bureaucracy. After the murder of her husband by a Chinese official, Trung Trac and her sister, Trung Nhi gathered supporters to push Chinese soldiers out of their village, attracting assistance from an army of disgruntled Vietnamese, many of them women. In the course of three years, the Trung sisters, using military skills learned at home from their soldier father, overthrew the Chinese and ruled northern Vietnam. In 43 AD, however, the Han Emperor dispatched Ma Yuan and a substantial force to crush the rebellion. In the ensuing battle, the Trungs lost and died, along with many of their followers.
>
> The Chinese fifth-century source, *Book of the Later Han* presents it as an illegal rebellion, defeated because men refused to follow women's leadership or because the Chinese cleverly fought naked and embarrassed the women. Vietnamese sources and folklore, like the *Complete Annals of Dai Viet* (1479), present them as fierce heroines revenging their family and people, who drowned themselves rather than be captured. The Trungs remained popular into modern times, with Communist propagandists especially focusing on elements of the story that encouraged female participation in guerrilla activity, like Phung Thi Chinh, who gave birth on the front line of the last battle, committed infanticide to keep fighting, and died with the Trungs. In contrast, Diem regime erected a stature of the Trungs in Saigon, modeled after Madame Nhu, the sister-in-law of the president. There are many temples dedicated to the Trungs in northern Vietnam, a street named after them in Hanoi, and annual celebrations of their memory.

well, and marched with the prisoner and the police to the station, chanting defiant revolutionary songs, mortifying the French authorities.

The Japanese and the French

In World War I, more than 100,000 men went to France as colonial subjects to serve as soldiers but more often as labor battalions, digging trenches, burying bodies, and supplying desperately needed manpower in a war of attrition. This cost 30,000 of them their lives and gained the Vietnamese no consideration from the French for increased autonomy or status as more than colonial subjects. Instead, as French investment in Indochina grew with dependence on the rubber, rice, and coal they produced, the exploitative weight grew larger and the tolerance for dissent even less. Nguyen Thi Minh Khai, a leading woman communist, who had been educated in Moscow and acted as Ho Chi Minh's deputy in Saigon, was arrested by the French and executed in early 1940s. The daughter of a Vietnamese railroad official, she had combined her knowledge of the transport system with her mother's wide-ranging network of social contacts to operate against the French.

France's defeat in 1940 placed Indochina in the hands of the Vichy government, which quickly lost control when the Japanese invaded Vietnam in 1941. With assistance from the Chinese, the Indochinese Communist Party set up a resistance, joining nationalist fighters to defy the Japanese. The Free French government and the American Office of Strategic Services also took interest in the movement and sent resources in order to hasten the defeat of the Japanese. Women worked as porters for the guerrillas, transporting thousands of pounds of food and supplies to remote posts, and a group of communist women led an attack on a Japanese grain depot, seizing supplies of food. General Giap had three women in his guerrilla unit, reinforcing for him their utility and abilities. This period allowed Ho Chi Minh to lay the foundation for a communist army, the Viet Minh, and a network of supporters across Vietnam. With the Chinese occupying the northern half of the country and supporting Ho Chi Minh's authority in Hanoi, and the French restored to power in Saigon, backed by the British and Americans, a second war broke out for control of the whole country.

This conflict, which lasted until 1954, saw the expansion of tactics that had been used against the Japanese. Women made up substantial numbers of the 840,000 soldiers in the North and 140,000 in the South, including Vo Thi Sau, who began her guerrilla career at 14, throwing a grenade at a group of French soldiers, killing two. In 1949, she attempted to assassinate a Vietnamese official tasked with executing insurgents and was arrested and herself executed. At the Battle of Dien Bien Phu, women porters made up as much as two-thirds of the Dan Cong labor brigades, which laboriously dragged supplies, ammunition, and artillery pieces to the high ground around the French base, allowing the guerrillas to fire on French supply planes using the runway and down into the base itself. Talks in Geneva divided Vietnam into North and South, with promises to hold elections in the near future to decide the political leadership of a united country. Instead, both sides prepared to fight—Ho Chi Minh leaving communists in place across the South. The war against the French, which would significantly affect their approach to their colonial conflict in Algeria, segued into a war with the South Vietnamese government and the United States.

The American War

In North Vietnam, women kept the prewar industrial and agricultural levels up throughout the 1960s, despite the loss of the labor of men fighting in the

North Vietnamese army (NVA). For the defense of Hanoi against American bombing, women also crewed antiaircraft guns, becoming so effective that pilots equated those runs to attacking Berlin in World War II for risk of being shot down, and in northern propaganda, they were praised as a "fine hairnet" guarding the population. A photo from 1972 epitomized this clash: A diminutive North Vietnamese woman in fatigues, Thi Kim Lai Nguyen, leads a tall, stunned American pilot, Capt. William Robinson, to the authorities using a gun. Women achieved "heroic" status in propaganda and recognition for losing three or more children to the conflict, a tragic condition after decades of fighting and huge numbers of deaths.

The Indochinese Communist Party had left behind some of its most skilled cadre in the South, where they applied their organizing and fighting skills to disruption and protest against the South Vietnamese government. In 1960, Nguyen Thi Dinh, an experienced guerrilla who had fought the French and survived a 1940–1943 term in prison, led a passive resistance against abuses by South Vietnamese troops against peasants at Ben Tre. The highly disciplined passive resistance made it difficult to end the opposition without damaging the regime's moral authority. Ut Tich, another veteran of the war against the French, had been assigned with her husband to live in the South and organize. Along with recruiting, scouting, and participating as a combatant in 23 battles, she spectacularly captured an outpost by approaching as a harmless local old woman and getting the soldiers drunk. Recalled to the North to participate in a Congress of Heroic Soldiers, she was celebrated in propaganda but died in 1965 in a bombing strike.

As members of and support for the Viet Cong guerrillas, thousands of women made up a "long haired army" of logistics, intelligence, and construction labor. These "water buffalo of the revolution" carried 200 pound loads along the Ho Chi Minh Trail and worked in engineering teams to repair the damage from bombing so that the roads remained passable. When this proved impossible, they might, like Ngo Thi Tuyen, carry 90 kg ammunition boxes to batteries across rivers on their backs, as she did at Dragon's Jaw Bridge in 1965. For years afterward, disbelieving propaganda officers and Eastern Bloc dignitaries demanded that she demonstrate her physical feat, eventually causing herself crippling injuries. Sympathetic village women might collect intelligence from the marketplace, where South Vietnamese and American enemies could not break into the oblique conversations of commerce, and they often acted as "foster mothers" to young women guerrillas, improving their morale and protecting them from the authorities by offering alibis and claiming them as family members, raising village protests and clamor when searches and arrests were attempted.

American military intelligence experts were fascinated by the women of the Viet Cong and eagerly studied captured diaries from the Bravo 8/3 Female Mortar Platoon, which fell into their hands after the unit's defeat and death in the early 1970s. Named for the date of International Women's Day, the journals of these teenagers revealed the day-to-day grueling lives in the field, from loneliness to abject terror, as well as the exhaustion and sickness that rendered them sexless and unable to conceptualize their male comrades as anything but comrades. Women defused bombs, carried radios, fought in tunnels, hid fugitives in pigsties, and during Tet in 1968, plausibly claimed to have destroyed four American tanks. At Cu Chi, 1969, Tran Thi Gung led a group of commandos who surprised a U.S. unit, killing 38 and destroying their helicopters.

The South Vietnamese

The governments of South Vietnam, whether Emperor Bao, the Diem family, or the junta of generals who overthrew Ngo Dinh Diem and ruled until the fall of Saigon in 1975, also fielded an army, which included some women, especially those who followed a husband and who had fought the Japanese and the French. One example was Ho Thi Que, eventually the master sergeant of the 44th Rangers, who earned the nicknames "Tiger Lady" and "Black Death" as an anti-Japanese guerrilla and transferred her allegiance away from the communists and to the South Vietnamese government. Tragically, her husband, angry that she overshadowed his own military career, murdered her in an incident of domestic violence in 1965. The South Vietnamese police also opened their ranks to police women, with about 3,000 serving in the 1960s.

The continual presence of French and then American troops in large concentrations had turned Saigon, and everywhere there was a garrison, into a camp town, replete with bars, brothels, and a flourishing economy of vice. The intersection of this with an existing image of Asian women as exotic offended Madame Nhu, the sister-in-law of Diem, who herself was portrayed by the press as a "Dragon Lady." When her daughter turned 18, she founded the South Vietnamese Army Corps and supervised the training of 3,000 "paramilitary girls" to make more men available for field duty by stepping into medical, clerical, and social welfare jobs. Long tours away from family had begun to strain South Vietnamese male officers' feeling of duty toward their parents and children, and it lifted some of the pressure to have military social workers assure their well-being. Additionally, the women trained in firearms, parachute qualifications, and small unit tactics, sometimes under the direction of Madame Nhu, and in 1962, two units, at Hoc Mon and Kong Loc, engaged with Viet Cong and emerged victorious. Madame Nhu, who had earlier overseen the new family laws that banned polygamy and concubinage and required daughters to receive inheritances, pushed the implementation of blue laws in 1962, aimed at forcing women to leave camp town jobs and serve in the South Vietnamese military. Some of the women recruited served in development teams, sent to rural villages to conduct educational campaigns against communism.

When communist forces took over, many of the women who had worked for the American military as secretaries and clerks were priority targets for retaliation and reeducation, along with South Vietnamese uniformed personnel. The woman colonel commanding the Women's Corps died in a prison camp in the late 1970s. Those who fled found that their organizational skills and discipline were an advantage in refugee camps and, as they immigrated to the United States and Australia, remained attached to their military service. In Australia, this has taken the form of adopting Anzac Day commemorations as a vehicle for memorializing South Vietnamese valor and holding reunions, which began in 1998. Lt. Col. Nguyen Hanh Nhon is the head of a nongovernmental organization (NGO), which collects money from the South Vietnamese diaspora to locate and aid disabled veterans and the widows of South Vietnamese soldiers, traveling several times a year to Vietnam to disburse money and oversee projects like the construction of ramps for housing.

The Postwar World

After 1975, Vietnam faced the devastation left by generations of warfare. At least a million combatants had died, with even more killed by disease, in bombings, or from starvation, and there were 200,000 people reported missing. There were also 300,000 orphans and countless displaced people, including Amerasian children born to military personnel and their Vietnamese partners. For supporters of the communist government in the North, actual reunion with them, and their austere and developed bureaucratic processes, was difficult for those who had lived as guerrillas in the South. The Vietnamese army, recruited by mandatory male conscription and women volunteers, sent troops to conflicts with the Chinese in 1974 and 1979 and occupied Cambodia in 1978 to contain the Khmer Rouge. During the war, women had taken over many agricultural communes using new techniques and modernized methods, which clashed with traditional elders. Men returning from being soldiers found that their female partners had more established or more high-ranking jobs. During the 1980s, 250,000 Vietnamese workers went to the Middle East and the Eastern Bloc, further disrupting the gender balance of those left behind.

Following the end of the war, many women found that their exposure to Agent Orange and other trauma had rendered them infertile or that they were unable to find partners. Not being able to have a family placed them in a scorned position in traditional society, so some turned to forming communes with other women and adopting orphans, seeking artificial insemination, or becoming pregnant through polygamous liaisons. The general consensus, although disapproving, has been that the women were owed a family and that they had the right to acquire one through any means. For those with posttraumatic stress disorder (PTSD), Buddhist nuns at specific temples have become known for offering helpful counseling and meditative treatment.

Rhetoric about women's leadership has not matched actual appointments to powerful positions. Nguyen Thu Binh, the "general of the long-haired army," served as a negotiator at the Paris talks in 1973, head of the Women's Union (a job in which she was symbolically awarded General Westmoreland's old office), minister of education, and vice president of Vietnam (1994–1997), but her career has been unusual. Women veterans head the Federation of Labor Unions, and the head of the Department of Tourism, in the case of tourism, supervising women expert in English because they had been American army employees in the 1960s. The 1986 revisions to the family law were largely negotiated by the Women's Union, but even 1994 policies of affirmative action and quotas have not seen Vietnamese women in the top tier of government or the military.

As in America, Vietnamese writers and filmmakers used the creative arts to grapple with the experience of the war. Nguyen Thi Duc Hoan, a volunteer soldier until chosen to act in propaganda films, developed into a director and producer in the 1970s, especially of films that address the women's experience of conflict. In *Love and Distance*, her protagonist struggles to love her husband, who was disfigured in the fighting. Duong Thi Hong's novels, *Paradise of the Blind* (1988) and *Novel without a Name* (1995), offering graphic accounts of wartime suffering and its aftermath, caused her ejection from the Communist Party of Vietnam over their content critical of the government. Bao Ninh, who served in the Glorious 27th Youth Brigade beginning in 1969, wrote the semi-autobiographical *Sorrows of War* (1990), which sees the continuing effects of the war on participants and their loved ones, especially women.

The end of the Soviet Union cut off financial support and the market for Vietnamese goods, as well as their exchange programs for education and consumer products. Pensions, already low, fell in the new economy to levels that sent veterans back to work in the "doi moi" or "renovations" of the 1990s. Some women veterans have leveraged technical expertise or regional networks to do well in the new economy, founding companies after acquiring microfinance loans from NGOs or overseeing the privatization of state firms. Others have been reduced to poverty and feel cast aside. Younger women, especially from rural areas, are prey for prostitution and marriage brokers, who come from Taiwan and China looking for sex workers and brides for farmers unable to afford a competitive dowry at home. This new world is not the one for which they picked up guns and fought to rid Vietnam of colonial oppressors.

Further Reading

Demery, Monique Brinson. *Finding the Dragon Lady: The Mystery of Vietnam's Madame Nhu*. New York: Public Affairs, 2014.
Ho, Hue-Tam Tai. *The Country of Memory: Remaking the Past in Late Socialist Vietnam*. Berkeley: University of California Press, 2001.

Lawrence, Mark Atwood. "Origins of the Vietnam War: Foreign Intervention Has a Long History in Vietnam." *Oklahoma Humanities* 10, no. 2 (Winter 2017): 12–14.
Luong, Hy V., ed. *Postwar Vietnam: Dynamics of a Transforming Society*. Lanham, MD: Rowman and Littlefield, 2003.
McKelvey, Robert S. *The Dust of Life: America's Children Abandoned in Vietnam*. Chiang Mai, Thailand: Silkworm Books, 2000.
Neu, Charles E. *After Vietnam: Legacies of a Lost War*. Baltimore, MD: Johns Hopkins University Press, 2000.
Nguyen, Nathalie Huynh Chau. *South Vietnamese Soldiers: Memories of the Vietnam War and After*. Santa Barbara, CA: Praeger, 2016.
Nguyen, Nathalie Huynh Chau. "South Vietnamese Women in Uniform." *Minerva Journal of Women and War* 3, no. 2 (2009): 8–33. doi:10.3172/min.3.2.8.
Nguyễn, Thị Đinh. *No Other Road to Take: Memoir of Mrs. Nguyễn Thị Đinh*. Edited by Huong Nam. Translated by Mai V. Elliot. Ithaca, NY: Cornell University Press, 2003.
Pike, Douglas. "The People's Army of Vietnam." In *The Armed Forces in Contemporary Asian Societies*, edited by Edward Olsen and Stephen Jurika, 123–37. Boulder, CO: Westview Press, 1986.
Stur, Heather Marie. *Beyond Combat: Women and Gender in the Vietnam War Era*. New York: Cambridge University Press, 2011.
Taylor, Keith Weller. *The Birth of Vietnam*. Berkeley: University of California Press, 1983.
Teerawichitchainan, Bussarawan. "Trends in Military Service in Northern Vietnam, 1950–1995: A Sociodemographic Approach." *Journal of Vietnamese Studies* 4, no. 3 (Fall 2009): 61–97. doi:10.1163/2468-1733_shafr_sim170180044.
Tétreault, Mary Ann. "Women and Revolution in Vietnam." In *Women and Revolution in Africa, Asia, and the New World*, edited by Mary Ann Tétreault, 111–36. Columbia: University of South Carolina Press, 1995.
Turner, Karen. "Soldiers and Symbols: North Vietnamese Women and the American War." In *A Soldier and a Woman: Sexual Integration in the Military*, edited by Gerard DeGroot and Corinna Peniston-Bird, 185–204. London: Longman, 2000.
Turner, Karen Gottshalk. *Even the Women Must Fight: Memories of War from North Vietnam*. New York: John Wiley & Sons, 1998.
Vasavakul, Thaveeporn. "Vietnam: From Revolutionary Heroes to Red Entrepreneurs." In *Coercion and Governance: The Declining Political Role of the Military in Asia*, edited by Muthiah Alagappa, 336–56. Stanford, CA: Stanford University Press, 2001.
White, Christine Pelzer. "State, Culture and Gender: Continuity and Change in Women's Position in Rural Vietnam." In *Women, State, and Ideology: Studies from Africa and Asia*, edited by Haleh Afshar, 226–34. Albany: State University of New York Press, 1987.

Index

Page numbers in **bold** indicate the location of main entries.

Abboud, Loula, 216
Abd, Meysa, 173
Aberdeen Proving Ground, 274
   sexual harassment at, 282, 285
Abortion, 239
   Rome Statute, 146
   United States military policy, 285
Abramov, Hani, 140
Abu Ghraib Prison, 284
Abu Sayyaf, 225
Addario, Lynsey, 2
Adi, Ghazi, 1
Afabet, Battle of (1988), 61
Afghanistan, **1–7**
   Canadian military in, 31
   German military in, 80
   Great Britain military in, 93
   Hungarian military in, 103
   Italian military in, 150
   Norwegian military in, 204–205
   Queen Soraya and reforms of, 1
   relations with Pakistan, 210
   Soviet Invasion of (1979), 1, 210, 239
   Swedish military in, 262
   United Arab Emirates military in, 272
   United States invasion of, 122, 274, 275, 283
Afghan Women's Council, 3
African American women, 276–277, 279, 284
African National Congress (ANC), 250–251
Afrikaans, 249, 250
Agent Orange, 294
Agricultural work, wartime
   Australia, 20
   Germany, 79
   Great Britain, 89
   Greece, 98
   Vietnam, 291, 294
Aguinaldo, Emilio, 221
Aisha, 181
Aisha, Darine Abu, 218
Akhter, Yasmeena, 111
Alamo, Zarghuna, 1
Al-Bakr, Ahmed Hassan, 120
Albania, 278
Alcazar Plan, 36
Aldige, Claire, 75
Al-Dulaimi, Nazhia, 119
Alexievich, Svetlana, 240
Al-Falsai, Afrah, 271
Alfonsin, Raul, 15

Algeria, **9–13**
  French COIN tactics in, 15, 71–72, 74, 291
Algerian Civil War, 11
Algerian War (1954–1962), 9
Algiers, Battle of (1956–1957), 10
Allende, Salvador, 35
All-Women's Association of Nepal, 186, 189
al-Majid, Ali Hassan ("Chemical Ali"), 172
Al-Mansouri, Mariam, 272
Al-Najar, Fatima, 219
Al-Nakba (the Palestinian "catastrophe"), 215
Al-Qaeda
  Afghanistan, 4
  Iraq, 124
  Philippines, 225
al-Rehibat al-Thawriyat "Revolutionary Nuns," 182
al-Saltaneh, Taj, 113
Altincekie, Leman, 267
Al-Wazir, Khalil, 217
al-Zahawi, Asma and Jamal, 119
al-Zawahiri, Ayman, 124
Ambuhl, Megan, 284
American Civil Liberties Union (ACLU), 285
American Civil War, 129, 274
American Colonization Society, 175
American Revolution, 27, 273
  effect on Australia, 19
  Loyalists in, 243, 273
Anarchists, 235
Anderson, Anne, 134
Anderson, Martina, 131, 133
Andrabi, Asiya, 111
Andre, Valerie, 72, 74, 75
Anfal genocide, 121, 172
Angel of Kobane, 170
Angola
  Cuban aid to, 48
Anjou, Margaret of, 87

Anti-aircraft crew, women as
  Finland, 68
  Germany, 81
  Great Britain, 90
  Vietnam, 292
Anti-militarism, women and
  Canada, 29
  Great Britain, 91
Anti-Nazi Resistance, women and
  Denmark, 51
  France, 72, 74
  Greece, 98
  Norway, 203
Anti-nuclear movement, women and
  Australia, 21
  Great Britain, 91
  Japan, 155
Anzac Day, 294
Apartheid, 249, 250, 251
Aquino, Corazon, 224, 226
Arab Revolt (1936), 137, 215
Arafat, Yassir, 215, 218
Aragon, Catherine of, 87
Arbel, Ziva, 141
Archer, Norma, 279
Ardartissa, 98
Ardjoune, Fatima Zohra, 12
Argentina, **15–18**
Arif, Abdul Salam, 119
Armed Forces Revolutionary Council (Liberia), 245
Armenian genocide, 266
Asfaw, Queen Menen, 63
Ashrawi, Hanan, 218
Assyrians, 172, 266
Astor, Nancy, 90
Ataturk, Mustafa Kemal, 266–267
  influence on Iran, 113–114
Australia, **19–24**
  cultural contrast to New Zealand, 193
  military deployment to Iraq, 156
  Vietnamese diaspora population in, 294
Australian Army Nursing Service, 19

Index

Australian Defense Force Academy, 22
Austria, 229
Auxiliary Territorial Service (ATS), 90
  as a model for CHEN, 138–139
Azanian People's Liberation Army, 251

Ba'athism, 119, 120, 123
  attitude toward Kurds, 172
Bachar, Oshrat, 140
Bachelet, Michelle, 36
Baden-Powell, Lord Robert, 230, 249
Bader-Meinhof Gang, 83
Badshah, Shahida, 211
Bager, Suzanne Bach, 52
Baldwin, Janice, 285
Balfour Declaration, 136, 215
Banat e-Ayesha ("Daughters of
  Ayesha"), 111
Bandaranaike, Sirimavo, 255
Bandaranaike, S.W.R.D., 255
Bangsamoro Women's Committee, 224
Bani-Etemad, Rakhshan, 114
Barayeva, Khava, 236
Bar Giora, 136
Barhoum, Saara, 216
Barry, James, 89
Barton, Clara, 274
Barzani, Asenath, 169
Battle for the Roads, 138
Battle of the Bulge, 278
Bay of Pigs, 48
Bedell, Zoe, 285
Behenji, Farida, 111
Bell, Gertrude, 119
Bendjedid, Chadli, 11
Ben-Gurion, David, 138
Berlin Airlift, 82
Beslan School, 240
Bethune, Mary McLeod, 277
Bhutto, Benazir, 210, 211
Bhutto, Zulfikar Ali, 209, 210, 211
Biafra, 198
Binh, Nguyen Thu, 295
Bin Laden, Osama, 225

Birth control, demographic effects of
  China, 43
  Ethiopia, 65
  Great Britain, 91
  Hungary, 103
  North Korea, 163
  South Korea, 165, 166
Black, Allison, 283
Black Mambas, 251
Black Tigers, 256
Blackwater, 20
Blackwell, Elizabeth, 274
Blais, Karine, 32
Bloody Sunday (1972), 131
Blue Star, 261
Bochkareva, Maria "Yasha," 236, 237
Boer War, 193, 230, 249
  Australia, 19
  Canada, 27
Boiko, Alecksandra, 238
Boko Haram, 200
  #BringBackOurGirls, 200
Bolshevik Revolution, 113, 136, 237
  Finland, 67
Bose, Subhas Chandra, 107
Bosnia, 197, 204–205, 232, 282
Botha, P.W., 250
Bottomly, Norah, 30
Bouboulina, Laskarina, 98
Boudica, 87
Boudouani, Fatima, 12
Boumediene, Hourai, 11
Bowser, Mary Elizabeth, 275
Boxer, Barbara, 280
Boxer Rebellion, 40
Boy Scouts, 129
Brasseur, Deanna, 30
Bravo 8/3 Female Mortar Platoon, 292
Bray, Linda, 28
Brazil, **25–26**
Breastfeeding, military mothers and, 136
Brecht, Bertolt, 244
Bremer, Paul, 123
Brestrup, Britt, 206

Brittain, Vera, 89
Broderick, Elizabeth, 22
Brothels, 152, 244, 293
Brown, Georgia Ann, 30
Brown, Holly, 30
Brown, Monica Lin, 283
Browne, Felicia, 90
Bubong, Zenadia, 225
Buddhism, 110, 253, 256
   treatment of PTSD, 294
Bullwinkel, Vivian, 21
Burkina Faso, 245
Bush, George W., 122, 123
Bush, Laura, 123
Bushbye, Sarah, 93
Bussani, Diadora, 149
Byron, Beverly, 280
Byte Mawada, 182

Cai Chang, 41
Calvinism
   Ireland, 132
   Scotland, 127
Camacho, Luzviminda, 226
Cambodia, 155, 294
Cammermeyer, Margrethe, 283
Canada, **27–34**
Canadian Airborne Regiment, 31
Canadian Human Rights Tribunal, 30
Canadian Women's Army Corps, 29
Canadian Women's Auxiliary Air
   Force, 29
Cansiz, Sakine, 171
Cantinières and sutlers, 71, 79, 101
Caracal Battalion, 140
Carignan, Jeannie, 32
Carvalho, Dalva Maria, 26
Castile, Isabella of, 87
Castle, Barbara, 91
Castro, Fidel, 47, 48, 49
Castro, Raul, 49
Catholicism
   Algeria, 9
   Argentina, 16

Chile, 35
Cuba, 47
Ireland, 127, 128, 130
Italy, 145
Philippines, 221, 223, 224
Poland, 232
Vietnam, 289
Cavalry Maiden, The (1836), 235
Cavazza, Lina, 145, 146
Cavell, Edith, 89
Cazneau, Jane, 2
Celler, Emanuel, 280
Central Intelligence Agency (CIA),
   171, 277
   operations in Chile, 25
   operations in Iran, 114
Chaldeans, 172
Chand Bibi, 105
Chapelle, Georgette "Dickey," 2
Chaplains, 280
Chapple, Phoebe, 19
Charter of Rights and Freedoms, 30
Chaturvedi, Avani, 109
Chaulagai, Bindi, 188
Chechnya, 236, 239, 240, 245
   "Black Widows," 236
CHEN, 139, 141
Child soldiers
   Liberia, 176
   Sierra Leone, 246
   Sri Lanka, 254
Chile, **35–37**
China, **39–45**
   conflicts with Vietnam, 289, 290,
      294–295
   military aid to Eritrea, 60
   military aid to Iranian Fedaian, 115
   occupation by Japanese, 158
Chizik, Sarah, 137
Chollima, 162
Christie, Agatha, 89
Church of England, 127
Cichociemni ("Silent Unseen"), 231
Ciller, Tansu, 268

Citadel, 281
Civil defense, women in wartime
  Afghanistan, 4
  Australia, 20
  Cuba, 48
  Germany, 81, 83
  Great Britain, 90
  Israel, 140
  Japan, 153
  Norway, 203
Civil Rights Act (1964), 279
Civil Rights Movement (US), 130
Clay, Wendy, 30
Coast Guard Women's Reserve (SPARS), 277
Cochrane, Jacqueline, 278
Collette, Ashley, 32
Combat Action Badge, 283
Combat Related Employment of Women (CREW) Trials, 30
"Comfort women," 42, 152, 158, 161
Commission on the Future of Women in the Armed Forces (1981), 75
Communism, women's role in
  Afghanistan, 3
  Chile, 35
  China, 41–42
  Finland, 69
  India, 109
  Iraq, 119
  Italy, 147
  Nepal, 185–186
  Philippines, 222, 224
  Poland, 231, 232
  Vietnam, 293
Communist Party of the Philippines, 222
Communist Party of Vietnam, 289, 290–291
Communist women, negative stereotypes of
  Finland, 68
  Germany, 81
  United States, 278

Conflict policing, 106
Confucianism
  China, 39
  Korea, 161, 163
  Vietnam, 289
Congo, 262
Congressional Medal of Honor, 275, 282
Conscription, male
  Algeria, 11
  China, 43
  Finland, 68
  France, 75
  Great Britain, 91
  Hungary, 102
  Iraq, 121
  Israel, 127
  Italy, 147
  New Zealand, 194
  North Korea, 163
  Poland, 231, 232
  Russia, 232, 235
  South Africa, 250
  South Korea, 164
  Sweden, 262
  Turkey, 266, 268
  United Arab Emirates, 271
  United States, 280
  Vietnam, 294
Conscription, of women
  Eritrea, 61
  Israel, 137, 140
  Norway, 206
Constitution of Rojava, 172
Control Orders, 210
Convention on the Elimination of All Forms of Discrimination against Women (CEDAW), 154
Cornum, Rhonda, 282
Coughlin, Paula, 281
Counter-insurgency (COIN), 10, 131, 226, 268
Courage Under Fire (1996), 282
Courbold, Linda, 22

Coyle, Marion, 131
Crawford v. Cushman (1976), 280
Crimean War, 71, 88, 169, 236, 274
Cross-dressing, women serving in male disguise by
 Brazil, 25
 France, 71
 Great Britain, 89
 Iraq, 124
 Russia, 235
 United States, 273, 276
Cryptography, 74, 91
Cuba, **47–50**
 military aid to Ethiopia, 63
 military aid to Iranian Fedaian, 115
 military aid to IRA, 131
 military aid to ANC, 250
 in Spanish-American War, 276
Culala, Felipa "Dayang Dayang," 223
Cultural Revolution, 40, 43, 223, 225
Curie, Marie, 229
Cyprus
 Canadian memorial, 28
 Canadian peacekeepers in, 31
 Great Britain's occupation of, 91
 Greece and Turkey, conflict over, 99, 268
 Irish peacekeepers in, 133
 Norwegian peacekeepers in, 204

Daetz, Jennifer, 22
Daughters of Faith, 110
Daughters of Iraq, 124
Daughters of Ireland, 129
DeBeers Company, 243
Deborah, 135
Decemberist Uprising, 235
Declaration 137 (Iraq), 123
Declaration of the Rights of Women and the Female Citizen, 71
De Gaulle, Charles, 73, 74
Degauque, Muriel, 124
De Gouge, Olympe, 71
Dehghani, Ashraf, 115

De Jesus, Gregoria, 221
De Jesus, Maria Quiteria, 25
De Klerk, F.W., 251
De la Cruz, Arlene, 226
Demirel, Suleyman, 268
Denmark, **51–53**
Derg, 63, 64, 65
De Soyza, Niromi, 254
Dhanu (code name), 256
Diamond, Black, 178, 179
Diaspora community, conflict and women in
 Afghanistan, 3–4
 Iran, 116
 Iraq, 122, 123
 Ireland, 128
 Kurds, 172
 Philippines, 225
 Sri Lanka, 258
Diem, Ngo Dinh, 290
Dien Bien Phu, Battle of (1954), 290
Dinh, Nguyen Thi, 292
Diocolano, Giobay, 224
Dirty War (Argentina), 15–16
Disarmament, demobilization and reintegration programs (DDR), women and
 Ethiopia, 64
 Liberia, 178, 179
 Nepal, 189
 Nigeria, 198
 Philippines, 225
 Sierra Leone, 246
 Sri Lanka, 258
Dix, Dorothea, 274
Dobis, Tracy, 22
Doce, Lidia, 48
Doctors Without Borders, 198
Doe, Samuel, 175, 176
Doi Moi economic reforms, 295
Doll's House, A (1879), 203
Domestic violence, women as targets of
 Afghanistan, 3
 Chile, 36

Egypt, 56
Iraq, 123
Ireland, 132
Israel, 140
Nepal, 185, 189
Sierra Leone, 246
United States, 285
Vietnam, 293
Dominican Republic, 279
Don't Ask/Don't Tell Policy, 283
Drachler, Devorah, 137
Drahonowska-Malkowska, Olga, 230
Dubrovka Theater, 236, 240
Duchemin, Marie-Angelique-Josephine, 71
Duckworth, Tammy, 284
Duerk, Alene, 280
Dugdale, Rose, 131
Dunwoody, Ann, 284
Durova, Nadezhda, 235

Easter Rising (1916), 129
East Timor, 22, 156
Echegoyen-McCabe, Terran, 136
Economic boycotts, women and, 199, 251, 273
Economic Community of West African States Monitoring Group (ECOMOG), 178, 245
Edib, Halide, 266
Education and literacy, women's
  Afghanistan, 3–4
  Algeria, 11
  Denmark, 51
  Eritrea, 59
  Ethiopia, 64, 65
  Greece, 99
  Iran, 116
  Iraq, 119, 122
  Liberia, 176
  Libya, 182
  Nepal, 185
  Turkey, 266

Eelam People's Revolutionary Liberation Front (EPRLF), 253
Egypt, **55–57**
El-Banat, Suraj, 1
El-Shazly, Shahdan, 55
Emergency Regulation 15A (Sir Lanka), 254
England, Elizabeth I of, 87
England, Lyddie, 284
English Civil War, 87, 127
Equal Pay Act (NZ), 194
Equal Rights Amendment (US), 280
Equipment, women using military
  Canada, 31
  Sweden, 262, 263
  United States, 274
Erdogan, Recep Tayyip, 269
Eritrea, **59–62**
Eritrean Liberation Front (ELF), 59–60
Eritrean Liberation Movement (ELM), 59–60
Eritrean People's Liberation Front (EPLF), 60
Erxleben, Heather, 30
Espin, Vilma, 49
Esther, 135
Ethiopia, **63–66**
  aid from Cuba, 48
  conflict with Eritrea, 60–61
Ethiopian People's Liberation Front (EPLF), 61
European Court of Justice, 84, 93, 149, 150
European Union, 75, 99, 132, 171, 269
Executive Outcomes, 245

Factory work, women and wartime
  Australia, 20
  Canada, 27–28
  Finland, 68
  France, 73
  Germany, 79
  Great Britain, 89, 90
  Hungary, 101

Ireland, 130
Italy, 145
Japan, 151
North Korea, 162
South Korea, 164
United States, 278
Vietnam, 291
Falklands War, 15, 92
Family support services, military
  Australia, 22
  Canada, 31
  Denmark, 52
  Germany, 80, 84–85
  Greece, 100
  Italy, 150
  United States, 284
Fanon, Frantz, 10, 115
Farhat, Mariam, 219
Farkas, T., 103
Farrell, Mairead, 131
Fascism, women under
  Ba'athist, 120
  Germany, 81
  Greece, 98
  Italy, 145
Fatah, 215, 218
Fatimah, 115
Fatima the Black, 169
Federal Security Service (FSB), 240
Federation of Cuban Women, 48
Federation of Labor Unions (Vietnam), 295
Fedian (Iran), 115
Female engagement teams, 10, 283
Female genital mutilation (FGM)
  Egypt, 56
  Eritrea, 60
  Liberia, 177
  Philippines, 222
Feminism
  Australia, 21
  China, 41
  France, 74
  Great Britain, 91

Nigeria, 198–199
Philippines, 223
Russia, 237
Feminist Association of Hungary, 101
Ferrals, Clodomira Acosta, 48
Ferrity, Geraldine, 132
Fianna Eireann, 129
Field Manual 3–24 (FM 3–24), 10
Finland, **67–70**
First Aid Nursing Yeomanry (FANY), 91
First Gulf War
  Canada, 31
  France, 75
  Germany, 84
  Great Britain, 88
  Hungary, 102
  Israel, 140
  Japan, 155, 156
  Kurds, 172
  Norway, 204, 205
  South Korea, 166
  United States, 281–282
First Intifada, 139, 216–217
First Lebanon War, 139, 141
First Russian Women's Battalion of Death, 236, 237
586th Fighters, 238
588th Night Bombers, 238
France, **71–77**
  military actions in Algeria, 9
  military actions in Vietnam, 289
Franco-Prussian War (1870–1), 72
Free French Forces, 74
Free women of Misrata, 182
French Foreign Legion, 74
French Revolution, 71, 127
Frontier mentality, women and
  Australia, 19
  Canada, 27
Front-line female comrade (tank), 238
Ft. Leonard Wood, 282
Fu Hao, 39
Fukushima, 156, 157

Fuller, Margaret, 2
Futaba, Yamakawa, 151

Gabbard, Tulsi, 284
Gaddafi, Muammar, 121, 181–183
Galula, David, 10
Gandhi, Indira, 107–108, 109, 110
Gandhi, Rajiv, 256
Gao, Ramon, 226
Garibaldi, Anita, 145
Garibaldi, Giuseppe, 145
Garin Program, 141
Gauthier, Isabelle, 30
Gauthier, Marie-Claude, 30
Gbowee, Leymah, 176
Geneva Convention, 146
Gensuikin, 155
Gensuikyo, 155
Germany, **79–86**
  invasion of Poland, 229–230
  unification of used as a model by Argentina, 15
Gettysburg, Battle of (1863), 275
GI Bill, 278
Giesbrecht, Kristal, 32
Gifford, Grace, 129
G. I. Jane (1997), 282
Gilane (2005), 114
Girls Scouts and Girl Guides, 20, 230
Gjerde, Ingrid, 205
Glenholmes, Evelyn, 131, 133
Goddard, Nichola, 31, 32
  Canadian reactions to her death, 32
Godot, Gal, 141
Gokcen, Sabiha, 266–267
Golan Heights, 155, 206
Gomez, Remedios, 223
Good Friday Agreement, 133
Gozen, Tomoe, 151
Grau, Ramon, 47
Great Britain, **87–95**
  Control Orders in, 210
  Great Britain, Elizabeth II of, 90, 91
  Great Britain, Victoria of, 87

Greater Japan National Defense Women's Association, 151
Great Leap Forward, 43
Great Trek, 249
Greece, **97–100**
  conflict with Turkey, 268
Greek Communist Party (KKE), 98
Greenhow, Rose O'Neill, 275
Gregory, Augusta, 129
Grozny, 240
Gruppo Donna Soldate (GDS), 150
Guinea, 245
Gul, Reza, 6
Gunay, Senay Ciper, 267
Gung, Tran Thi, 293
Gun-jeong, Hwang, 166
Gurkahs, 189, 190
Guthrie, Woody, 238
Gyllenstierna, Kristina, 261

Hadley, Eleanor, 153
Haganah, 137, 138
Hague Convention (1954), 120
Haile Selassie, 59, 60, 63
Haiti, 26, 282
Hall, Virginia, 278
Hamas, 216–219
Hammer, Julie, 22
Harding, Peter, 93
Haring, Ellen, 285
Harman, Sabrina, 284
Ha Sharon Prison, 219
Hashd al-Shaabi, 124
Hashomer, 136
Haslett, Caroline, 90
Hassoun, Paulina, 119
Hays, Anna Mae, 280
Hays, Molly Ludwig "Molly Pitcher," 273
Heads of state, women as
  Germany, 80
  Great Britain, 92
  India, 108
  Israel, 139

Liberia, 176
Sri Lanka, 255
Turkey, 268
Hegar, Mary Jennings, 285
Hernandez, Melba, 47
Herrick, Ruth, 194
Hester, Leigh Ann, 283
Hezb-e-Islam, 6
Hezbollah, 140
Hijackings, women conducting, 216, 217
Hinduism
　India, 105, 109
　Nepal, 185
　Sri Lanka, 253–254
Hiroshima, 155
HIV/AIDS, 65
Hoan, Nguyen Thi Duc, 295
Hobby, Oveata Culp, 277
Ho Chi Minh Trail, 292
Hoisington, Elizabeth P., 280
Holguin, Battle of, 47
Holm, Jeanne, 280
Hong, Duong Thi, 295
Ho-suk, Choe, 163
Hotak, Mirwais, 1
Hotonu, Itunu, 199
Houlden, Joseph G., 30
Howard, Michelle, 284
Hua Mulan, 39, 41
Hukbalahap, 223
Humanitarian operations, women in, 222
　Chile, 36
　Italy, 147
　Japan, 155, 157, 158
Humanitarian Relief and Iraq Reconstruction Special Measures Law, 156
Human Rights Act (Canada), 30
Human Rights Act (EU), 93
Human Systems Integration Project, 274
Hungarian Uprising (1956), 102

Hungary, **101–104**
　integration of women contrasted with Poland, 232
Hussein, Saddam, 92, 117, 120, 122–124, 172, 218
Hyon-hee, Kim, 162

Iatta, Leonhilda, 147
Idris, Wisal, 218
Illegitimate children, women and wartime conception of
　Sierra Leone, 246
　South Korea, 165
　Vietnam, 294
Il-sung, Kim, 162, 163
Improvised explosive devices (IED), 5, 32, 205
India, **105–112**
　colonial legacies of Great Britain, 87
　conflict with China, 43
　intervention in Sri Lanka, 253, 256
　peacekeepers in Liberia, 108
Indian Formed Police Unit, 106
Indian Military Nursing Service, 105
Inkatha Freedom Party, 251
Intelligence work, women performing
　China, 42
　Great Britain, 91
　Italy, 147
　Korea, 162, 165
　New Zealand, 194
　Nigeria, 198
　United States, 275, 279, 284
　Vietnam, 292
International Brigades, 73, 90, 194
International Women's Day, 43, 293
International Year of the Woman (1975), 21
Iran, **113–118**
　Kurdish minority population, 169
　Israeli and U.S. training of SAVAK, 115
　seizure of British sailors by, 94
Iranian Revolution (1979), 116

Index

Iran-Iraq War, 114, 116, 121, 170, 172
Iraq, **119–125**
   Australian military in, 22
   Canadian military in, 31
   German military in, 80
   Great Britain's military in, 93
   Italian military in, 150
   Japanese military in, 156
   Kurdish minority population, 169
   Norwegian military in, 205–206
   United States invasion of, 274, 275
Iraq, Faisal I of, 119
Ireland, **127–134**
   potato famine and emigration from, 128
Irgun, 138
Irish Civil War, 130
Irish Republican Army (IRA), 92, 128, 129, 130–133
Irish Volunteers, 129
Iron Cross (Germany), awarded to women, 81
Irving, Sibyl, 21
Isaksson, Charlotte, 262
Islam
   Egypt, 55
   Eritrea, 60
   India, 105, 110
   Iran, 113
   Iraq, 122, 124
   Israel, 135
   Nigeria, 197
   Pakistan, 209
   Palestine, 219
   Philippines, 221, 224
   Russia, 239
   Wahabi, 225, 236
Islamic State (ISIS), 120, 170, 173, 225, 272
Israel, **135–143**
Israel Defense Force (IDF), 217–218
Italy, **145–150**
   colonization of Eritrea, 59
   colonization of Ethiopia, 63
   colonization of Libya, 181

Jamahiriya, 181
Jammu, 106
Janos Bolyai Military Technical College, 103
Japan, **151–159**
   postwar occupation of, 194
Jeong-hwa, Won, 162
Jewish Brigades, 138
Jhansi Girls Brigade, 106
Jhansi, Lakshmi Bai of, 105
Jineology, 171
Jinnah, Fatima, 209
Jinnah, Mohammad Ali, 209
Jin Qiu, 41
Joan of Arc, 71, 223
John Paul II, 16, 149
Johnson, Shoshana, 284
Jonathan, Goodluck, 199
Jong-il, Kim, 163
Jong-nam, Kim, 162
Jong-suk, Ho, 163
Jong-suk, Kim, 162
Jong-un, Kim, 162, 163, 164
Jordan, 210, 215, 218
Joseph, Eleanor, 140
Jowett, Vida, 194
Joya, Malalai, 4
Joyce, Neryl, 20
Juche, 163
Judith, 135
Jung-suk, Yang, 167

Kaine, Frances, 194
Kalam, Meena, 3
Kale, Aderonke, 199
Kane, Kerry, 275
Kanth, Bhawana, 109
Karazi, Hamid, 4–5, 32
Karbala, Battle of (680), 115
Karman, Tawakkol, 176
Karpinski, Janice, 284

Kashmir, 106, 108–111
Kashmir Islamic Front, 111
Katipunan, 221
Kemalism, 266
Kenya, 244
Khadawi, Lame'a Abed, 123
Khadka, Devi, 188
Khai, Nguyen Thi Minh, 290
Khaled, Leila, 216, 217
Khalifa, Mohammed Jamal, 225
Khan, Abdur Rahman, 1
Khan, Amanullah, 1
Khan, Mohammad Daoud, 1–2
Khar, Hina Rabbani, 212
Khawlah bint al-Azwar School, 271
Khmer Rouge, 294
Khomeini, Ayatollah, 116–117
Kidnapping children as COIN tactic
   Argentina, 16
   Philippines, 223
Kilo Sierra II Plan (1998), 187
Kim, Helen, 164
Kindertransport, 90
King, Olive, 19
Klump, Andrea, 83
Koc, Nilufer, 172
Kondakova, Yelena, 238
Korea, **161–168**
Korean Air 858, 162
Korean War, 162, 164
   Australia, 21
   Canada, 21, 29
   China, 43
   Great Britain, 91
   Greece, 99
   Japan, 152
   New Zealand, 194
   Turkey, 267
   United States, 279
Korean Women's Rights Organization, 161
Korea Special Tourist Association, 165
Kosovo, 102, 275, 272, 282
Krabbe, Frederike, 83

Krabbe, Hanna-Elise, 83
Kraszewska-Ancerewicz, Wanda, 231
Krawczyk, Eliana Maria, 16
Kreil, Tanja, 84
Krey, Solveig, 205
Kumaratunga, Chandrika, 255
Kurdish National Congress, 172
Kurdistan Regional Government, 172
Kurdistan Workers Party (PKK), 171, 172, 268
Kurds, **169–174**
   Iran, 116
   Iraq, 121–122
   Turkey, 268
Kuwait, 121, 155, 206
Kwa Zulu, 251

LaLonde, Romeo, 31
Lansdale, Edward, 223
Lashkar-e-Taiba, 111
Law to Rid the Armies of Useless Women (1793), 71
Lebanese Civil War (1975–1990), 215, 216
Lebanon, 279
   Italian peacekeepers in, 149
   Norwegian peacekeepers in, 204–205
   PKK training camps in, 171
Legislative representation, women's
   Afghanistan, 4
   Ethiopia, 65
   Germany, 80
   Iran, 117
   Iraq, 123
   Ireland, 129
   Kurds, 171
   Libya, 183
   United States, 280
LeMay, Curtis, 279
LGBTQ population, in military
   Argentina, 16
   Denmark, 52
   Great Britain, 88, 94
   United States, 282–283

Index

Liang Hongyu, 39
Liberation Tigers of Tamil Eelam (LTTE), 109, 132, 253–258
Liberia, **175–179**
    Indian peacekeepers in, 106
Liberians United for Reconciliation and Democracy (LURD), 178
Libya, **181–183**
    compared to Iraqi state feminism, 121
    Great Britain, intervention in, 93
    United States intervention in, 275
Likud, 140, 217
Lioness Program, 10, 283
Lions of Jordan, 183
Li Zhen, 42
Logistical support, women providing to military operations
    Algeria, 9
    Greece, 98
    Ireland, 132
    Israel, 139
    South Africa, 250
    Vietnam, 291–292
Lombardi, Jane, 279
Long March, 42
LORAN navigation system, 276
Lotta Svard Organization, 67–68, 261
    used as model for Nazi women's organization, 81
Love, Nancy Harkness, 278
Luciani, Filomena, 147
Luna, Christina, 136
Lund, Kristen, 204
Lust, Caution (2007), 42
Lutheranism, 51, 261
Luxemburg, Rosa, 81
Lynch, Jessica, 283
Lysistrata, 97

Mackerras, Mabel Josephine, 21
Madhya Samana Battalion, 186
Madison, Dolley, 273
Magsaysay, Ramon, 223
Malalay, 1
Malayan Emergency, 194
Malik, Shahida, 211
Maltseva, Olga, 240
Mandela, Nelson, 251
Mandela, Winnie, 250
Manhattan Project, 277
Mannerheim, Carl, 67
Mannerheim, Sophie, 67
Maoism
    Eritrea, 60
    Nepal, 186
    Philippines, 224, 226
Maori, 193, 194
Mao Tse-tung, 42–43
Marcos, Ferdinand, 224, 226
Margai, Albert, 243
Margai, Milton, 243
Maria Clara (*Noli Me Tangere*), 221
Mariam, Mengistu Haile, 63
Mariana Grajales Platoon, 47, 49
Markievicz, Constance, 129
Marshall, George C., 277
Marshall Plan, 99
Martyrdom, 218, 219, 255
Marxism
    Ethiopia, 63
    Korea, 163
    Philippines, 223
    Soviet Union, 235
    Sri Lanka, 253, 255
Masako, Hojo, 151
*M*A*S*H*, 279
Masoud, Marwa, 219
Mavrogenous, Manto, 98
May Fourth Movement, 41
McAffee, Mildred, 277
McGee, Anita Newcomb, 276
McGrath, Amy, 284
Meiji Restoration (1868), 151
Mein, Joanne, 23
Meir, Golda, 108, 139
Memorials, women included in
    Canada, 28, 32

Nepal, 189
  Sri Lanka, 258
Mendes, Michelle, 32
Merkel, Angela, 80
Merlinettes, 74
Mesfin, Azeb, 65
Metis Rebellion, 27
Mexican-American War, 2, 129, 273
Meyer, Barbara, 83
Michel, Louise, 72
Military contractors, 20, 246
Military medicine
  Australia, 21
  China, 44
  Cuba, 48
  Egypt, 55
  Eritrea, 61
  France, 72
  Germany, 83
Military spouses, changing role of
  Argentina, 16
  Chile, 36
  Italy, 150
  United States, 285
Miller, Alice, 140
Million, Charles, 75
Mindano National Liberation Front (MNLF), 224
Minh, Ho Chi, 289–290
Modise, Joe, 251
Modise, Thandi, 250, 251
Moganada Masreya (Female Egyptian Conscripts), 56
Mohammadzai, Khatool, 5
Molony, Helena, 129
Momoh, Joseph, 244
Monmouth, Battle of (1778), 273
Morale, women and responsibility for military
  Australia, 21
  Finland, 67
  France, 73
  India, 107
  Japan, 151

New Zealand, 194
  Sweden, 261
  Vietnam, 292
Moro Islamic Liberation Front (MILF), 224–225
Moros, 221, 224
Morrison, David, 22
Mosaddegh, Mohammad, 114
Mosher, Leah, 30
Mossad, 139
Mother Courage (1939), 244
Motherhood, challenges of military, 136
Mothers of the Plaza de Mayo, 15, 16
Mowlam, Mo, 133
Mozambique, 155
Mugrabi, Bilal, 216
Mujahedin (Iran), 115–116, 117
Mujahideen, diaspora from Afghanistan, 3, 110
Mukhtar, Marium, 212
Mu Lu, 39
Mumbai Massacre, 111
Munich Olympics (1972), 139, 215
Muslim League, 209
Mussolini, Benito, 145
Muttahida Qaumi Movement (MQM), 211

Naibi, Zarif Shaan, 6
Namibia, 20
Napoleonic Wars, 71, 235, 249, 253
Nasser, Gamal Abdel, 55, 119, 215
National Association of Women Soldier Aspirants (ANANDOS), 149, 150
National Liberation Army of Iran, 117
National Liberation Front (FLN), 9, 10, 11
National Patriotic Front of Liberia (NPFL), 177
Naxalites, 109
Nazari, Aziza, 6
Nehru, Jawaharlal, 108

Nepal, **185–191**
Nesbitt, Kate, 93
New Deal, 277
New People's Army, 223, 224
New Soviet Woman, 237
New Zealand, **193–195**
New Zealand Army Nursing Service, 193
Nguyen, Thi Kim Lai, 292
Nhon, Nguyen Hanh, 294
Nhu, Madam, 290, 293
Nicaragua, 48
Nie Li, 44
Niger Delta Women for Justice, 199
Nigeria, **197–201**
   intervention in Liberia, 178
   intervention in Sierra Leone, 245
   protests against US invasion of Iraq, 199
Nigerian Civil War, 198
Nigerian Defense Academy, 199
Nightingale, Florence, 67, 88, 274
Night witches, 238
Ninh, Bao, 295
Nobel Peace Prize, 176
Non-governmental organizations (NGOs), women and
   Afghanistan, 4–5
   Iraq, 124
   Ireland, 133
   Liberia, 146
   Nepal, 188
   Philippines, 224, 225
   Vietnam, 294, 295
Nordic Center for Gender in Military Operations, 262
Nordic Women Mediation Network, 204
Norris, Michelle, 93
North Atlantic Treaty Organization (NATO)
   Germany, 80, 84
   Great Britain, 88
   Greece, 99–100
   Hungary, 103, 103
   Italy, 150
   Military forces in Afghanistan, 4
   New Zealand, 195
   Norway, 204, 205
   Poland, 232
   Sweden, 262
   Turkey, 267, 268
North Vietnamese Army (NVA), 292
Norway, **203–207**
Nottage, Lynn, 244
Noy, Lt., 140
Nur Jahan, 105
Nursing, women and military
   Afghanistan, 3
   Algeria, 9
   Australia, 19, 21
   Brazil, 25
   Canada, 27, 28
   Chile, 35
   China, 42
   Cuba, 47
   Finland, 67
   France, 73
   Germany, 79, 83
   Great Britain, 88, 90
   Greece, 98, 99
   Hungary, 101
   India, 107
   Japan, 153
   Korea, 165, 166
   Libya, 183
   New Zealand, 193, 194
   Russia, 236
   South Africa, 250
   Sweden, 261
   United States, 274, 276, 278

Oakley, Annie, 276
Ocalan, Abdullah, 171
O'Donnell, Liz, 133
O'Dwyer, Ella, 131
Office of Strategic Services (OSS), 98, 277, 290

Okinawa, 152
Okinawa Women Act Against Military Violence, 152
Oktyabrskaya, Mariya, 238
O'Loan, Nuala, 128, 134
Omar, Mullah, 124
Operation Juliet, 262
Operation Just Cause (Panama), 281
Operation Odyssey Dawn (Libya), 284
Operation Urgent Fury (Grenada), 281
Oron, Israela, 139
Orthodox Christianity
    Eritrea, 60
    Russia, 235–236
Orthodox Judiasm, 141
Oskouei, Marzieh Ahmadi, 115
Oslo Accords (1993), 217
Ottoman Empire, 88, 119, 135, 169, 215, 265–266
Oxfam, 222

Pahlavi, Ashraf, 115
Pahlavi, Farah, 115
Pahlavi, Mohammad, 114
Pahlavi, Reza, 113, 114
Paige, Caroline, 88
Pakistan, **209–213**
    conflict with Afghanistan, 2
Pakistan People's Party, 211
Palestine, **215–220**
Palestine Liberation Organization (PLO), 215, 218
    aid to Eritrea, 60
    aid to IRA, 131
    aid to Iran, 116
Palestinian Authority (PA), 216, 218
Palmach, 138
Pankhurst, Emmaline, 89, 237
Paradise of the Blind, 295
Parents of Disappeared Persons, 110
Partition of India (1947), 107
Partnership for Peace Program, 102
Pavlichenko, Lyudmila, 238

Peacekeepers and peacekeeping
    Argentina, 15
    Australia, 22
    Brazil, 26
    Canada, 28, 31
    Chile, 36
    Finland, 69
    Germany, 80
    India, 106
    Ireland, 133
    Italy, 147, 148
    Japan, 155, 157
    Nepal, 187, 188
    New Zealand, 195
    Norway, 204, 206
    Philippines, 226
    Poland, 232
    South Africa, 251
    Sri Lanka, 256
    Sweden, 262, 263
    United Arab Emirates, 272
People's Defense Force (YPG), 173
People's Democratic Party of Afghanistan, 2–5
People's Liberation Army (China), 43
People's Liberation Army (Nepal), 187, 188
People's Liberation Organization of Tamil Elote (PLOTE), 253
Perez, Mireya, 36
Perron, Sandra, 31
Perry, Ruth Sando, 178
Peshmerga, 171, 173
Philippine Military Academy, 226
Philippines, **221–227**
    US prisoners of war in WWII, 278
Phipps, Anita, 277
Pilsudski, Josip, 229
Pinochet, Augusto, 35
Piotrowiczowa, Maria, 229
Plan Beersheba (Australia), 22
Plater, Emilia, 229
Poland, **229–233**

Index

Police, women working as
  Afghanistan, 3, 6, 29, 124
  Canada, 29
  Chile, 36
  China, 44
  France, 75
  Great Britain, 91
  Greece, 100
  India, 107, 108
  Iraq, 124
  Israel, 140
  Italy, 147, 150
  Libya, 183
  Nepal, 189
  Pakistan, 212
  Palestine, 218
  Philippines, 224, 225, 226
  Poland, 232
  Sierra Leone, 245, 246
  South Africa, 250
  Vietnam, 293
Polish Home Army, 230–231
Polish Legion, 229
Polish Military Union, 230
Polish Socialist Party, 229
Pontecorvo, Debra, 16
Pope, Barbara, 281
Popular Front for the Liberation of Palestine, 216
Post-traumatic Stress Disorder (PTSD), 114, 294
Prabhakaran, Velupillai, 253, 256, 257
Pregnancy, military women and
  Australia, 21
  Canada, 31
  China, 42
  Eritrea, 60
  Great Britain, 92
  Israel, 139
  Korea, 165
  Nepal, 189
  Philippines, 226
  United States, 280
  Vietnam, 294

Pregnancy, used as a ruse for suicide bombing
  Ireland, 132
  Sri Lanka, 256
Prevention of Terrorism Act (1979), 254
Prevention of Terrorism Act (2005), 210
Price, Marian and Dolours, 131
Prisoners of war, women as
  Australia, 21
  China, 42, 43
  United States, 282, 283, 284
Propaganda, women featured in
  China, 40
  Nepal, 186
  Sri Lanka, 254
  Vietnam, 290, 292
Prostitution, women and
  Afghanistan, 6
  Japan, 152
  Korea, 165
  Sierra Leone, 246
  Vietnam, 293, 295
Provisional Irish Republican Army (PIRA), 131, 132, 133, 134
Przysposobienie Wojskowe Kobiet (Female Military Training), 230, 231
Puebla, Tete, 49
Putin, Vladimir, 122, 239

Qasim, Abd el Karim, 119
Qasim, Leyla, 172
Que, Ho Thi, 293
Queen of Sheba, 63

Ra'ana, Begum, 209
Rahab the Harlot, 135
Rahmani, Niloofar, 6
Rai, Pabin, 190
Rajavi, Maryam, 117
Rambo, Julia, 179
Rani of Jaipur Regiment, 107

Rape
  Algeria, 10–11
  Canada, 31
  Germany, 81
  Liberia, 177, 178
  Libya, 182
  Nigeria, 198
  Okinawa, 152
  Philippines, 224
  prosecution for under Rome Statute, 146
  Sri Lanka, 256
Rape of Nanjing, 42
Raskova, Maria, 238
Rathbun-Nealy, Melissa, 282
Reagan, Ronald, 3, 280
Red Army, 238, 239
  used as a model by Chinese, 43
Red Army Faction, 83
Red Crescent, 119, 218, 265
Red Cross, 20, 28, 61, 73, 89, 98, 101, 129, 222, 236, 258
Red Detachment of Women (1964), 40
Redmond, John, 129
Regev, Miri, 140
Reid, Elizabeth, 21
Reifenstahl, Leni, 81, 82
Reiffenstein, Anne, 30
Republic Act 7192 (1993), 226
Reserve Officer Training Corps (ROTC), 280
  Korea, 166
Reunification of Germany (1990), 83
Revolution of 1830 (France), 72
Revolution of 1830 (Poland), 229
Revolutionary Armed Forces of Columbia (FARC), 26
Revolutionary Guard (Iran), 116
Revolutionary United Front (RUF), 244
Revolutionary Women of Afghanistan (RAWA), 3
Revolutions of 1848, 2, 79, 101
Robinson, William, 292
Rogers, Edith Nourse, 277, 278

Rojas, Marta, 47
Rome Statute, 146
Roosevelt, Eleanor, 238, 278
Rosie the Riveter, 278
Roulettes, 23
Roxelana Hurrem Sultan, 265
Royal Commission on the Status of Women in Canada, 30
Royal Military College of Canada, 30
Royal Ulster Constabulary (RUC), 130, 131, 133
Ruined, 244
Russia, **235–241**
  invasions of Poland, 229, 230
  peacekeepers in Sierra Leone, 245
  relations with Iran, 113
  Russo-Finnish War, 67
Russia, Catherine II of, 235
Russia, Peter I of, 235
Russia, Peter III, 235
Russian Civil War, 237
Russian Revolution (1905), 235
Russo-Japanese War, 151
Rwanda, 22, 31

Salud Algabre, 221
Samar, Sima, 4, 5
Sampson, Deborah, 273
Sanchez, Celia, 47
Sandhurst, 92, 271
Santamaria, Haydee, 47
Sarmiento, Lina, 226
Sarojini Naidu, 107
Sassari Regiment, 150
Sau, Vo Thi, 290
Saudi Arabia, 282
SAVAK, 115, 116
Savitskaya, Svetlana, 238
Scholl, Sophie, 81
Schroeder, Patricia, 280
SEALs, 282
Second Intifada, 218
Second Lebanon War, 136, 140
Security Service Law (1949), 138

Sedibe, Jackie, 250, 251
Selective Service, 277
Seminole Wars, 273
Sepoy Mutiny (1857), 87
September 11, 2001 attacks, reaction to
  Afghanistan, 4
  Canada, 31
  Japan, 156
  Nepal, 188
  United States, 283
Serova, Elena, 238
Servicewomen in Non-traditional Environments and Roles (SWINTER) Trials, 30
Sethi, Nargis, 212
Seven Years' War, 27, 221
Sexual assault, 20, 281, 282, 285
Sexual harassment
  Australia, 22
  Israel, 140
  Sweden, 262
  United States, 282, 285
Seymour, Helen, 93
Sgt. Fatma, 265
Shadbolt, Rene Mary, 194
Shah, Fath Ali, 113
Shah, Nasir al-Dinh, 113
Sharia Law, 1, 122, 271
Shariati, Ali, 115, 116, 117
Sharon, Ariel, 218
Shello, Margaret George, 172
Shochat, Manya, 137
Shrum, Linda, 30
Shuo Zhen Chen, 39
Shuras, 5, 262
Sierra Leone, **243–247**
  relationship with Liberia, 178
Sikhs, 105, 108
Silang, Gabriela, 221
Silver Star, 283
Siman, Sandra, 225
Sinclair, Jeffery, 285
Singh, Mohana, 109
Sinn Fein, 129

Sirdar, Angela Maria, 93
Sirleaf, Ellen Johnson, 176
Sirota, Beate, 153
Six-Day War (1967), 55, 120, 139
Sky Fighters (2011)
Slander campaigns, 73, 278
Slanger, Frances, 278
Smith, Margaret Chase, 279
Smithsonian Institution, 120
Snipers, women as
  Ireland, 131
  Kurds, 170
  Russia, 238
Soldiers' Mothers Association, 239, 240
Solidarity Movement, 230, 231
Somalia, 64, 84, 272, 282
Soong Qing Ling, 42
Sorrows of War, 295
South Africa, **249–252**
South African Army Women's College, 250
South African Defense Force, 251
South Sudan, 157
South Vietnamese Army Corps, 293
Soviet Union, effects of collapse (1989)
  Afghanistan, 3
  Cuba, 49
  Ethiopia, 64
  Hungary, 102
  India, 110
  North Korea, 163
  Vietnam, 295
Soviet Union, space program, 238
Spain, 272
Spanish-American War, 221, 276
Spanish Civil War, 73, 90, 194
Sparta, Gorgo of, 97
Sparta, women in, 98
Special Operations Executive (SOE), 21, 91, 98
Sri Lanka, **253–260**
Stalinism, 238
State feminism
  Iraq, 121

Libya, 181–182
Turkey, 266
St. Cyr, 271
Stevens, Siaka, 243
Stigma, attached to women's military service
  Algeria, 10
  Eritrea, 61
  Ethiopia, 65
St. Olga of Kiev, 235
Submarines, women serving on
  Argentina, 16
  Australia, 22
  Canada, 31
  France, 75
  Germany, 84
  United States, 285
Subong Bangsa Bai, 224
Sudan, 2, 251
Suffrage, women's
  Canada, 28
  Cuba, 47
  Denmark, 51
  Finland, 67
  France, 74
  Germany, 80
  Great Britain, 89, 90
  Iran, 114, 115
  New Zealand, 193
  Philippines, 222
  Poland, 230
  Russia, 237
  Turkey, 266
Suffrajitsu, 89
Suicide bombers, male, 212, 218, 256–257
Suicide bombers, women
  Afghanistan, 6
  Chechnya, 236, 239
  Iraq, 124
  Kashmir, 111
  Kurds, 171
  Palestine, 218, 219, 220
Sulieman the Magnificent, 265

Sun Tzu, 39
Sun Yat-sen, 41
Surratt, Mary, 275
Swaminathan, Lakshmi, 107
Sweden, **261–263**
Sykes-Picot Agreement, 136, 215
Syrian Civil War, 100, 169, 172, 173
Szabo, Violette, 91
Szilagyi, Ersebet, 101

Tahrir Square (2011), 56
Tailhook Scandal, 281, 285
Tai-ping Rebellion, 39
Taiwan, 43, 295
Taliban, 4–6, 211
Tanks Crushed My Mom, The, 60
Tarabi, 105
Tara Devi, 106
Taraki, Nur Mohammad, 3
Taylor, Charles, 175, 176, 244
Tehrik-e-Taliban, 212
Telegraph and telephone operators, women, 29, 42, 73, 145, 276
Telemark Battalion, 206
Tendler, Keren, 140
Terrorism Prevention and Investigation Measures (2011), 210
Terrorist and Disruptive Acts Order, 188
Tet Offensive, 279, 293
Thakur, Pragya Singh, 111
Thatcher, Margaret, 92, 268
Third Kuban Women's Shock Battalion, 237
Thirty Years' War, 79
Tich, Ut, 292
Tigrayan Peoples Liberation Front (TPLF), 64
Timor-Leste, 128
Tokyo War Crimes Trials, 21
Tolbert, William, 175, 176
Tomorrow's Pioneers, 216
Toronka, Adama "Cut-hand," 245, 246

Torture of women political dissidents
　Algeria, 10
　Argentina, 15, 16
　Brazil, 25
　Chile, 36
　Greece, 99
　Iran, 115, 116
　Iraq, 122
　Sri Lanka, 255
Tourism work, women in, 49, 295
Traeholt, Lone, 52
Travers, Susan, 74
Trung Sisters, 290
Tubman, Harriet, 275
Turkey, **265–270**
　Abkhazian minority in, 268
　Kurds in, 169
Turney, Faye, 94
Tuyen, Ngo Thi, 292

Uganda, 20, 31, 244
Ukraine, 230
Ulster Defense Association, 131
Ulster Defense Force, 132
Ulster Volunteer Force, 131
Um Jihad, 217
Umkhonto we Sizwe (Spear of the Nation), 250, 251
Underground Railroad, 275
Uniforms, women and military
　Great Britain, 91, 93
　India, 107
　Japan, 154
　Korea, 166
　Philippines, 225
　South Africa, 215
　Sri Lanka, 257
　United States, 277, 278, 282
Union of South Africa, 249
United Arab Emirates, **271–272**
　effect of woman UAE pilot on Egypt, 56
United Nations, 161, 204, 245, 258, 267, 272
　post-conflict work in Nepal, 189
　sanctions on Iraq, 121, 122
United Nations Children's Fund (UNICEF), 179, 198
United Nations Educational, Scientific and Cultural Organization (UNESCO), 120
United Nations Security Council Resolution (UNSCR) 1325, 100, 133, 154, 178
United Nations Women Executive Board, 134
United States, **273–287**
　policy toward Kurds, 170, 172
　target of Nigerian protests against Texaco/Chevron, 199
　training of Palestinian Authority Presidential Guard, 218
　training of SAVAK, 115
　Vietnamese refugees in, 294
United States Military Academy West Point (USMA), 199, 271, 280
Universal Military Duty Law (1939), 238
Usakhgil, Latife, 266

Van Lew, Elizabeth, 275
Varena, Blanda of, 261
Vargas, Getulio, 25
Vatican, 146
Veiling of women
　Afghanistan, 1, 4
　Algeria, 9
　Chechyna, 236
　Egypt, 55
　Iran, 113, 116, 117
　Iraq, 122
Venezuela, 49
Vichy France, 74, 138, 290
Viet Cong, 292, 293
Viet Minh, 290
Vietnam, **289–296**
　Chinese hegemony over, 43
　French colonial regime in, 72, 74

US tactics in used as model by Argentina, 15
Vietnam War
  Australia, 21
  Canada, 29
  Great Britain, 91
  Japan, 152
  Korea, 165
  New Zealand, 194
  Sweden, 262
  United States, 279, 280
Vikings, 261
Virginia Military Academy, 281
Volpi argentate (silver fox), 147
Voluntary Legion of Women, 230
Von der Leyen, Ursula Albrecht, 80
Von Weymarn, Verena, 83

Wahlgren, Lars Eric, 205
Wake, Nancy, 21, 91
Walentynowicz, Anna, 231
Walesa, Lech, 231, 232
Walker, Mary, 274, 275
War of 1812, 27, 273
War of Independence (1948), 138, 140
War of the Pacific (1879–1884), 35
War reporting, women and, 2, 47
Warsaw Pact, 102, 231, 232, 267
Warsaw Uprising (1944), 231
Wegener, Corine, 120
West, Alan, 93
Western Sahara, 22, 166
White Revolution (Iran), 115
Wilde, Jane, 129
Williams, Duvall, 281
Winter War (1939), 238
Witt, Margaret, 283
Wittek, Maria, 230, 231, 232
Wolfenbarger, Janet, 284
Wollstonecraft, Mary, 203
Woman Hero, 60
Woman in Berlin, A, 81
Woman Platoon Leader, A, 166

Women, duty to be mothers of potential soldiers
  France, 71
  Greece, 99
  Iran, 116
  Israel, 138, 139
  Korea, 163
  Russia, 239
Women Accepted for Volunteer Emergency Service (WAVES), 277
Women Air Force Service Pilots (WASP), 278
Women and Democracy Initiative, 123
Women and Society Commission (1973), 83
Women for a Free Iraq, 122
Women of Liberia Mass Action for Peace, 178
Women's Armed Service Integration Act (1948), 279
Women's Army Corps (Japan), 154
Women's Army Corps (WAC), 277
Women's Auxiliary (Philippines), 225
Women's Auxiliary Army Corps (New Zealand), 194
Women's Auxiliary Ferrying Squadron, 278
Women's Detachments (YPJ), 173
Women's Institute (WI), 90
Women's League for Peace and Freedom, 194
Women's National Guard (Pakistan), 209
Women's Royal Army Corps (UK), 91
Women's Royal Canadian Naval Service, 29
Women's Union (Vietnam), 289, 295
Women's Worker Battalions (Ottoman), 265
Woodward, Margaret, 284
World War I (WWI)
  Canada, 28
  cultural destruction resulting from, 120

France, 71, 73
Germany, 79
Great Britain, 89
Greece, 98
Hungary, 101
India, 106
Iraq, 119
Ireland, 129, 130
Israel, 136
Italy, 145
Japan, 151
New Zealand, 193
Nigeria, 197
Norway, 203
Poland, 229, 230
Russia, 235
South Africa, 250
Sweden, 261
Turkey, 265
United States, 276
Vietnam, 290
World War II (WWII)
  Australia, 20, 21
  Brazil, 25
  Canada, 28–29
  China, 42
  cultural destruction resulting from, 120
  Denmark, 51
  Eritrea, 59, 60
  Germany, 81
  Great Britain, 90–92
  Hungary, 102
  India, 107
  Iran, 114
  Ireland, 130
  Israel, 137, 138
  Italy, 146, 147
  Japan, 151, 152, 154
  Korea, 161
  New Zealand, 194
  Nigeria, 197
  Norway, 203

Philippines, 222
Poland, 230, 231
Russia, 238
South Africa, 250
Sweden, 261, 262
Turkey, 267
United States, 277

Xanim, Adile, 169
Xanzad, 169
Xatun, Meyan, 169
Xiang, Jian Gou, 41

Ya'akobi, Keren, 140
Yacob, Elsa, 60
Yarmouk, Battle of (636 CE), 271
Yassin, Sheik Ahmed, 218
Yasukuni Shrine, 154
Yeltsin, Boris, 239
Yo-Jong, Kim, 164
Yom Kippur War (1973), 139
Young Pioneers, 230
Young Turks, 265, 266
Young Women's Christian Association (YWCA), 63, 276
Youth Report, 166
Yugoslavia, 84

Zana, Leyla, 171
Zardari, Asif, 212
Zasulich, Vera, 235
Zawadzka, Anna, 230
Zawadzka, Elzbieta, 231, 232
Zaynab, 115
Zaynab's Commandos, 116
Zheng Pingru, 42
Zia, Muhammad, 209
Zina Ordinance (1979), 209
Zinky Boys, 239
Zionism, 135, 136, 215
Zrinyi, Ilona, 101
Zulus, 249

About the Author

Dr. Margaret D. Sankey is the director of research and electives for the U.S. Air Force Air War College.